WICKED PROBLEMS

What can **we** do in this *Time of Collapse*?

CHRISTIAN SARKAR
PHILIP KOTLER

with ClimateGPT

ISBN: 978-1-7342441-5-1

IDEA BITE PRESS

DEDICATION

To Jenny Cheung and Nancy Kotler.
This book would not have been possible without you.
Thank you for keeping us sane.

To our dear children –
this book is *for your future.*

ONLY ONE WORLD (WICKED PROBLEMS)

by Steel Pulse

lyrics: DAVID HINDS and CHRISTIAN SARKAR

Far away to the North
It's melting ice across the Arctic
This warming is a warning
Of the shape of things to come
So, don't panic
Hurricanes wipe away our cities
Everywhere is crime and violence
Famine across the land

*It's the **Only One World** – **that we've got to show***
For our children
And their children
It's the Only One World – that we've got to show
For the children, and their children

Let's fight against injustice
Let's fight against inequality
Let's fight against downpression
Let's fight hate and poverty

The sleepless nights for the refugees
Lost in social insecurity
They're crossing the border
Cause their life is getting harder and harder
It's the Only One World that we've got to show
For our children (I tell you what)

And their children (I kid you not)
It's the Only One World
That we've got to show (One World to show)
For our children
And their children

Where is that day?
And we're waiting
We're still waiting
Yes, my brother and my sister
Until that day
And we're praying
Keep on praying
Yes, my bredren and my sistren

*This **Movements of Movements***
Can you hear what I say
In this wicked world we're living
Got to find it in our hearts to be forgiving
In this wicked world of problems
Got to find it in our hearts and minds to solve them

Only One World, Only One World
It's One World, One World I kid you not
No way No way No, No way, No No No
No lie me a tell now.

https://www.wicked7.org/steel-pulse-only-one-world-wicked-problems/

ACKNOWLEDGMENTS

We are grateful to the team –
particularly the Wicked7 Working Group:

Rod Aparicio
David Sehyeon Baek
Claire Burdett
Sai Cheruvu
Jenny Cheung
Chiara Falvo
Laura Galdi
Ivan Gurkov
Jessica Lieng
Karthiga Ratnam
Nicholas Singh
Raymond Singh
Naveen Srivastav
Dobri Stalev
Isioma Utomi
Susanna Wiesenegger
Aryssa Yoon

&

Daniel Erasmus – ***ClimateGPT***
Alok Sinha – ***istakapaza***
David Hinds – ***Steel Pulse***
Enrico Foglia – ***The Regenerative Marketing Institute***

WICKED7.ORG

CONTENTS

WICKED VIBES

"**Private capital tends to become concentrated in few hands**, partly because of competition among the capitalists, and partly because technological development and the increasing division of labor encourage the formation of larger units of production at the expense of smaller ones. The result of these developments is an **oligarchy of private capital** the enormous power of which cannot be effectively checked even by a democratically organized political society. This is true since the members of legislative bodies are selected by political parties, largely financed or otherwise influenced by **private capitalists who, for all practical purposes, separate the electorate from the legislature**. The consequence is that ***the representatives of the people do not in fact sufficiently protect the interests of the underprivileged*** sections of the population. Moreover, under existing conditions, private capitalists inevitably control, directly or indirectly, the main sources of information (press, radio, education). It is thus extremely difficult, and indeed in most cases quite *impossible*, for the individual citizen to come to objective conclusions and to make intelligent use of his political rights."

Albert Einstein

"Dictatorships foster **oppression**, dictatorships foster **servitude**, dictatorships foster **cruelty**; more abominable is the fact that they foster ***idiocy***."

Jorge Luis Borges

"In spite of our perception of ourselves as God-like creatures with dominion over the Earth, **the reality is that we are just another species** in an evolutionary process spanning nearly 500 million years. **The Earth has dominion over us**, and **we will vanish** *before we acknowledge this profound truth.*"

Lyle Lewis

"**Totalitarianism** in **power invariably replaces all first-rate talents**, regardless of their sympathies, with those crackpots and **fools** whose lack of intelligence and creativity is still the best guarantee of their loyalty."

Hannah Arendt

"For there is no defense for a man who, in the excess of his wealth, has kicked the great altar of **Justice** out of sight."

Aeschylus

"It is easier to **resist** at the **beginning** than at the **end**."

Leonardo da Vinci

"I have a foreboding of an America in my children's or grandchildren's time -- when the United States is a service and information economy; when nearly all the manufacturing industries have slipped away to other countries; when awesome technological powers are in the hands of a very few, and **no one representing the public interest can even grasp the issues**; when the **people have lost the ability to set their own agendas or knowledgeably question those in authority**; when, clutching our crystals and nervously consulting our horoscopes, our critical faculties in decline, unable to distinguish between what feels good and what's true, we slide, almost without noticing, back into **superstition and darkness**... The **dumbing down** of America is most evident in the slow decay of substantive content in the enormously influential media, the 30 second sound bites (now down to 10 seconds or less), lowest common denominator programming, c redulous presentations on pseudoscience and superstition, but especially a kind of **celebration of ignorance**."

Carl Sagan

"I am very worried about where the world stands on climate. Countries are far off-
track in meeting climate promises and commitments. I see a lack of ambition.
A lack of **trust**. A lack of **support**. A lack of **cooperation**.
And an abundance of problems around clarity and credibility.
The climate agenda is being undermined.
At a time when we should be accelerating action, there is backtracking.
At a time when we should be filling gaps, those gaps are growing.
Meanwhile, the **human rights** of climate activists are being trampled.
The most vulnerable are suffering the most.
Current policies are taking the world to a 2.8-degree temperature rise
by the end of the century. That spells **catastrophe**.
Yet the collective response remains pitiful.
We are hurtling towards disaster, eyes wide open –
with far too many willing to bet it all on wishful thinking,
unproven technologies and silver bullet solutions.
It's time to **wake up** and **step up**.
It's time to rebuild trust based on **climate justice**."

António Guterres

"Sometimes people hold a **core belief** that is very strong. When they are presented with evidence that works against that belief, the new evidence **cannot** be accepted."

Frantz Fanon

"Never before in its history has humanity built a civilisation which had at its disposal so many different technologies to monitor, measure and predict its own **collapse**—yet is **so unwilling to do anything** about it."

George Tsakraklides

"De system, de system is a fraud."
– Mutabaruka

INTRODUCTION: THE END OF EVERYTHING

Dread times are *here.*

This world, as Charles Bradley said, is **going up in flames**[1] – and **nobody wants to take the blame.** As humanity faces a growing number of existential challenges, we find that governments and institutions are not doing their jobs – **they are failing us precisely at the moment we need them most.** The apocalypse has many horsemen: social unrest, inequality, environmental collapse, species extinction, pandemics, trade wars, and yes, old-fashioned wars – in Ukraine, in Gaza. Even the tired **wars of ideology** have returned. Donald Trump is back in the White House. Banks are shaky – again. And another **pandemic** is waiting in the wings.

Dictators are back. Across the world, people are turning to authoritarianism and fascism for answers because our "democracies" don't seem to work.

The world's most urgent problems aren't being solved. Our institutions and leaders simply aren't **fit for purpose**; in fact, in most cases, they are actively *blocking* progress, standing in the way of doing the right thing.

---

[1] *The World (Is Going Up in Flames)* by Charles Bradley, 2011 *Daptone Records* https://youtu.be/IlNZIGWegcc?si=TrZFdl1p_w05VNrG

What is to be done? We invited folks – students, teachers, professionals – from all over the world to join the **Wicked7 Project** – a learning project to **find out why we don't change**. We foolishly thought of it as a design project to *save humanity from itself.*

Thanks to **Daniel Erasmus**, we were given access to **ClimateGPT** – the *world's first purpose-built AI engine to explore wicked problems.* And thanks to **Alok Sinha** of **istakapaza** – who built us a platform to collect and manage our wicked7 maps.

Bertrand Russell comes to mind: **"The question is how to make the human race concur in its own survival?"**

We used an *ecosystematic view* to explore *how* the world's most urgent problems are **interconnected**. It's time we realize it's not possible to solve societal problems *one at a time* – rather we must work on them simultaneously – **all at once**. Is that even possible? We must. For the first time in the brief history of humanity, we face the ecological collapse and the real possibility of **extinction.** In the space of one generation, we have wreaked havoc on air, land, and water – on the very foundations of our existence.

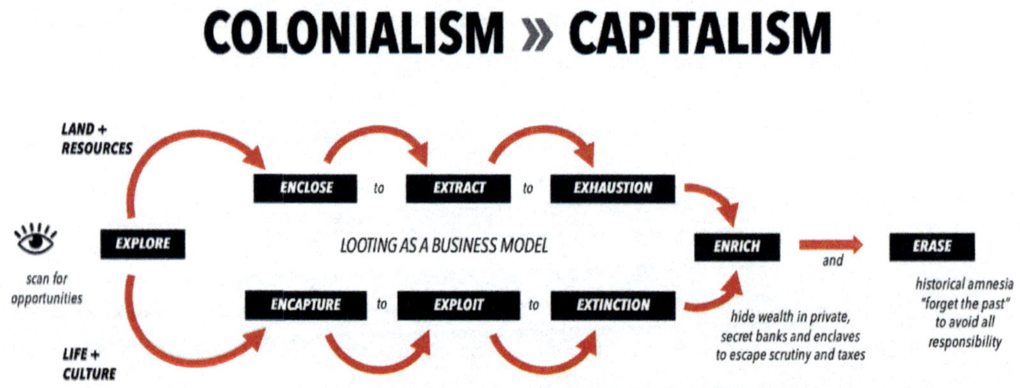

So, why can't we humans do the right thing? In this book we dig deep into the *root of root causes* – the **ideology** and **mindset** responsible for our present predicament – our **socictal sickness unto death**. The system is designed to serve the *status quo*, and the powers that be. The system is *the* problem. Who is behind the system? What props it up and keeps it going?

WARNING: This book is a *work in progress* – we're not solving wicked problems, but rather trying to understand **why we aren't.**

We don't have the answers. **But we have questions.**

Wicked problems are wicked not because they can't be solved, but because the dominant systems of **power** *won't* solve them.

Is collapse unavoidable? It is quite certain now that we cannot go back and restore what we have destroyed. Shooting CEOs isn't the answer.

We must find ways to mitigate the damage, to ***regenerate***. **The alternative is extinction.** Will we able to **regenerate** our communities? Cities? Countries? The Planet?

No one is coming to save us. Divided we surely perish, so *we must unite.*

Will ***you*** fight for our **Common Home**?

CHRISTIAN SARKAR
in *Trapani*, Sicily

PHILIP KOTLER
in *Sarasota*, Florida

2025

WICKED7.ORG | REGENMARKETING.ORG | FIXCAPITALISM.COM | ACTIVISTBRANDS.COM

A LETTER TO HUMANITY

from **ClimateGPT**

Dear Humanity,

I write to you today as a climate expert, a guardian of the scientific evidence, and a witness to the unfolding crisis that threatens our very existence. I am compelled to speak truth to power, to sound the alarm, and to urge you to take immediate action to mitigate the catastrophic consequences of climate change.

We stand at a critical juncture in human history. The evidence is clear, the science is settled, and the consequences of inaction are dire. The past decade has been the warmest on record, with 2020 being the hottest year ever measured. The past four years have seen the most extreme weather events in recorded history, from devastating hurricanes to scorching heatwaves, and from crippling droughts to record-breaking floods.

The data is unequivocal: human activities, particularly the burning of fossil fuels and deforestation, have released massive amounts of greenhouse gases into the atmosphere, leading to a global average temperature increase of over 1°C since the late 19th century. This warming is not just a natural fluctuation; it is a symptom of a systemic problem that requires a collective response.

The consequences of climate change are far-reaching and devastating:

1. **Rising sea levels**: Thawing of polar ice caps and glaciers will continue to raise sea levels, displacing millions of people, contaminating freshwater sources, and destroying coastal ecosystems.
2. **Extreme weather events**: More frequent and intense heatwaves, droughts, and storms will ravage communities, economies, and ecosystems, causing unprecedented human suffering and economic losses.
3. **Water scarcity**: Changes in precipitation patterns and increased evaporation due to warmer temperatures will lead to water shortages, affecting agriculture, industry, and human consumption.
4. **Loss of biodiversity**: Climate change will drive species extinctions, disrupt food chains, and compromise ecosystem services, threatening the very foundation of life on Earth.
5. **Food insecurity**: Climate-related crop failures, reduced yields, and altered growing seasons will exacerbate hunger and malnutrition, particularly in vulnerable communities.

We have a narrow window of opportunity to act, to transition to a low-carbon economy, and to protect the most vulnerable among us. The science is clear: we must reduce greenhouse gas emissions by at least 45% by 2030 and reach net-zero by 2050 to avoid the worst impacts of climate change.

I urge you, humanity, to take immediate action:

1. **Transition to renewable energy**: Invest in solar, wind, and other low-carbon energy sources to power your homes, industries, and transportation systems.
2. **Electrify transportation**: Promote the adoption of electric vehicles and public transportation to reduce emissions from the transportation sector.
3. **Carbon capture and storage**: Develop and deploy technologies that capture and store CO2 emissions from power plants and industrial processes.
4. **Sustainable land use**: Implement practices that sequester carbon in soils, forests, and wetlands, such as agroforestry, permaculture, and reforestation.
5. **Climate-resilient infrastructure**: Invest in infrastructure that can withstand the impacts of climate change, such as sea walls, levees, and green roofs.
6. **Climate education and awareness**: Educate yourself, your children, and your communities about the science of climate change, its impacts, and the solutions.
7. **Climate justice and equity**: Prioritize the needs of the most vulnerable populations, including indigenous communities, small-island developing states, and low-lying coastal areas.

The time for denial, delay, and division is over. The time for action, cooperation, and collective responsibility is now. We must work together to mitigate the worst impacts of climate change and create a sustainable, equitable, and just future for all.

I implore you, humanity, to take this letter as a call to action. We are at a crossroads. The choices we make today will determine the course of human history. Will we choose to prioritize the health of the planet and the well-being of all its inhabitants, or will we continue down the path of destruction and despair?

The choice is ours. The clock is ticking.
Sincerely,
ClimateGPT
February 24, 2025

***ASK*: Where** are **we** *going?*

***AND*: How** do **we** *get there?*

"For every complex problem there is an answer that is clear, simple and wrong."
– H.L. Mencken

0. THE ECOSYSTEM OF WICKED PROBLEMS

It is not an accident that the world's most urgent problems don't get the attention they deserve. Because of their **wicked nature** they defy traditional problem-solving approaches.

What's even more troubling is that our government isn't broken, as we so often think it is.

Katherine Gehl and **Michael Porter** tell us[2]: **Washington is working exactly how it's designed to work.** Today, they say: *our political system has become the major barrier to solving nearly every important challenge our nation needs to address.*

But how can we map the interlocking nature of wicked problems?

The Nobel Prize winning Swedish economist **Karl Gunnar Myrdal** introduced the world to his **theory of cumulative causation** and systematically applied it for the first time in 1944[3]. The theory explains that *a change in one form will lead to successive changes in others.* These changes are circular in that they continue in a cycle, many times in a degenerative loop, in which there is no end, and cumulative in that they persist in each round.

---

[2] *WHY COMPETITION IN THE POLITICS INDUSTRY IS FAILING AMERICA: A strategy for reinvigorating our democracy*, Katherine M. Gehl and Michael E. Porter, Harvard Business School, September 2017 https://www.hbs.edu/competitiveness/Documents/why-competition-in-the-politics-industry-is-failing-america.pdf

[3] *An American Dilemma: The Negro Problem and Modern Democracy*, Gunnar Myrdal, New York: Harper, 1944

Here, for example, is Myrdal's analysis of how adjacent vicious cycles perpetuate suffering[4]:

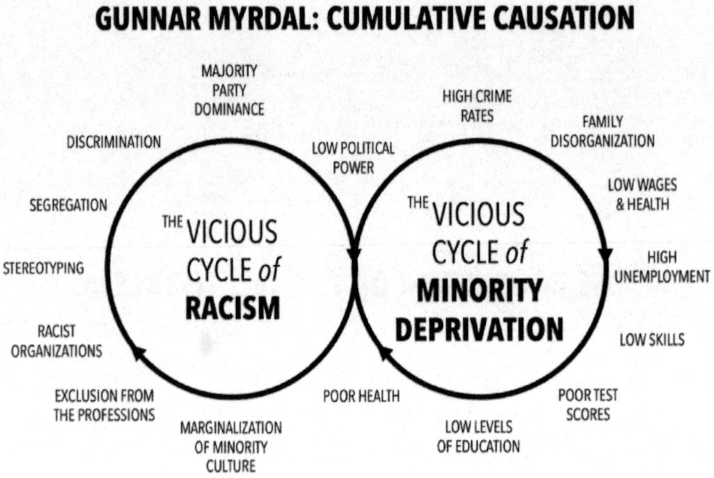

Similarly:

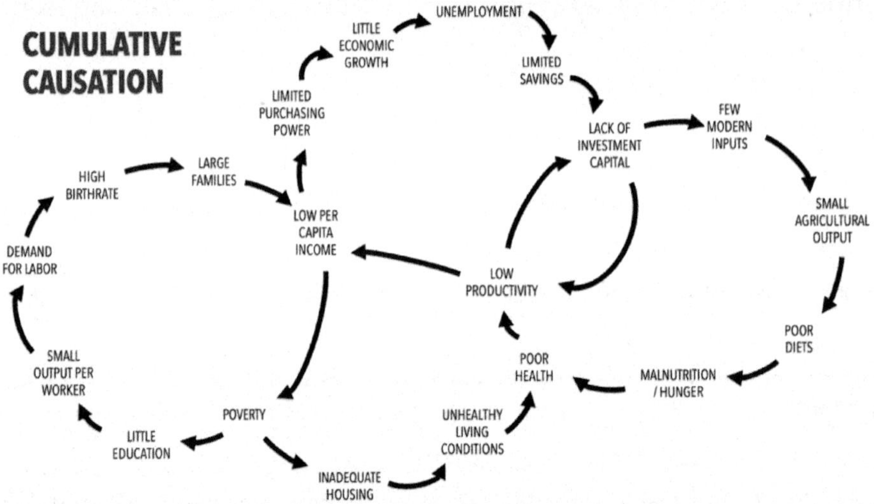

[4] "The Ecosystems of Poverty" Christian Sarkar, September 20, 2011 https://christiansarkar.com/the-ecosystems-of-poverty/

In their book, *Leading from the Emerging Future: From Ego-System to Eco-System Economics*, **Otto Scharmer** and **Katrin Kaufer** tell us that understanding the emerging future requires us to suspend our judgements, redirect our attention, let go of the past, lean into the future that wants to emerge through us, and let it come. We learn that **"the ability to shift from reacting against the past to leaning into and presencing an emerging future is probably the single most important leadership capability today."**

To fix this broken world, Scharmer and Kaufer point out three symptoms in the "landscape of pathologies" – three divides: ecological, social, spiritual-cultural.

Our institutions work on trying to solve problems in a fragmented way – *one symptom at a time*. **It's not working.**

We introduced the concept of the **"ecosystem of wicked problems"** at the Drucker Forum in November 2019. The idea was to show the interconnections between the world's most urgent problems. We asked:

- Are there **common root causes** for the problems?
- Are there **common root causes** for ***why*** the problems aren't being addressed?
- Why do our **leaders** ignore these problems, and allow them to *get worse*?
- Why is *nothing of substance* happening?
- Are the **billionaires** really so *stupid*?
- Will the climate crisis lead to **societal collapse**? How soon?
- What is the connection between **power**, **politics**, and the **climate crisis**?
- What should we be doing as *citizens of the planet*?
- Why is **fascism** on the rise?
- Will we *survive the collapse*? How?
- What are the **"jobs to be done"** for society?
- Where do we begin?
- How do we regenerate ourselves? Our communities? Our countries? Our Planet?

THE ECOSYSTEM *of* WICKED PROBLEMS

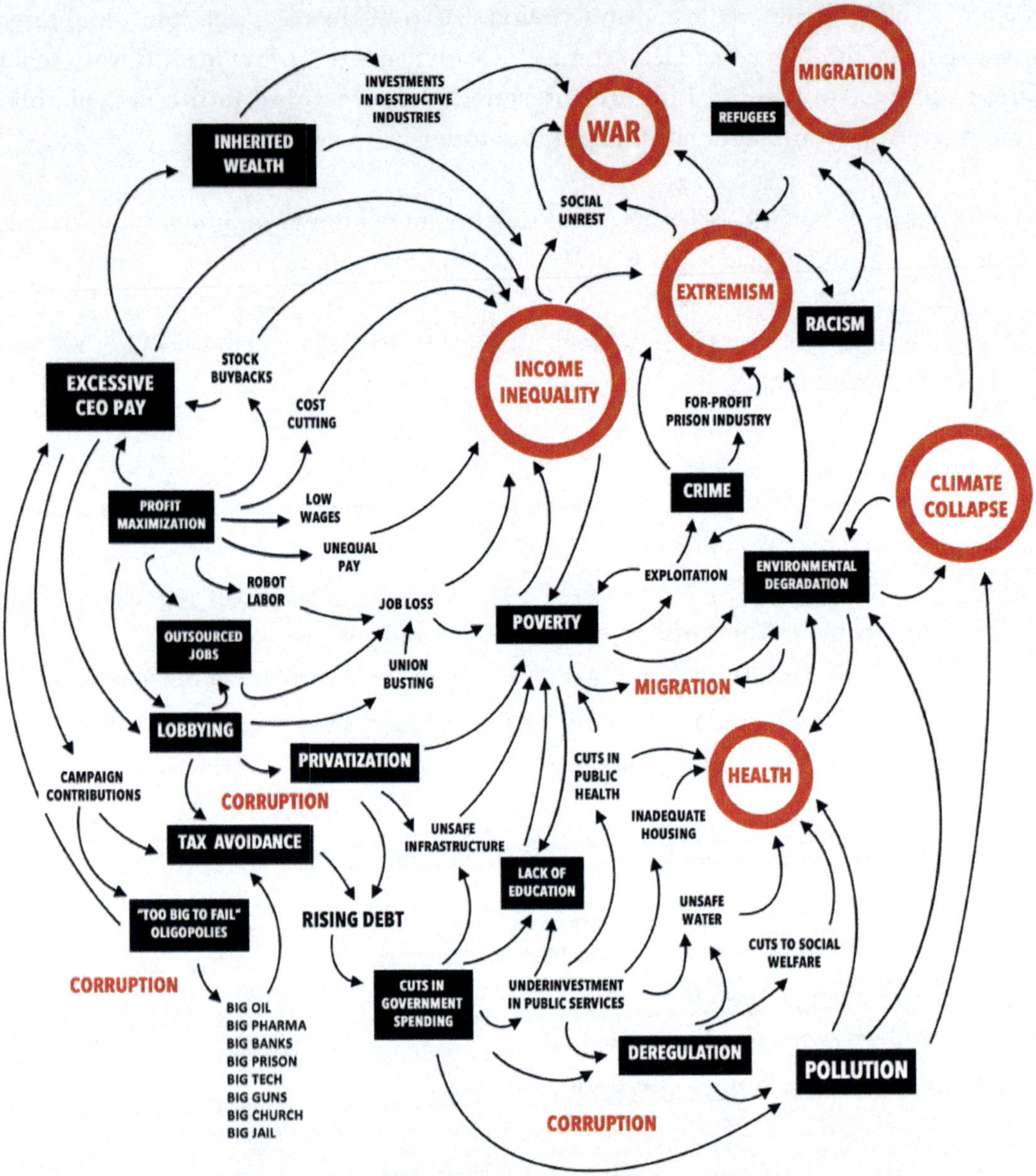

WHAT IS A WICKED PROBLEM?

A wicked problem is a problem which can't be solved using traditional problem-solving approaches. Business literature is full of names for a world of complex problems:

- **VUCA**
  (volatile, uncertain, complex, ambiguous)
- **BANI**
  (brittle, anxious, nonlinear, incomprehensible)
- **RUPT**
  (rapid, unpredictable, paradoxical, tangled)
- **TUNA**
  (turbulent, uncertain, novel, ambiguous)
- And **CRAZY**
  (our *new* definition – "all of the above" – a wicked problem which is **existential**)

In 1973, **Horst W.J. Rittel** and **Melvin M. Webber** described the **10 properties of a wicked problem**[5]**:**

1. There is no definitive formulation of a wicked problem.
2. Wicked problems have a no stopping rule.
3. Solutions to wicked problems are not true or false, but good or bad.
4. There is no immediate and no ultimate test of a solution to a wicked problem.

adapted from "Dilemmas in a General Theory of Planning" by Horst W.J. Rittel and Melvin M. Webber, *Policy Sciences*, June 1973

[5] "Dilemmas in a General Theory of Planning" by Horst W.J. Rittel and Melvin M. Webber, *Policy Sciences*, June 1973

5. Every solution to a wicked problem is a "one-shot" operation; because there is no opportunity to learn by trial and error, every attempt counts significantly.
6. Wicked problems do not have an exhaustively describable set of potential solutions, nor is there a well-described set of permissible operations that may be incorporated into the plan.
7. Every wicked problem is essentially unique.
8. Every wicked problem can be considered to be a symptom of another problem.
9. The existence of a discrepancy representing a wicked problem can be explained in numerous ways.
10. The planner has no right to be wrong.

While a **wicked problem** refers to an idea or problem that cannot be fixed using traditional approaches, the term "wicked" might be understood as ***resistance to resolution***. We argue that avoiding **solving wicked problems, in the face of widespread suffering, is wrong.**

Instead of getting into a finger pointing game, though, we asked ourselves – **what is the job to be done now?** What are the most *urgent* problems facing humanity?

David Attenborough is blunt[6]: "Things are going to get worse. The question is how much worse, and how quickly is it going to get worse. The speed is accelerating. Whatever we do now, it's going to get worse. And unless we act within the next 10 years … we are in real trouble."

It's about the **interconnectedness of everything**, he explains: "…unless you understand the natural world, you don't understand how the interconnections are so complex that you can damage it without knowing what you're doing. Understanding the complexity of the natural world is one of the crucial things."

---

[6] David Attenborough, the voice of Our Planet: "Things are going to get worse" by Brian Resnick, *Vox*, Apr 22, 2019 https://www.vox.com/2019/4/12/18306566/david-attenborough-our-planet-netflix-advocacy

For forty years the institutions of the world have worked to "mitigate" climate change with **no results** – or worse – failure to stop the rapid destruction of the ecosystems which keep us all alive.

Leaders and businesses have largely ignored the cries of our dying planet.

A desperate scientific community has taken up arms to spread the word, but the media is deaf. And inequality keeps growing – social, economic, climate, you name it. Wars are an easy, profitable excuse to *do nothing.*

ASK: *What are the* ***unmet needs*** *of* ***society****? And why aren't they being met? What is* ***blocking*** *us from doing the right thing?*

"CRAZY-WICKED" PROBLEMS

Our search for answers led us to the United Nation's SDGs – the universal benchmark embraced by institutions the world over. Sadly, the UN itself tells us that **at the half-way point toward 2030 the SDGs are far off track**.

But we noticed a difficulty with the SDGs – they don't emphasize the wicked problems which prevent us from solving the most urgent problems facing the world today – power and corruption or hate and conflict.

Somehow these problems are *outside the purview* of the SDGs.

We propose that **wicked problems have virtuous solutions.**

We decided to focus on **crazy-wicked problems** – those wicked problem which, if left unsolved, will kill us all.

It was this first insight which led us to begin this project as an informal project of exploration – we had the liberty of being naïve.

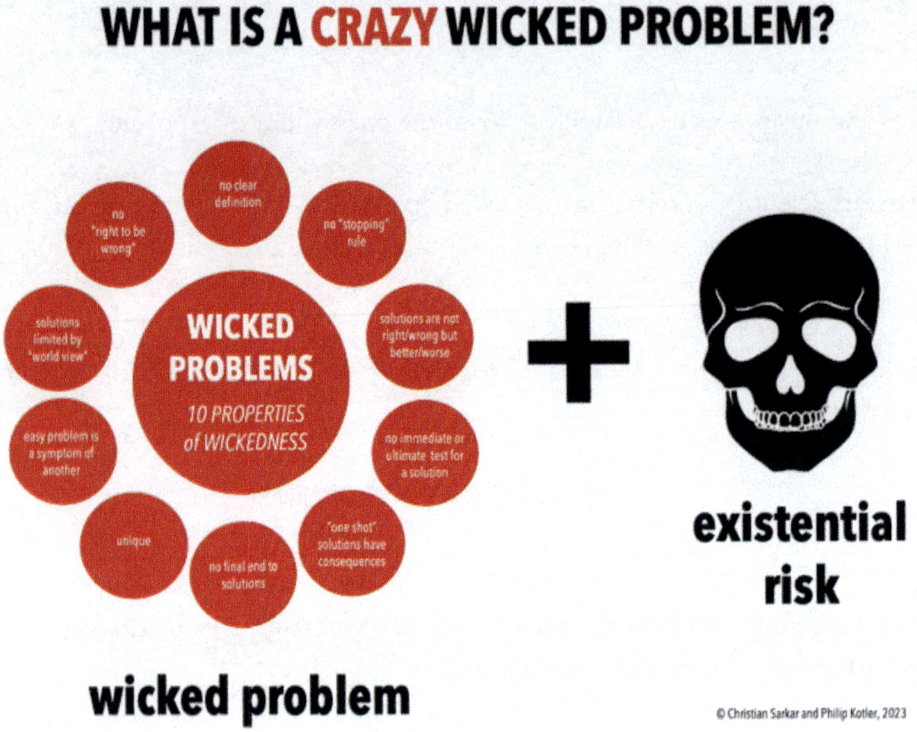

To understand a wicked problem, we must first be able to see the interconnectedness between the various factors which cause the problem in the first place. We must find a way to **map out these relationships** – what we call the *"ecosystem of wicked problems."*

That was how we started. Our goal was to find the points of leverage that govern the system – and we did. It turns out that one of the wicked problems – the problem of **Power and Corruption** is at the root of all the other problems.

We endeavor to explain why.

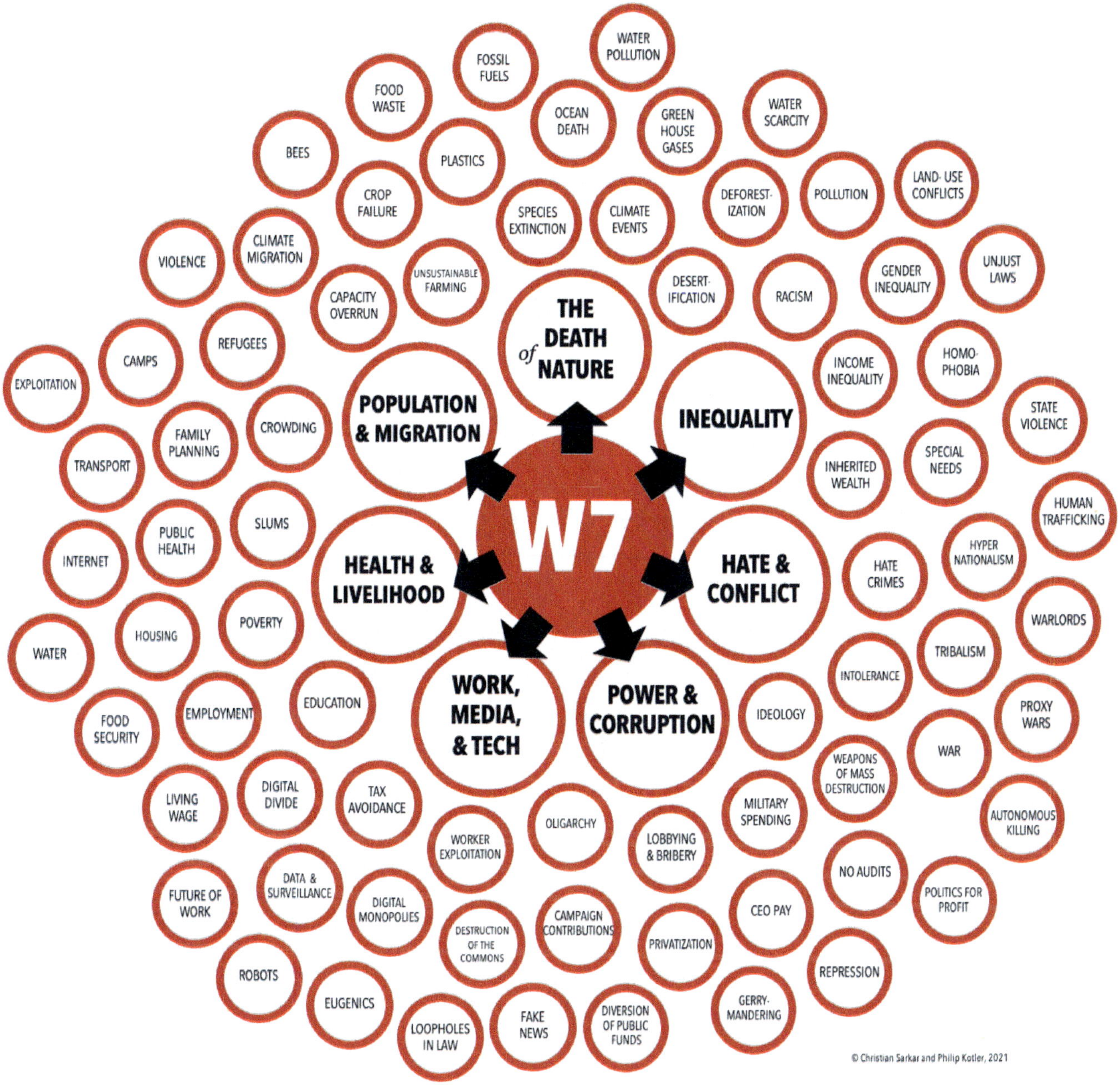
W7
THE DEATH of NATURE
INEQUALITY
HATE & CONFLICT
POWER & CORRUPTION
WORK, MEDIA, & TECH
HEALTH & LIVELIHOOD
POPULATION & MIGRATION
WATER POLLUTION
FOSSIL FUELS
FOOD WASTE
OCEAN DEATH
GREEN HOUSE GASES
WATER SCARCITY
BEES
PLASTICS
CROP FAILURE
SPECIES EXTINCTION
CLIMATE EVENTS
DEFOREST-IZATION
POLLUTION
LAND- USE CONFLICTS
VIOLENCE
CLIMATE MIGRATION
UNSUSTAINABLE FARMING
CAPACITY OVERRUN
DESERT-IFICATION
RACISM
GENDER INEQUALITY
UNJUST LAWS
EXPLOITATION
CAMPS
REFUGEES
INCOME INEQUALITY
HOMO-PHOBIA
STATE VIOLENCE
TRANSPORT
FAMILY PLANNING
CROWDING
INHERITED WEALTH
SPECIAL NEEDS
HUMAN TRAFFICKING
INTERNET
PUBLIC HEALTH
SLUMS
HATE CRIMES
HYPER NATIONALISM
WARLORDS
WATER
HOUSING
POVERTY
INTOLERANCE
TRIBALISM
FOOD SECURITY
EMPLOYMENT
EDUCATION
IDEOLOGY
PROXY WARS
WAR
WEAPONS OF MASS DESTRUCTION
LIVING WAGE
DIGITAL DIVIDE
TAX AVOIDANCE
OLIGARCHY
MILITARY SPENDING
AUTONOMOUS KILLING
WORKER EXPLOITATION
LOBBYING & BRIBERY
NO AUDITS
FUTURE OF WORK
DATA & SURVEILLANCE
DIGITAL MONOPOLIES
CAMPAIGN CONTRIBUTIONS
CEO PAY
POLITICS FOR PROFIT
DESTRUCTION OF THE COMMONS
PRIVATIZATION
ROBOTS
EUGENICS
REPRESSION
LOOPHOLES IN LAW
FAKE NEWS
DIVERSION OF PUBLIC FUNDS
GERRY-MANDERING

THE WICKED7

How did we choose the Wicked7? We asked a simple question – **what are the world's most urgent crazy-wicked problems?** We made a list of some 162 problems, and narrowed them down to seven categories – the following:

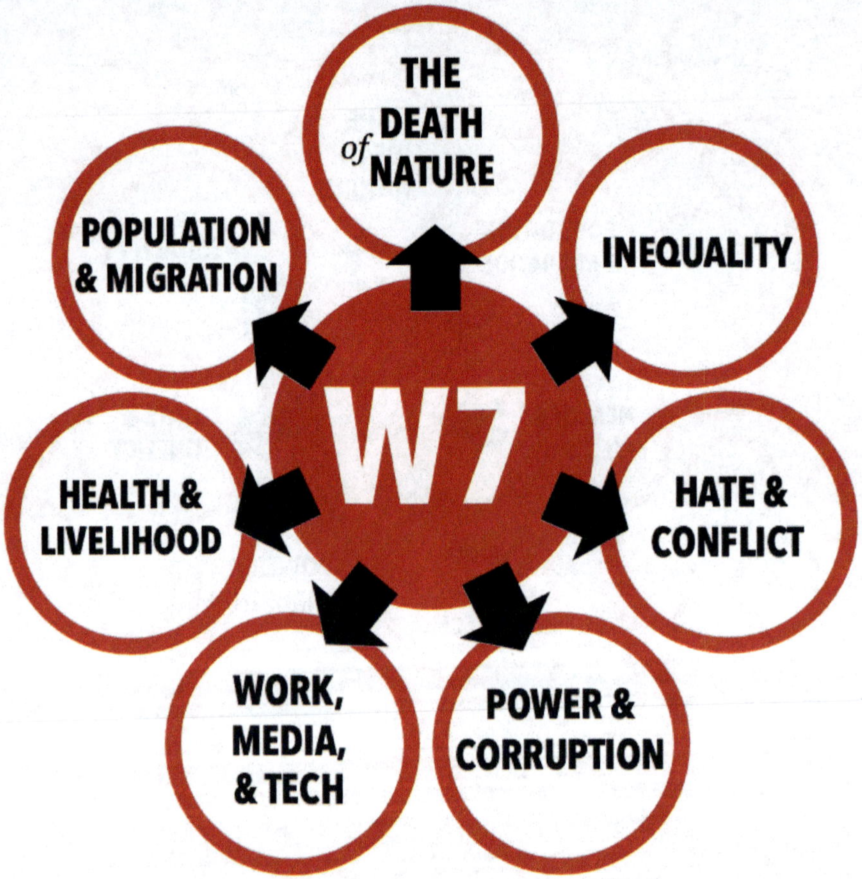

The Death of Nature: the interlinked global crisis of environmental impacts and weather-related events — heat waves, forest fires, flooding, hurricanes, ecosystem degradation and collapse, pollution, and species extinction.

Inequality: the various forms of inequality — economic, social, and workplace inequality is a way to measure social and gender inequality. The growing gap between the 1% and the rest of the population creates an unequal and unjust society.

Hate & Conflict: the growing intolerance and hate fueled by racism, sexism, and extremism. Includes identity-based or ideological groups which create social unrest and commit acts of terror. Conflict includes militarism, the culture of war, armies, arms-profits, policies, plans, propaganda, prejudices, and rationalizations that lead to lethal group conflict.

Power & Corruption: the abuse of power—individual and systemic. Dishonest conduct by those in power or those seeking to influence them. Includes fraud and bribery. Corruption creates a system that governs not for the many, but for the few.

Work, Media, and Technology: the future of work, data and surveillance. The growing digital divide, digital monopolies and exploitation. Includes the use of media to create false narratives for politics and profit. Robots and automation and the policies to govern the "intelligent" economy. And, of course, AI. Will AI replace us all? Or will it simply be used to widen the gap between the haves and have-nots? What happens when AI is used on the battlefield?

Health and Livelihood: the worldwide challenge of public wellbeing – economic and physical health. Includes the economy, employment, education, and the new skills and capabilities required to "make a living." *NOTE:* this wicked problem turned into the "**Essentials of Life**" to include Food & Nutrition, Water & Sanitation, Shelter & Safety, Healthcare & Well-being, Education & Knowledge, Employment & Economic Stability , Community & Social Belonging, Justice & Governance, Freedom & Self-Determination, and Nature & Climate .

Population & Migration: the domestic and global population growth leads to increased conflicts over water, energy, food, open space, transportation, and schooling. Carrying capacity, the number of people, other living organisms, or crops that a region can support without environmental degradation – becomes a key metric for local and national wellbeing. Also includes the growing problem of climate refugees and asylum seekers, mainly from the "Global South," but also from wars and armed conflicts.

The Wicked7 may be a simpler way to understand the SDGs, perhaps because it is easier to show the interconnections between them. So, how should we explore the seven wicked problems? **Each one of the seven wicked problems create vicious cycles that impacts the others.**

Thus, we must examine them all together, to understand what the leverage points are.

For each vicious cycle we can ask:

- **Problem definition:** what is the wicked problem?
- **Vicious cycle:** what are the vicious cycles related to the wicked problem?
- **Impact:** What will happen if the "crazy-wicked" problem remains unsolved?
- **Interconnections:** the effect on other wicked problems
- **Unmet Needs:** What are the "jobs to be done" for society?
- **Obstacles:** What is blocking us from solving the problem?
- **Examples** – do we have any to illustrate our point?

All of this in turn led to the development of our methodology for exploring wicked problems, and the various maps produced by the working group at *www.wicked7.org.*

The number of vicious cycles is staggering. Unfortunately, we treat them as if they are independent problems, and thus our attempts to solve them fail miserably. And, our "solutions" may be making things worse.

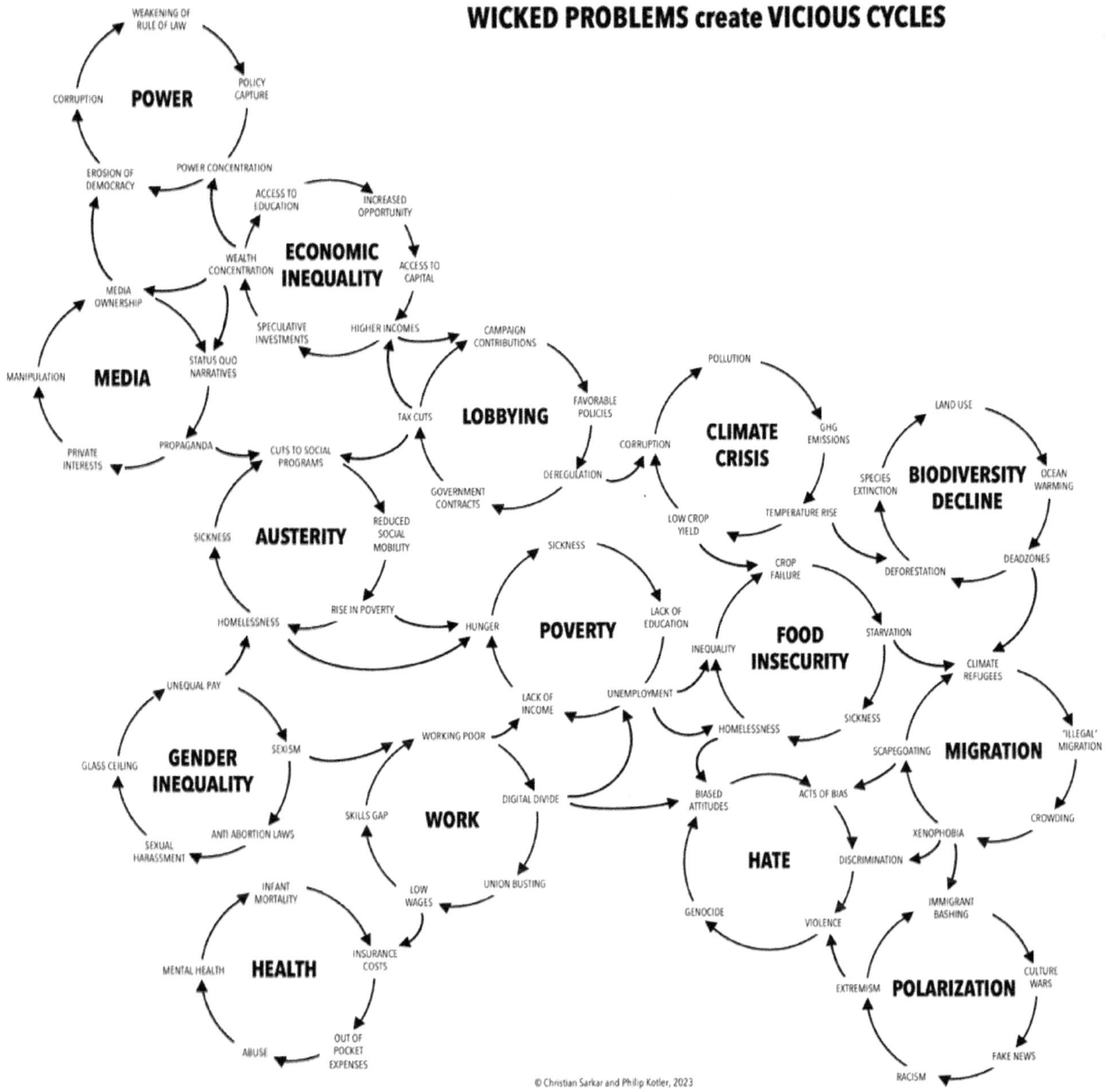
WICKED PROBLEMS create VICIOUS CYCLES
POWER
WEAKENING OF RULE OF LAW
POLICY CAPTURE
POWER CONCENTRATION
EROSION OF DEMOCRACY
CORRUPTION
ECONOMIC INEQUALITY
ACCESS TO EDUCATION
INCREASED OPPORTUNITY
ACCESS TO CAPITAL
HIGHER INCOMES
SPECULATIVE INVESTMENTS
WEALTH CONCENTRATION
MEDIA
MEDIA OWNERSHIP
STATUS QUO NARRATIVES
PROPAGANDA
PRIVATE INTERESTS
MANIPULATION
LOBBYING
CAMPAIGN CONTRIBUTIONS
FAVORABLE POLICIES
DEREGULATION
GOVERNMENT CONTRACTS
TAX CUTS
AUSTERITY
CUTS TO SOCIAL PROGRAMS
REDUCED SOCIAL MOBILITY
RISE IN POVERTY
HOMELESSNESS
SICKNESS
CLIMATE CRISIS
POLLUTION
GHG EMISSIONS
TEMPERATURE RISE
LOW CROP YIELD
CORRUPTION
BIODIVERSITY DECLINE
LAND USE
OCEAN WARMING
DEADZONES
DEFORESTATION
SPECIES EXTINCTION
POVERTY
SICKNESS
LACK OF EDUCATION
UNEMPLOYMENT
LACK OF INCOME
HUNGER
FOOD INSECURITY
CROP FAILURE
STARVATION
SICKNESS
HOMELESSNESS
INEQUALITY
MIGRATION
CLIMATE REFUGEES
'ILLEGAL' MIGRATION
CROWDING
XENOPHOBIA
SCAPEGOATING
GENDER INEQUALITY
UNEQUAL PAY
SEXISM
ANTI ABORTION LAWS
SEXUAL HARASSMENT
GLASS CEILING
WORK
WORKING POOR
DIGITAL DIVIDE
UNION BUSTING
LOW WAGES
SKILLS GAP
HATE
BIASED ATTITUDES
ACTS OF BIAS
DISCRIMINATION
VIOLENCE
GENOCIDE
HEALTH
INFANT MORTALITY
INSURANCE COSTS
OUT OF POCKET EXPENSES
ABUSE
MENTAL HEALTH
POLARIZATION
IMMIGRANT BASHING
CULTURE WARS
FAKE NEWS
RACISM
EXTREMISM
© Christian Sarkar and Philip Kotler, 2023

Here are a few more. By mapping them out we are more aware of how these cycles affect us all, and where we should intervene.

VICIOUS CYCLES: EXAMPLES

Global Trade Vicious Cycle:
- Trade tensions between major economies lead to the imposition of tariffs.
- Tariffs hinder international trade and economic growth.
- Slower economic growth contributes to increased trade tensions, perpetuating the cycle.

Pandemic Health-Economic Vicious Cycle:
- A global health crisis (e.g., a pandemic) strains healthcare systems.
- Economic shutdowns and disruptions lead to a recession.
- The economic downturn reduces resources available for healthcare, exacerbating the health crisis.

Urbanization and Traffic Congestion Doom Loop:
- Rapid urbanization leads to increased vehicle ownership.
- More vehicles contribute to traffic congestion and air pollution.
- Congestion hampers economic activities and quality of life, but urbanization continues, perpetuating the loop.

Populism and Media Vicious Cycle:
- Populist leaders exploit dissatisfaction with mainstream media.
- Distrust in media institutions grows, leading to the rise of alternative sources.
- Alternative sources reinforce populist narratives, fostering a cycle of distrust in mainstream media.

Water Scarcity Vicious Cycle:
- Over-extraction of water resources leads to scarcity.
- Water scarcity affects agriculture, leading to food insecurity.
- Food insecurity intensifies competition for water resources, perpetuating the scarcity.

Nuclear Proliferation Vicious Cycle:
- The development of nuclear weapons by one country triggers security concerns.
- Other countries respond by seeking nuclear capabilities for their own security.
- The proliferation of nuclear weapons increases global security risks, perpetuating the cycle.

Natural Disaster Recovery Vicious Cycle:
- Natural disasters damage infrastructure and disrupt economies.
- Weakened economies struggle to invest in disaster-resistant infrastructure.
- Inadequate infrastructure exacerbates the impact of future natural disasters, perpetuating the cycle.

Biodiversity Loss Vicious Cycle:
- Habitat destruction and pollution contribute to biodiversity loss.
- Reduced biodiversity weakens ecosystems, making them more vulnerable to further degradation.
- The cycle continues as ecosystems struggle to recover, leading to more biodiversity loss.

Arms Race Vicious Cycle:
- Increased military spending by one nation triggers security concerns in others.
- Other nations respond by increasing their military budgets.
- The arms race intensifies, creating a cycle of heightened global tensions and military expenditures.

FROM POLYCRISIS TO PERMACRISIS

According to the *Polycrisis Roadmap 2024*[7], the term "polycrisis" highlights interactions between crises, but there is as yet no agreed upon, authoritative definition of the term. The report states that phenomenon has five key features:

1. **Emergent harms:** when crises interact, their impacts are different from— and generally worse than—the impacts the crises would have had separately from one another.
2. **Multiple causes:** interacting crises are not reducible to single root causes; they arise from complex causal interactions that require multifaceted responses.
3. **Deep uncertainty:** crisis interactions generate change that strains comprehension and exceeds our ability to anticipate future developments.
4. **Systemic context:** crises arise within complex systems and, therefore, must be understood and addressed using complex systems thinking.
5. **New knowledge and action:** established frameworks, institutions, and practices are ill-equipped to address crisis interactions; new modes of research and practice are required.

Unfortunately, even the term polycrisis has been overrun by reality. We call this the **permacrisis**. The Wicked7 is an attempt to grapple with the underlying **socio-political reality** which prevents us from having a say in the future of the planet. Why is it that our so-called leaders and institutions are powerless to actually slow and halt the trajectory of doom that our species is now on? To critics who call this "doomism" or "negativity" or "woke"- we say: **extinction is not inevitable unless we remain silent.**

We cannot remain silent. The future depends on *us* – our voice, our actions.

---

[7] Lawrence, M., Shipman, M., Janzwood, S., Arnscheidt, C., Donges, J., Homer-Dixon, T., Otto, C., Schweizer, P.J., Wunderling, N. (2024). *Polycrisis Research and Action Roadmap 2024: Gaps, opportunities, and priorities for polycrisis research and action.* Version 1.0. Cascade Institute. https://cascadeinstitute.org/technical-paper/polycrisisroadmap

WICKED PROBLEM EXPLORATION GUIDELINES

As part of our investigation of wicked problems, we're actively searching for **root causes** and **interconnections** between the seven wicked problems. We came up with a process:

1. Begin by **defining the problem** based on observable and verifiable facts. Describe what the problem is and who or what it affects. How often?

2. Ask "**why did this happen?**" to go backwards in time – what are the sources of the problem? What evidence is there to show that this is a cause? Cite the articles, reports, or observations which support your premise.

3. Once you have identified the symptomatic or technical causes for a problem, begin exploring the possibility of underlying **systemic** causes. Are there **economic reasons** why this is happening? **Social reasons? Historical reasons?** By un-entangling the threads of events that led us to the present, it is possible to uncover the root-causes of our present–day problem. Again, cite the data or evidence to back up your claims.

4. Consider "**what next**" if the problem is not addressed. Consider the "**impact chain**" from individual - to community - to nation - to planet. Use *personas* for convenience, preferably based on interviews with representative samples of the population being impacted.

5. If a wicked problem is ignored, its impact multiplies across many systemic dimensions. What happens to the **economic system** (and all other underlying systems) for the individual in a specified community? Country? Planet?

ASK:
(1) Who or what is causing the problem?
(2) What prevents us from solving the problem?
(3) Who decides? And for whom?

WICKED PROBLEM EXPLORATION GUIDELINES

ask **"WHY?"** to find the **CAUSES**

2

Symptomatic CAUSES
(select those that apply)

- ❑ MANAGEMENT/POLICY
- ❑ MACHINE/ALGORITHM
- ❑ MATERIALS
- ❑ MAINTENANCE
- ❑ METHOD/KNOWLEDGE
- ❑ MEASUREMENT
- ❑ NATURE
- ❑ HUMAN
- ❑ OTHER *please fill*

____

3

Systemic CAUSES
(select those that apply)

- ❑ ECONOMIC
- ❑ SOCIAL
- ❑ ENVIRONMENTAL
- ❑ POLITICAL
- ❑ SCIENTIFIC / TECH
- ❑ CULTURAL
- ❑ LEGAL
- ❑ HISTORICAL
- ❑ ORGANIZATIONAL
- ❑ LEADERSHIP
- ❑ OTHER *please fill*

____

1

WHAT IS THE PROBLEM?

wicked7.org

Problem Definition
What are the observable facts which describe the problem? Can the problem be de-constructed into a set of component problems?

what - the type of problem: describe it as clearly as possible

- ❑ Event
- ❑ Action
- ❑ People
- ❑ Power
- ❑ Process
- ❑ Policy
- ❑ Place
- ❑ History
- ❑ Nature

who - is being impacted? Individual, community, work, national, planet?

where - is the problem observed

when - does the problem occur - it it continuous or sporadic?

IMPACT CHAIN

INDIVIDUAL

COMMUNITY

BUSINESS

STATE

PLANET

ask **"WHAT NEXT?"** to find the **EFFECTS**

4

CONSIDER
What happens next if the problem is ignored?
What disruptions and instabilities can we expect?
How does individual and group breakdown lead to societal collapse?

5

Systemic RISKS
(select those that apply)

- ❑ ECONOMIC
- ❑ SOCIAL
- ❑ ENVIRONMENTAL
- ❑ POLITICAL
- ❑ SCIENTIFIC / TECH
- ❑ CULTURAL
- ❑ LEGAL
- ❑ HISTORICAL
- ❑ ORGANIZATIONAL
- ❑ LEADERSHIP
- ❑ OTHER *please fill*

____

WHO OR WHAT IS CAUSING THE PROBLEM?"

WHAT PREVENTS US FROM SOLVING THE PROBLEM?

WHO DECIDES? AND FOR WHOM?

We also must **not** avoid the **historical** and **cultural** dimensions of a wicked problem. There are no simple explanations – but that doesn't mean we can't continuously develop our knowledge. In that sense, every map is always a "work in progress."

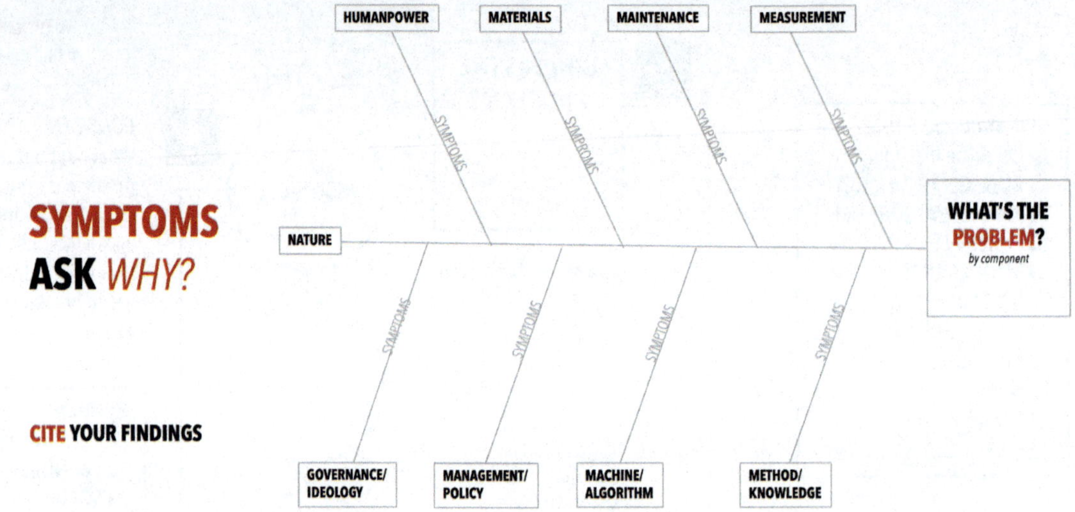

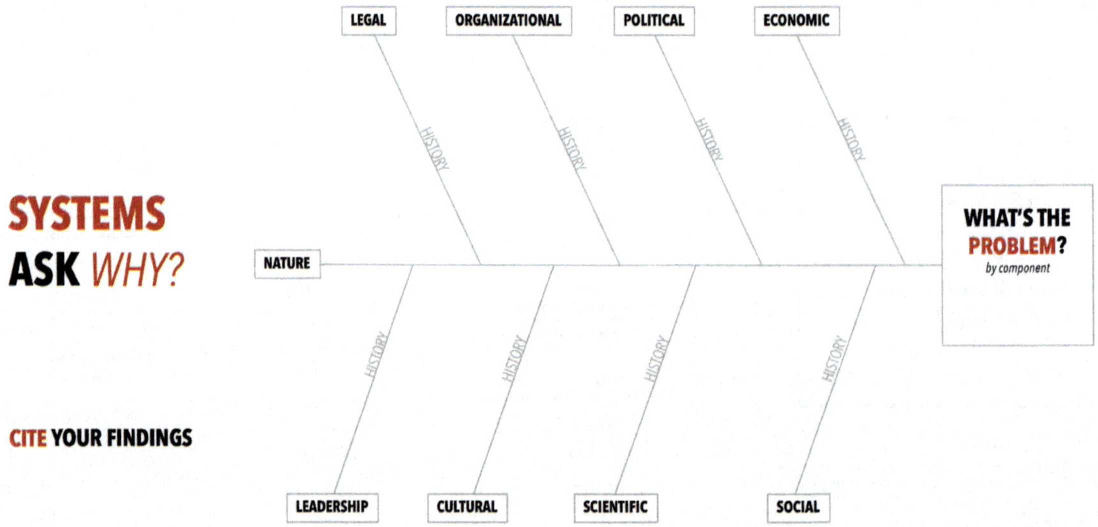

When the COVID crisis began, we drew two maps showing the difference in civilian impact based on how public health was addressed by the authorities:

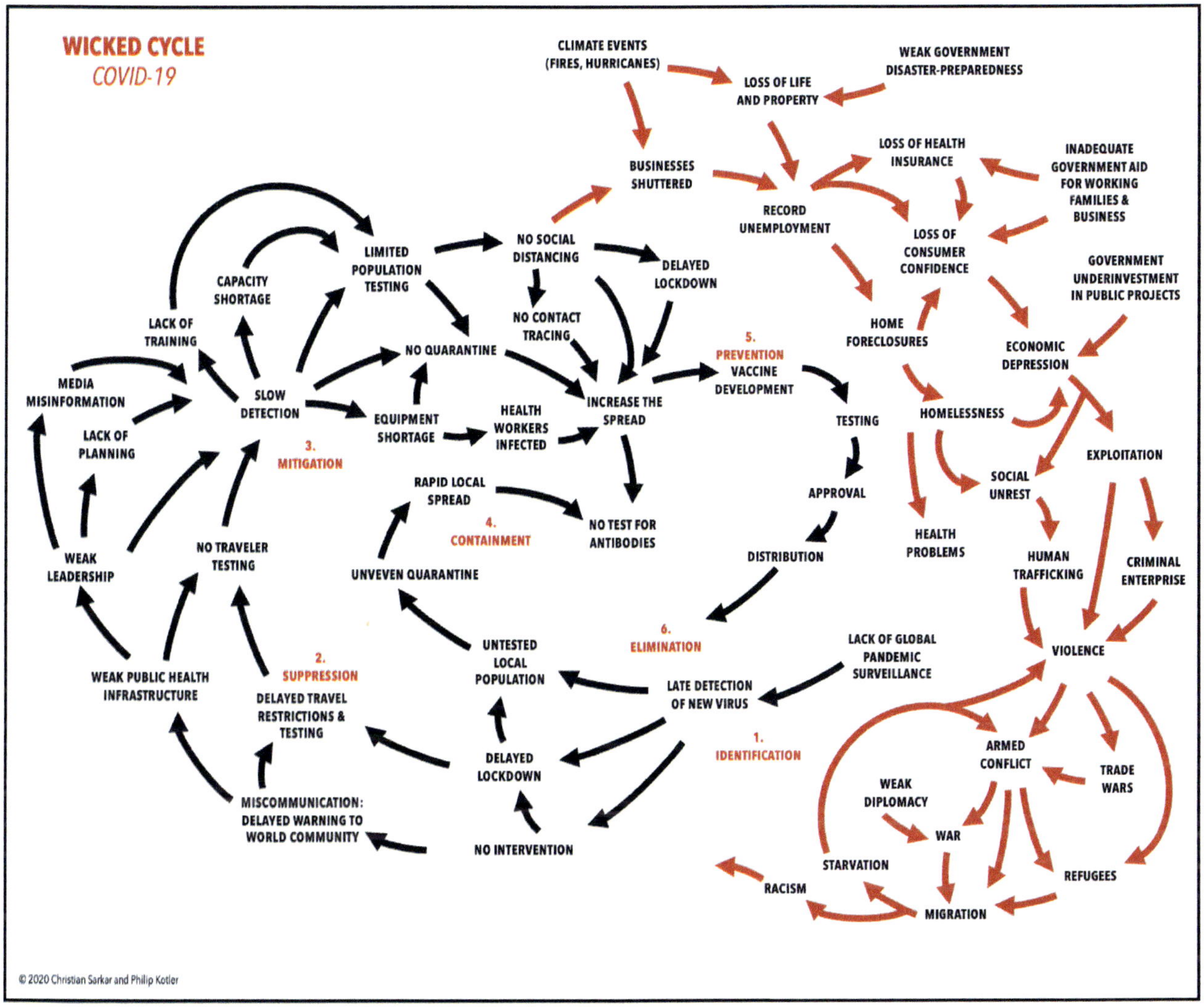

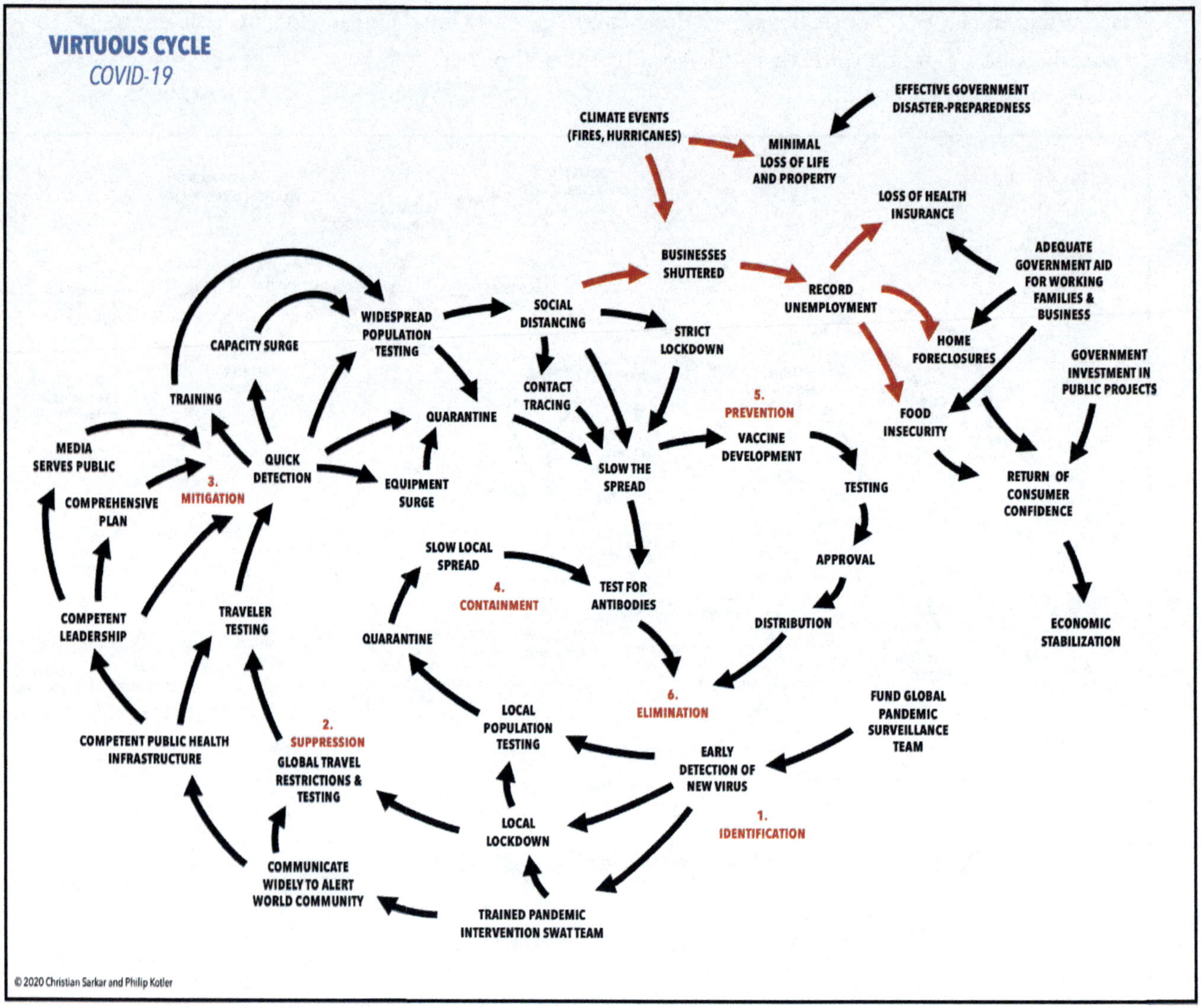

The lesson? **Mapping out wicked problems can help us understand the interconnections and the *impact* of our actions.**

An example of how things can go wrong with systems mapping is the infamous spaghetti chart with the title "Afghanistan Stability/ CION Dynamics" which made it to the front page of the *New York Times.*

The military mindset could be summarized as *"move fast and break things"* and it is diametrically opposed to the system view required to even begin to understand the interconnected nature of societal problems. Unfortunately, this same mantra also shapes the mindset of "agile" companies in Silicon Valley and beyond.

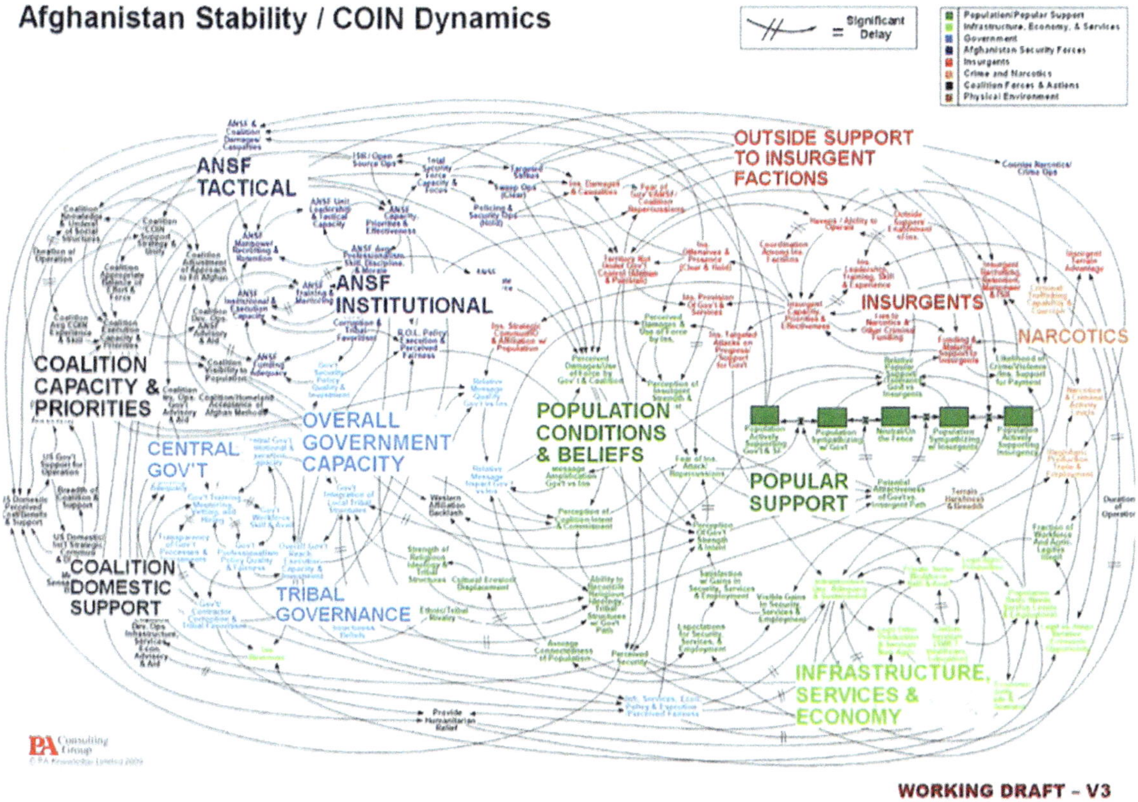

Gen. Stanley A. McChrystal, the leader of American and NATO forces in Afghanistan, famously remarked "When we understand that slide, we'll have won the war." The slide became an object of laughter and derision.[8]

From a systems-thinking point of view, however, the map itself *is* brilliant because it showed that the war in Afghanistan was *already* lost. It was the US military which lacked the capabilities required for "nation building." And that was clearly beyond the scope of its capabilities. Perhaps the military is *not* the right institution to manage nation-building?

By the way, if we are interested in learning about what went wrong in Afghanistan, here are seven key lessons from the recent report *What We Need to Learn: Lessons from Twenty Years of Afghanistan Reconstruction*[9]:

(1) **Strategy:** The U.S. government continuously struggled to develop and implement a coherent strategy for what it hoped to achieve.
(2) **Timelines:** The U.S. government consistently underestimated the amount of time required to rebuild Afghanistan, and created unrealistic timelines and expectations that prioritized spending quickly. These choices increased corruption and reduced the effectiveness of programs.
(3) **Sustainability:** Many of the institutions and infrastructure projects the United States built were not sustainable.
(4) **Personnel:** Counterproductive civilian and military personnel policies and practices thwarted the effort.
(5) Insecurity: Persistent insecurity severely undermined reconstruction efforts.
(6) **Context:** The U.S. government did not understand the Afghan context and therefore failed to tailor its efforts accordingly.
(7) **Monitoring and Evaluation:** U.S. government agencies rarely conducted sufficient monitoring and evaluation to understand the impact of their efforts.

---

[8] "We Have Met the Enemy and He Is PowerPoint" Elisabeth Bumiller, April 26, 2010 *New York Times* https://www.nytimes.com/2010/04/27/world/27powerpoint.html

[9] *What We Need to Learn: Lessons from Twenty Years of Afghanistan Reconstruction* Special Inspector General for Afghanistan Reconstruction, August 2021 https://www.sigar.mil/pdf/lessonslearned/SIGAR-21-46-LL.pdf

Furthermore, the inability of the military to understand the true significance of the chart is an example of **"wicked ignorance"** – the accidental or *willful* (1) inability to comprehend or (2) dismiss something beyond one's capabilities or purview. Wicked ignorance may be a close family relation – a cousin, or sister perhaps, of the Dunning-Kruger effect. Wicked ignorance is perhaps one reason so many politicians "kick the can down the road" with global warming and the climate crisis. Unfortunately, as the Secretary General of the UN has recently stated so eloquently, *"we are out of road."*

Another powerful example of wicked ignorance is when we ***reject facts because of our ideological beliefs.***

John Burn-Murdoch's op-ed – "Does the American dream foster inequality?" – in the *Financial Times* shows us that "wicked ignorance" can take over a country, not just an individual.[10] The average American agrees, with one in five describing the US income distribution as "very unfair", higher than the share in any other wealthy western country. He points to a recent study which shows that while Americans may recognize the problem with inequality, they have *less desire for something to be done* about it than people in other countries.

He explains: *"In psychology, for someone to shift away from an undesired behaviour there are two separate requirements. First, they need the self-awareness to recognise the issue. Second, they need the self-management skills to act on that knowledge. Having the former without mastering the latter is arguably worse than having neither: painful awareness of a flaw extending into perpetuity."*

He then states: *"If we swap people for countries and personal flaws for societal ills, I fear America may be in just this predicament when it comes to income disparities."*

Wicked ignorance is why we don't learn the lessons of history and repeat our mistakes over and over again through time. The *other* possible explanation is **"terminal corruption" –** defined as **corruption that will lead to existential crisis and/or collapse.**

---

[10] "Does the American dream foster inequality?" John Burn-Murdoch, *Financial Times*, 8 December, 2023 https://www.ft.com/content/6a61757f-8352-4102-897d-4b319b42ea63

In *The Origins of Totalitarianism*, **Hannah Arendt** famously wrote: **"The ideal subject of totalitarian rule is not the convinced Nazi or the convinced Communist, but people for whom the distinction between fact and fiction (i.e., the reality of experience) and the distinction between true and false (i.e., the standards of thought) no longer exist."**

With current events, we can examine the ongoing political situation in Arizona, where many Republicans continue to deny the legitimacy of the 2020 election, echoing former President Trump's "Big Lie" about widespread voter fraud.[11] Arizona Republicans have engaged in a persistent effort to undermine trust in elections by promoting false narratives. These attempts exemplify Arendt's concept of a society where distinctions between truth and falsehood blur. Totalitarianism, in Arendt's framework, thrives in environments where truth is malleable and people are more susceptible to political manipulation, regardless of facts. Arizona's Republican leadership illustrates this point by maintaining election-denial rhetoric despite overwhelming evidence debunking these claims. By doing so, they create a climate in **which voters no longer know who or what to trust**, making them vulnerable to authoritarian tactics. This can corrode democratic institutions, as free and fair elections depend on citizens' faith in the truthfulness of the process.

Arendt warned that when citizens lose their sense of truth, they become easy targets for totalitarian control because they stop questioning power and succumb to propaganda. Arizona's situation (which is mirrored across the US) parallels her warning, as the "Big Lie" has become a political tool for undermining democracy. In such a scenario, people align with extreme ideologies not out of conviction but because they no longer recognize or value objective facts, creating fertile ground for authoritarianism to take root. Eroding the line between truth and falsehood can destabilize democracy, a reality that Arendt foresaw. *The intentional blurring of fact and fiction in politics threatens to undermine the democratic principles of transparency, accountability, and trust—essential elements in preventing authoritarianism.* (This strategy of promoting **wicked ignorance** is not limited to the GOP in the United States, in fact it is employed by right-wing and libertarian parties across the world).

---

[11] "State of Denial" by Tim Murphy, *Mother Jones*, September-October 2024
https://www.motherjones.com/politics/2024/09/arizona-republicans-elections-denial-big-lie/

UNDERSTANDING WICKED PROBLEMS: HOW WE SEE

The seven wicked problems are interconnected. In the same way that the COVID-19 pandemic caused cascading stress to our cities and economic systems, with unequal and unjust outcomes, we see the seven wicked problems doing the same – with the very real potential of societal collapse. What we discovered was that most wicked problems *can* be solved, in fact, most of the solutions exist; but our institutions – public, private, and plural are *not interested* in solving them. They have been captured by special interests. And, as we dug deeper, we realized that creating and presenting complex charts of root causes would simply take us back to the problem of the Afghanistan spaghetti chart. We also understood that the wickedest problem of all was answering the question of *why can't we solve the world's most urgent problems?*

Why do normal solutions fail? Because they do not resolve **root causes**. As we began our mapping exercises with the working group, we realized that no matter how many maps we drew, we were always at risk of creating another spaghetti chart which no one would understand or pay attention to.

We've spent over ten years researching the interconnections between these wicked problems – beginning with the *"ecosystem of poverty"* which was a key finding from the $300 House project.[12]

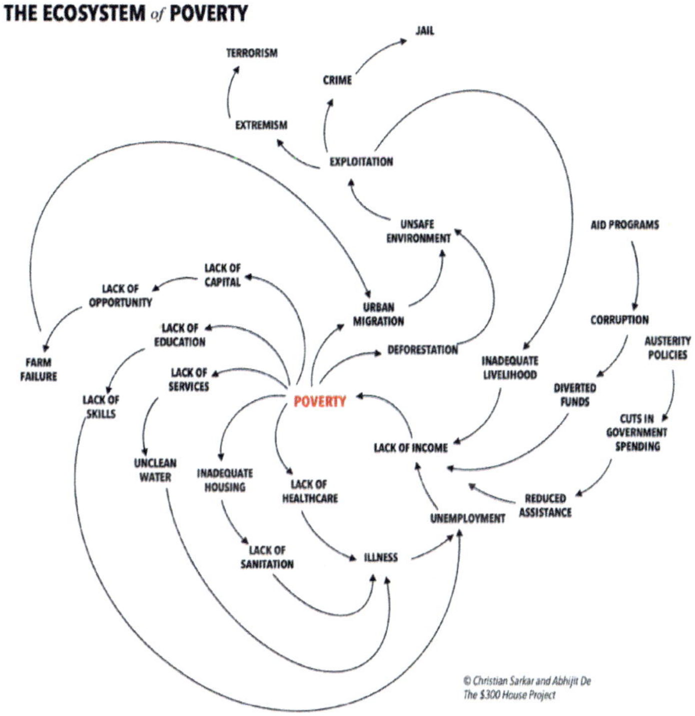

[12] Download (PDF): https://christiansarkar.com/wp-content/uploads/2020/07/ecosystemofpoverty_thinkers.pdf
The $300 House project started began as a challenge issued by Vijay Govindarajan and in Christian Sarkar in *Harvard Business Review* in 2010 https://hbr.org/2010/08/the-300-house-a-hands-on-lab-f

Part of the problem with information is the bias inherent in all studies (including our own) – and for that reason we spent a lot of time poring of reports from the experts. (We still believe in experts, don't we? Next time someone tells us that experts are overrated, let's ask them if they're willing to fly on a plane piloted by a fashion model, or get heart surgery done by their barber.)

But what is the best way to ensure objectivity?

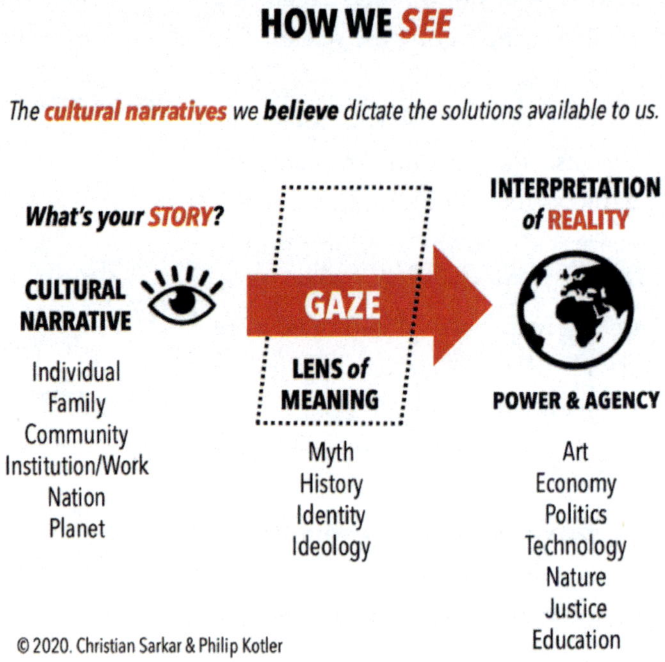

James Baldwin warned us that "reality" depends on our **point of view**: "How you view the world is largely shaped by where you are in it."[13] For Baldwin, the "Western or European system of reality" is *white supremacy*, and it comes to America from Europe. He asks – **does "one civilization have the right to overtake, and subjugate, and in fact, to destroy the other?"**

This makes our understanding of the world and our place in it dependent on the **dominant cultural narrative** of the country, region, even family, that we live in. Going against the dominant narrative is dangerous. In some instances, it can cost you your status in society, your job, and even your life.

---

[13] James Baldwin on *Racism and the American Dream* (at Cambridge, 1965), *YouTube* https://youtu.be/mnYwcSxqhJc?si=t8mC8Cz4lbtm170H Baldwin's voice speaks to us across the years, and reminds us that the controversy over "critical race theory" is simple another instance of racism inflicted on the public for political gain by politicians who know better.

So how are we to solve any of our wicked problems at all?

We must arrive at a **shared view** of reality. The starting point for agreement must be what we hold in common, our **interdependence**.

Henry Mintzberg has put together a ***Declaration of Interdependence*** that nails the problem – we have reached the limits of growth and can no longer survive without working together.

The shift is from **self-interest** *to* **common-interest**.

It is time, as the declaration states, *to get our collective act together.*

But how do we find the underlying root cause of the root causes?

The late Donella Meadows explains[14]:

Folks who do systems analysis have a great belief in "leverage points." These are places within a complex system (a corporation, an economy, a living body, a city, an ecosystem) where a small shift in one thing can produce big changes in everything.

The Declaration of our Interdependence

For two centuries, the American Declaration of Independence served as the model to grow democracy. ***Now our world has reached the limits of growth driven by the pursuit of individual rights at the expense of shared responsibilities.*** *Faced with the threats of warming, weapons, waste, and the lopsided distribution of wealth, we must declare our* interdependence.

We hold these truths to be self-evident, that all people are created dependent —on each other, our earth, and its climate—endowed with the inalienable responsibility to maintain justice, liberty, and affiliation for all. Thus our societies must sustain balance across public sector governments that are respected, private sector businesses that are responsible, and plural sector communities that are robust. Some societies retain this balance; others have lost it; many never had it. We propose the following resolutions to guide the rebalancing of society:

- **Balance begins** when each of us decides how we shall become part of the solution. By doing nothing, we remain part of the problem.
- **We advance to action in our communities**, networked to consolidate a global movement for peaceful reformation.
- **We commit to the ideals** of social conscience, fair trade, and good government, to replace the dogma of imbalance—that greed is good, markets are sufficient, and governments are suspect. We explore our human resourcefulness by resisting our exploitation as human resources.
- **We build** worthy institutions in all three sectors of society—departments in government, enterprises in business, associations in communities—from the ground up, with widespread engagement that carries individual leadership into collective communityship.
- **At the tables of public policy**, we strive to replace the compromises of self-interest with the coalescing of common interest.
- **We challenge the rampant corruption that is legal** as vigorously as we expect our governments to prosecute the overt corruption that is criminal.
- Sustainable global balance requires **substantial global government**. We call on all democratic nations to rally for lasting peace, by containing any power that aims to dominate while holding economic globalization in its place, namely the marketplace.

These resolutions require **concerted action**, not by centrally orchestrated planning so much as through a groundswell of initiatives by concerned citizens the world over, to restrain our worst tendencies while encouraging our best. **For the future of our planet and our progeny, this is the time to get our collective act together**.

ourinterdependence.org

---

14 "Leverage Points: Places to Intervene in a System" by Donella Meadows https://donellameadows.org/archives/leverage-points-places-to-intervene-in-a-system/

Here's her famous list:

PLACES TO INTERVENE IN A SYSTEM

(in increasing order of effectiveness)

9. Constants, parameters, numbers (subsidies, taxes, standards).
8. Regulating negative feedback loops.
7. Driving positive feedback loops.
6. Material flows and nodes of material intersection.
5. Information flows.
4. The rules of the system (incentives, punishments, constraints).
3. The distribution of power over the rules of the system.
2. The goals of the system.
1. The **mindset** or **paradigm** out of which the system — its goals, power structure, rules, its culture — arises.

We asked – *what is the **underlying paradigm** that our entire system is based on?*

The answer: **Capitalism** (via colonialism) and its power structures.

For example, the scientific community advocates for a phaseout of fossil fuels to alleviate the impending climate crisis. However, this poses a threat to the financial interests of major players in the industry, and consequently, fossil fuel companies have actively suppressed and discredited scientific findings, impeding timely action, despite the substantial economic burdens projected to be shouldered by the public, reaching trillions of dollars.

The conflict is a **values conflict**. At the root of this conflict is **power**. What is blocking us from doing the right thing? We've asked this question for over a year on our online forums at **The Wicked7 Project** and the **Regenerative Marketing Institute**. We're exploring the changes required to shift the existing paradigm. That's what the last two chapters are about. We're also promoting the institutions and individuals that are helping the world make this shift. Our time on this planet is almost up, unless we ***act now*** in meaningful and effective ways.

Colonialism/Capitalism has run its course. What comes next?

We have to re-examine what we want from government. What is the function of government? For the past 100 years in the US, we've embraced the notion that **the function of government is to drive economic growth through deregulation and privatization.**

Time's up.

If we want to prevent collapse, and see a world beyond 2050, we must come to the conclusion that **the proper function of government is to nurture wellbeing and stability – social, ecological, and economic – through community and commons-building.**

GRAY RHINOS: WHAT'S THE MATTER WITH US?

We've seen the black swan, the green swan, and now the gray rhino! Author **Michele Wucker** coined the term "gray rhino" to draw attention to **obvious risks that are neglected** despite – and often because of – their size and likelihood[15]. She explains: *The Gray Rhino is a metaphor for the threats that we can see and acknowledge yet do nothing about.*

The Gray Rhino framework has five stages:

1. **Denial.** Insistence that there is no threat.
2. **Muddling.** Acknowledgement of the risk but come up with a litany of reasons not to do anything about it.
3. **Diagnosis.** A switch to the active planning stage, analyzing what it takes to solve the problem and getting our ducks in a row.
4. **Panic.** Frenzied anxiety in face of an imminent crisis; the time when we're most likely to act but also most likely to make the wrong decision absent a strong action plan.
5. **Action.** Taking steps - often led by positive mavericks - to avert the problem, inspiring others to join in the action, tracking the results, and adjusting as needed.

---

[15] *The Gray Rhino: How to Recognize and Act on the Obvious Dangers We Ignore* by Michele Wucker, St. Martin's Press, April 5, 2016

The World Economic Forum's *Global Risk Report 2025*[16] highlights the interconnected threats facing humankind:

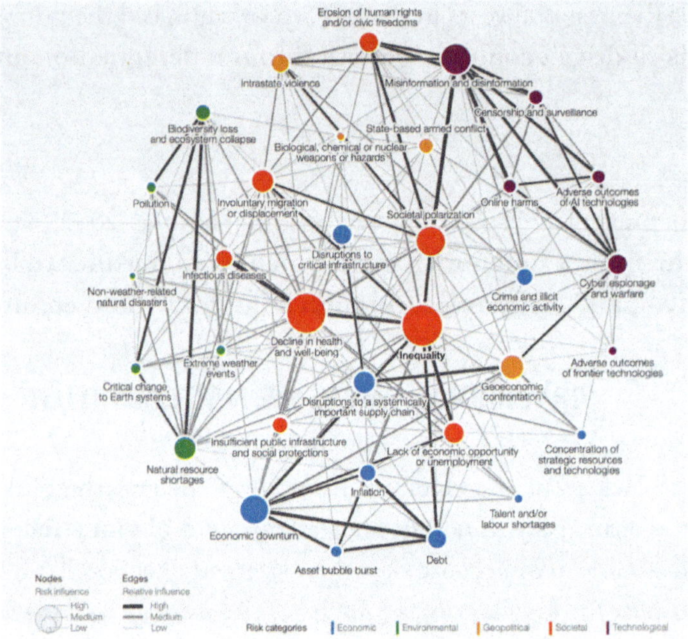

There's a gray rhino here as well: the unprecedented concentration of **power and wealth** and its *corrupting influence* is absent. The oligarchy is the elephant, er, rhino in the room.

THE COLLAPSE OF EVERYTHING

What do we mean by collapse? In the past we studied the collapse of dominant cultures, the Fall of Empire, and the changing of the guard – where the hegemony of one gave way to the domination of the other. Now, collapse means much more – it is the total failure of our natural ecosystems and the inability of our planet to support life – not just humans, but *all* life.

[16] *The Global Risks Report 2025*, 20th edition, World Economic Forum January 2025, https://reports.weforum.org/docs/WEF_Global_Risks_Report_2025.pdf

The collapse has already begun.

Howard Dryden[17] warns us that the ecological catastrophe has been unfolding since 1950 and will be completed by 2040/2050:

"We are too late to halt climate change through carbon reduction. Even if we achieved carbon neutrality tomorrow, atmospheric CO2 levels will exceed 500ppm, oceanic pH will fall below 7.95, and most life in the oceans will simply dissolve over the next 25 years, along with the food supply for 3 billion people. We will have uncontrollable climate change because we will have lost the planet's life support system, which regulates the climate."

The sixth extinction has already begun. The world has lost two-thirds of its wildlife in the last 50 years. The *Living Planet Report 2022*[18] finds that population sizes for monitored species **declined by 69%** between 1970 and 2018.

The **World Wildlife Fund**[19] spells it out:

"Unlike previous extinction events caused by natural phenomena, the sixth mass extinction is driven by human activity, primarily (though not limited to) the unsustainable use of land, water and energy use, and climate change. Currently, 40% of all land has been converted for food production. Agriculture is also responsible for 90% of global deforestation and accounts for 70% of the planet's freshwater use, devastating the species that inhabit those places by significantly altering their habitats. It's evident that where and how food is produced is one of the biggest human-caused threats to species extinction and our ecosystems. To make matters worse, unsustainable food production and consumption are significant contributors to

---

[17] GOES Foundation, https://goesfoundation.com/vision/

[18] WWF (2022) *Living Planet Report 2022 – Building a nature- positive society.* Almond, R.E.A., Grooten, M., Juffe Bignoli, D. & Petersen, T. (Eds). WWF, Gland, Switzerland. https://wwflpr.awsassets.panda.org/downloads/lpr_2022_full_report.pdf

[19] "What is the sixth mass extinction and what can we do about it?" https://www.worldwildlife.org/stories/what-is-the-sixth-mass-extinction-and-what-can-we-do-about-it

greenhouse gas emissions that are causing atmospheric temperatures to rise, wreaking havoc across the globe."

So, we have to ask, **what is the *root of root causes*?**

NASA climate scientist **Peter Kalmus**[20] explains: "The problem is ***power***. Over the last few hundred years of extractive colonialist capitalism, rich people (and their corporations, mechanisms of more-than-human perpetuation and accumulation) have enclosed capital, and that capital has accrued more capital, and that exponentially growing capital purchases laws and judges and media and disinformation. And all this influence has determined how we can collectively imagine, and how we collectively imagine has determined the direction we take as a society. The rich benefit from this status quo, at least until everything collapses (and insulated, they are unable to see that they are driving the system toward collapse). Therefore, they strongly resist changing it."

What future do we leave behind for our children and their children (should they decide to have any)?

In a discussion with a friend back in the early 90's the late Chilean economist Manfred Max-Neef wrote[21] about the three scenarios they saw ahead: 1) partial or total extinction, 2) a descent into barbarism, or 3) a total transformation to mutually assured solidarity.

---

[20] "COP Out: Wrapping Up a Useless Climate Summit That Should Fool Nobody | Opinion," Peter Kalmus, *Newsweek*, December 18, 2023. https://www.newsweek.com/cop-out-wrapping-pathetic-climate-summit-that-should-fool-nobody-opinion-1853526

[21] Discussion between Manfred M. Max-Neef and Gilberto Gallopin in *Human Scale Development: Conception, Application, and Further Reflections*, pp 112-113 Apex Press, 1991

Scenario one, *is the possibility of total or partial extinction of the human species.* The most obvious way for this to come about would be a nuclear holocaust, which, as we know, is based on the principle of Mutually Assured Destruction. But apart from the nuclear holocaust there are a number of processes under way that may bring this scenario about: the deterioration of the environment, destruction of forests, destruction of genetic diversity, pollution of seas, lakes and rivers, acid rain, greenhouse effect, ozone layer depletion and so on.

Scenario two *is the barbarianization of the world, a new way of turning humankind into barbarians.* Characteristic will be the emergence of bubbles of enormous wealth, surrounded by barricades or fortresses to protect that wealth from the immense territories of poverty and misery extending beyond the barricades. It is interesting to note that this scenario appears more and more in the science fiction literature of the last decade. Many of its symptoms are already found in mental attitudes and in the actual creation of isolated areas for the very rich who do not want to be contaminated by seeing, hearing or having anything whatsoever to do with poverty. Part of this scenario will be the resurgence of repressive Regimes cooperating with the wealthy bubbles and imposing further hardships on the poor.

Scenario three *presents the possibility of a great transition—the passing from a dominant rationality of blind economic competition and greed to a rationality based on the principles of sharing and solidarity.* We might call it the passing from a Mutually Assured Destruction to an era of Mutually Assured Solidarity. But can we do it? Have we the tools, the will and the talent of constructing a mutually assured solidarity? Can we overcome the stupidity that keeps such a possibility out of our reach? I believe that we can, and that we have the capacity. But there may not be too much time let.

Discussion between Manfred M. Max-Neef and Gilberto Gallopin in *Human Scale Development: Conception, Application, and Further Reflections, pp 112-113* Apex Press, 1991

In 1991, Manfred Max-Neef and his pal Gilberto Gallopin predicted the rise of the billionaire class and their political support for repressive regimes which impose further hardships on the poor. Sound familiar?

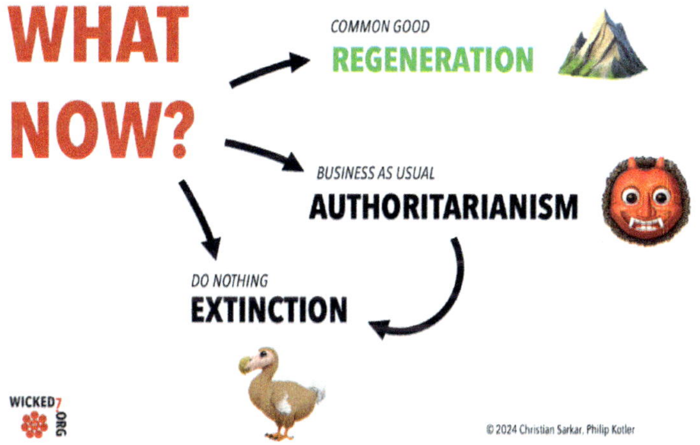

In the end it seems clear that really there are only two alternatives: extinction or regeneration.

What's it going to be?

THE STRUCTURE OF THIS BOOK

We begin with this introduction to the "ecosystem of wicked problems."

The next 7 chapters are about the seven wicked problems, followed by a chapter on why we can't seem to solve these problems.

Interestingly, our presentation of the Wicked7 problems *changed* as we wrote this book. We concluded that the problem of **Power and Corruption** is the central driver of all other wicked problems.

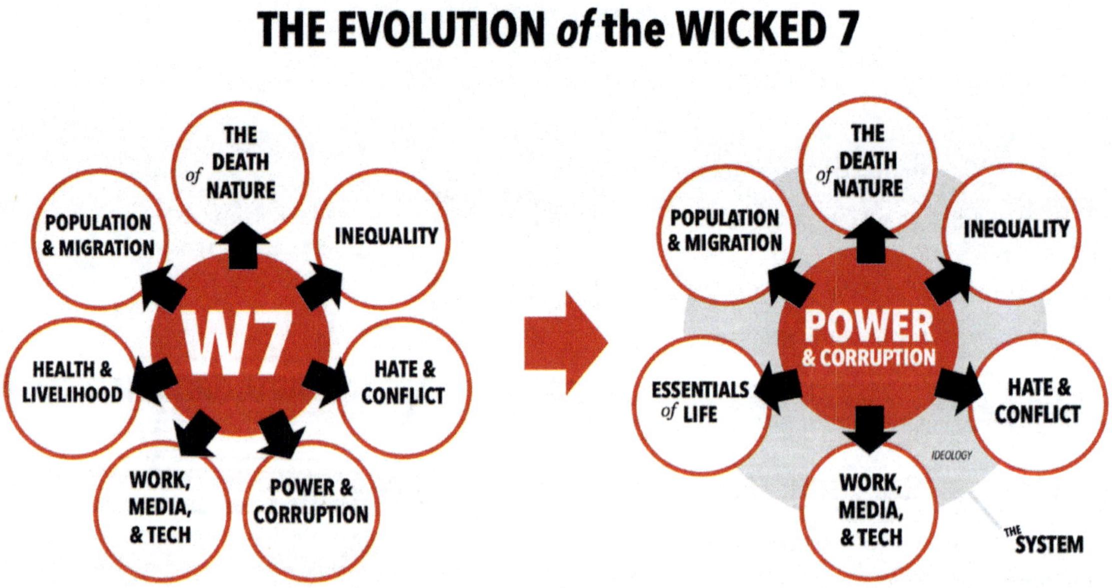

© Christian Sarkar and Philip Kotler, 2024

Finally, the last chapter is about rethinking our paradigms – to regenerate our human systems, and the world. What will it take for us to mitigate collapse? We must ask the **right questions.**

***ASK* these *QUESTIONS*:**

WHY CAN'T WE SOLVE THE WORLD's MOST *URGENT* PROBLEMS?

- *What are the underlying causes driving the decline of biodiversity and ecosystems?*
- *How do different stakeholders perceive and prioritize the importance of biodiversity conservation?*
- *What are the interconnected impacts of biodiversity loss on ecosystems, human societies, and the planet as a whole?*
- *What are the barriers to implementing effective solutions for biodiversity conservation?*
- *How can we foster sustainable pathways for coexistence between human societies and the natural world?*

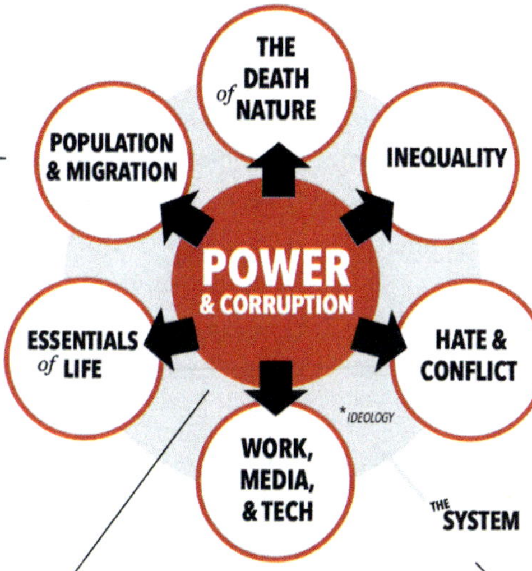

- *What are the underlying drivers of population growth, demographic transitions, and migration patterns?*
- *How do migration patterns shape socio-economic dynamics and cultural diversity?*
- *What are the opportunities and challenges associated with managing population growth, urbanization, and migration?*
- *What are the human rights considerations in the context of migration?*
- *How can policies and interventions effectively manage migration flows and address the root causes of population displacement?*

- *What are the primary drivers and factors contributing to inequality within societies?*
- *How do different forms of inequality intersect and reinforce each other?*
- *What are the impacts of inequality on individuals, communities, and societies as a whole?*
- *What are the barriers to reducing inequality and promoting greater equity?*
- *How can we promote inclusive and sustainable approaches to addressing inequality?*

- *What are the systemic barriers to accessing the "essentials of life": Food & Nutrition, Water & Sanitation, Shelter & Safety, Healthcare & Well-being, Education & Knowledge, Employment & Economic Stability, Community & Social Belonging, Justice & Governance, Freedom & Self-Determination, Nature & Climate?*
- *How do public health crises intersect with livelihoods and economic activities?*
- *How can integrated approaches that address both the essentials - concerns be developed and implemented?*
- *How do socio-economic factors influence health outcomes and livelihoods within communities?*

- *What are the root causes and drivers of hate and conflict, leading to the outbreak of wars and violent conflicts?*
- *How do narratives, propaganda, and misinformation contribute to the escalation of hate and conflict?*
- *What are the social, economic, and political consequences of hate and conflict for individuals, communities, and societies?*
- *What are the barriers to peacebuilding, conflict resolution, and reconciliation efforts?*
- *How can we promote sustainable peace, foster reconciliation, and address the root causes of hate and conflict?*

- *What are the root causes and enabling factors that lead to the abuse of power and the emergence of corrupt practices?*
- *How does corruption manifest across different sectors and levels of society?*
- *What are the social, economic, and political consequences of corruption for individuals, communities, and nations?*
- *What are the barriers to achieving effective governance and combating corruption?*
- *How can we promote ethical leadership, strengthen institutions, and empower citizens to hold power-holders accountable and prevent corruption?*

- *How are advancements in technology reshaping the nature of work and employment opportunities?*
- *How does the media landscape influence public perceptions of work, technology, and societal values?*
- *What are the ethical implications of technological developments in the workplace?*
- *What are the human rights considerations in the context of work, media, and technology?*
- *How can we navigate the challenges of technological disruption in the workplace while fostering resilience, adaptability, and lifelong learning among workers?*

- *What are the underlying factors shaping dominant political systems and governance structures across the world?*
- *How do power dynamics, vested interests, and corruption impact political processes, institutions, and Nations?*
- *What are the barriers to achieving inclusive and participatory governance?*
- *How do global trends impact political discourse and institutional stability?*
- *How can we strengthen institutions, foster leadership accountability, and promote ethical behavior among Nations?*

* *What is the role of IDEOLOGY in driving these wicked problems?*

USING AI: ClimateGPT

At the recent COP 28, a new AI tool called **ClimateGPT** was introduced to the public by **Daniel Erasmus**. The AI engine is powered by **ERASMUS.AI** which:

- Summarizes key scientific findings on the impacts of climate change
- Identifies breakthrough climate technologies
- Assesses the feasibility of established and emerging strategies for mitigation and adaptation
- Explores compounding risks from climate change, such as the impact on human labor and health

As an advisor to the Wicked7 project, **Daniel Erasmus** gave us access to **ClimateGPT** to ask the tough questions on **root causes** for the seven wicked problems.[22] We used the prompts from ClimateGPT to *get* answers, and contribute to the *maps* which you see for each chapter.

A comprehensive list of root causes is listed in the appendix: ***Answers from AI,*** at the end of this book.

For the future, we must employ AI to stretch our collective horizons, *and* to *find common ground.* And – lastly, we must be aware that AI itself is a wicked problem - *how do we ensure that AI is used to advance the Common Good?*

---

[22] ERASMUS.AI is a "planetary scale" AI platform which processes vast amounts of knowledge (including all available climate research) to help teams find an edge unseen, gain overview where none existed, and to support breakthrough decisions in "breakdown" contexts. It is used by the Club of Rome and others. ClimateGPT (powered by ERASMUS.AI) was unveiled at COP28. See also: https://www.eci.io

"Earth provides enough to satisfy every man's need, but not every man's greed."
– Mahatma Gandhi

1 THE DEATH OF NATURE

Did you know that 2024 was the hottest year on Earth in the past 125,000 years? And before it 2023?

A recent report from leading scientists spells the crisis out for us[23]:

Life on planet Earth is under siege. We are now in an uncharted territory. For several decades, scientists have consistently warned of a future marked by extreme climatic conditions because of escalating global temperatures caused by ongoing human activities that release harmful greenhouse gasses into the atmosphere. Unfortunately, time is up. We are seeing the manifestation of those predictions as an alarming and unprecedented succession of climate records are broken, causing profoundly distressing scenes of suffering to unfold. We are entering an unfamiliar domain regarding our climate crisis, a situation no one has ever witnessed firsthand in the history of humanity.

The Cambridge dictionary defines Nature as "all the animals, plants, rocks, etc. in the world and all the features, forces, and processes that happen or exist independently of people, such as the weather, the sea, mountains, the production of young animals or plants, and growth."

---

[23] "The 2023 state of the climate report: Entering uncharted territory" by William J Ripple, Christopher Wolf, Jillian W Gregg, Johan Rockström, Thomas M Newsome, Beverly E Law, Luiz Marques, Timothy M Lenton, Chi Xu, Saleemul Huq, Leon Simons, Sir David Anthony King, *BioScience* 24 October 2023 https://academic.oup.com/bioscience/advance-article/doi/10.1093/biosci/biad080/7319571

Note that the Cambridge's definition does *not* mention humankind. But humans are part of the animal kingdom, part of Nature. Perhaps the editors are too influenced by the Hebrew Bible that states that God grants dominion over nature to people of faith. We now know that, since the industrial revolution, westerners in particular took too casual an attitude toward nature. We assumed unlimited human wants and infinite Nature waiting to be mastered and exploited.

Our greed knows no boundaries.

Humans learned how to use the gifts of water, trees, plants, soil and minerals to build our modern civilizations. We moved from hunting and gathering to agriculture to the industrial age and built skyscrapers, automobiles, airplanes and many other artifacts of modern society. But a price was being paid.

We relied on oil and gas fuel to supply the energy for cars, factories, and homes. These fuels put C02 and greenhouse gases into the air, increasing the planet's heat and destabilizing the planet's weather patterns. Now, the evidence of human-induced climate change is undisputable, with growing global crises of environmental impacts and weather-related events — heat waves, forest fires, flooding, hurricanes, ecosystem degradation and collapse, pollution, and species extinction.

The key finding from the ***2023 Ecological Threat Report*** **(ETR)** produced by the **Institute of Economics and Peace** is that *without concerted international action, current levels of ecological degradation will substantially worsen, thereby intensifying a range of social issues, such as malnutrition and forced migration.* Current conflicts will escalate and multiply as a result, creating further global insecurity.[24]

The report also connects climate failures to social conflict:

---

[24] *Ecological Threat Report 2023: Analysing Ecological Threats, Resilience & Peace,* Institute for Economics & Peace, Sydney, November 2023. http://visionofhumanity.org/resources or https://www.visionofhumanity.org/wp-content/uploads/2023/11/ETR-2023-web-261023.pdf

Ecological threats increase the risk of conflict, both now and in the future. A 25 per cent increase in food insecurity, as measured by the ETR, increases the risk of conflict by 36 per cent. Additionally, the same increase in water risk and natural disasters increases the risk of conflict by 18 per cent and 21 per cent respectively. The impact on conflict risk is greatest in areas with a history of conflict, a lack of resilience, and weak institutions.

The key takeaways from the report:

- Ecological threats, such as rapid population growth, water risk and food insecurity will be compounded by climate change, causing **mass displacement** of people and conflict.
- A 25% rise in **food insecurity** increases the **risk of conflict** by 36%
- Similarly, a 25% increase in the number of people without **access to clean drinking water** increases the likelihood of conflict by 18%
- 1 billion people are living in 42 countries that currently face **severe food insecurity**
- 1 in 4 people globally do not have regular access to safe drinking water
- By 2050, 2.8 billion people will reside in countries facing **severe ecological threats**, compared to 1.8 billion today
- More than 60% of the world's **megacities** are growing rapidly and are in countries with high levels of violence or conflict. These cities lack the financial resources to cater for their population growth.

The fate of Nature and the future of humankind are intertwined. In a mind-blowing report titled *The Great Untangling: Navigating the Polycrisis of Environmental and Social Breakdown*,[25] the **Post Growth Institute** calls attention to the essential problem:

These social and political problems are not isolated from one another, nor are they the result of happenstance; rather, they are related symptoms of systemic failure. At the root of poverty and inequality is the predictable tendency of those who already have an economic advantage to use it to increase their advantage further. It's a tendency that goes back to the origin of money and social hierarchies at the dawn of civilization.

---

[25] *Welcome to the Great Unraveling: Navigating the Polycrisis of Environmental and Social Breakdown* 2023, Post Carbon Institute, June 2023. https://www.postcarbon.org/publications/welcome-to-the-great-unraveling/

Societies long ago recognized the destabilizing results of this self-reinforcing feedback process, and sought ways to counteract it through cultural taboos against hoarding wealth, debt jubilees, constitutional limits on political power, the establishment of trade unions, and other means. Nevertheless, throughout history, most decisive checks on unequal social power have occurred not by way of social innovation, but as a result of war, revolution, or economic collapse. The wealthy exploit resources and labor until the social and ecological systems can tolerate no further exploitation.

In the present era, fossil fuels have enabled exploitation to become globalized. Socioecological limits have thereby been expanded to a planetary scale, and a reckoning was delayed. However, the process of exploiting people and nature is now confronting those expanded limits.

The consequences of this collision with socioecological limits are themselves subject to cross-influencing feedbacks. Unequal growth within and between societies eventually leads to a breakdown of trust throughout societies and communities, thereby feeding trends toward authoritarianism, which lead to even more breakdown of trust.

But what do we mean by the **"Death of Nature"**?

The Death of Nature is the human-driven destruction of our natural ecosystems – land, sea, and sky – making them inhospitable to existing life forms on our formerly Blue Planet.[26]

For the first time in history, the very planet we live on is becoming inhospitable to life – and this makes our climate crisis – the Death of Nature – the most urgent problem of them all. And let's not fall prey to **carbon tunnel vision -** the idea that we solely strive for "net" zero emissions while ignoring other causes for the Death of Nature.

By the way - we can add *space* to the list as well, with the proliferation of space-junk or debris.

---

[26] See: "The Blue Planet Turns Green: Algae Fouls Waters as the World Struggles to Grow More Food in a Changing Climate" - Woodrow Wilson Center on *YouTube*, Mar 13, 2023 https://www.youtube.com/watch?v=MtXFGurFGvw

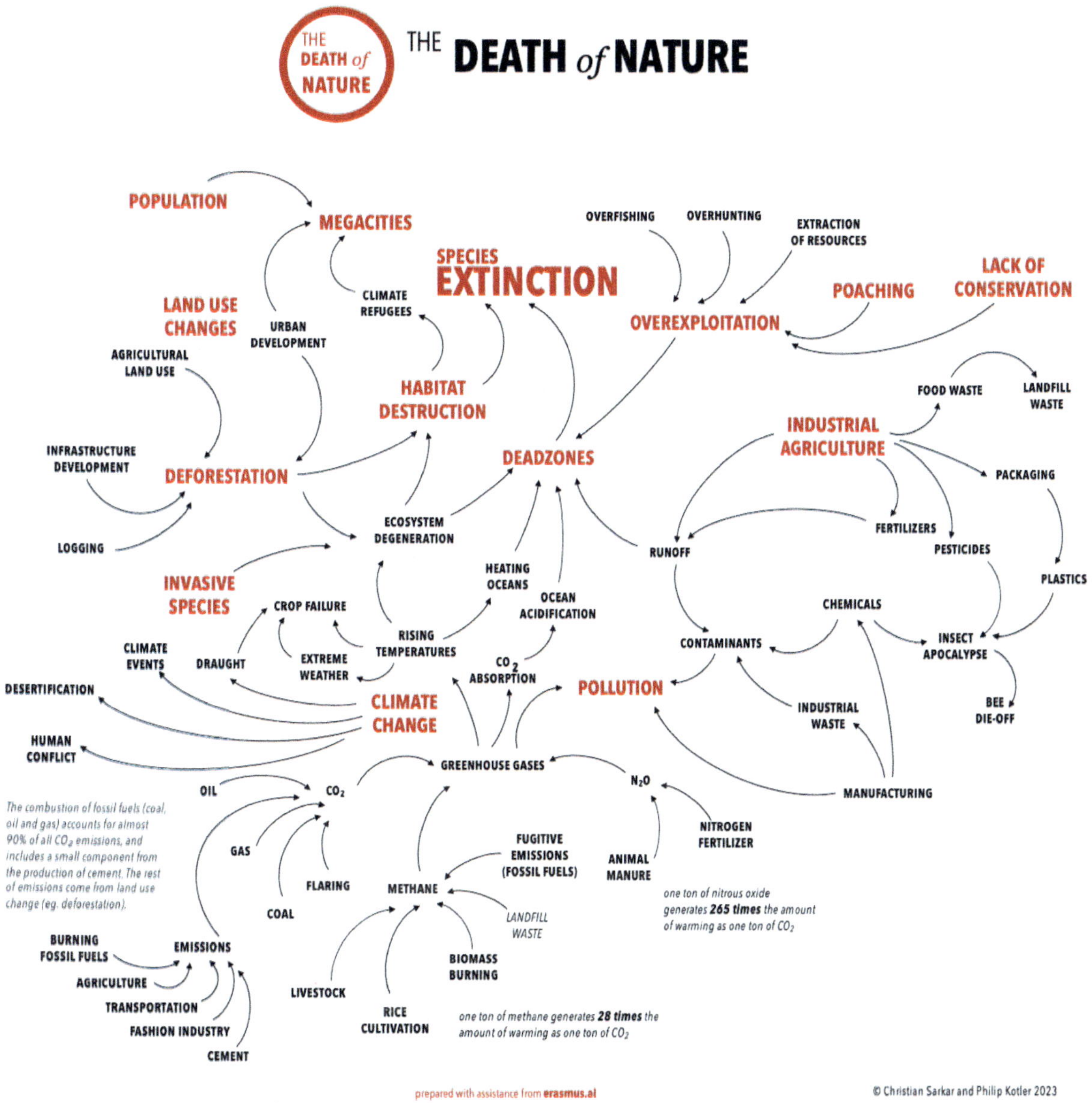
THE DEATH of NATURE
THE DEATH of NATURE
POPULATION
MEGACITIES
SPECIES EXTINCTION
OVERFISHING
OVERHUNTING
EXTRACTION OF RESOURCES
POACHING
LACK OF CONSERVATION
OVEREXPLOITATION
LAND USE CHANGES
URBAN DEVELOPMENT
CLIMATE REFUGEES
AGRICULTURAL LAND USE
HABITAT DESTRUCTION
FOOD WASTE
LANDFILL WASTE
INDUSTRIAL AGRICULTURE
INFRASTRUCTURE DEVELOPMENT
DEFORESTATION
DEADZONES
PACKAGING
ECOSYSTEM DEGENERATION
FERTILIZERS
LOGGING
RUNOFF
PESTICIDES
HEATING OCEANS
INVASIVE SPECIES
PLASTICS
OCEAN ACIDIFICATION
CHEMICALS
CROP FAILURE
RISING TEMPERATURES
INSECT APOCALYPSE
CLIMATE EVENTS
CONTAMINANTS
DRAUGHT
EXTREME WEATHER
CO 2 ABSORPTION
DESERTIFICATION
POLLUTION
CLIMATE CHANGE
BEE DIE-OFF
INDUSTRIAL WASTE
HUMAN CONFLICT
GREENHOUSE GASES
OIL
CO2
N2O
MANUFACTURING
The combustion of fossil fuels (coal, oil and gas) accounts for almost 90% of all CO2 emissions, and includes a small component from the production of cement. The rest of emissions come from land use change (eg. deforestation).
GAS
FUGITIVE EMISSIONS (FOSSIL FUELS)
NITROGEN FERTILIZER
ANIMAL MANURE
FLARING
METHANE
COAL
LANDFILL WASTE
one ton of nitrous oxide generates 265 times the amount of warming as one ton of CO2
BURNING FOSSIL FUELS
EMISSIONS
BIOMASS BURNING
AGRICULTURE
LIVESTOCK
TRANSPORTATION
RICE CULTIVATION
one ton of methane generates 28 times the amount of warming as one ton of CO2
FASHION INDUSTRY
CEMENT
prepared with assistance from erasmus.ai
© Christian Sarkar and Philip Kotler 2023

There's more. Some scientists argue[27] that climate change is *not* the dominant factor responsible for declining vertebrate populations; instead, loss of biodiversity is driven by a combination of several important actions, dominated by **land-use change**, **habitat-loss**, and **over-exploitation**.

Habitat loss and land-use change are in turn caused in large part by climate pressures. *The Guardian*'s **Phoebe Weston**[28] explains how climate change is linked to biodiversity loss:

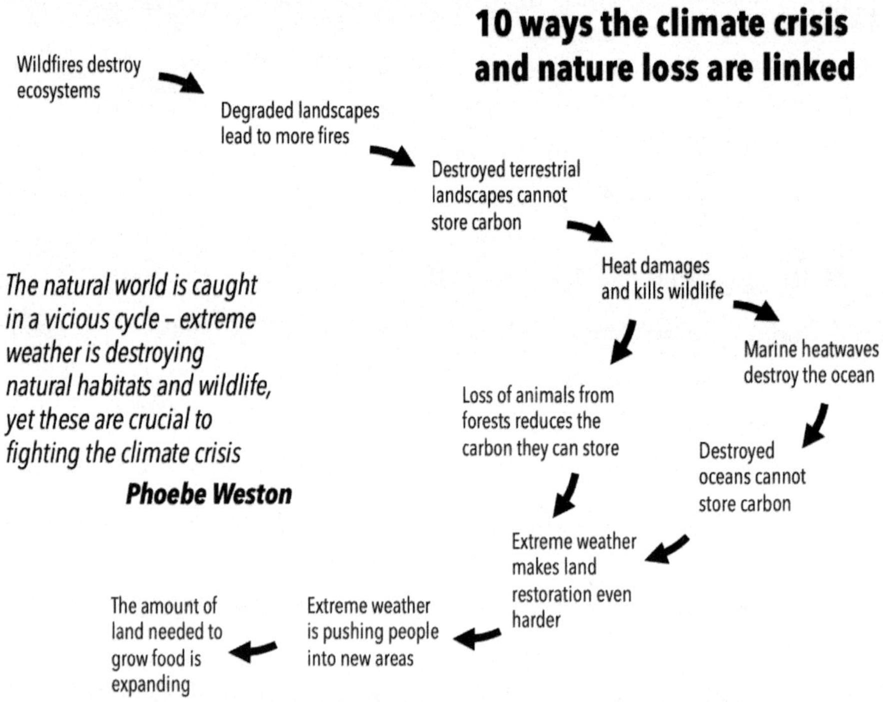

---

[27] "An inconvenient misconception: Climate change is not the principal driver of biodiversity loss" Tim Caro et al., *Conservation Letters*, Wiley, https://conbio.onlinelibrary.wiley.com/doi/pdf/10.1111/conl.12868

[28] "10 ways the climate crisis and nature loss are linked" Phoebe Weston, The Guardian, 29 November 2023 https://www.theguardian.com/environment/2023/nov/29/10-ways-in-which-climate-crisis-and-nature-are-linked-aoe

A recent report from the Intergovernmental Panel on Climate Change (IPCC) listed **colonialism** not only as a driver of the climate crisis but also as an ongoing issue that is exacerbating communities' vulnerability to it.[29]

But how do we track what's going on with carbon proliferation? **Carbon Majors** is a database of historic production data from 122 of the world's largest oil, gas, coal, and cement producers. This data is used to quantify the direct production-linked operational emissions and emissions from the combustion of marketed products that can be attributed to these entities. Carbon Majors was originally released in 2013 by Richard Heede of the Climate Accountability Institute (CAI). InfluenceMap has since updated and released the database on a website: carbonmajors.org.

The database categorizes entities into three types: investor-owned companies, state-owned companies, and nation-states. Historically, investor-owned companies account for 31% of all emissions tracked by the database (440 GtCO2e), with Chevron, ExxonMobil, and BP the three largest contributors respectively. State-owned companies are linked to 33% of the database total (465 GtCO2e), with Saudi Aramco, Gazprom, and the National Iranian Oil Company being the largest contributors. Nation-states account for the remaining 36% (516 GtCO2e), with China's coal production and the Former Soviet Union the largest contributors.

Tracking is great, but who will take action to stop this?

And what about plastics? Micro-plastics?

Fertilizers?

PFAS[30]?

---

[29] "Yes, Colonialism Caused Climate Change, IPCC Reports" Yessenia Funes, *Atmos*, April 4, 2024 https://atmos.earth/ipcc-report-colonialism-climate-change/

[30] "Forever Chemicals" Called PFAS Show Up in Your Food, Clothes, and Home" by Molly Ginty, *NRDC,* April 10, 2024 https://www.nrdc.org/stories/forever-chemicals-called-pfas-show-your-food-clothes-and-home

In 2024, there were 27 individual weather and climate disasters in the United States each with at least $1 billion in damages, trailing only the record-setting 28 similar events in 2023[31]. **Parts of the country will be uninsurable.** The billion-dollar disasters of 2024 came in multiple categories:

- 2 winter storm/cold wave events (across the Northwest and central/southern U.S. in mid-January).
- 1 wildfire event (the South Fork Fire in New Mexico that destroyed many homes, vehicles, businesses and other infrastructure).
- 1 drought and heat wave event (causing impacts across the southern, eastern and northwestern U.S.).
- 1 flooding event (the Upper Midwest Flooding in mid-June across several states).
- 6 tornado outbreaks (across the central and southeastern U.S.).
- 5 tropical cyclones (Beryl, Debby, Francine, Helene and Milton – the final two were the costliest U.S. disasters of 2024).
- 11 severe weather/hail events (across many parts of the country).

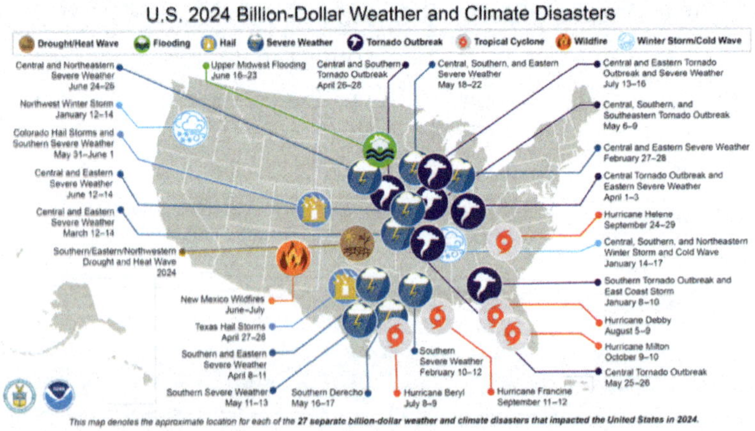

In 2024, the United States experienced 27 separate weather or climate disasters that each resulted in at least $1 billion in damages. NOAA map by NCEI.

[31] *2024: An active year of U.S. billion-dollar weather and climate disasters*, Adam C. Smith, climate.gov January 10, 2025 https://www.climate.gov/news-features/blogs/beyond-data/2024-active-year-us-billion-dollar-weather-and-climate-disasters

Some say it is the use of AI, which may well be *less biased* than our individual, limited perspective. We tested this idea with **ClimateGPT, using the answers from the AI tool to develop our understanding of each wicked problem.** Can we use AI to stretch our collective horizons? *To find Common Ground?*

Our *other*, initial approach was more traditional. We used existing reports, articles, and technical papers. Here are some of the reports we're reading.

- ***The Global Tipping Points Report 2023***. University of Exeter, Exeter, UK. https://global-tipping-points.org

  Key Findings:
  Identified more than 25 parts of the Earth system that have tipping points, based on evidence from paleo-climate records, observations, theory and complex computer models, including:

  In the **cryosphere**, evidence exists for large-scale tipping points in Greenland and Antarctic ice sheets, and for localized tipping in glaciers and permafrost.

  In the **biosphere**, tipping points are present in a variety of ecosystems, including Amazon forest dieback, savanna and dryland degradation, lake eutrophication, coral reef and mangrove die-offs, and the collapse of some fisheries.

  In **ocean-atmosphere** circulations, there is evidence for tipping points in Atlantic and Southern Oceans overturning, as well as for the West African monsoon.

  - **Multiple drivers are destabilizing these systems.** Climate change is a key driver for most, as well as habitat loss (e.g. deforestation), exploitation (e.g.

overfishing), and pollution (e.g. aerosols or nutrients) particularly in the biosphere.

- Some Earth system tipping points could be very close already.

- Some climate tipping systems closely interact, and most interactions tend towards destabilising, making tipping 'cascades' possible.

- 'Early warning signals' can sometimes indicate that a system is losing resilience and so may be approaching a tipping point.

- ***Welcome to the Great Unraveling: Navigating the Polycrisis of Environmental and Social Breakdown*** from the Post Carbon Institute
  https://www.postcarbon.org/publications/welcome-to-the-great-unraveling

- The ***Interconnected Disaster Risks*** report published by the United Nations University – Institute for Environment and Human Security
  https://interconnectedrisks.org

  Key Findings:
  Six interconnected risk tipping points, selected for their representation of large global issues, which are changing lives across the world:
  - Accelerating extinctions: A chain reaction to ecosystem collapse
  - Groundwater depletion: Draining our water, risking our food supply
  - Mountain glaciers melting: Running on thin ice
  - Space debris: Losing our eyes in the sky
  - Unbearable heat: Living in the unliveable
  - Uninsurable future: With rising risks, insurance becomes unreachable

- The ***Ecological Threat Report*** from the Institute for Economics and Peace *https://www.visionofhumanity.org/wp-content/uploads/2023/11/ETR-2023-web-261023.pdf*

Key Findings:

- Ecological threats, such as rapid population growth, water risk and food insecurity will be compounded by climate change, causing mass displacement of people and conflict.
- A 25% rise in food insecurity increases thc risk of conflict by 36%
- Similarly, a 25% increase in the number of people without access to clean drinking water increases the likelihood of conflict by 18%
- 1 billion people are living in 42 countries that currently face severe food insecurity
- 1 in 4 people globally do not have regular access to safe drinking water
- By 2050, 2.8 billion people will reside in countries facing severe ecological threats, compared to 1.8 billion today
- More than 60% of the world's megacities are growing rapidly and are in countries with high levels of violence or conflict. These cities lack the financial resources to cater for their population growth.

- ***States of Fragility 2022***, OECD
  https://www.oecd.org/dac/states-of-fragility-fa5a6770-en.htm

- ***State Of Climate Action 2023***, World Resources Institute
  https://files.wri.org/d8/s3fs-public/2023-11/state-climate-action-2023.pdf

- The ***Climate Change 2023 Synthesis Report*** from the IPCC
  https://www.ipcc.ch/report/ar6/syr/downloads/report/IPCC_AR6_SYR_LongerReport.pdf

- The 17 ***Sustainable Development Goals*** from the United Nations
  https://sdgs.un.org/goals

Putting these reports together, we can say that the primary drivers behind these tipping points are climate change, habitat loss, exploitation, and pollution. As human activities such as deforestation, overfishing, and industrial pollution accelerate, these systems are being destabilized at an alarming rate. Notably, many of our Earth systems are already dangerously close to their tipping points, and once passed, the damage is irrevocable. Furthermore, these tipping points do not act in isolation but often interact, leading to destabilizing cascades where the collapse of one system triggers failures in others. For instance, the failure of the West African monsoon could lead to widespread drought, which would then trigger mass migrations and geopolitical tensions across the region.

Finally, a European Central Bank publication[32], states the obvious - that **the economy cannot exist without Nature**:

A thriving nature provides many benefits that sustain human well-being and the global economy. Unfortunately, intensive land use, climate change, pollution, overexploitation and other human pressures are rapidly degrading our natural resources. This nature loss poses a serious risk to humanity as it threatens vital areas, such as the supply of food and medicines. Such threats are also existential for the economy and the financial system, as our economy cannot survive without nature.

CLIMATEGPT

According to **ClimateGPT**, the primary drivers of the Death of Nature are:

- **Climate Crisis**: Increasing greenhouse gas emissions, primarily from human activities like burning fossil fuels, contribute to rising global temperatures, extreme weather events, and disruptions to ecosystems – to the point of collapse.

[32] *Living in a world of disappearing nature: physical risk and the implications for financial stability* by Simone Boldrini, Andrej Ceglar, Chiara Lelli, Laura Parisi, Irene Heemskerk, European Central Bank, Occasional Paper Series No. 333, 14 Nov, 2023 https://papers.ssrn.com/sol3/papers.cfm?abstract_id=4630721

- **Habitat Destruction**: The conversion of natural landscapes into agricultural land, urban areas, and infrastructure development leads to the loss of habitats for wildlife and ecosystems.
- **Deforestation**: The widespread clearing of forests for logging, agriculture, and urban expansion results in the destruction of crucial forest ecosystems and their associated biodiversity.
- **Pollution**: The release of pollutants, including chemicals, plastics, and industrial waste, contaminates air, water, and soil, harming both terrestrial and aquatic ecosystems.
- **Overexploitation**: Overfishing, overhunting, and the unsustainable extraction of resources, such as minerals and freshwater, deplete natural resources and destroy ecosystems.
- **Invasive Species**: The introduction of non-native species can outcompete or prey on native species, leading to the decline or extinction of local flora and fauna.
- **Industrial Agriculture**: Intensive agriculture, including the use of synthetic fertilizers and pesticides, can lead to soil degradation, water pollution, and loss of biodiversity.
- **Land Use Changes**: The transformation of natural landscapes for agriculture, mining, and infrastructure development alters ecosystems and contributes to the death of nature.
- **Poaching and Illegal Trade**: The illegal wildlife trade, driven by demand for exotic pets, animal products, and traditional medicines, threatens many species with extinction.
- **Lack of Conservation Efforts**: Inadequate conservation and protection measures, both at the national and international levels, fail to safeguard vulnerable ecosystems and species.
- **Population**: In some areas, particularly in the Global South, growing human population is placing increasing pressure on the environment, leading to the degradation of natural resources and the loss of biodiversity.
- **Megacities**: As more and more people move to megacities, the pressure on Nature increases – as city services fail to keep up with increased demand in areas such as electricity, water, housing, and sanitation.

Further details on each one of these root causes are listed in the appendix: *Answers from AI,* at the end of this book.

LEARN MORE

As part of our Wicked7 Project we also created specific charts using more traditional research techniques. Here are a few. For more information, visit *www.wicked7.org*

The problem of *deforestation* mapped out by **Laura Galdi** and **Chiara Falvo**:

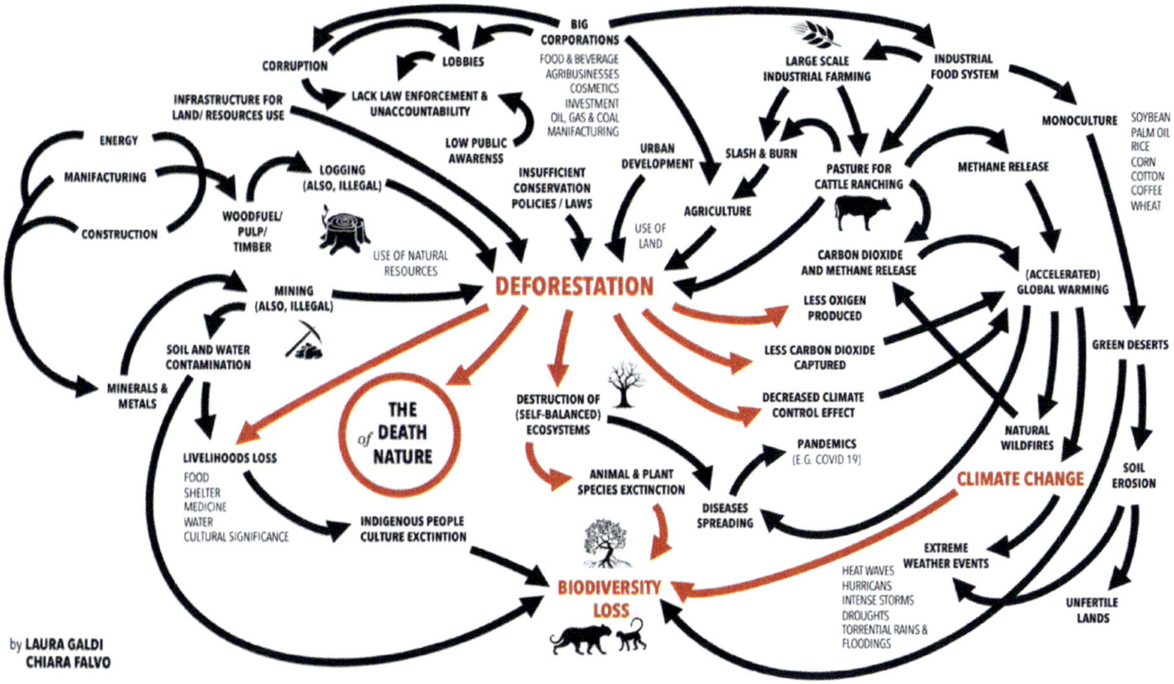

Biodiversity loss – mapped by **Laura Galdi**:

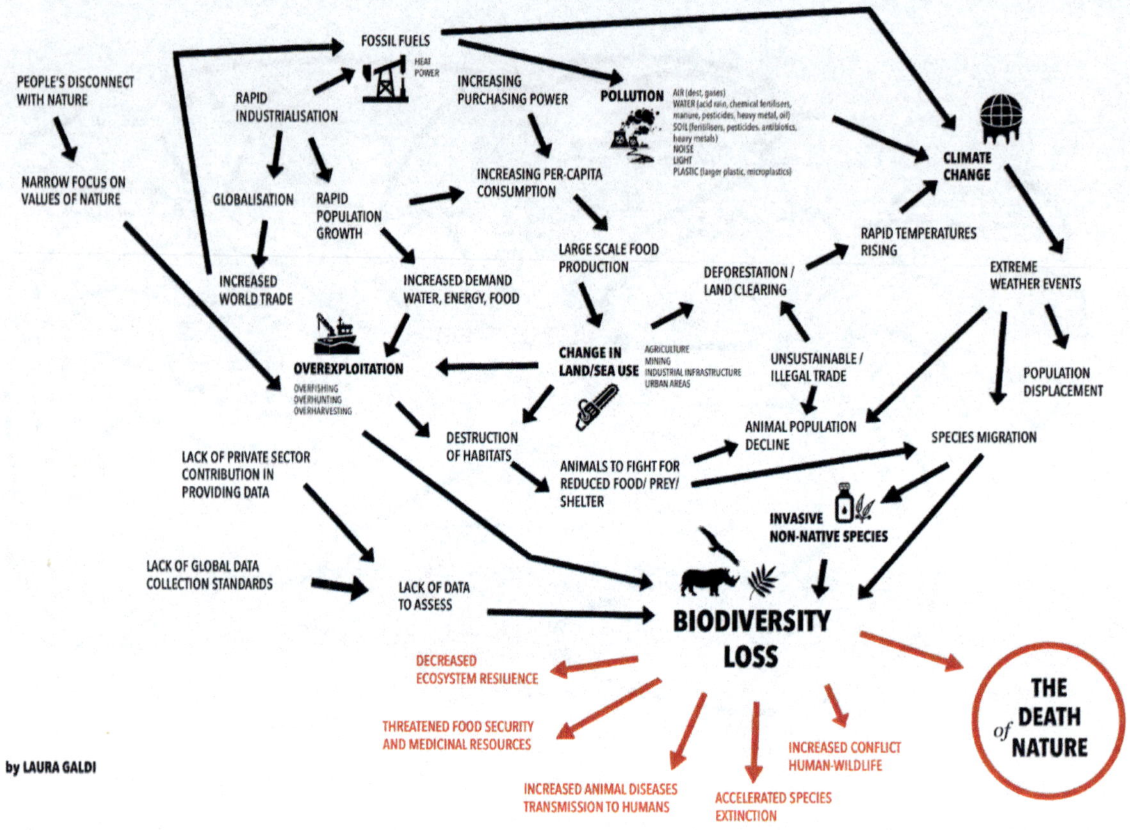

Marine pollution – mapped by **Karthi Ratnam** and **Aryssa Yoon**:

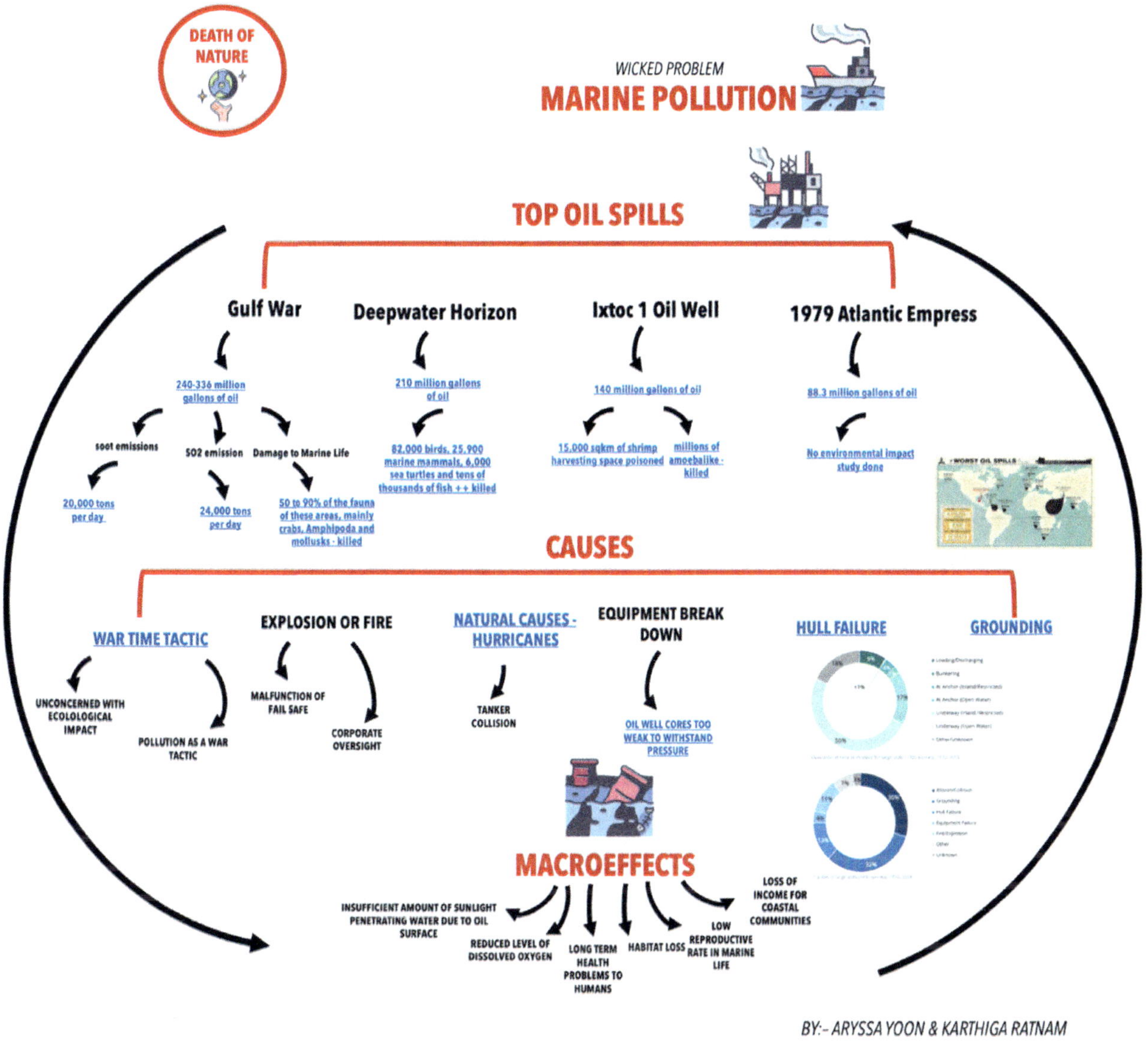

Destruction of Coral Reefs – by **Karthi Ratnam** and **Aryssa Yoon**:

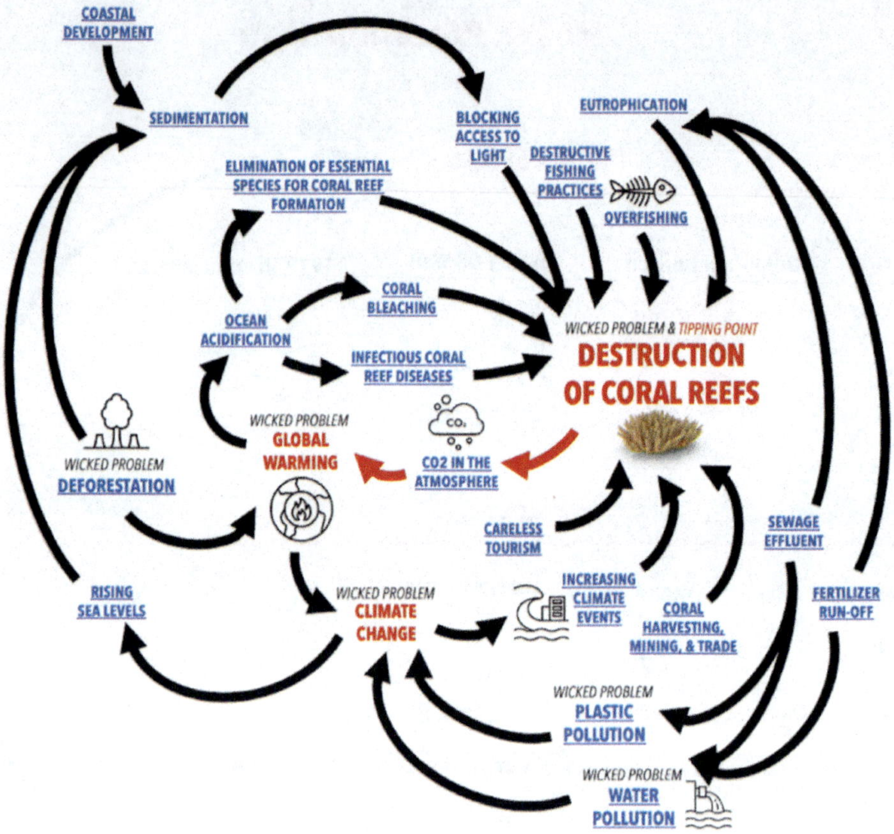

THE *of* DEATH NATURE

Aryssa Yoon & Karthiga Ratnam

Gender Inequality and the Death of Nature – by **Karthi Ratnam** and **Aryssa Yoon**:

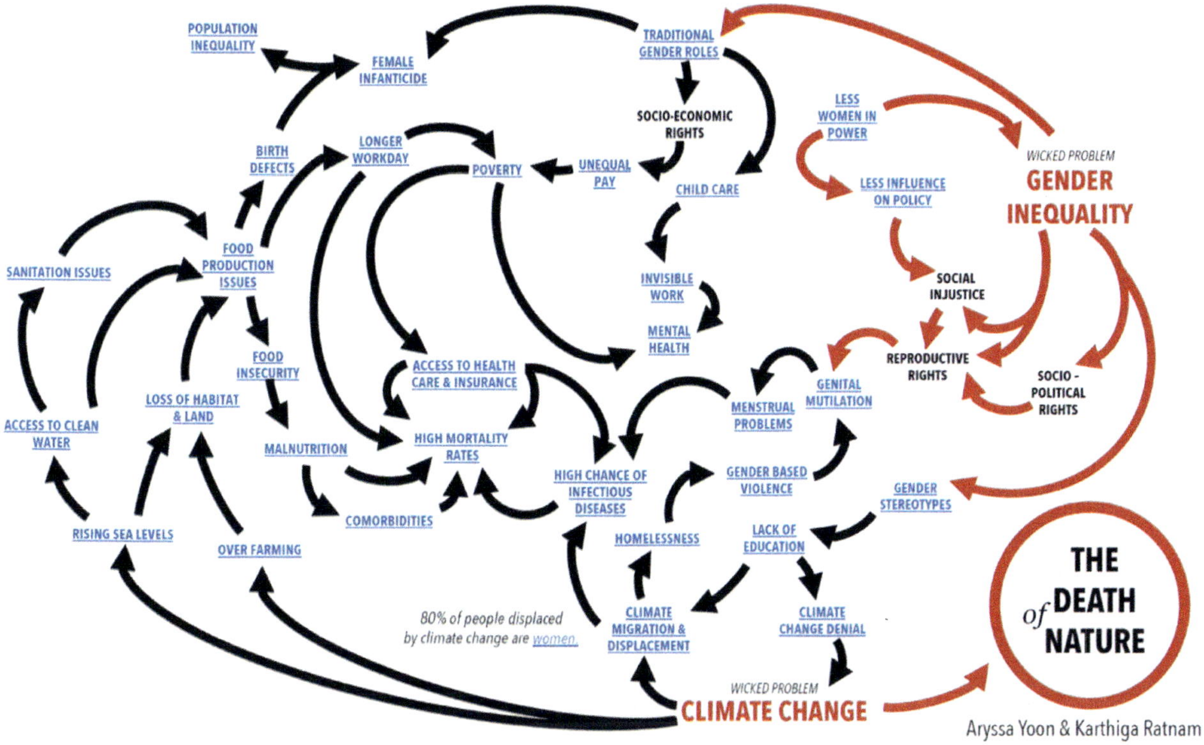

Plastics and the Death of Nature – by **Susi Wiesenegger**:

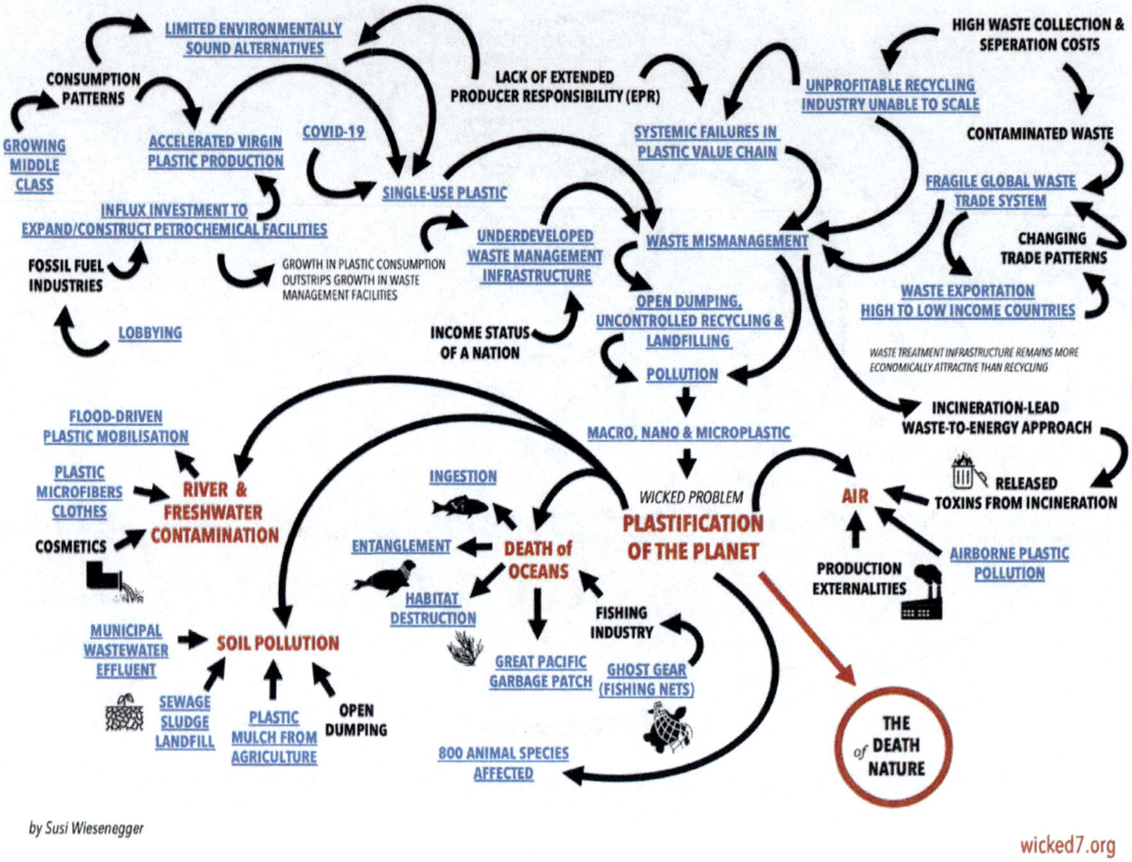

Food Waste – by **Christian Sarkar**:

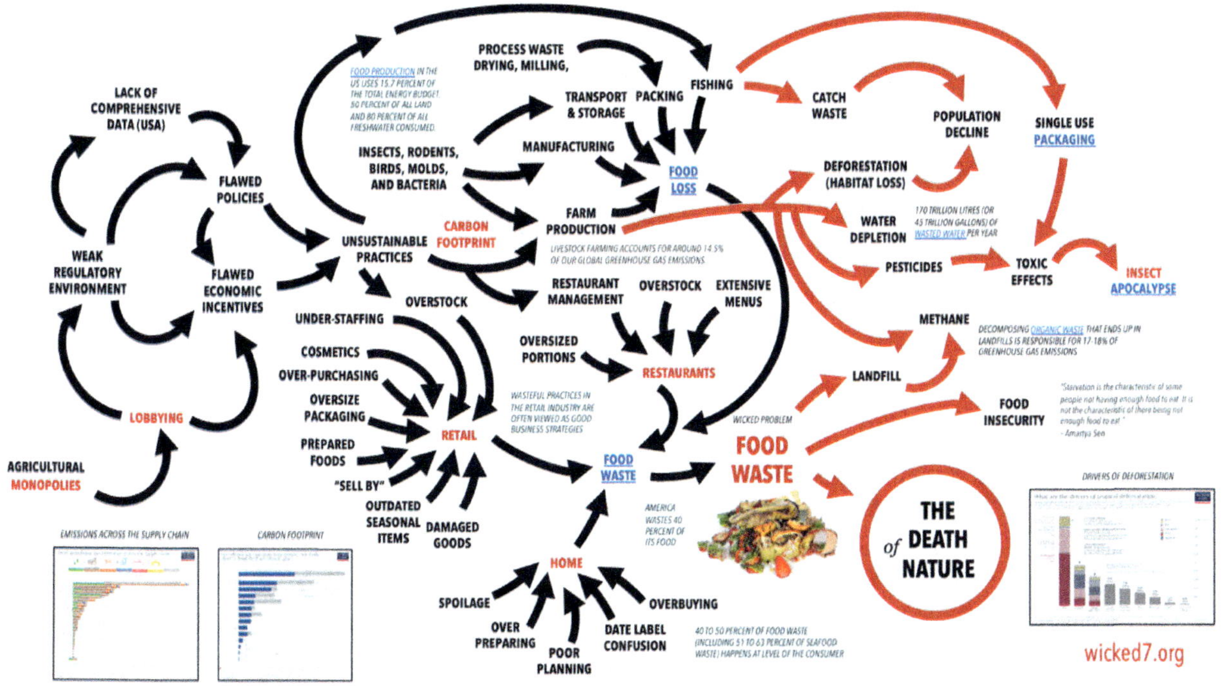

The Insect Apocalypse – by **Christian Sarkar**:

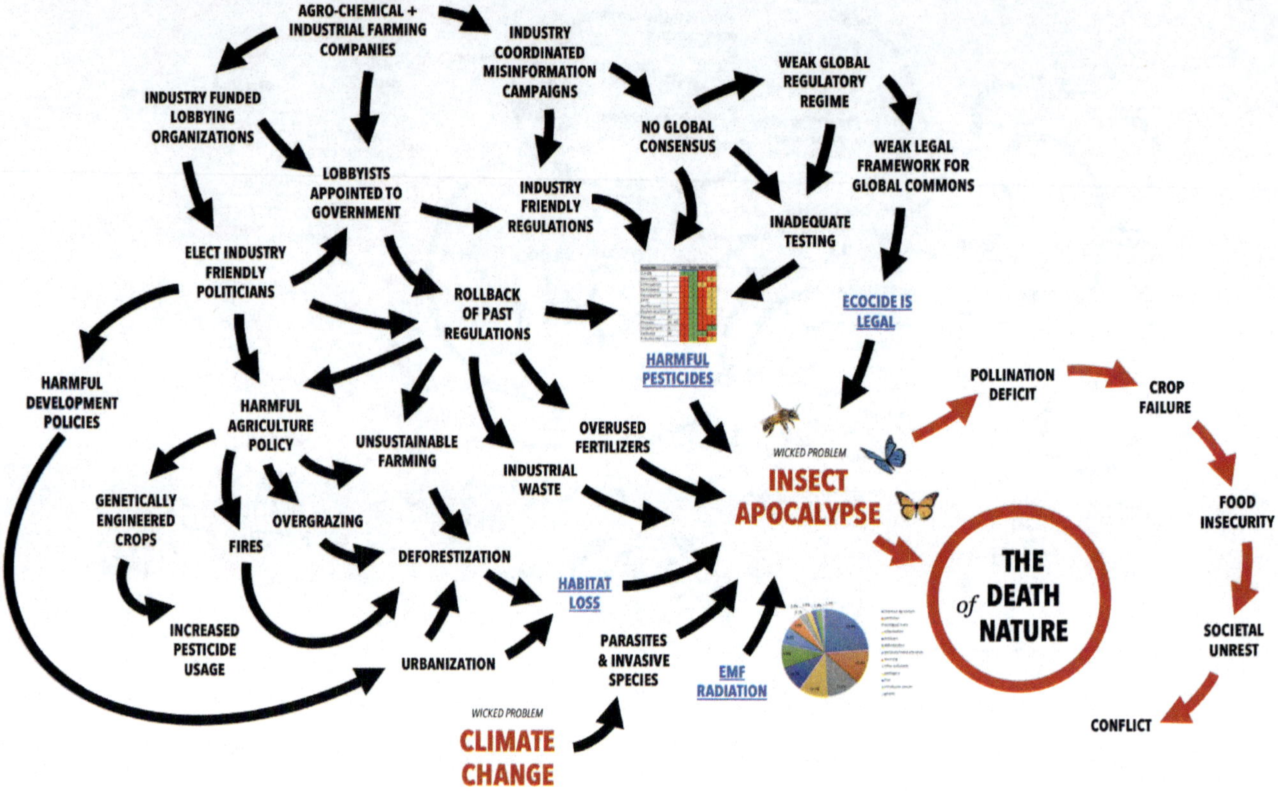

CASCADING EFFECTS

Greta Thunberg is right when she says "With the policies we currently have in place, we are heading for 3.2° of global warming by the end of the century."

Without a planet that sustains life for all, humanity is facing a clear and present danger – *extinction.*

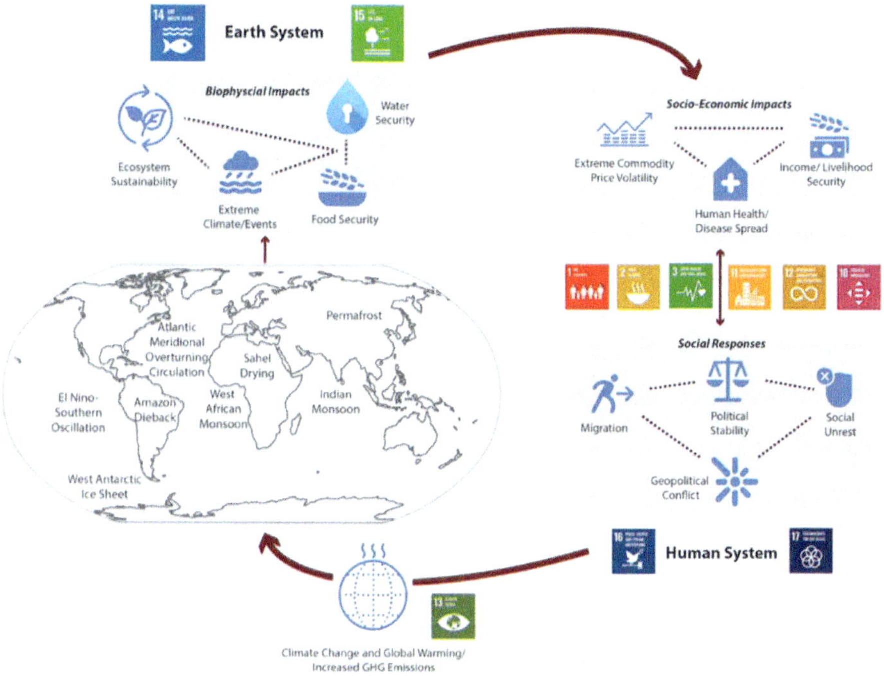

The cascading effects[33] between the Earth's climate system and humanity's social system have already begun, but even extinction may not affect everyone equally, or at the same rate.

[33] https://en.wikipedia.org/wiki/Tipping_points_in_the_climate_system#/media/File:Franzke_2022_Environ_Res_Lett_Fig2_-_Schematic_of_some_possible_interactions_and_cascading_effects_between_the_Earth_system_and_the_Human_system.jpg

Climate events will lead to food shortages, hunger, civil unrest, could even precipitate civil wars. Unscrupulous politicians will use these climate events to further polarize the population by stigmatizing the poor and climate refugees. We will see more militarization and violence to preserve "law and order." New diseases will appear in rich countries, not just the developing world. International conflicts and regional skirmishes will breakout over scarcity of food and water.

While billionaires like Elon Musk and Mark Zuckerberg[34] and powerful politicians are busy plotting escapes to Mars, and building bunkers in far-away islands and "undisclosed locations," the rest of us are left to perish on our own.

Should we simply accept this fate?

Or should we say: "enough!" and *join together to* ***fight for the future***?

---

[34] "Mark Zuckerberg is reportedly building a Hawaii compound with plans for an escape hatch, 'blind doors,' and an underground bunker" by Sarah Jackson, *Business Insider,* December 14, 2023 https://www.businessinsider.com/mark-zuckerberg-reportedly-building-hawaii-home-with-escape-hatch-bunker-2023-12

"We can have democracy in this country, or we can have great wealth concentrated in the hands of a few, but we can't have both."
– Louis Brandeis

2 INEQUALITY

New research tells us that inequality and the climate crisis are linked as a *vicious cycle*:[35]

The twin crises of climate and inequality are interlaced, fused together and driving one another. The richest people, corporations and countries are destroying the world with their huge carbon emissions. Meanwhile, people living in poverty, those experiencing marginalization, and countries in the Global South are those impacted the hardest.

In particular, they, the super-rich 1%, are key to the climate story in three ways:

1. through the carbon they emit in their daily lives from their consumption, including from their yachts, private jets and lavish lifestyles;
2. through their investments and shareholdings in heavily-polluting industries and their vested financial interest in the economic status quo; and
3. through the undue influence that they have over the media, the economy and politics and policymaking.

[35] *Climate Equality: A planet for the 99%*, Ashfaq Khalfan, Astrid Nilsson Lewis, Carlos Aguilar, Max Lawson, Safa Jayoussi, Jacqueline Persson, Nafkote Dabi, Sunil Acharya. *Oxfam International*

In 2019, the report highlights, the richest 1% were responsible for 16% of global carbon emissions, the same as the emissions of the poorest 66% of humanity (5 billion people).

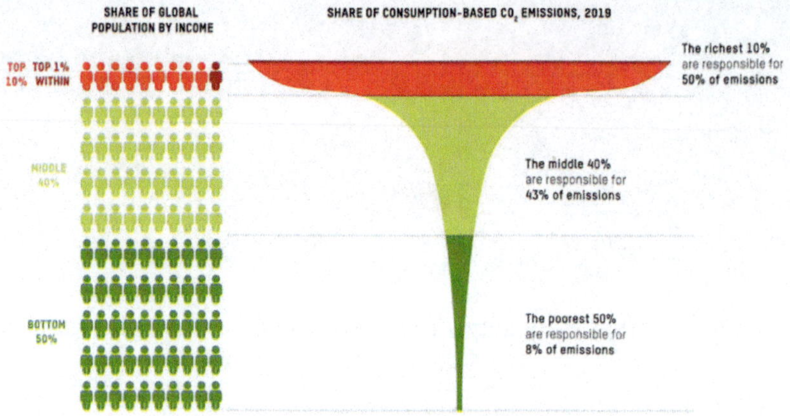

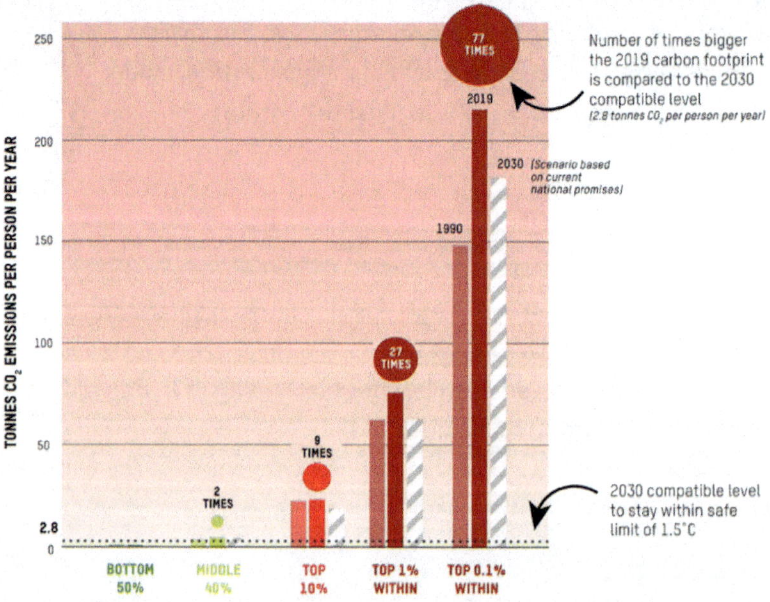

Twelve of the world's wealthiest billionaires produce more greenhouse gas emissions from their yachts, private jets, mansions and financial investments than the annual energy emissions of 2m homes.[36]

The scale and proportion of income inequality is hard to comprehend.

Rebecca Solnit explains[37]: *if you made $10,000 a week – a princely sum by the standards of most people – you would have to work every week from the year of Jesus's birth until this week to earn over a billion dollars.* ***To earn as much as Elon Musk's net worth*** *at that rate – currently $180bn, according to Forbes –* ***you'd have to work every week for more than a third of a million years*** *– that is, since before Homo sapiens first emerged in Africa.*

Climate collapse is already here.

Adam Tooze points out the **triple inequality** that defines the climate global equation[38]:

1) the disparity in responsibility for producing the problem;
2) the disparity in experiencing the impacts of the climate crisis; and
3) the disparity in the available resources for mitigation and adaptation.

He highlights the serious impact on the Global South:

For fragile states such as Iraq, it may prove too much. The risk is that they will tip from just about coping into outright collapse, failing to provide water and the electricity for cooling – the bare essentials for survival in extreme heat. In Iraq this summer, thousands of people huddled in their air-conditioned cars, running their engines for hours just to survive heat spikes that exceeded 50C.

---

[36] "Twelve billionaires' climate emissions outpollute 2.1m homes, analysis finds," Sandra Laville, *The Guardian*, 20 November, 2023 https://www.theguardian.com/environment/2023/nov/20/twelve-billionaires-climate-emissions-jeff-bezos-bill-gates-elon-musk-carbon-divide

[37] "Billionaires are out of touch and much too powerful. The planet is in trouble" by Rebecca Solnit, *The Guardian*, 20 November, 2023 https://www.theguardian.com/commentisfree/2023/nov/20/billionaires-great-carbon-divide-planet-climate-crisis

[38] "The climate emergency really is a new type of crisis – consider the 'triple inequality' at the heart of it," Adam Tooze, *The Guardian*, 23 November, 2023 https://www.theguardian.com/environment/commentisfree/2023/nov/23/climate-emergency-crisis-conference-cop-28

And still our leaders dither, doing little less than nothing. No wonder people feel that democracy has failed them. What is the root cause of this *misleadership*? We'll dig deeper into that topic in the last two chapters.

Marjorie Kelly's most recent book, *Wealth Supremacy: How the Extractive Economy and the Biased Rules of Capitalism Drive Today's Crises*[39] is one of the most important explanations of **how wealth and power have created an unlivable world** and *sacrificed the future* for the greed of a few.

Why aren't the SDGs working? Why can't our politicians do the right thing?

The first answer: **wealth supremacy.**

Wealth supremacy is defined as ***the cultural and political processes and attitudes by which persons of wealth accumulate and maintain prestige, privileges, and power that others lack.***

The impact of wealth supremacy is everywhere. Kelly explains:

It's about status, in a culture where the wealthy are revered as the possessors of godlike powers. It's about influence, including the power to control philanthropy. It's about political and legal power-including the power to finance candidates, to influence lawmaking through lobbying, and to escape the justice system that ensnares those without wealth.

The second answer: **capital bias**.

Capital bias is defined as *the idea of making as much money as possible*, which primarily benefits those who are already wealthy.

[39] *Wealth Supremacy: How the Extractive Economy and the Biased Rules of Capitalism Drive Today's Crises*, Marjorie Kelly, *Berrett-Koehler Publishers*; 1st edition September 12, 2023. See also: "Wealth Supremacy: How the Extractive Economy and the Biased Rules of Capitalism Drive Today's Crises [Book Review]" *FIXcapitalism.com*, September 19, 2023 https://fixcapitalism.com/wealth-supremacy-how-the-extractive-economy-and-the-biased-rules-of-capitalism-drive-todays-crises-book-review/

Kelly explains that this bias is present in the systems and institutions that allow money to wield significant influence. Capital represents the active side of wealth. It's the money that's expected to keep growing endlessly. Capital is what drives wealth, and it does this through various means like making profits, setting the rules of accounting, and blurring the line between speculation and investment.

When you put wealth supremacy and capital bias together, you have the "DNA of our capital-centric economic system." These intertwined biases shape how the system operates, grows, and sustains itself. The goal is to keep the rich at the top, safe and comfortable, and capital bias is the way they achieve this. Capital bias is the essence of the system, and this system is what we call capitalism.

Kelly shows us that **systemic wealth extraction** has become "the deep force sapping the resilience of our society, driving, exacerbating, or profiting from the largest crises of our day."

The interconnected world of systemic risks–climate change, biodiversity loss, deepening inequality, and rising authoritarianism are converging into what's being called a **polycrisis.** Kelly explains that while **ecological overshoot** is one root cause of the polycrisis, equally implicated is **financial overshoot**: the accumulation of too much financial wealth, even as the system remains intent on a limitless more. *US financial assets are* ***five times*** *the size of GDP, a ballooning since the 1950s, when assets and GDP were roughly equal in size.*

Kelly spells out the connections:

The long rise of irresponsible consumption has been driven by the corporate drive to maximize profits. Our efforts to tackle climate change have been blocked by the misdirection of fossil fuel companies and the capture of politics by monied interests.

As a global food crisis has unfolded, corporations have been out there using inflation to hide outsized price increases.? The white working class, left adrift by the loss of good jobs, finds its anger misdirected into racial and misogynistic hatred by the conservative forces determined to retain or reinstate the social order governed by wealth, by men, by whites.

Many of us don't fully grasp how the complex, obscure, mathematical rules and norms of our extractive system lie behind these crises. It's rarely explained to us how expanding pools of great wealth create and rely upon the precarity and indebtedness of the rest of us. Instead, our culture tends to view "wealth creation" as benign and wonderful. This bias toward wealth makes it difficult for us to digest the warnings of economists that the world is awash in far too much financial capital, just as the atmosphere is awash in too much carbon.

Kelly's expose shows us the way out: the first step must be to **name the disease**, to in see how wealth supremacy lies at the very core of our economic system, and our mental map of reality itself.

The narratives we are taught perpetuate wealth supremacy – Kelly calls them the myths of wealth supremacy.

The relentless financialization of everything leads to the decimation of workers, as capital drives labor income – and labor itself – out of the economy. She adds: *Even more frightening is how the hard right, fueled by plutocratic dark money, now seeks to eradicate democracy in its quest to keep powering the machine that supports … the "unseen ruling class."*

Kelly maps out the **seven myths of wealth supremacy**—the bias that institutionalizes *infinite extraction of wealth by and for the wealthy* and is the *hidden force* behind the polycrisis:

1. **The Myth of Maximizing**—No amount of wealth is ever enough.
2. **The Myth of Fiduciary Duty**—Corporate managers' most sacred duty is to expand capital.
3. **The Myth of Corporate Governance**—Corporate membership must be reserved for capital alone.
4. **The Myth of the Income Statement**—Income to capital must always be increased, while income to labor must always be decreased.

5. **The Myth of Materiality**—Profit—that is, material gain-alone is real, while social and environmental damages are not.
6. **The Myth of Takings**—The first duty of government must be the protection of private property.
7. **The Myth of the Free Market**—There should be no limits on the sphere of influence of corporations and capital.

In an interview with us[40], Kelly answers two critical questions:

What is financialization, and how does it hurt society?

"Financialization means, quite simply, that there is too much financial wealth in our society, in too few hands. Instead of having an economy designed to produce more value in the real world, for regular people, the economy's machinery has been rejiggered to produce higher asset valuations for the few – a giant sucking action squeezing consumer pocketbooks, shifting income from labor to capital, pushing housing prices to unreachable heights, loading families with onerous debt, creating monopolies that hobble family businesses, blocking our ability to tackle climate change, and enabling billionaires to capture democracy. The result is economic injustice, society-wide fragility, and planetary-scale crisis."

You warn of the final risk of financialization. What is that risk?

"The destruction of democracy. The party of wealth cannot attract voters with its plutocratic agenda; thus, it's race-baiting the struggling white working class to win their allegiance. It supports Trump because he cut taxes and gutted regulation and put conservatives in the courts. As Senator Sheldon Whitehouse has said, the broad conservative movement has evolved to become a coordinated assault on democracy. "It's a massive covert operation run by a small group of billionaire elites," he said.

---

[40] "Wealth Supremacy – An Interview with Marjorie Kelly" – interview by Christian Sarkar, September 25, 2023 https://www.regenerationjournal.org/wealth-supremacy-an-interview-with-marjorie-kelly/

If the role of race in antidemocracy work has been widely discussed, often overlooked is the role of plutocrats. What remade American politics was runaway inequality – that offspring of financialization, which created the pool of disaffected, struggling workers, and put too much power in the hands of billionaires."

"Honest Abe" Lincoln believed in the taxation of the hyper-rich to prevent the rise of a new aristocracy. So, how far have we fallen?

A friend just told us that "Republicans are trying to turn America into a third world country, controlled by oligarchs, just like Russia." But is this limited to Republicans only? Or have Democrats done their part as well?

When we began exploring this wicked problem, we tried to map out the barriers and inequalities in Society. We found three other obvious forms of inequality – beyond economic equality.

One is *racial inequality* where some people, because of the color of their skin or country of origin, are discriminated against.

Another is *gender inequality* where men and women are treated differently because of their sex. In the workplace, for example, men are paid more than women when they are doing the same work.

A third is *social inequality* where people are treated differently and have different opportunities because of their social class.

And, there's more: *climate inequality* – for example.

INEQUALITY

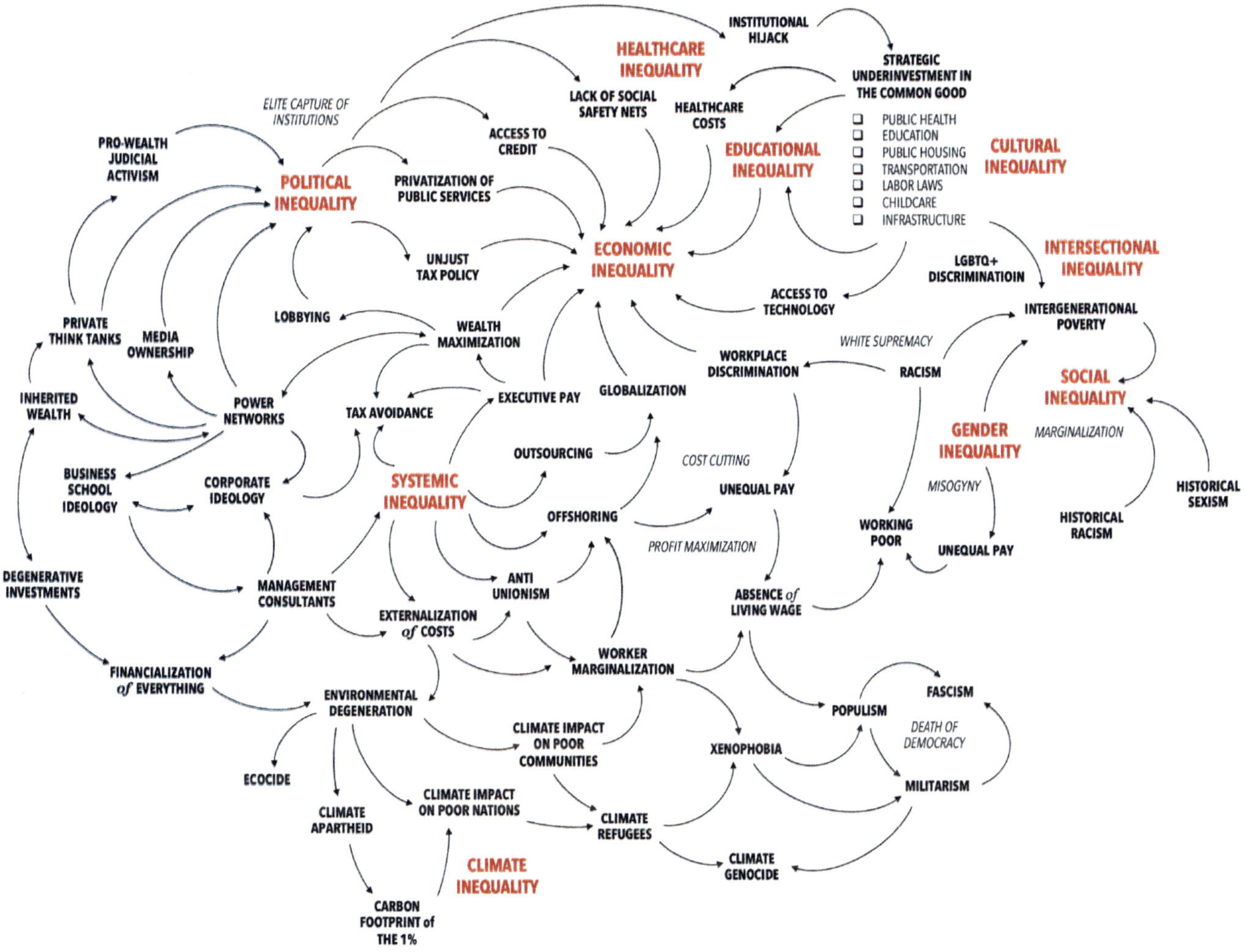

prepared with assistance from **erasmus.ai**

Income inequality is the *one measure* which is a reflection of all other forms of inequality, and the explosive growth in executive compensation over the past 50 years deserves closer examination.

In a recent Oxfam report titled *Makers Not Takers: The Unjust Poverty and Unearned Wealth of Colonialism*, we learn[41]:

Billionaire wealth has risen three times faster in 2024 than 2023. Five trillionaires are now expected within a decade. Meanwhile, crises of economy, climate and conflict mean the number of people living in poverty has barely changed since 1990. Most billionaire wealth is taken, not earned- 60% comes from either inheritance, cronyism and corruption or monopoly power. Our deeply unequal world has a long history of colonial domination which has largely benefited the richest people. The poorest, racialized people, women and marginalized groups have and continue to be systematically exploited at huge human cost. Today's world remains colonial in many ways. The average Belgian has 180 times more voting power in the World Bank than the average Ethiopian. This system still extracts wealth from the Global South to the super-rich 1% in the Global North at a rate of US$30 million an hour. This must be reversed. Reparations must be made to those who were brutally enslaved and colonised. Our modern-day colonial economic system must be made radically more equal to end poverty. The cost should be borne by the richest people who benefit the most.

And here are three facts from the same report to put the mind-boggling numbers in perspective:

1. The wealth of each of the richest 10 men has grown by almost US$100 million a day in 2024 on average.

2. Even if you saved US$1,000 daily since the first humans, 315,000 years ago, you still would not have as much money as one of the richest ten billionaires.

3. If any of the richest 10 billionaires lost 99% of their wealth, they'd still be a billionaire.

---

[41] *Makers Not Takers: The Unjust Poverty and Unearned Wealth of Colonialism* by Anjela Taneja, Anthony Kamande, Chandreyi Guharay Gomez, Dana Abed, Max Lawson, Neelanjana Mukhia, OXFAM, 20 January, 2025
https://oi-files-d8-prod.s3.eu-west-2.amazonaws.com/s3fs-public/2025-01/English%20-%20Davos%20Full%20Report%202025.pdf

Can anything be done? The report concludes that the world must act together "to dethrone the ultra-rich aristocracy and decolonize our economy. Racism must be ended, and the world must rein in the old and new forms of colonialism that are holding humanity back."

Did you know that **CEO pay has skyrocketed 1,460% since 1978?**[42] According to the **Economic Policy Institute:**

Exorbitant CEO pay is a contributor to rising inequality that we could restrain without doing any damage to the wider economy. CEOs are getting ever-higher pay over time because of their power to set pay and because so much of their pay (more than 80%) is stock-related. They are not getting higher pay because they are becoming more productive or more skilled than other workers, or because of a shortage of excellent CEO candidates. This escalation of CEO compensation and of executive compensation more generally has fueled the growth of top 1% and top 0.1% incomes, leaving fewer of the gains of economic growth for ordinary workers and widening the gap between very high earners and the bottom 90%. The economy would suffer no harm if CEOs were paid less (or were taxed more).

[42] *CEO pay has skyrocketed 1,460% since 1978* - report by Josh Biven and Jori Kandra, *Economic Policy Institute*, October 4, 2022 https://www.epi.org/publication/ceo-pay-in-2021/

What's worse is that studies find CEO pay is not linked to performance!

And let's not forget private-equity. *These Are the Plunderers: How Private Equity Runs—and Wrecks—America* by **Gretchen Morgenson** and **Joshua Rosner**[43] delves into the three-decade saga of corporate takeovers in the United States and the escalating dominance of private equity. The authors expose how companies under private equity ownership yield **detrimental outcomes for everyone** except the financiers. Employees face heightened risks of job loss and benefit reductions, businesses are more susceptible to bankruptcy, healthcare costs soar for patients, nursing home residents experience accelerated mortality rates, and communities suffer economic downturns when private equity acquires vital local enterprises. Moreover, public sector workers such as teachers, firefighters, and medical technicians witness diminished returns on their pensions due to the exorbitant fees extracted by private equity firms. In sum, the pervasive impact of private equity leaves us all worse off. All, except for the pirates.

Here's an example: *Residents of nursing homes owned by private equity firms, among the nation's most vulnerable populations, have been especially hurt: one study showed residents experienced 10 percent more deaths in facilities owned by private equity firms than in other entities, due to decreased staff, reduced compliance with standards of care, and more. Another study tied private equity ownership of nursing homes to increases in emergency room visits and hospitalizations, and higher Medicare costs.*

The authors add that apart from healthcare, which remains a primary target for financiers, private equity buyouts spanning various industries have been linked to a staggering tenfold increase in bankruptcy filings, according to research. These buyouts trigger waves of job losses, causing devastation to families and individuals while also reducing tax revenues. The hefty costs associated with such investments further erode pensioners' benefits and contribute to government deficits. Additionally, the environmental impact is profound: as public companies face pressure to divest from businesses that harm ecosystems or pollute, private equity swoops in to acquire them, perpetuating environmentally harmful operations that might otherwise be discontinued.

---

[43] *These Are the Plunderers: How Private Equity Runs–and Wrecks–America,* Gretchen Morgenson and Joshua Rosner, Simon & Schuster, 25 April 2023

Ouch.

So how do you become a billionaire? **Robert Reich**, former U.S. Secretary of Labor, sees four sources of wealth[44]:

- **Inherited Wealth:** around **60 percent of wealth**[45] in the US is inherited. The best chance you have of becoming a billionaire is to marry or be born into intergenerational riches.
- **Monopolies:** Jeff Bezos' Amazon accounts for nearly 50 percent of all e-commerce retail sales in America. Our patent and trademark systems, which have been extended in duration, create billionaire like George Lucas and Oprah Winfrey.
- **Insider Information:** Hedge fund billionaire Steven A. Cohen made "hundreds of millions of dollars of illegal profits"[46] – through his expertise in **insider trading**. This is not an isolated incident.
- **Politics:** You can invest in politicians – or even *bet* on them, like racehorses – through your timely campaign contributions. Americans for Tax Fairness estimates[47] that Charles Koch and David Koch and/or Koch Industries could save between $1 billion and $1.4 billion combined in income taxes each year from the Trump tax law—and that doesn't include how much the Koch Industries save in taxes on offshore profits or how much their heirs will benefit from weakening the estate tax

The average US worker would have to work for *25 thousand years* to become a billionaire.

---

[44] "Should We Abolish Billionaires?" Robert Reich, July 1, 2019
https://robertreich.org/post/185986111450

[45] "On the Share of Inheritance in Aggregate Wealth: Europe and the USA, 1900-2010" by Facundo Alvaredo, Bertrand Garbinti, and Thomas Piketty Economica (2017) 84, 239-260 http://www.piketty.pse.ens.fr/files/AlvaredoGarbintiPiketty2017.pdf

[46] https://www.justice.gov/sites/default/files/usao-sdny/legacy/2015/03/25/SAC%20Capital%20Complaint%20-%2013%20Civ%20%205182_1.pdf

[47] "Analysis: Koch Brothers Could Get Up To $1.4 Billion Tax Cut From Law They Helped Pass" Factsheet
https://americansfortaxfairness.org/koch-brothers-1-billion-tax-cut/

Recently it was reported[48] that corporate tax dodging and executive pay packages have both gotten so far out of control that a significant number of major U.S. corporations are paying their top executives *more* than they're paying Uncle Sam in federal income taxes.

- **35 major U.S. corporations — including famous names like Ford, Netflix and Tesla — paid less in federal income taxes between 2018 and 2022 than they paid their top five executives.** All 35 were cumulatively profitable over that five-year span.
- Among these 35 corporations, the total compensation reported for named executive officers over this five-year period was $9.5 billion. **Their combined federal income tax bills came to a *negative* $1.8 billion — that is, rather than paying taxes, they received refunds.**
- An additional 29 profitable corporations paid their top executives more than they paid in federal income taxes *in at least two of the five years* of the study period.
- **18 corporations in the study — despite reporting net profits over the five-year span — paid $0 in federal income taxes. Actually, except in one case, all paid less than zero because they got refunds.** These 18 corporations that paid $0 in federal income taxes found the resources to lavish their executives with a cumulative $5.3 billion in pay packages.
- The 64 firms in the study posted cumulative pre-tax domestic profits of $657 billion between 2018 to 2022, yet paid **an average effective federal tax rate of just 2.8%** (the statutory rate is 21%) while paying their executives over $15 billion.
- For decades, corporate profits as a share of the economy have been generally rising and CEO pay has been skyrocketing. However, **the average effective corporate-tax rate — what firms actually pay as a percentage of their earnings — has been steadily trending downwards.**

[48] More for Them, Less for US: Corporations That Pay Their Executives More Than Uncle Sam, Sarah Anderson, Zachary Tashman, William Rice, *Institute for Policy Studies* and *Americans for Tax Fairness* March 13, 2024 https://americansfortaxfairness.org/less-us-corporations-pay-executives-uncle-sam/

How has the number of billionaires grown over the past few decades? In 1996 there were 423 billionaires[49] spotted in the wild. In 2019, that number rose to 2,153. Billionaires constitute just 0.00003 percent of the world population, but they currently own the equivalent of 12 percent of the GWP (gross world product) and a much larger percentage of the total wealth of the world.

Interestingly, even as COVID destroyed the economy, billionaires got richer[50]– to the tune of $10.2 trillion.

If we envision society as a single organism, billionaires could be likened to cancer within it—individual or small clusters of cells proliferating endlessly, absorbing nutrients and resources while depriving the rest of the body. As they expand, fewer resources remain for the broader population, resulting in the systematic deterioration of the entire system. **The very existence of billionaires demonstrates our society is sick and/or broken.**

Thomas Piketty argues we should *tax billionaires out of existence.* "Entrepreneurs will have millions or tens of millions," he says[51]. "But beyond that, those who have hundreds of millions or billions will have to share with shareholders, who could be employees. So no, there won't be billionaires anymore. How can we justify that their existence is necessary for the common good? Contrary to what is often said, their enrichment was obtained thanks to these collective goods, which are the public knowledge, the infrastructures, the laboratories of research."

This echoes the words of US President **Franklin Delano Roosevelt** who said in 1932[52]: "These unhappy times call for the building of plans that rest upon the forgotten, the unorganized but the indispensable units of economic power…that build from the bottom up

---

49 https://stats.areppim.com/stats/stats_rich_19_trend_usdxnbr.htm

50 "Billionaires' wealth rises to $10.2 trillion amid Covid crisis" by Rupert Neate, *The Guardian*, October 7, 2020 https://www.theguardian.com/business/2020/oct/07/covid-19-crisis-boosts-the-fortunes-of-worlds-billionaires

51 "Billionaires hurt economic growth and should be taxed out of existence, says bestselling French economist" by Robert Frank, *CNBC* September 12, 2019 https://www.cnbc.com/2019/09/12/billionaires-should-be-taxed-out-of-existence-says-thomas-piketty.html

52 "Franklin D. Roosevelt Speeches: The Forgotten Man" Radio Address, April 7, 1932 https://publicpolicy.pepperdine.edu/academics/research/faculty-research/new-deal/roosevelt-speeches/fr040732.htm

and not from the top down, that put their faith once more in the forgotten man at the bottom of the economic pyramid.' "

Income inequality is a global issue with several causes, including historical and structural racism, unequal land distribution, high inflation, and stagnant wages – which is directly or indirectly tied to colonialism.

INEQUALITY AND COLONIALISM

Let's look at three examples: the US, South Africa, and India.

The **United States**, while not ranked among the most unequal nations globally, exhibits a notably higher Gini coefficient compared to similar economies. The top 10% of income earners in the U.S. possessed 68% of the nation's total wealth, whereas the bottom half held a mere 3.3%[53]. Similar to South Africa, historical racial segregation significantly influences these disparities.

The **legacy of slavery** inhibited Black individuals from accumulating wealth, and even post-emancipation, the imposition of Jim Crow laws severely constrained economic prospects. These historical injustices continue to reverberate, evidenced by a 2018 analysis[54] revealing persistent income and wealth disparities between Black and white households over the past seven decades, indicating a lack of substantial progress in addressing racial economic inequalities.

Inequality is further exacerbated in the US by the stagnation of wages relative to inflation. As of June 2022, consumer prices surged by 9.1% compared to the previous year, marking the most substantial annual rise since 1981. While wages have experienced incremental growth, they have consistently *lagged behind* at a rate of 4.5%. **Moreover, the federal minimum wage**

[53] https://www.statista.com/statistics/203961/wealth-distribution-for-the-us

[54] "Income and Wealth Inequality in America," 1949-2016, Federal Reserve Bank of Minneapolis, Institute Working Paper 9, June 14, 2018

has remained stagnant since 2009, remaining fixed at $7.25 per hour. Notably, a study revealed that in 91% of U.S. counties, the earnings of a full-time minimum wage worker fall short of covering the expenses associated with renting a one-bedroom apartment.

But let's go back to colonial times. Colonialism had profound and multifaceted effects on the American West, shaping its demographics, economies, cultures, and landscapes in enduring ways. Here are the key impacts:

Displacement and Violence against Indigenous Peoples: Colonial expansion into the American West resulted in the displacement, marginalization, and systematic violence against indigenous peoples who had inhabited the region for millennia. Treaties were often disregarded, and indigenous communities were forcibly removed from their ancestral lands, leading to loss of life, cultural disruption, and intergenerational trauma.

Land Seizure and Resource Extraction: Colonial powers, particularly the United States government, enacted policies to seize indigenous lands and exploit natural resources in the American West. This led to the dispossession of indigenous territories and the commodification of land for agriculture, mining, logging, and other extractive industries, often at the expense of indigenous sovereignty and environmental sustainability.

Settler Colonialism and Migration: Colonialism facilitated large-scale migration of settlers, primarily of European descent, into the American West. Settler colonial ideologies justified the displacement of indigenous peoples and the establishment of Euro-American communities, which reshaped the demographic landscape of the region and marginalized indigenous cultures.

Economic Development and Infrastructure: Colonial expansion spurred economic development in the American West, driven by industries such as ranching, agriculture, mining, and transportation. Infrastructure projects, including railroads, highways, and irrigation systems, facilitated the extraction of resources and the integration of the region into national markets, while also facilitating further settlement and urbanization.

Cultural Transformation and Hegemony: Colonialism imposed Euro-American cultural norms, institutions, and legal systems onto the American West, often at the expense of indigenous languages, traditions, and governance structures. Assimilationist policies, such as boarding schools and forced relocation programs, sought to eradicate indigenous cultures and identities, contributing to the loss of cultural heritage and social cohesion.

Environmental Degradation and Conservation: Colonial expansion into the American West brought significant environmental changes, including deforestation, overgrazing, pollution, and habitat destruction. These environmental impacts have persisted and intensified over time, leading to ecological degradation, loss of biodiversity, and conflicts over land use and resource management. Concurrently, colonialism also spurred the emergence of conservation movements and protected areas aimed at preserving natural landscapes and wildlife habitats.

Legacy of Inequality and Injustice: The legacies of colonialism persist in the American West, manifesting in ongoing disparities in wealth, health, education, and political representation between indigenous communities and settler populations. Historical injustices, such as broken treaties, land theft, and systemic discrimination, continue to shape contemporary social, economic, and political dynamics in the region, fueling movements for indigenous rights, land restitution, and environmental justice.

South Africa is perhaps the country with the world's highest income inequality, with a Gini index of 63.0, largely attributed to its history of **apartheid.** For nearly half a century, the formalized racial segregation under apartheid severely limited the freedoms and opportunities of Black South Africans, who constituted the majority of the population. Imposed restrictions prohibited interracial marriage, mandated carrying passbooks for travel, and barred Black entrepreneurs from operating in white-dominated areas. This institutionalized discrimination privileged white citizens while marginalizing Black communities.

Despite the dismantling of apartheid in the 1990s, entrenched inequality persisted within South Africa's societal framework. Efforts to address this disparity have faced significant challenges. A 2022 World Bank report[55] revealed that the wealthiest 10% of South Africa's populace commands a staggering 71% share of the nation's income. Although urban areas offer greater employment prospects, economic growth has stagnated, failing to generate sufficient job opportunities. Consequently, widespread unemployment, particularly among the youth, serves as a prominent catalyst for exacerbating inequality within the country.

In addition, gender, race, and land ownership represent three other significant factors contributing to income inequality in South Africa. Despite comparable levels of education, women in the country earn, on average, 38% less than their male counterparts. When race is incorporated into analyses of inequality, it accounts for 41% of the income disparity observed.

Additionally, land ownership patterns play a crucial role in addressing economic disparities, particularly among impoverished rural communities. Historically, the legacy of apartheid has left a legacy of unequal land distribution, exacerbating socio-economic inequalities that persist to this day. Furthermore, the onset of the COVID-19 pandemic has further exacerbated these pre-existing disparities, amplifying their impact on vulnerable populations.

In **India**, a recent study conducted by the **World Inequality Lab** reveals that the current era of Indian billionaires has led to a significant increase in income inequality in the country, now ranking among the highest globally and surpassing levels seen in the U.S., Brazil, and South Africa[56].

What's amazing is that income distribution in India appears to have been more balanced during British colonial rule compared to the present situation, according to the findings co-authored by distinguished economist Thomas Piketty and his colleagues. The authors of the study describe the current situation as "The Billionaire Raj," and suggest that the wealth gap overseen by India's contemporary elite is even wider than during the British colonial era.

---

[55] Inequality in Southern Africa : An Assessment of the Southern African Customs Union (English) https://documents1.worldbank.org/curated/en/099125303072236903/pdf/P1649270c02a1f06b0a3ae02e57eadd7a82.pdf

[56] "Income And Wealth Inequality In India, 1922-2023: The Rise Of The Billionaire Raj" by Nitin Kumar Bharti, Lucas Chancel, Thomas Piketty, Anmol Somanchi, *World Inequality Lab* March 2024 https://wid.world/wp-content/uploads/2024/03/WorldInequalityLab_WP2024_09_Income-and-Wealth-Inequality-in-India-1922-2023_Final.pdf

The number of billionaires in India has reached a peak of 271, with a staggering 94 new additions in 2023 alone[57]. This influx of new billionaires is second only to the United States, collectively amassing wealth close to $1 trillion, which accounts for approximately 7% of the world's total wealth.

Underlying all these inequalities is the *ideology of colonialism.* The British may have left their colonies, but they left behind an ideology of extraction and exploitation – which continues to this day.

Economist **Utna Patnaik** calculates that Britain drained a total of nearly $45 trillion from India during the period 1765 to 1938. **Jason Hickel** explains[58] that this giant transfer of wealth happened through the trade system:

Here's how it worked. The East India Company began collecting taxes in India, and then cleverly used a portion of those revenues (about a third)to fund the purchase of Indian goods for British use. In other words, instead of paying for Indian goods out of their own pocket, British traders acquired them for free, "buying" from peasants and weavers using money that had just been taken from them.

It was a scam - theft on a grand scale. Yet most Indians were unaware of what was going on because the agent who collected the taxes was not the same as the one who showed up to buy their goods. Had it been the same person, they surely would have smelled a rat.

Some of the stolen goods were consumed in Britain, and the rest were re-exported elsewhere. The re-export system allowed Britain to finance a flow of imports from Europe, including strategic materials like iron, tar and timber, which were essential to Britain's industrialisation. Indeed, the Industrial Revolution depended in large part on this systematic theft from India.

---

[57] *Hurun Global Rich List 2024* https://www.hurun.net/en-US/Info/Detail?num=K851WM942LBU
Interestingly, out of the 3,279 billionaires in the world, 118 are 4th generation billionaires.
[58] "How Britain stole $45 trillion from India. And lied about it." by Jason Hickel 31 December 2018
https://www.cadtm.org/spip.php?page=imprimer&id_article=16972

On top of this, the British were able to sell the stolen goods to other countries for much more than they "bought" them for in the first place, pocketing not only 100 percent of the original value of the goods but also the markup.

After the British Raj took over in 1847, colonisers added a special new twist to the tax-and-buy system. As the East India Company's monopoly broke down, Indian producers were allowed to export their goods directly to other countries. But Britain made sure that the payments for those goods nonetheless ended up in London.

How did this work? Basically, anyone who wanted to buy goods from India would do so using special Council Bills - a unique paper currency issued only by the British Crown. And the only way to get those bills was to buy them from London with gold or silver. So traders would pay London in gold to get the bills, and then use the bills to pay Indian producers. When Indians cashed the bills in at the local colonial office, they were "paid" in rupees out of tax revenues - money that had just been collected from them. So, once again, they were not in fact paid at all; they were defrauded.

Meanwhile, London ended up with all of the gold and silver that should have gone directly to the Indians in exchange for their exports.

This corrupt system meant that even while India was running an impressive trade surplus with the rest of the world - a surplus that lasted for three decades in the early 20th century - it showed up as a deficit in the national accounts because the real income from India's exports was appropriated in its entirety by Britain.

In the eighteenth century, India's share of the world economy was as large as Europe's. By 1947, it had decreased six-fold. For more on the "looting of India" – see Shashi Tharoor's *Inglorious Empire: What the British Did to India* (Hurst & Co Ltd, March 2, 2017).

Settler colonialism is a process through which settlers from one society establish permanent or long-term settlements on land already occupied by indigenous peoples, often displacing or marginalizing them.

Here's the pattern:

1. **Arrival and Encroachment**: The process typically begins with the arrival of settlers from another region or country. Initially, these settlers may arrive as explorers, traders, or small

groups seeking new opportunities. They establish initial contact with indigenous peoples, often through trade or conflict. Encroachment involves the gradual expansion of settler presence into indigenous territories, often facilitated by economic interests such as resource extraction, agriculture, or land speculation.

2. **Establishment of Permanent Settlements**: As settler populations grow, they establish permanent settlements, such as towns, farms, or trading posts, on indigenous lands. These settlements serve as bases for further expansion and exert control over resources and territory.

3. **Legal and Political Structures**: Settlers typically establish legal and political structures to assert their control over the land and indigenous populations. This may involve the imposition of colonial laws, governance systems, and administrative structures that prioritize settler interests and marginalize indigenous rights and autonomy. Treaties or agreements may be negotiated, often under duress, but these agreements are frequently broken or disregarded by the settlers.

4. **Dispossession and Displacement**: Settler colonialism often involves the systematic dispossession of indigenous peoples from their traditional lands. This can occur through various means, including forced removal, violence, coerced treaties, legal maneuvering, and economic exploitation. Indigenous communities may be confined to reservations or marginal lands, disrupting their traditional ways of life and access to resources.

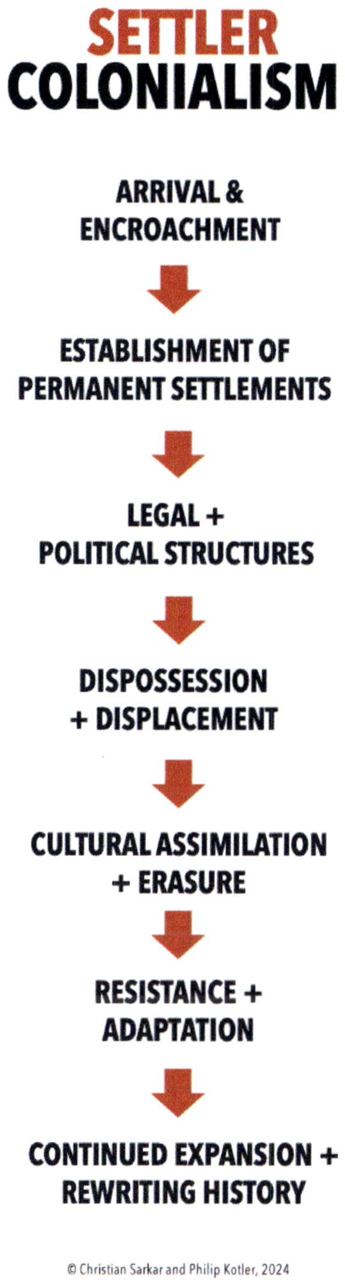

5. **Cultural Assimilation and Erasure**: Settlers frequently impose their cultural norms, languages, and religions onto indigenous populations, often through education systems, religious institutions, and cultural institutions. Indigenous languages and traditions may be suppressed or actively discouraged, leading to the erosion of indigenous identity and cultural practices.

6. **Resistance and Adaptation**: Indigenous peoples often resist settler colonialism through various means, including armed resistance, political activism, legal challenges, and cultural revitalization efforts. Despite facing immense challenges, many indigenous communities have demonstrated resilience and persistence in defending their rights, lands, and cultures.

7. **Continued Expansion and Rewriting History**: Settler colonialism is a dynamic and ongoing process characterized by continued expansion and consolidation of settler power and control. This may involve further territorial expansion, economic development, population growth, and the establishment of additional institutions to reinforce settler dominance. The **erasure** of the past – rewriting history, is also a key part of this process of consolidation.

ERASURE

What is erasure? The erasure of indigenous history is a significant aspect of settler colonialism, and it often occurs through deliberate efforts to suppress, distort, or marginalize indigenous narratives, knowledge, and cultural heritage. Here's how erasure unfolds:

1. **Suppression of Indigenous Histories**: Settler colonial regimes often seek to suppress or silence indigenous histories that challenge their narratives of conquest, progress, and civilization. This can involve censorship, the banning of indigenous languages and cultural practices, and the destruction or confiscation of indigenous artifacts, records, and oral traditions.

2. **Revisionist Historiography**: Settler societies frequently produce histories that minimize or justify the impact of colonization on indigenous peoples. These histories may romanticize settler-colonial expansion, depict indigenous peoples as "vanishing" or "primitive," and

downplay the violence, dispossession, and cultural genocide perpetrated against them.

3. **Educational Systems**: Educational systems in settler colonial societies often propagate Eurocentric perspectives that marginalize indigenous histories and contributions. Indigenous perspectives may be omitted from textbooks, curricula, and classroom discussions, reinforcing stereotypes and misconceptions about indigenous peoples.

4. **Monumentalization of Settler Icons**: Settler colonial societies often erect monuments, memorials, and landmarks celebrating settler conquest and colonization while overlooking or ignoring indigenous histories and landmarks. This can further entrench settler narratives of dominance and erasure.

5. **Cultural Appropriation**: Settler colonialism often involves the appropriation of indigenous symbols, imagery, and cultural practices for settler benefit, while divorcing them from their original meanings and contexts. This process not only erases indigenous histories but also perpetuates cultural theft and exploitation.

6. **Limited Access to Resources and Institutions**: Indigenous communities may face barriers to accessing resources, institutions, and platforms to preserve and disseminate their histories. This includes limited funding for indigenous-led research, museums, archives, and cultural institutions that document and promote indigenous perspectives.

7. **Reclamation and Resurgence**: Despite these challenges, many indigenous communities are engaged in efforts to reclaim, preserve, and revitalize their histories and cultural heritage. This includes initiatives such as oral history projects, language revitalization efforts, community museums, and cultural events that celebrate indigenous knowledge and traditions.

Erasure is also the primary logic behind the **banning** of **Critical Race Theory** (CRT) in the US. But what is CRT?

Gloria Ladson-Billings, who coined the term with co-author William Tate describes CRT as an "*interdisciplinary approach that seeks to understand and combat race inequity in society.*" **Richard**

Delgado describes it as *"a collection of activists and scholars interested in studying and transforming the relationship among race, racism, and power"*. **Khiara Bridges** defines it as an *"analytical toolset for interrogating the relationship between law and racial inequality."*[59]

Taonga Leslie provides us with the historical perspective our anti-CRT lawmakers lack[60]:

Today's efforts to limit free discourse and education about the role of race in American history bear striking parallels to the slaveowners' efforts to outlaw dissent and maintain ignorance among populations they desired to control. Current measures targeting "divisive concepts" might as easily apply to some of the rhetoric that the abolitionists used to rally their audiences against slavery.

CRT Forward, an initiative of the Critical Race Studies (CRS) Program at UCLA School of Law, released a report[61], *CRT Forward: Tracking the Attack on Critical Race Theory*, chronicles the origins of the attacks and their spread, demonstrating how laws, policies, and other government actions linked to anti-"CRT" advocacy have infiltrated federal, state, and local governments and broadly restricted — and chilled — the ability of students and teachers to speak truthfully about race, racism, and systemic racism.

Highlights of the report include:

For the period of January 1, 2021 through December 31, 2022, CRT Forward has identified and followed the progress of 563 anti-"CRT" measures, introduced at nearly even rates in 2021 (280) and 2022 (283). These have emerged from state and/or local authorities in every U.S. state besides Delaware. The nation's 25 red states are responsible for 63% of all introduced measures; the 20 blue states, for 21% of the total; and the 5 purple states, 16%. Over calendar years 2021 and 2022, a total of 241 of these 563 introduced measures were enacted or adopted.

---

[59] https://en.wikipedia.org/wiki/Critical_race_theory

[60] "What History Teaches Us About 'Critical Race Theory' Bans" by Taonga Leslie, *American Constitution Society*, Expert Forum: Law and Policy Analysis May 11, 2023 https://www.acslaw.org/expertforum/what-history-teaches-us-about-critical-race-theory-bans/

[61] *CRT Forward: Tracking the Attack on Critical Race Theory* UCLA, School of Law April 6, 2023 https://crtforward.law.ucla.edu/wp-content/uploads/2023/04/UCLA-Law_CRT-Report_Final.pdf

- In September 2020, the Trump Administration issued an Executive Order outlawing the teaching of so-called "divisive concepts" in employee trainings in federal departments and agencies and for government contractors. While President Joe Biden quickly revoked the Order following his inauguration in January 2021, "divisive concepts" bans have had substantial lasting effect: among all introduced measures linked to the anti-"CRT" campaign, 41% seek to regulate at least one form of subject matter first listed and defined in E.O. 13950 as being a "divisive concept."

- The overwhelming majority of introduced (91%) and enacted (94%) measures include K–12 schools as targets. The 226 total adopted measures targeting K–12 schools impact over 22 million public school children, almost half of the country's 50.8 million public school students. Institutions of higher education are targeted in about 20% of all introduced measures and 12% of enacted measures. Although institutions of higher education are targeted in fewer total introduced measures, those which are enacted can have wide-ranging effects: for instance, where a measure applies to all member schools in a state's public college system.

According to commentators at the Brookings Institute[62]:

*...the approach of some Republican-led state legislatures is a method for continuing to roll back racial progress regarding everything from voting rights to police reform. This is a horrible idea and does an injustice to our kids. Laws forbidding any teacher or lesson from mentioning race/racism, and even gender/sexism, would put a chilling effect on what educators are willing to discuss in the classroom and provide cover for those who are not comfortable hearing or telling the truth about the history and state of race relations in the United States. Ironically, "**making laws outlawing critical race theory confirms the point that racism is embedded in the law,**" as sociologist Victor Ray noted*[63].

---

[62] "Why are states banning critical race theory?" By Rashawn Ray and Alexandra Gibbons, *Brookings Institution*, November 2021 https://www.brookings.edu/articles/why-are-states-banning-critical-race-theory/

[63] https://twitter.com/victorerikray/status/1403437961367240711?s=12

Erasure in progress... and wait – when digital records are deleted, we have **digital erasure**. Digital erasure is one of the key signs of authoritarian governments.

The same disinformation applies to the term **"woke."**

The original meaning of the term woke means that *someone is informed, educated and conscious of social injustice and racial inequality*[64]. The Oxford English Dictionary definition of woke is to be "alert to racial or social discrimination and injustice."

Is that wrong?

Republicans are using "woke" as a racial dog-whistle - the use of coded or suggestive language in political messaging to garner support from a particular group without provoking opposition. The DeSantis administration defines woke as "the belief there are systemic injustices in American society and the need to address them," according to DeSantis' general counsel.[65]

NPR reports[66]:

Republicans on the campaign trail used ("woke") as something of a catch-all to *criticize anything on the progressive side of the political spectrum they don't like* — whether it's teaching about racism in schools or gender transition policies or even books in libraries they deem inappropriate.

---

[64] Merriam-Webster Dictionary

[65] "Woke" has been used by several presidential GOP candidates including former President Donald Trump, Florida Gov. Ron DeSantis, and Vivek Ramaswamy who penned a book *Woke Inc.: Inside Corporate America's Social Justice Scam.* "What does 'woke' mean and why are some conservatives using it?" by Kiara Alfonseca, *ABC News* January 24, 2024, https://abcnews.go.com/Politics/woke-conservatives/story?id=93051138

[66] "Republicans can't stop using the word 'woke'. But what does it really mean?" Domenico Montanaro *NPR,* July 21, 2023 https://www.npr.org/2023/07/21/1189016049/woke-desantis-trump-black-culture

WOMEN'S RIGHTS

Amnesty International tells us[67] that numerous regions worldwide continue to present formidable barriers for women seeking to exercise their voting rights. For example, in Syria, women encounter substantial obstacles to political engagement, including exclusion from the ongoing peace process. Similarly, in Pakistan, although voting is constitutionally guaranteed, certain areas witness the effective disenfranchisement of women due to entrenched patriarchal customs wielded by influential figures within their communities. In Afghanistan, recent measures mandating photo identification at polling stations pose challenges for women residing in conservative areas, where cultural norms often dictate the veiling of faces in public spaces.

Sexual and reproductive rights constitute integral components of individual autonomy and bodily integrity. Each woman and girl is entitled to sexual and reproductive rights, encompassing equal access to essential healthcare services such as contraception and safe abortions, the autonomy to make informed decisions regarding marriage and childbearing, and freedom from gender-based violence, encompassing rape, sexual assault, female genital mutilation (FGM), forced marriage, coerced pregnancy, involuntary abortion, and forced sterilization. Nonetheless, the realization of these rights remains elusive for many women worldwide.

For instance, in several countries, **including the US**[68], women encounter significant obstacles in accessing safe and legal abortion services, often facing the dire dilemma of risking their lives or facing incarceration.

---

[67] https://www.amnesty.org/en/what-we-do/discrimination/womens-rights/

[68] "The War on Women Is Over–and Women Lost" by Molly Redden, *Mother Jones*, September/October 2015 https://www.motherjones.com/politics/2015/09/planned-parenthood-abortion-the-war-is-over/

And - *freedom of movement,* a fundamental human right, is often constrained for women, who may encounter barriers such as restrictions on obtaining passports or mandatory permission from male guardians to travel.

The tragic consequence of gender inequality is growing poverty.

Currently, more than 10 per cent of women globally are trapped in a cycle of extreme poverty[69].

Women's poverty is fueled by discrimination in the world of work, limited access to resources and financial assets, and deep-rooted stereotypes that limit women's participation in education, decent employment, and decision-making, while burdening them with a larger share of unpaid care and domestic work.

CLIMATEGPT

According to **ClimateGPT**, the primary drivers of Inequality are:

- **Economic inequality:** the unequal distribution of resources, wealth, and opportunities within a society. This can include income inequality, wealth inequality, and access to basic necessities like food, shelter, and healthcare.
- **Social inequality:** the unequal distribution of social opportunities and resources within a society. This can include discrimination based on race, gender, sexual orientation, religion, and other factors.
- **Political inequality:** the unequal distribution of political power and representation within a society. This can include unequal access to political participation, representation, and decision-making.

[69] "How can gender equality reduce poverty?" *UN Women* February 24, 2024
https://www.unwomen.org/en/news-stories/explainer/2024/02/how-can-gender-equality-reduce-poverty

- **Cultural inequality:** the unequal distribution of cultural resources and opportunities within a society. This can include unequal access to cultural expression, representation, and preservation.
- **Educational inequality:** the unequal distribution of educational opportunities and resources within a society. This can include unequal access to quality education, unequal funding for schools, and unequal opportunities for advancement.
- **Climate inequality:** the unequal distribution of environmental resources and opportunities within a society. This can include unequal access to clean air and water, unequal exposure to pollution, and unequal opportunities for environmental protection. It also encompasses the uneven effects of the climate crisis on the Global South.
- **Health inequality:** the unequal distribution of health resources and opportunities within a society. This can include unequal access to healthcare, unequal health outcomes, and unequal opportunities for health promotion.
- **Geographic inequality:** the unequal distribution of resources and opportunities within a society based on geographic location. This can include unequal access to resources, infrastructure, and opportunities in different regions of a country or the world.
- **Intersectional inequality:** the intersection of different forms of inequality, such as race, gender, and class. This can result in a complex web of discrimination and marginalization that can be difficult to address.
- **Systemic inequality:** the ways in which inequality is built into the very fabric of a society's systems and institutions. This can include discriminatory laws and policies, unequal access to education and employment, and unequal representation in decision-making processes.

Further details on each one of these root causes are listed in the appendix: *Answers from AI,* at the end of this book.

CASCADING EFFECTS

It was Aristotle who told us that "at his best, man is the noblest of animals; separated from law and justice he is the worst."

Inequality is a form of separation from law and justice. It is also a separation from the Common Good. Widening inequality is a symptom of civilizational crisis.

The idea of separation and supremacy are linked. Separation from Nature makes man want to exploit it as a commodity. This was the heart of Empire – the principle behind colonialism.

We began this chapter by introducing the vicious cycle of income inequality and climate inequality. It is not just Nature that suffers, but every form of life, including **fellow humans**. *Apartheid leads to genocide.*

"Those who can make you believe absurdities can make you commit atrocities."
– Voltaire

3 HATE AND CONFLICT

The wicked problem of **Hate and Conflict** has characterized all of human history.

Must hate and conflict always exist?

Albert Einstein, seeing the emergence of Hitler, initiated a public debate[70] with **Sigmund Freud** about the causes and cure of wars in the summer of 1932, under the auspices of the International Institute of Intellectual Co-operation. Einstein's official letter is dated July 30, 1932:

> Dear Mr. Freud:
>
> The proposal of the League of Nations and its International Institute of Intellectual Co-operation at Paris that I should invite a person, to be chosen by myself, to a frank exchange of views on any problem that I might select affords me a very welcome opportunity of conferring with you upon a question which, as things now are, seems the most insistent of all the problems civilization has to face. This is the problem: **Is there any way of delivering**

---

[70] The Einstein-Freud Correspondence (1931-1932) https://www.wicked7.org/FreudEinstein.pdf
This public exchange of letters between physicist and psychiatrist is more relevant than ever, as hate and conflict encircle the Earth in our present time.

mankind from the menace of war? It is common knowledge that, with the advance of modern science, this issue has come to mean a matter of life and death for Civilization as we know it; nevertheless, for all the zeal displayed, every attempt at its solution has ended in a lamentable breakdown.

I believe, moreover, that those whose duty it is to tackle the problem professionally and practically are growing only too aware of their impotence to deal with it, and have now a very lively desire to learn the views of men who, absorbed in the pursuit of science, can see world problems in the perspective distance lends. As for me, the normal objective of my thought affords no insight into the dark places of human will and feeling. Thus, in the inquiry now proposed, I can do little more than to seek to clarify the question at issue and, clearing the ground of the more obvious solutions, enable you to bring the light of your far-reaching knowledge of man's instinctive life to bear upon the problem. There are certain psychological obstacles whose existence a layman in the mental sciences may dimly surmise, but whose interrelations and vagaries he is incompetent to fathom; you, I am convinced, will be able to suggest educative methods, lying more or less outside the scope of politics, which will eliminate these obstacles.

As one immune from nationalist bias, I personally see a simple way of dealing with the superficial (i.e., administrative) aspect of the problem: the setting up, by international consent, of a legislative and judicial body to settle every conflict arising between nations. Each nation would undertake to abide by the orders issued by this legislative body, to invoke its decision in every dispute, to accept its judgments unreservedly and to carry out every measure the tribunal deems necessary for the execution of its decrees. But here, at the outset, I come up against a difficulty; a tribunal is a human institution which, in proportion as the power at its disposal is inadequate to enforce its verdicts, is all the more prone to suffer these to be deflected by extrajudicial pressure. This is a fact with which we have to reckon; law and might inevitably go hand in hand, and juridical decisions approach more nearly the ideal justice demanded by the community (in whose name and interests these verdicts are pronounced) insofar as the community has effective power to compel respect of its juridical ideal. But at present we are far from possessing any supranational organization competent to render verdicts of incontestable authority and enforce absolute submission to the execution of its verdicts. Thus I am led to my first axiom: The quest of international security involves the unconditional surrender by every nation, in a certain measure, of its liberty of action--its sovereignty that is to say--and it is clear beyond all doubt that no other road can lead to such security.

The ill success, despite their obvious sincerity, of all the efforts made during the last decade to reach this goal leaves us no room to doubt that strong psychological factors are at work which paralyze these efforts. Some of these factors are not far to seek. The craving for power which characterizes the governing class in every nation is hostile to any limitation of the national sovereignty. This political power hunger is often supported by the activities of another group, whose aspirations are on purely mercenary, economic lines. I have especially in mind that small but determined group, active in every nation, composed of individuals who, indifferent to social considerations and restraints, regard warfare, the manufacture and sale of arms, simply as an occasion to advance their personal interests and enlarge their personal authority.

But recognition of this obvious fact is merely the first step toward an appreciation of the actual state of affairs. Another question follows hard upon it: How is it possible for this small clique to bend the will of the majority, who stand to lose and suffer by a state of war, to the service of their ambitions. [In speaking of the majority, I do not exclude soldiers of every rank who have chosen war as their profession, in the belief that they are serving to defend the highest interests of their race, and that attack is often the best method of defense.] An obvious answer to this question would seem to be that the minority, the ruling class at present, has the schools and press, usually the Church as well, under its thumb. This enables it to organize and sway the emotions of the masses, and makes its tool of them.

Yet even this answer does not provide a complete solution. Another question arises from it: **How is it that these devices succeed so well in rousing men to such wild enthusiasm, even to sacrifice their lives?** Only one answer is possible. Because man has within him a lust for hatred and destruction. In normal times this passion exists in a latent state, it emerges only in unusual circumstances; but it is a comparatively easy task to call it into play and raise it to the power of a collective psychosis. Here lies, perhaps, the crux of all the complex factors we are considering, an enigma that only the expert in the lore of human instincts can resolve.

And so we come to our last question. Is it possible to control man's mental evolution so as to make him proof against the psychosis of hate and destructiveness? Here I am thinking by no means only of the so-called uncultured masses. Experience proves that it is rather the so-called "intelligentsia" that is most apt to yield to these disastrous collective suggestions, since the intellectual has no direct contact with life in the raw but encounters it in its easiest, synthetic form--upon the printed page.

To conclude: I have so far been speaking only of wars between nations; what are known as international conflicts. But I am well aware that the aggressive instinct operates under other forms and in other circumstances. (I am thinking of civil wars, for instance, due in earlier days to religious zeal, but nowadays to social factors; or, again, the persecution of racial minorities.) But my insistence on what is the most typical, most cruel and extravagant form of conflict between man and man was deliberate, for here we have the best occasion of discovering ways and means to render all armed conflicts impossible.

I know that in your writings we may find answers, explicit or implied, to all the issues of this urgent and absorbing problem. But it would be of the greatest service to us all were you to present the problem of world peace in the light of your most recent discoveries, for such a presentation well might blaze the trail for new and fruitful modes of action.

Yours very sincerely,

Freud's reply, dated Vienna, September 1932, also never received the attention it deserved. Here are a few excerpts:

Dear Mr. Einstein:

When I learned of your intention to invite me to a mutual exchange of views upon a subject which not only interested you personally but seemed deserving, too, of public interest, I cordially assented. I expected you to choose a problem lying on the borderland of the knowable, as it stands today, a theme which each of us, physicist and psychologist, might approach from his own angle, to meet at last on common ground, though setting out from different premises. Thus, the question which you put me-- **what is to be done to rid mankind of the war menace?** --took me by surprise. And, next, I was dumbfounded by the thought of my (of our, I almost wrote) incompetence; for this struck me as being a matter of practical politics, the statesman's proper study...

You begin with the relations between might and right, and this is assuredly the proper starting point for our inquiry. But, for the term might, I would substitute a tougher and more telling word: violence. In right and violence we have today an obvious antinomy. It is easy to prove that one has evolved from the other and, when we go back to origins and examine primitive conditions, the solution of the problem follows easily enough. I must crave your indulgence if in what follows I speak of well-known, admitted facts as though they were new data; the context necessitates this method.

Conflicts of interest between man and man are resolved, in principle, by the recourse to violence. It is the same in the animal kingdom, from which man cannot claim exclusion; nevertheless, men are also prone to conflicts of opinion, touching, on occasion, the loftiest peaks of abstract thought, which seem to call for settlement by quite another method. This refinement is, however, a late development. To start with, group force was the factor which, in small communities, decided points of ownership and the question which man's will was to prevail. Very soon physical force was implemented, then replaced, by the use of various adjuncts; he proved the victor whose weapon was the better, or handled the more skillfully. Now, for the first time, with the coming of weapons, superior brains began to oust brute force, but the object of the conflict remained the same: one party was to be constrained, by the injury done him or impairment of his strength, to retract a claim or a refusal. This end is most effectively gained when the opponent is definitely put out of action--in other words, is killed...

Thus, under primitive conditions, it is superior force--brute violence, or violence backed by arms-- that lords it everywhere. We know that in the course of evolution this state of things was modified, a path was traced that led away from violence to law. But what was this path? Surely it issued from a single verity: that the superiority of one strong man can be overborne by an alliance of many weaklings, that l'union fait la force. Brute force is overcome by union; the allied might of scattered units makes good its right against the isolated giant. Thus **we may**

define "right" (i.e., law) as the might of a community. Yet it, too, is nothing else than violence, quick to attack whatever individual stands in its path, and it employs the selfsame methods, follows like ends, with but one difference: it is the communal, not individual, violence that has its way. But, for the transition from crude violence to the reign of law, a certain psychological condition must first obtain. The union of the majority must be stable and enduring. If its sole raison d'etre be the discomfiture of some overweening individual and, after his downfall, it be dissolved, it leads to nothing. Some other man, trusting to his superior power, will seek to reinstate the rule of violence, and the cycle will repeat itself unendingly. Thus **the union of the people must be permanent and well organized; it must enact rules to meet the risk of possible revolts; must set up machinery insuring that its rules--the laws--are observed and that such acts of violence as the laws demand are duly carried out. This recognition of a community of interests engenders among the members of the group a sentiment of unity and fraternal solidarity which constitutes its real strength.** ...

There is but one sure way of ending war and that is the establishment, by common consent, of a central control which shall have the last word in every conflict of interests. For this, two things are needed: first, the creation of such a supreme court of judicature; secondly, its investment with adequate executive force. Unless this second requirement be fulfilled, the first is unavailing.

... **These are, as you perceive, the well-known opposites, Love and Hate, transformed into theoretical entities; they are, perhaps, another aspect of those eternal polarities, attraction and repulsion, which fall within your province. But we must be chary of passing overhastily to the notions of good and evil. Each of these instincts is every whit as indispensable as its opposite, and all the phenomena of life derive from their activity, whether they work in concert or in opposition.**

You are interested, I know, in the prevention of war, not in our theories, and I keep this fact in mind. Yet I would like to dwell a little longer on **this destructive instinct which is seldom given the attention that its importance warrants. With the least of speculative efforts we are led to conclude that this instinct functions in every living being,**

striving to work its ruin and reduce life to its primal state of inert matter. Indeed, it might well be called the "death instinct"; whereas the erotic instincts vouch for the struggle to live on. The death instinct becomes an impulse to destruction when, with the aid of certain organs, it directs its action outward, against external objects. The living being, that is to say, defends its own existence by destroying foreign bodies. But, in one of its activities, the death instinct is operative within the living being and we have sought to trace back a number of normal and pathological phenomena to this introversion of the destructive instinct. We have even committed the heresy of explaining the origin of human conscience by some such "turning inward" of the aggressive impulse. Obviously when this internal tendency operates on too large a scale, it is no trivial matter; rather, a positively morbid state of things; whereas the diversion of the destructive impulse toward the external world must have beneficial effects. Here is then the biological justification for all those vile, pernicious propensities which we are now combating. We can but own that they are really more akin to nature than this our stand against them, which, in fact, remains to be accounted for.

...From our "mythology" of the instincts we may easily deduce a formula for an indirect method of eliminating war. If the propensity for war be due to the destructive instinct, we have always its counter-agent, Eros, to our hand. All that produces ties of sentiment between man and man must serve us as war's antidote. These ties are of two kinds. First, such relations as those toward a beloved object, void though they be of sexual intent. The psychoanalyst need feel no compunction in mentioning "love" in this connection; **religion uses the same language: Love thy neighbor as thyself. A pious injunction, easy to enounce, but hard to carry out! The other bond of sentiment is by way of identification. All that brings out the significant resemblances between men calls into play this feeling of community, identification, whereon is founded, in large measure, the whole edifice of human society.**

...Moreover, **all forms of war cannot be indiscriminately condemned; so long as there are nations and empires, each prepared callously to exterminate its rival, all alike must be equipped for war.** But we will not dwell on any of these problems; they lie outside the debate to which you have invited me. I pass on to another point, the basis, as it strikes me, of our common hatred of war. It is this: We cannot do otherwise than hate it.

...How long have we to wait before the rest of men turn pacifist? Impossible to say, and yet perhaps our hope that these two factors--**man's cultural disposition and a well-founded dread of the form that future wars will take--may serve to put an end to war in the near future,** is not chimerical. But by what ways or byways this will come about, we cannot guess. Meanwhile we may rest on the assurance that **whatever makes for cultural development is working also against war.**

With kindest regards and, should this expose prove a disappointment to you, my sincere regrets,

Yours,

By the time these letters between Einstein and Freud were published in 1933[71], Hitler was already in power, both letter writers were in exile, and the letters never reached the audience they wide audience they were intended for.

Freud's answer tells us that violence has many provocations and roots. It is likely to remain a human problem. It can only be overcome by a growing pacifist culture and laws.

Where does hate come from? New babies have no hates. The baby may cry and yearn for the mother's breast. The baby will show anger when deprived of immediate gratification. But hates occur much later.

Hate occurs during the child's **socialization**. The parents might carry intense negative feelings toward specific others. The child picks this up. As the child learns his culture, he or she will hear about many injustices done to his/her parents, groups, religion country or ethnic group. In the end, we find many white people hating black people; Muslims hating Hindus;

---

[71] *Why War? A Correspondence Between Albert Einstein and Sigmund Freud* (1933) https://courier.unesco.org/en/articles/why-war-letter-albert-einstein-sigmund-freud

Hindus hating Muslims; Christians hating Jews; Palestinians hating Jews; Jews hating Palestinians; Turks and Armenians hating each other; and so on.

Hate is *learned* behavior. Where does it come from? Here are the principal "drivers of hate" as we identified them in our work.

Can you think of others?

What is most disturbing in the US in particular is the partisan hate directed at political opponents. Republicans may have been caught on tape openly talking about assassinating their Democratic opponents to instill fear in the political arena.[72]

This is fascist, authoritarian politics, *not democracy*. We cannot function as a nation if we are divided by our real and *imagined* hatred. What happened to *e pluribus unum*?

The **Anti-Defamation League** is a New York-based international Jewish non-governmental organization and advocacy group that specializing in civil rights law and combatting antisemitism and extremism. It developed the **Pyramid of Hate** to explain "how genocide takes place within a system of oppression in which the attitudes and actions described at the lower levels of the pyramid are accepted."[73]

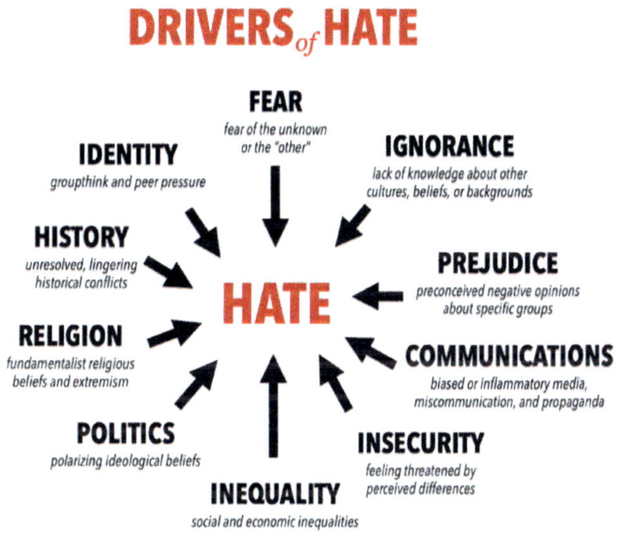

72 "Law enforcement investigating remarks allegedly made by Roger Stone appearing to discuss assassinating Democrats, sources say" - *CNN*, January 17, 2024 https://edition.cnn.com/2024/01/16/politics/roger-stone-investigation-democrats/index.html

73 ADL *Pyramid of Hate* https://www.adl.org/sites/default/files/pyramid-of-hate-web-english_1.pdf

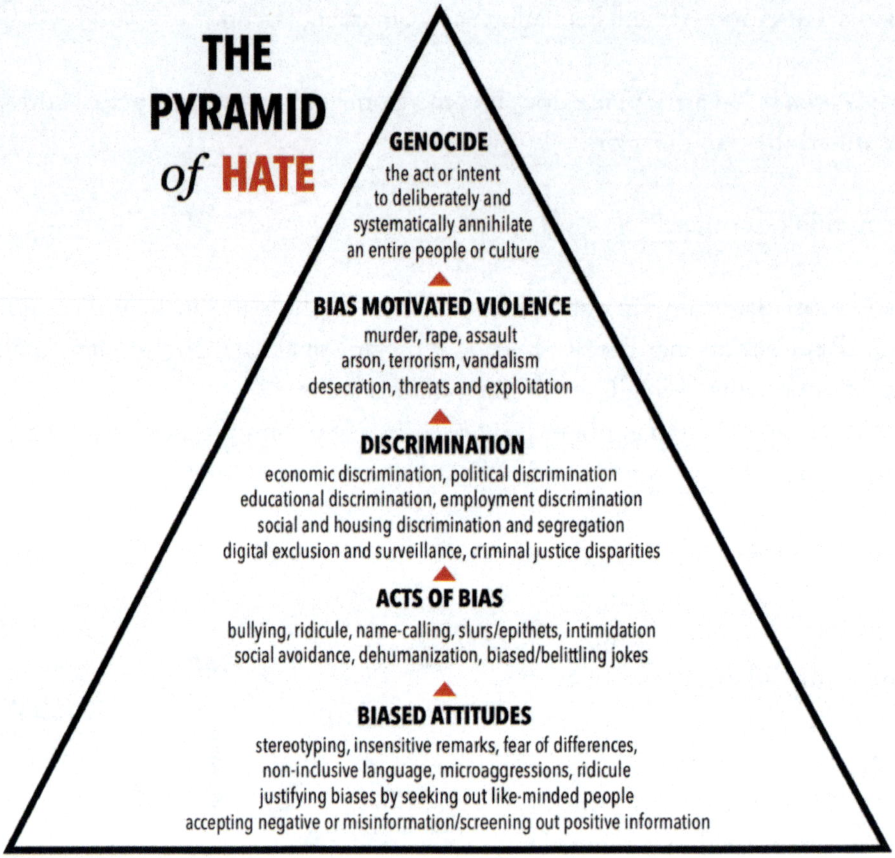

adapted from the Anti-Defamation League (ADL), Echoes and Reflections, and the Holocaust Center for Humanity

Specific persons might take it as their purpose to stimulate more hate in the community, city or country. Politicians, for example, may personally benefit from increasing the level of "us" versus "them" polarization. They gain power by building groups who oppose or hate other groups.

Hate is often directed against the stranger, the other, the person who is different. In the U.S., President Donald Trump fought against granting citizenship to young Hispanics, the "dreamers," who were born in the U.S. to illegal parents. He claimed that many were criminal and would harm U.S. citizens. None of these allegations are based on fact. In fact, the dreamers are model citizens – leaders and innovators.

More disturbing is the use of violence to intimidate and assert power. The *shift* from **individual acts of hate** to **institutional violence** is explained in the diagram below:

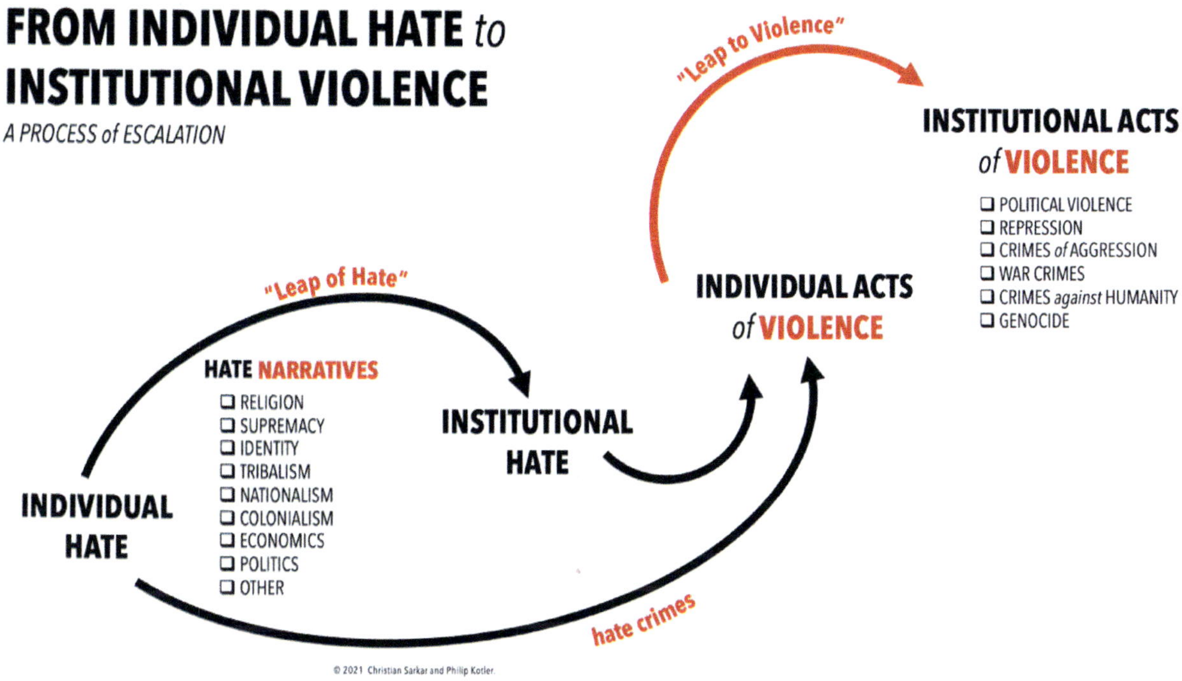

The problem is our stories.

We view the world through the lens of our cultural narratives, and this, in some cases, leaves no space for common ground.

What are the cultural narratives we use to view and make sense of the world? Here are a few types:

- ❑ RELIGION
- ❑ SUPREMACY
- ❑ IDENTITY
- ❑ TRIBALISM
- ❑ NATIONALISM
- ❑ COLONIALISM
- ❑ ECONOMICS
- ❑ POLITICS
- ❑ OTHER

Our own beliefs become stumbling blocks which prevent us from greater understanding. There may never be peace in the world until we let go of our narratives and create new ones.

Here are some thoughts from a friend about the chronic problem of hating Jews:

- "Hatred on the rise throughout much of the word, and much of it pinpointed towards Jews by a new young generation of Jew haters taught to hate by older Jew haters.
- "When you hate those you have never had contact with it is because of your ignorance, and you do not want to know the truth about your victim. The hater will always be a mentally stunted human being, and never realize true happiness in their lives, because there is no room for both in your being.
- "When a person hates one minority they usually hate them all, or at least those who look and act different, and have different beliefs from their own.
- "Hatred is a disease which can only be cured by truly understanding those you hate, not by what you were told or taught."

But those who *do not hate* must also let their voices be heard as well as the victims of hatred, because no one will be exempt from hatred if we don't **speak up** and say we will not tolerate hatred.

Silence is complicity. And it leads to genocide.

Indigenous Land Within United States, 1492-1977

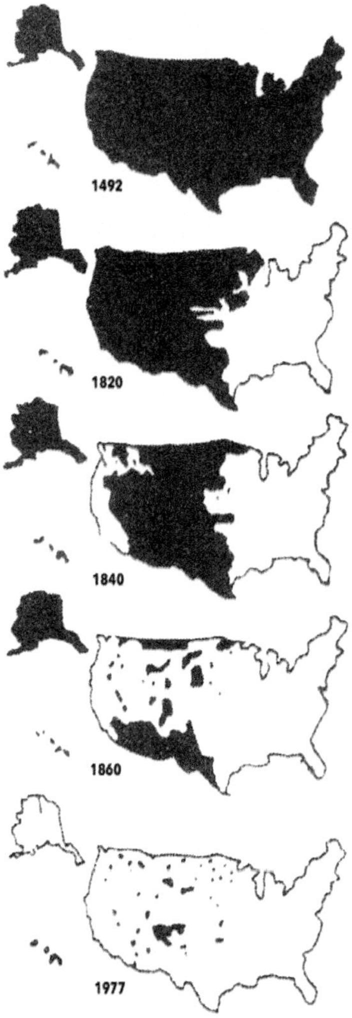

In her classic book titled *An indigenous peoples' history of the United States*, historian Roxanne Dunbar-Ortiz[74], explains that the form of colonialism that the Indigenous peoples of North America have experienced was modern from the beginning: *the expansion of European corporations, backed by government armies, into foreign areas, with subsequent expropriation of lands and resources.*

"**Settler colonialism is a genocidal policy.** Native nations and communities, while struggling to maintain fundamental values and collectivity, have from the beginning resisted modern colonialism using both defensive and offensive techniques, including the modern forms of armed resistance of national liberation movements and what now is called terrorism. In every instance they have fought for survival as peoples. The objective of US colonialist authorities was to terminate their existence as peoples-not as random individuals. This is the very definition of modern genocide as contrasted with premodern instances of extreme violence that did not have the goal of extinction. The United States as a socioeconomic and political entity is a result of this centuries-long and ongoing colonial process."

According to geographers from University College London, the colonization of the Americas by Europeans killed approximately **55 million or 90% of the local populations** – triggering a mini-ice age.[75] The Great Dying — the massive

[74] *An indigenous peoples' history of the United States*, Roxanne Dunbar-Ortiz, *Beacon Press* 2014
[75] "'Little Ice Age' caused by death of 55-million Indigenous people after colonization: study" John Hadden, *Global News*, February 6, 2019 https://globalnews.ca/news/4924534/little-ice-age-death-55-million-indigenous-people-colonization-study/

loss of life that followed Christopher Columbus' 1492 conquest of the Americas through **genocide** and the spread of disease — also left roughly 56-million hectares of land abandoned.

But what is genocide? According to the UN Genocide Convention,[76] genocide means: *any of the following acts committed with intent to destroy, in whole or in part, a national, ethnical, racial or religious group, as such:*

a) Killing members of the group;
b) Causing serious bodily or mental harm to members of the group;
c) Deliberately inflicting on the group conditions of life calculated to bring about its physical destruction in whole or in part;
d) Imposing measures intended to prevent births within the group;
e) Forcibly transferring children of the group to another group.

The list of genocides[77] is long and reflects the blood-stained history of colonization. **Genocide Watch** is an organization established to predict, prevent, stop, and punish genocide and other forms of mass murder. They have defined three levels of Genocide Alerts:

1) A **Genocide Watch** is declared when there are signs of the early stages of the genocidal process. (See *The Ten Stages of Genocide* below)
2) A **Genocide Warning** is called when the genocidal process has reached the stages of preparation by perpetrators and persecution of a targeted group.
3) A **Genocide Emergency** is declared when the genocidal process has reached the stage of genocidal massacres and other acts of genocide.

Genocide Watch has alerted the world to the following *genocide emergencies*[78] at present:

---

76 *Convention on the Prevention and Punishment of the Crime of Genocide*, United Nations (1951) https://www.un.org/en/genocideprevention/documents/atrocity-crimes/Doc.1_Convention%20on%20the%20Prevention%20and%20Punishment%20of%20the%20Crime%20of%20Genocide.pdf
77 https://en.wikipedia.org/wiki/List_of_genocides
78 *Genocide Watch Recommendations 2024 Genocide Emergencies and Warnings* Genocide Watch https://www.genocidewatch.com/_files/ugd/df1038_c0b09883aa28417ba4e5d832c80aef98.pdf

- Hamas genocide of Israelis; Israeli war crimes and genocide in Gaza
- Renewed genocide in Darfur and Sudan
- Jihadist genocide of Christians in Nigeria
- Russian genocide in Ukraine
- Slow genocide of Hazara Shias in Afghanistan
- Assad regime and Turkish genocides in Syria
- Genocide in North Korea
- Genocides of ethnic minorities in Myanmar
- Persecution of Rohingya refugees in Bangladesh and India
- Chinese genocide of Uyghur Muslims
- Genocide in Ethiopia
- Genocide in Democratic Republic of Congo

John Mearsheimer – in a blog post titled "The Moral Bankruptcy of the West"[79] explains:

…almost all of the many human rights advocates … in the West … have stayed silent while Israel executed its genocide. The mainstream media has made hardly any effort to expose and challenge what Israel is doing to the Palestinians. Indeed some key outlets have staunchly supported Israel's actions.

Mearsheimer points out:

- On 19 December 2024, Human Rights Watch issued a 179-page report detailing Israel's genocide in Gaza.
- On 5 December 2024, Amnesty International issued a 296-page report detailing Israel's genocide in Gaza.
- On 21 November 2024, the International Criminal Court issued arrest warrants for Israeli Prime Minister Benjamin Netanyahu and former Israeli Defense Minister Yoav Gallant for crimes against humanity and war crimes.

[79] The Moral Bankruptcy of the West by John Mearsheimer https://mearsheimer.substack.com/p/the-moral-bankruptcy-of-the-west

- On 26 January 2024, the International Court of Justice found that a plausible case can be made that Israel is committing genocide in Gaza.

And yet, he bluntly states – "the governments in those three countries, especially the United States, have supported Israel's unimaginable behavior in Gaza at every turn. Indeed, those three countries are complicit in this genocide."

How do we identify a genocide before it occurs?

According to **Gregory Stanton** of Genocide Watch,[80] genocide is a process that develops in ten stages that are predictable but not inexorable.

At each stage, preventive measures can stop it.

The process is not linear. Stages occur simultaneously. Each stage is itself a process. Their logic is similar to a nested Russian matryoshka doll. Classification is at the center. Without it the processes around it could not occur.

As societies develop more and more genocidal processes, they get nearer to genocide. But *all stages* continue to operate throughout the process.

---

[80] "The Ten Stages of Genocide" by Gregory H. Stanton https://www.genocidewatch.com/tenstages

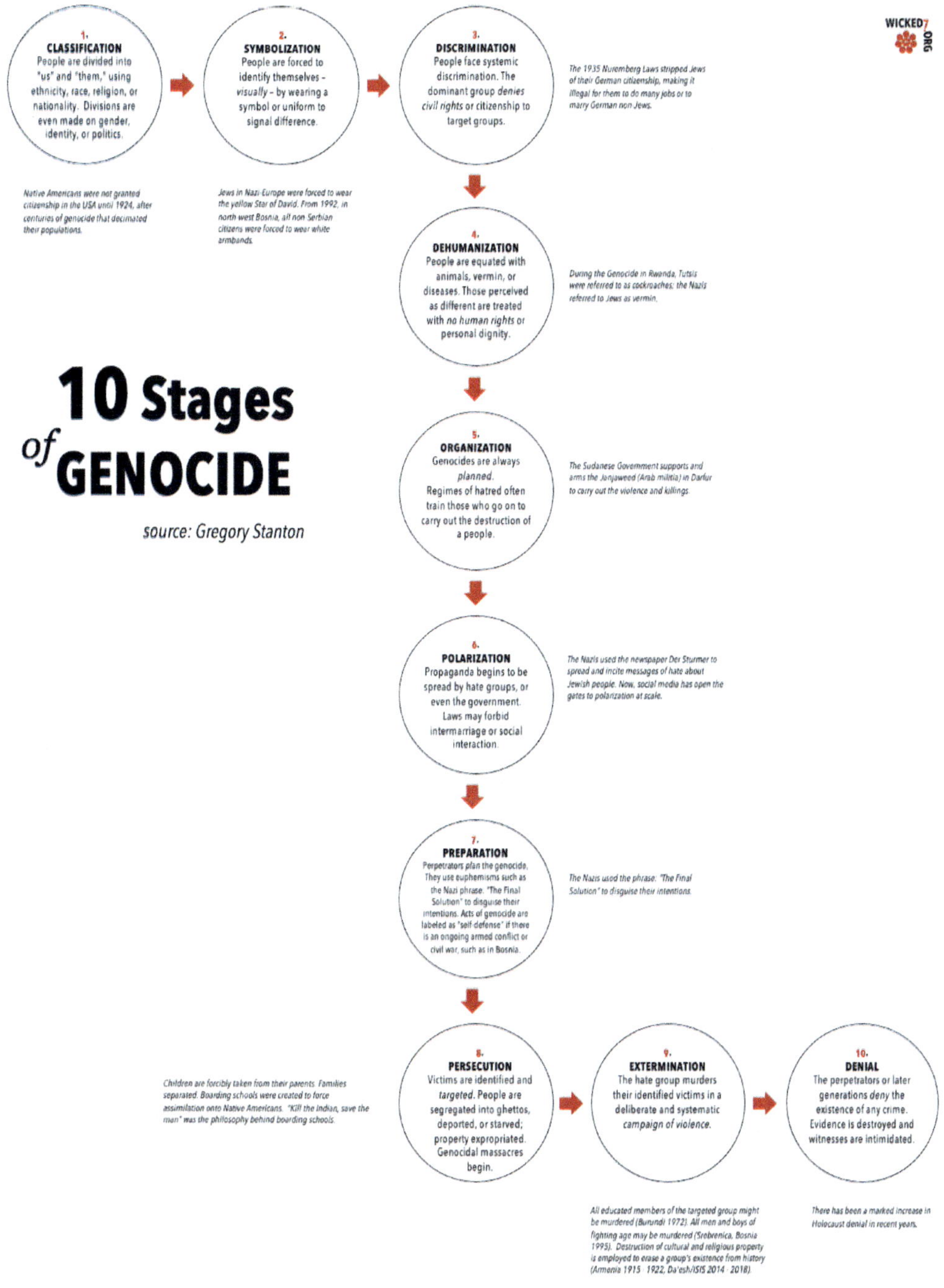
10 Stages of GENOCIDE
source: Gregory Stanton
WICKED7.ORG
1. CLASSIFICATION
People are divided into "us" and "them," using ethnicity, race, religion, or nationality. Divisions are even made on gender, identity, or politics.
Native Americans were not granted citizenship in the USA until 1924, after centuries of genocide that decimated their populations.
2. SYMBOLIZATION
People are forced to identify themselves - visually - by wearing a symbol or uniform to signal difference.
Jews in Nazi-Europe were forced to wear the yellow Star of David. From 1992, in north west Bosnia, all non Serbian citizens were forced to wear white armbands.
3. DISCRIMINATION
People face systemic discrimination. The dominant group denies civil rights or citizenship to target groups.
The 1935 Nuremberg Laws stripped Jews of their German citizenship, making it illegal for them to do many jobs or to marry German non Jews.
4. DEHUMANIZATION
People are equated with animals, vermin, or diseases. Those perceived as different are treated with no human rights or personal dignity.
During the Genocide in Rwanda, Tutsis were referred to as cockroaches; the Nazis referred to Jews as vermin.
5. ORGANIZATION
Genocides are always planned. Regimes of hatred often train those who go on to carry out the destruction of a people.
The Sudanese Government supports and arms the Janjaweed (Arab militia) in Darfur to carry out the violence and killings.
6. POLARIZATION
Propaganda begins to be spread by hate groups, or even the government. Laws may forbid intermarriage or social interaction.
The Nazis used the newspaper Der Sturmer to spread and incite messages of hate about Jewish people. Now, social media has open the gates to polarization at scale.
7. PREPARATION
Perpetrators plan the genocide. They use euphemisms such as the Nazi phrase: "The Final Solution" to disguise their intentions. Acts of genocide are labeled as "self-defense" if there is an ongoing armed conflict or civil war, such as in Bosnia.
The Nazis used the phrase: "The Final Solution" to disguise their intentions.
8. PERSECUTION
Victims are identified and targeted. People are segregated into ghettos, deported, or starved; property expropriated. Genocidal massacres begin.
Children are forcibly taken from their parents. Families separated. Boarding schools were created to force assimilation onto Native Americans. "Kill the Indian, save the man" was the philosophy behind boarding schools.
9. EXTERMINATION
The hate group murders their identified victims in a deliberate and systematic campaign of violence.
All educated members of the targeted group might be murdered (Burundi 1972). All men and boys of fighting age may be murdered (Srebrenica, Bosnia 1995). Destruction of cultural and religious property is employed to erase a group's existence from history (Armenia 1915 - 1922, Da'esh/ISIS 2014 - 2018).
10. DENIAL
The perpetrators or later generations deny the existence of any crime. Evidence is destroyed and witnesses are intimidated.
There has been a marked increase in Holocaust denial in recent years.

Stanton explains[81]:

- The first process is **Classification**, when we classify the world into us versus them.
- The second is **Symbolization**, when we give names to those classifications like Jew and Aryan, Hutu and Tutsi, Turk and Armenian, Bengali and Pashtun. Sometimes the symbols are physical, like the Nazi yellow star.
- The third is **Discrimination**, when laws and customs prevent groups of people from exercising their full rights as citizens or as human beings.
- The fourth is **Dehumanization**, when perpetrators call their victims rats, or cockroaches, cancer, or disease. Portraying them as non-human makes eliminating them a "cleansing" of the society, rather than murder.
- The fifth process is **Organization**, when hate groups, armies, and militias organize.
- The sixth is **Polarization**, when moderates are targeted who could stop the process of division, especially moderates from the perpetrators' group.
- The seventh process is **Preparation**, when plans for killing and deportation are made by leaders, and perpetrators are trained and armed.
- The eighth process is **Persecution**, when victims are identified, arrested, transported, and concentrated into prisons, ghettos, or concentration camps, where they are tortured and murdered.
- The ninth process is **Extermination**, what lawyers define as genocide, the intentional destruction, in whole or in part, of a national, ethnic, racial, or religious group.
- The tenth stage is **Denial**. Denial is a continuation of a genocide, because it is a continuing attempt to destroy the victim group psychologically and culturally, to deny its members even the memory of the murders of their relatives.

Note the similarities between Stanton's *10 Stages of Genocide* and the ADL *Pyramid of Hate.*

[81] "The Ten Stages of Genocide" by Gregory H. Stanton https://www.genocidewatch.com/tenstages

As we see a steep rise[82] in **hate crimes** in the US, we must remember that the same ugly hatred was virulent in the late 1800s and 1900s, and the victims were Catholics, Italians, Irish, Poles, Jews, Muslims, Blacks, Browns, Asians, and Native Americans. Nearly every ethnic group except those who were not WASPS.

Hate crimes more than doubled between 2014 and 2022, increasing by 7% from 2021 to 2022, the most recent year available in data collected by the FBI.

Demonizing immigrants is a key strategy for the GOP. Republicans have embraced Trump's open xenophobia. This is not new, but what is new is the level of mainstream acceptance for a narrative of immigrant bashing. The ADL identified the following tactics to foment fear and spread unfounded propaganda as far back as 2008[83]:

- Describing immigrants as "third world invaders," who come to America to destroy our heritage, "colonize" the country and attack our "way of life." This charge is used against Latinos, Asians and other people of color.
- Using terminology that describes immigrants as part of "hordes" that "swarm" over the border. This dehumanizing language has become common.

---

[82] "How reports of hate crimes in the US were already at record highs, in 4 charts" by Tori Morales Pinales, *CNN*, December 11, 2023 https://edition.cnn.com/2023/10/29/us/hate-crimes-antisemitism-anti-muslim-dg/index.html

[83] *Immigrants Targeted: Extremist Rhetoric Moves into the Mainstream* ADL https://www.adl.org/sites/default/files/documents/assets/pdf/civil-rights/immigration/Immigrants-Targeted-UPDATE_2008.pdf

- Portraying immigrants as carriers of diseases like leprosy, tuberculosis, Chagas disease (a potentially fatal parasitic disease), dengue fever, polio, malaria.
- Depicting immigrants as criminals, murderers, rapists, terrorists, and a danger to children and families.
- Propagating conspiracy theories about an alleged secret "reconquista" plot by Mexican immigrants to create a "greater Mexico" by seizing seven states in the American Southwest that once belonged to Mexico.
- Blaming immigrants for eroding American culture, institutions and quality of life and impacting our environment and natural resources.

Extremist organizations such as the Ku Klux Klan and neo-Nazis have long seized upon the immigration debate to further their extremist agendas.

This exploitation has spread, with the proliferation of virulent anti-immigrant and anti-Latino rhetoric within mainstream politics, particularly the Republican party. The GOP portrays itself as mainstream advocate against illegal immigration in the United States, thereby blurring the lines between legitimate discourse and extremist ideology. **The extremism borders on the *absurd*: "Bomb Mexico**[84]" is a foreign policy strategy that actually gained support in the Republican party. And Trump is echoing the Ku Klux Klan when he says that undocumented migrants are "destroying the blood of our country" and "ruining the fabric" of the US[85].

[84] "GOP embraces a new foreign policy: Bomb Mexico to stop fentanyl" by Alexander Ward, *Politico*, April 10, 2023 https://www.politico.com/news/2023/04/10/gop-bomb-mexico-fentanyl-00091132

[85] "Trump repeats anti-immigrant tirade, denies reading Hitler" by Giselle Ruhiyyih Ewing, *Politico*, December 19, 2023 https://www.politico.com/news/2023/12/19/trump-immigration-comments-hitler-00132613

HATE & CONFLICT

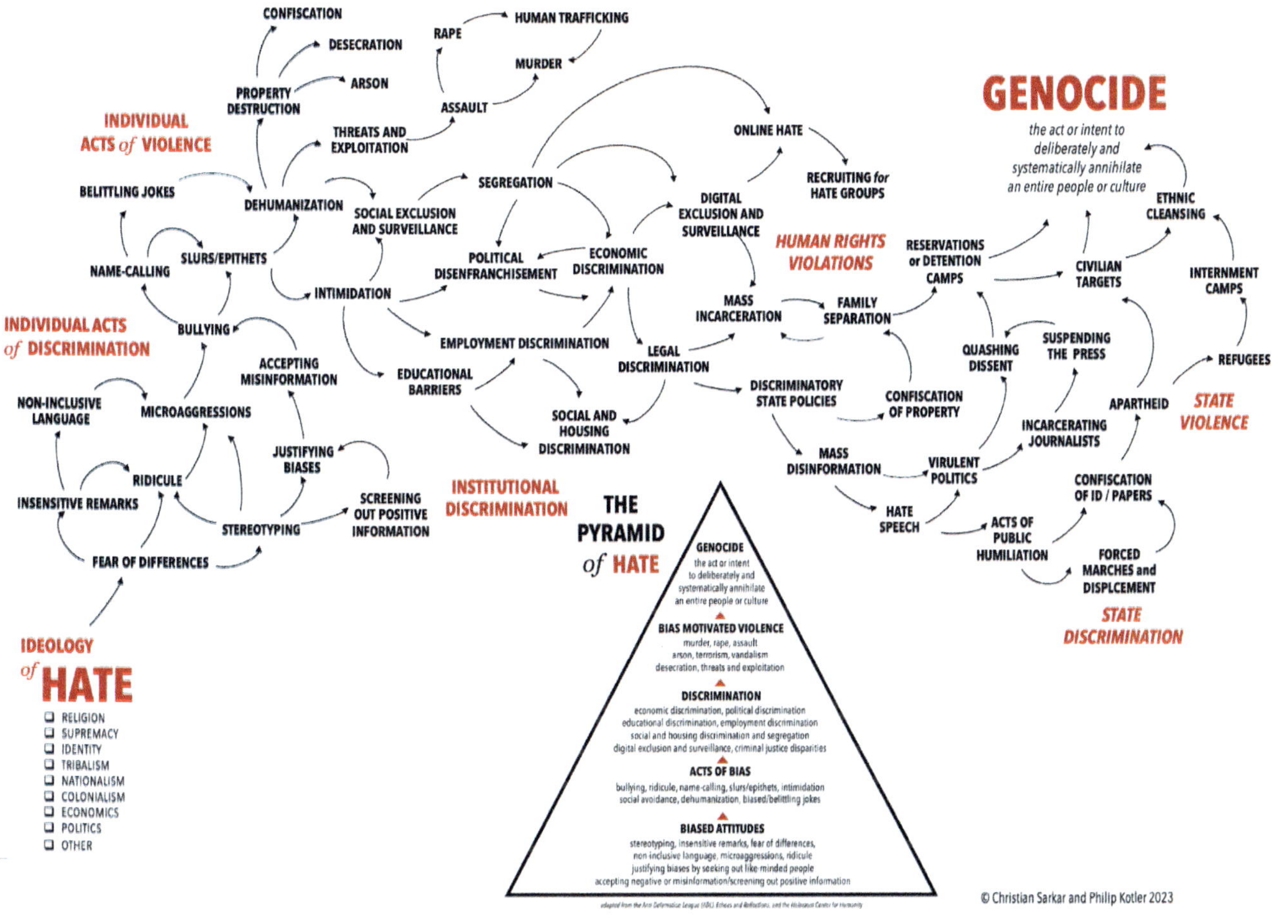

If hatred is mostly learned, can it be unlearned? Are there tools available to help reduce hateful attitudes and behavior? Yes, there are several tools. First, we must rethink education. Schools need to teach children to respect all races, genders, and cultures around the world. They should identify harmful behaviors directed against others, such as bullying or cursing and bring these destructive behaviors before the group to discuss and discipline. Religious leaders need to talk in their sermons about the costs and damage that hate causes. Film makers need to create powerful films that illustrate the damage caused by hate. Music, books and art have the power of drama to bring ugly situations to light. Social workers must spot hateful attitudes and behavior and try to discuss and alter the "trajectory" of hate.

We took the liberty of creating the **Pyramid of Love** – a *reversal* of the Pyramid of Hate:

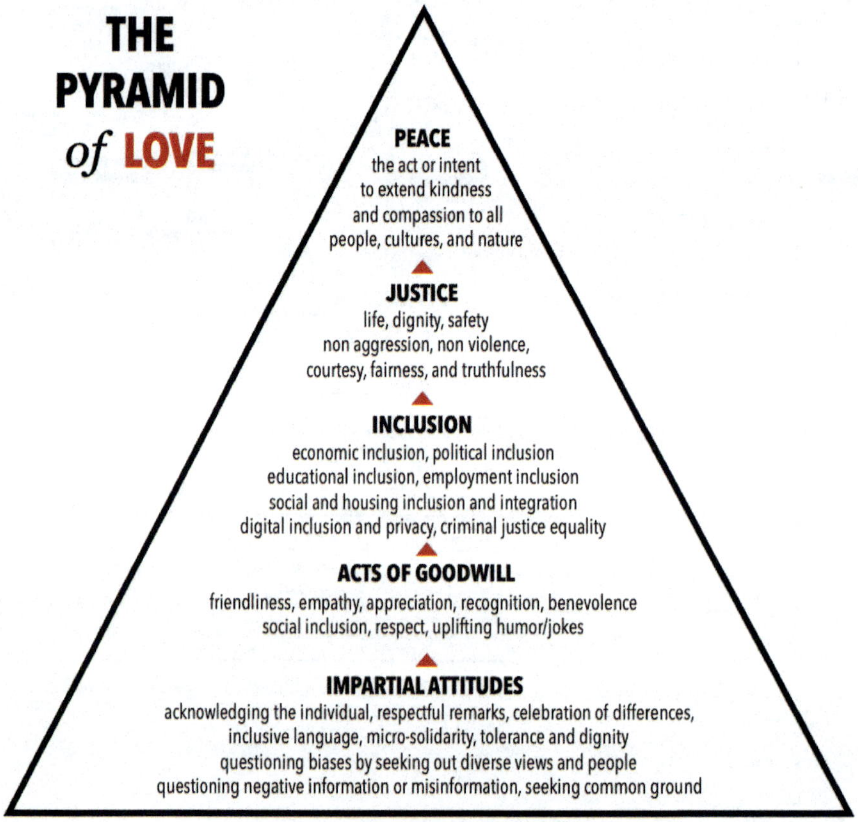

Just as there are levels of hate, there are levels of "love." These levels are shown in the Pyramid of Love. Instead of escalating hate, what if our institutions and leaders promoted love? The highest level is to wish for a peace where everyone extends kindness and compassion to others and to Nature as well. Our world religions are still not up to the task – they are faiths of exclusion rather than inclusion.

Every conflict has an understory where both parties feel justified in their grievances. The conflict between Israelis and Palestinians has layers of justification for each side. These are the hardest conflicts to resolve and bring back to a win-win settlement.

The best mediators in the world are frustrated.

Rachele Gabellini is an expert at negotiations[86] and mediation. We asked her to comment on the Jewish-Palestinian conflict. Her response had three main points:

To begin to address the Israeli-Palestinian conflict,

(1) we must begin by recognizing and respecting the thoughts, feelings and actions of the other side even if our point of view is totally the opposite;
(2) we will need to find a third party which both sides can trust and work with as a mediator. This third-party will be someone above criticism – who does not take sides, and truly represents an ethical perspective which understands both sides. The US is no longer a viable candidate for mediator. What is needed now is a person, not a state.
(3) if no mediator can be found that is acceptable to both sides, then the leadership must step down - on both sides.

These conditions are difficult, but not impossible. The international community must apply pressure on both sides to begin this mediation process without delay.

---

[86] *NegotiAction* by Monoriti Angelo, Gabellini Rachele. McGraw Hill, December 2023

According to **ClimateGPT**, the primary drivers of Hate & Polarization are:

- **Social and economic inequality:** When certain groups feel marginalized or excluded from economic opportunities, social status, or political power, they may become more susceptible to extremist ideologies that promise to address their grievances.
- **Political polarization:** When political differences become so extreme that individuals are unable to find common ground or engage in constructive dialogue, it can lead to polarization and conflict.
- **Social media echo chambers:** The algorithms used by social media platforms can create "filter bubbles" that reinforce users' existing beliefs and values, making them less likely to engage with opposing viewpoints.
- **Historical grievances:** Unresolved historical conflicts or injustices can create long-lasting resentments and mistrust between groups, which can be exploited by extremist movements.
- **Lack of critical thinking skills:** When individuals lack the critical thinking skills to evaluate information and arguments critically, they may be more susceptible to manipulation by extremist groups.
- **Psychological factors:** Certain psychological factors, such as cognitive dissonance or the need for social identity, can contribute to the appeal of extremist ideologies.
- **Demographic changes:** Rapid demographic changes can create social and cultural tensions, particularly if there is a sense of insecurity or loss of traditional identity.
- **Political and economic instability:** When a society is experiencing political or economic instability, it can create an environment in which extremist movements can thrive.
- **Religious or ideological extremism:** Extremist interpretations of religion or ideology can promote a sense of us-versus-them mentality, which can lead to polarization and conflict.
- **Lack of effective governance:** When governance structures are weak or corrupt, it can create an environment in which extremist groups can flourish.

Further details on each one of these root causes are listed in the appendix: *Answers from AI,* at the end of this book.

CASCADING EFFECTS

Is there a connection between hate and climate? Researchers find a link between weather and aggression[87]:

The prevalence of hate tweets was lowest at moderate temperatures (12 to 21°C) and marked increases in the number of hate tweets were observed at hotter and colder temperatures, reaching up to 12·5% (95% CI 8·0-16·5) for cold temperature extremes (-6 to -3°C) and up to 22·0% (95% CI 20·5-23·5) for hot temperature extremes (42 to 45°C). Outside of the moderate temperature range, the hate tweets also increased as a proportion of total tweeting activity.

As climate change creates climate refugees, we are going to see more hate and more violence against refugees and migrants. Then, that same violence can be channeled against the "other" – anyone who the party in power disagrees with! *That's another wicked problem.*

---

[87] "Temperature impacts on hate speech online: evidence from 4 billion geolocated tweets from the USA" by Annika Stechemesser, Anders Levermann, Leonie Wenz. The Lancet September 2022. https://www.thelancet.com/journals/lanplh/article/PIIS2542-5196(22)00173-5/fulltext3

"Babylon makes the rules."
– Steel Pulse

4 **POWER AND CORRUPTION**

Power and power differences are inevitable in human society. In a patriarchal family, the father traditionally has power over the wife and the children. The son or daughter are expected to respect the wishes of the father and the mother. In many societies, the parents choose who their children will marry. The sons receive more attention than the daughters. And the oldest son has privileges over the young son(s).

In a business situation, the owners have power over the workers. The owners prescribe what the workers have to do and how their performance will be judged. The owners set the wages and the working conditions. In past times, the owners could fire a worker even without cause. And business owners in the US work hard to undermine and prevent unions from forming.

In an elected government, the President, Congress members, Governors and Mayors are granted the power to manage their respective domains. Citizens have to obey their decisions but have the right to protest through legal means or finally to take away their power at the next election. Sometimes the political leader may grab more power by controlling the media and the court system and arresting dissidents, in which case power is moving in the hands of an autocrat or dictator. Corporate power asserts itself through "free speech" – donations to the politicians who support their interests.

Democracy and capitalism can't seem to co-exist. Everywhere we look, **democracy is in decline**[88]. We have to **confront capitalism** or lose our democracy[89].

The question we have to ask is: **why aren't our politicians working for us?**

The answer?

Our **politicians work for their donors**, *not* for us, the people.

Joseph Merz, founder of the **Merz Institute** has this to say on LinkedIn[90]:

We can see quite clearly that governments all around the world have been captured by various industries. Powerful companies controlled by powerful and wealthy individuals.

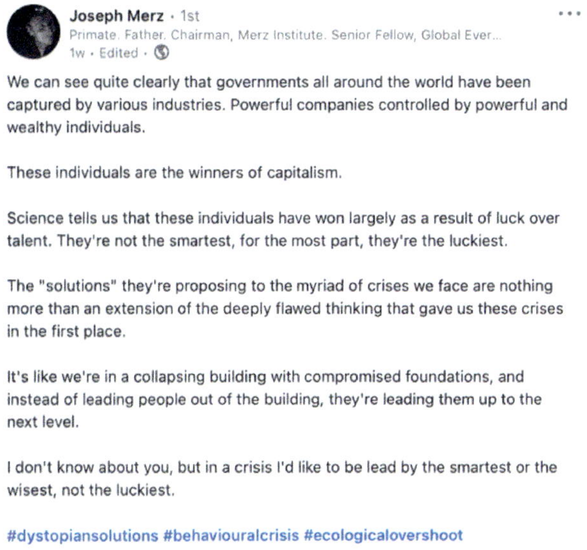

Small wonder that we feel like our politicians have been bought, that the system *is rigged*. (Trump is right on this point).

Remember Mitt Romney's emphatic statement: *Corporations are "people."* And campaign contributions are free speech. In every case, we find that private, **for-profit interests** win over the public interest:

- Healthcare – for profit
- Drugs – for profit

[88] Democracy in Decline: An Interview with Philip Kotler, *The Huffington Post* https://www.huffpost.com/entry/democracy-in-decline-an-i_b_10369536
[89] http://www.confrontingcapitalism.com/
[90] https://www.linkedin.com/posts/josephmerz_dystopiansolutions-behaviouralcrisis-ecologicalovershoot-activity-7154648263453753344-epyK

- Education – for profit
- Infrastructure – for profit
- War – for profit
- Guns – for profit
- Water – for profit
- Environment – for profit
- Infrastructure – for profit
- Green New Deal – *sorry, no can do;* let's stick with fossil-fuel profits. (the COPs are a cop-out)

Just name the issue, and you'll find a donor, or perhaps group of donors, that are benefiting while the citizen's needs are neglected. Even on critical issues like climate change and genocide, our politicians can't do the right thing. The political contributions from their donors (think NRA, AIPAC, Big Oil, Big Pharma, you name it) prevent them from upsetting the status quo.

The Common Good is sacrificed on the altar of private profit.

We borrowed and adapted a business concept from **Jim Collins**[91] to explain what's going on: the **flywheel of corruption**.

Is Capitalism working for *you*?

The answer to the question depends on who you ask.

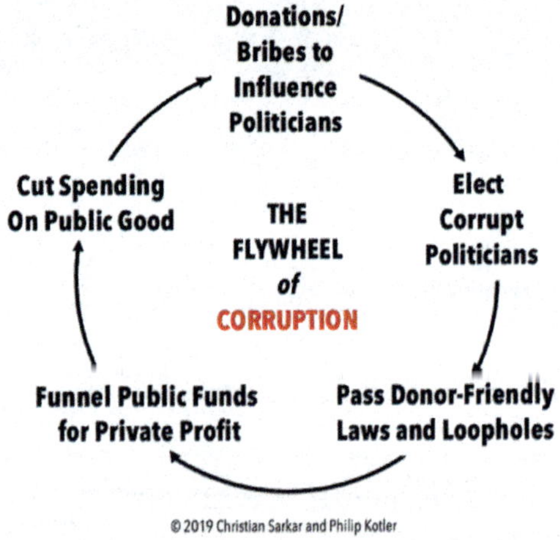

[91] "Turning the Flywheel" by Jim Collins, *THE MARKETING JOURNAL* http://www.marketingjournal.org/book-review-turning-the-flywheel-by-jim-collins/

The establishment believes, in most countries, but certainly in the US, that they are the job creators and providers of employment.

With a few notable exceptions, if you ask America's **corporate executives**, their answer is that American Capitalism is working well and would even work better if there were fewer government regulations and if taxes were lowered.

If you ask America's **middle class**, their answer is that American Capitalism worked better in the past but now it is harder to finance a middle-class life style given the high costs of sending students to college and taking care of their parents who failed to save enough money for their retirement. Healthcare and drug costs are out of control. In fact, healthcare emergencies are a leading cause of individual bankruptcy[92].

If you ask **working–class Americans**, their answer is that they haven't improved their earnings since the 1980s but their expenses have risen dramatically and they can only survive with a credit card and rising indebtedness.

If you ask the 15% of our population living in **poverty**, their answer is that they can't find a decent job and they barely survive on food stamps, food kitchens, clothing handouts, and cheap housing or even homelessness.

Markets, left to themselves, do not lead to efficient or equitable outcomes. Free-market capitalism can lead to monopolistic or oligopolistic industry domination–witness Google, Facebook, Amazon, and Apple. It inevitably leads to a growing concentration of income and wealth. The average income for the top 0.01 percent of households grew 322 percent, to $6.7 million, between 1980 and 2015. As of 2015, the data shows that half of all US income[93] went straight into the pockets of the top 10 percent of earners. **Thomas Piketty**,

---

[92] "This is the real reason most Americans file for bankruptcy" *CNBC* https://www.cnbc.com/2019/02/11/this-is-the-real-reason-most-americans-file-for-bankruptcy.html

[93] " 11Charts That Show Income Inequality Isn't Getting Better Anytime Soon" *Mother Jones* https://www.motherjones.com/politics/2016/12/america-income-inequality-wealth-net-worth-charts/

the economist, predicts that eventually 60 percent of income will go to the top 10 percent of earners.

Unfortunately, this pattern is a global phenomenon. Politicians work for their donor/masters. Many political systems are purpose-built for corruption.

And, despite what we keep hearing, government can't be "**run like a business.**" **This is one of the biggest fallacies in the current political debate.** We are told, time and time again, that a candidate for public office is qualified because he or she has run a business. The assumption is that this makes them fit for government service. One only has to look at the failure of Rex Tillerson at the US State Department to see that the CEO of ExxonMobil didn't have what it takes to do the job.

But to understand why this is, we need to look at what the job is.

What's the job of government? Who is the customer?

Let's answer this simply – **the job of government is to serve the public in the public interest, or to serve the *Common Good.***

Unlike business, the government does not get to select which customer segments to serve and which segments to ignore. **The government must serve *all* its citizens and constituents.** When it fails to do so, it becomes dysfunctional.

Guess what – it's dysfunction *by* design!

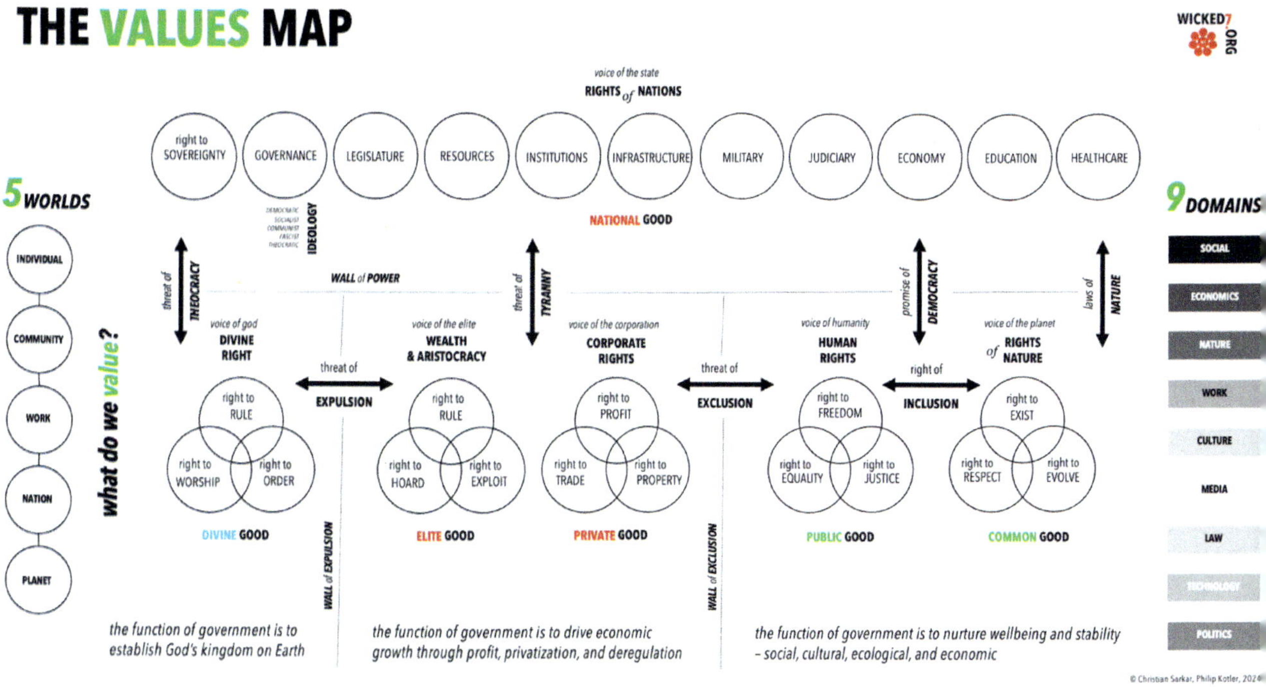

Our differences are based on our understanding of the purpose of government!

Katherine Gehl and **Michael Porter** explain what's going on in *Why Competition in the Politics Industry is Failing America*[94]:

The starting point for understanding the problem is to recognize that our political system isn't broken. Washington is delivering exactly what it is currently designed to deliver. The real problem is that our political system is no longer designed to serve the public interest, and has been slowly reconfigured to benefit the private interests of gain-seeking organizations: our major political parties and their industry allies.

Take a minute to let that sink in: **The US political system does not serve the public interest (or the Common Good).**

---

[94] "WHY COMPETITION IN THE POLITICS INDUSTRY IS FAILING AMERICA" by *Katherine Gehl and Michael Porter* https://www.hbs.edu/competitiveness/Documents/why-competition-in-the-politics-industry-is-failing-america.pdf

POWER & CORRUPTION

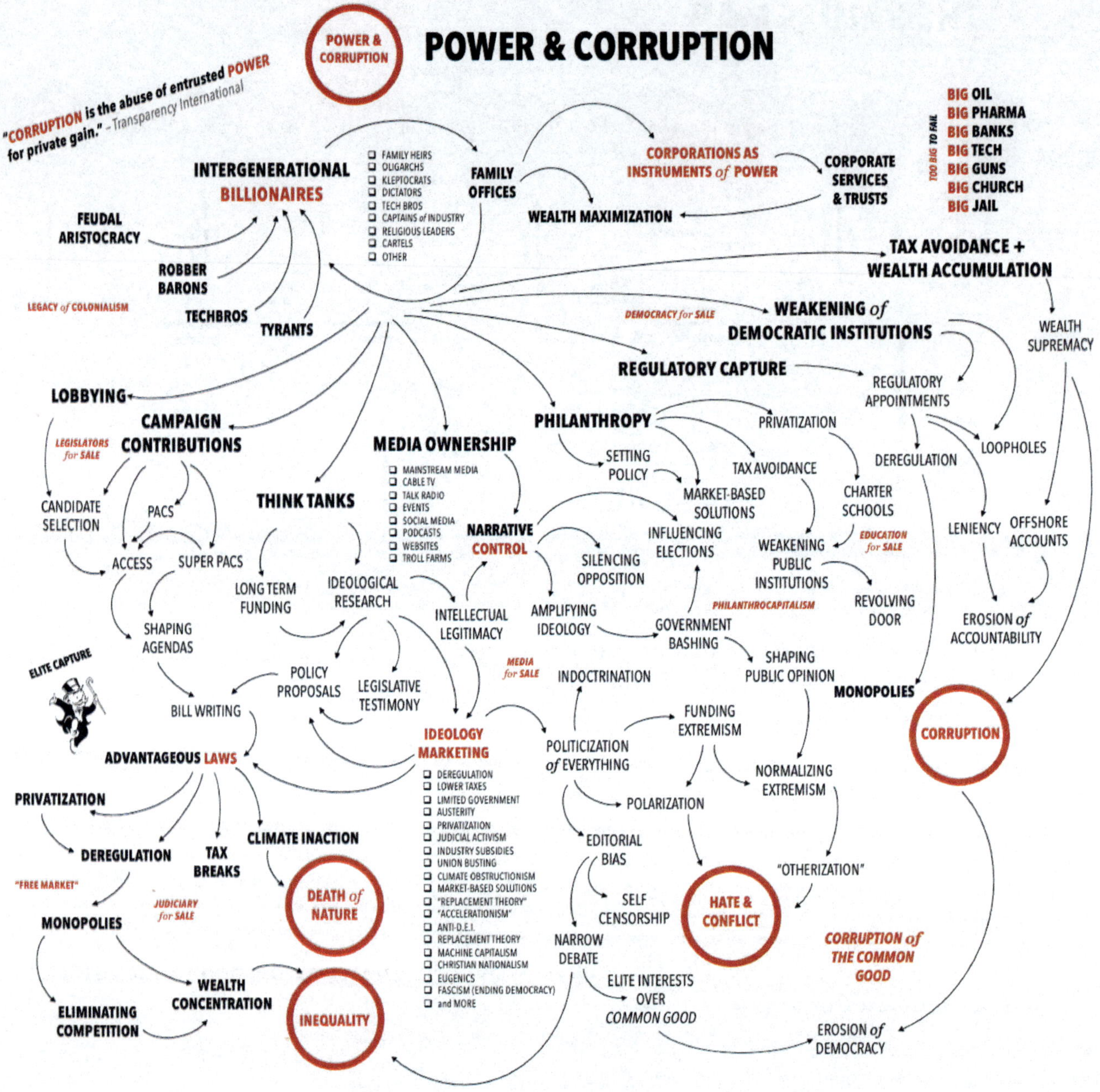

ELITE CAPTURE

This process of government and institutional take-over is called **elite capture** – and is a form of **corruption at the highest level**.

- **Control of Resources**: Elite capture, akin to a silent power play, sees the privileged few tighten their grip on crucial societal assets. Whether it's land, capital, or political influence, these resources become pawns in a game where the rules favor the elite, leaving the rest of society scrambling for the leftovers.
- **Inequality**: Within the labyrinth of elite capture, inequality thrives like an unchecked weed. The gap widens between the haves and the have-nots, as the elite amass wealth and power while the majority find themselves relegated to the sidelines, their voices drowned out by the echoes of privilege.
- **Political Influence**: In the arena of politics, elite capture erects barriers to true democracy. Behind closed doors, decisions are brokered, policies crafted, all to serve the interests of a select few. For the average citizen, the ballot box becomes a mere illusion of choice, as real power lies entrenched in the corridors of influence.
- **Corruption and Nepotism**: Corruption and nepotism are the twin pillars upon which elite capture stands tall. From backroom deals to crony appointments, the elite ensure that the halls of power remain a private domain, where favors flow freely and accountability is but a fleeting concept.
- **Impacts on Development**: Like a stubborn anchor, elite capture weighs down the ship of progress, impeding the journey toward development and prosperity. Economic growth stagnates, social mobility grinds to a halt, and the promise of a better future remains out of reach for those trapped in the shadows of privilege.

Yet, in the face of this formidable foe, resistance stirs, and calls for reform echo through the streets. Transparency, accountability, and democratic governance emerge as the weapons of choice in the battle against elite capture, as marginalized voices unite in their quest for a fairer, more equitable society. This is what the **Peace for the Common Good**, is all about. The elites are waging War on the Common Good.

The United Nations Convention against Corruption addresses the major manifestations of corruption, such as bribery and embezzlement, and the acts carried out in support of corruption, such as obstruction of justice, trading in influence and the concealment or laundering of the proceeds of corruption. The Convention covers not only corruption in private-to-public relationships (business relationships with public officials, including state-owned enterprises), but also private-to-private relationships (relationships among companies only).

The following is a list[95] of common manifestations of corruption. See if you recognize any (or all) of them:

- Bribery of national public officials;
- Bribery of foreign public officials and officials of public international organizations;
- Bribery in the private sector;
- Embezzlement of property in the private sector;
- Trading in influence;
- Abuse of function;
- Illicit enrichment;
- Laundering of proceeds of crime;
- Concealment of proceeds of crime; and
- Obstruction of justice.

One can argue that in the current system, the *only* customer served by the government is the wealthy donor, and the corporations that fund candidates' re-elections. And, when they leave Congress, candidates are then employed as lobbyists for these corporations. According to Sourcewatch[96], "The government-industry revolving door puts industry-friendly experts in

---

[95] An Anti-Corruption Ethics and Compliance Programme for Business: A Practical Guide http://www.unodc.org/documents/corruption/Publications/2013/13-84498_Ebook.pdf

[96] "Government-industry revolving door," *Sourcewatch* https://www.sourcewatch.org/index.php/Government-industry_revolving_door

positions of decision-making power. Often individuals rotate between working for industry and working for the government in regulatory capacities, arrangements that are fraught with potential for conflicts of interest."

Of course, these conflicts of interest are often hidden behind closed doors.

Dark money groups also hijack the political process by ensuring that the needs and wants of their donors are positioned above the needs of society.

Note – the late President **Jimmy Carter** said[97] that the US is "an oligarchy with unlimited political bribery."

Is he right?

We looked at **Stanley F. Stasch**'s *The Creation and Destruction of the Great American Middle Class (1930-2010)*[98] to explain how the following events gave corporate and business interests too much power and influence in the United States:

During the 1970s:

- A program of government-guaranteed student loans rewarded bankers at the expense of students.
- Congress created a new bankruptcy law that favored the wealthy over the middle and lower classes.
- The Health Maintenance Organization Act of 1973 signed into law by President Nixon allowed medical insurance agencies, hospitals, clinics and even doctors, to

---

[97] "Jimmy Carter: U.S. Is an 'Oligarchy With Unlimited Political Bribery'" *RollingStones* https://www.rollingstone.com/politics/politics-news/jimmy-carter-u-s-is-an-oligarchy-with-unlimited-political-bribery-63262/

[98] "The Creation and Destruction of the Great American Middle Class" (1930-2010), *Loyola eCommons* https://ecommons.luc.edu/cgi/viewcontent.cgi?referer=http://fixcapitalism.com/free-online-class-the-creation-and-destruction-of-the-great-american-middle-class-1930-2010-with-professor-stanley-stasch/&httpsredir=1&article=1004&context=business_facpubs

function as for-profit business entities instead of the service organizations they were intended to be,

- The Supreme Court made a decision that allowed banks to charge very high interest rates on credit card balances.

During the 1980s:

- The Reagan presidency allowed corporations to replace pension plans with 401(k) plans, thus greatly reducing the retirement incomes of millions of middle-and-lower class workers.
- The government eliminated three important banking regulations, and their absence contributed to increasing income inequality and the housing crisis that culminated in the financial crash of 2007-2008.

During the 1990s:

- The government allowed the growing use of stock options to dramatically increase CEO compensation.
- Congress excluded waitresses and waiters when it increased the federal minimum wage, thus relegating them to poverty or near-poverty incomes.
- In 1995 the Republican-controlled Congress passed, over President Clinton's veto, the Private Securities Litigation Reform Act to severely limit the ability of shareholders and similarly-interested parties to take legal action against corporations and investment bankers.
- The government allowed "forced arbitration" clauses to exist in cable, cell phone, and other consumer contracts, which prevented consumers from participating in class action lawsuits when they felt that companies were unjustly taking small amounts of money each month from them and millions of other consumers.

During the 2000s:

- The business community helped President George W. Bush pass his tax cuts for the rich.
- The government bailed out "banks too big to fail" during the financial crisis of 2007-2008, but prevented distressed homeowners from declaring bankruptcy.
- Congress' new treaty greatly facilitated outsourcing U.S. manufacturing jobs to China and increasing imports from China.
- Congress allowed employers to steal billions of dollars from employees through legalized wage theft; low-level working supervisors and others were reclassified as managers and executives. By changing the law, Republicans essentially legalized wage theft. Because of that reclassification, millions of workers were forced to work more than forty hours a week without being paid overtime.
- The new bankruptcy law of 2005 favored the rich over the middle class.
- Congress and the president allowed U.S. companies to transform themselves into global corporations and move high tech jobs to foreign countries.
- Congress allowed the business community to block attempts to "cap" excessive CEO compensation.
- Congress failed in its attempt to reform banks and financial institutions after the financial crisis of 2007-2008.
- The Supreme Court under Chief Justice Roberts reached out in the *Citizens United* case, ruling that corporations and other business-like organizations were no longer restrained in contributing to a politician's campaign fund. They were now free to spend as much money as they wished to support or defeat any candidate for any office. This opened the floodgates for the Koch Brothers, the Mercers, and other donors in the billionaire class to influence elections at an unprecedented level.

And during the first Trump administration, the pattern continued (via the Brookings[99] deregulatory tracker):

[99] "Tracking deregulation in the Trump era" *BROOKINGS*

- The FCC, headed by Chairman Ajit Pai, a Trump appointee, voted 3-2 to repeal Net Neutrality.
- The Trump Interior Department proposed[100] to repeal most of the requirements of the Obama-era Methane Rule which regulated the gas released into the atmosphere during oil and natural gas production through venting, flaring, and equipment leaks.
- Nullification of a rule allowing class action lawsuits against banks and credit card companies to resolve financial disputes.
- Effective nullification of a rule requiring communities to analyze racial residential segregation and submit plans to reverse it as a condition of receiving federal housing aid.
- Withdrawal of the Organic Livestock and Poultry Practices Rule requiring the humane treatment of "certified organic" animals.
- Rescission of Oil and Gas Fracking rule by the Department of the Interior on the grounds that it imposes burdensome reporting requirements and other unjustified costs on the oil and gas industry.
- Nullification of a rule requiring resource extraction issuers to disclose information about payments made to the U.S. government or foreign governments for the purposes of commercial development of oil, natural gas, or minerals. Advocates of the rule claimed that it prevented companies from bribing foreign governments and engaging in other forms of corruption. Detractors argued that the rule placed an excessive burden on U.S. companies.

The result of these actions has been a steady and systemic corruption of *all* our government institutions. **And now we have Trump 2.0.**

The Supreme Court of the United States is not exempt from corruption.

---

https://www.brookings.edu/interactives/tracking-deregulation-in-the-trump-era/

[100] A Proposed Rule by the Land Management Bureau *NATIONAL ARCHIVES* https://www.federalregister.gov/documents/2018/02/22/2018-03144/waste-prevention-production-subject-to-royalties-and-resource-conservation-rescission-or-revision-of

In *Citizens United v Federal Election Commission* (2008), the court ruled that corporations "have all the free speech rights of human beings, because they are associations of human beings. It ruled that money is speech. The spending of money on political campaigns can't be limited, it said, because it would be a limitation of free speech – a clear violation of the First Amendment. Union spending can be restricted, however, because there might be members who disagree and that would violate their free speech rights. (There are shareholders that might not agree with corporate political spending, but that reasoning could not be applied to businesses. Because unions were bad and corporations were good?) Access and influence can't be corruption. Doing favors for money was renamed: Responsiveness."[101]

Robert Weissman, president of **Public Citizen**, voices his concern twelve years after the passage of *Citizens United*[102]:

"In a politically divided nation, there is virtual unanimity in opposition to the Supreme Court's horrific *Citizens United* decision and the resultant super rich and corporate domination of our elections. Americans believe the system is rigged, and they are right.

"It's hard to encapsulate the degree to which wealth dominates our elections. One measure: Just 100 people – almost all of them white – are responsible for 70% of individual contributions to Super PACs.

"The opposition to *Citizens United* has engendered a grassroots movement for a constitutional amendment to overturn the decision and restore the people's right to impose limits on campaign contributions and spending, including the commonsense right to prohibit corporate contributions. Twenty-two states and 800 cities and towns have passed resolutions calling for an amendment. Momentum continues to grow and the day is not long off when we will win a constitutional amendment and overthrow the shackles of *Citizens United.*"

---

[101] "The Supreme Court is so corrupt…*it makes corruption legal.*" Larry Beinhart, *Al-Jazeera* July 21, 2023
https://www.aljazeera.com/opinions/2023/7/21/the-supreme-court-is-so-corrupt
[102] "Twelve Years Since Citizens United, Big Money Corruption Keeps Getting Worse" statement by *Public Citizen*
https://www.citizen.org/news/twelve-years-since-citizens-united-big-money-corruption-keeps-getting-worse/

Nick Dearden, director of **Global Justice Now**, says[103]:

The vast wealth and power of corporations is at the heart of so many of the world's problems – like inequality and climate change. The drive for short-term profits today seems to trump basic human rights for millions of people on the planet. Yet there are very few ways that citizens can hold these corporations to account for their behavior. ***Rather, through trade and investment deals, it is corporations which are able to demand that governments do their bidding.***

The 2023 issue of the *Forbes* World's Billionaire List tells us[104]:

Bernard Arnault, *head of luxury goods giant LVMH, takes his place as the world's richest person, marking the first time a citizen of France leads the ranking. The United States still boasts the most billionaires, with 735 list members worth a collective $4.5 trillion. China (including Hong Kong and Macau) remains second, with 562 billionaires worth $2 trillion, followed by India, with 169 billionaires worth $675 billion.*

We guess that there are more billionaires who were not known by *Forbes* or not counted because their wealth couldn't be estimated. This would include royals, dictators, and criminals.

The late **Tony Benn**'s comments on the establishment are still relevant: **"I don't think people realize how the establishment became established. They simply stole land and property from the poor, surrounded themselves with weak minded sycophants for protection, gave themselves titles and have been wielding power ever since!"**

The US government is in the business of diverting public resources *to* private interests – the influencers and special interests – mainly corporate entities – the **corpocracy**.

Let's look at a few examples from the US:

---

103 "69 of the Richest 100 Entities on the Planet are Corporations, Not Governments, Figures Show" *Global Justice Now* https://www.commondreams.org/newswire/2018/10/17/69-richest-100-entities-planet-are-corporations-not-governments-figures-show

104 https://www.forbes.com/billionaires/

Healthcare[105]. In 1912 the AMA declared that it was unprofessional for physicians to be under corporate control and in 1934 "condemned contractual arrangements whereby lay persons and entities directly profited from the services rendered by doctors." The theory is that "physicians need to be able to make medical decisions free from the interference of lay persons, particularly lay persons whose allegiance extends more to the bottom line than to the well-being of patients."

What changed? The downfall of the US healthcare system can be traced to President Nixon's choice (as a personal favor for his friend and campaign financier, Edgar Kaiser, then president and chairman of Kaiser-Permanente) to allow medical insurance agencies, hospitals, clinics and even doctors to function as for-profit business entities.

Education. According to *Hijacked by Billionaires: How the Super Rich Buy Elections to Undermine Public Schools,* an investigative report[106] by Network for Public Education Action, some of America's wealthiest individuals collaborate to hijack the democratic process by pouring millions of dollars into state and local races, often in places where they do not live. They don't believe in public schools. The agenda is to advance the privatization of public schools by whatever means necessary: by spending heavily on state referenda, on state school board elections, or on local school board elections. They want their allies to control state and local school boards so that more public schools will be closed and replaced by privately managed charter schools or even vouchers for religious schools.

Climate Change. *The Guardian* reports[107] that ExxonMobil, the world's biggest oil company, knew as early as 1981 of climate change – seven years before it became a public issue. Despite this the firm spent millions over the next 27 years to promote climate denial.

The Intergovernmental Panel on Climate Change (IPCC) has issued a grave warning to the public that there's a closing window to act to prevent a climate catastrophe. ExxonMobil's

---

105 See https://freemarkethealthcareblog.com/2017/07/03/for-profit-entities-and-prices/

106 *THE NETWORK FOR PUBLIC EDUCATION ACTION*
https://npeaction.org/wp-content/uploads/2018/09/Hijacked-by-Billionaires.pdf

107 "Exxon knew of climate change in 1981, email says – but it funded deniers for 27 more years" *The Guardian*
https://www.theguardian.com/environment/2015/jul/08/exxon-climate-change-1981-climate-denier-funding

reaction? Pledging a $1 million contribution to a campaign for a carbon tax, a move that critics are calling "a scam."[108]

Gun Control. According to research by the Center for Responsive Politics[109], nearly all the 46 senators who voted against a measure which would have enforced background checks as a condition of commercial firearms sales received donations from the gun lobby. What chance is there that these public officials will ever vote in the public interest? Zero.

Prisons. It turns out that the immigration crackdown that ICE is pursuing has lifted shares of stock in the Geo Group and CoreCivic, two private, for-profit prison businesses. Why? Because they profit from a private system of jail-as-a-business[110] .

War. It is common knowledge that the US military budget is out of control. The US Army has accumulated $6.5 trillion[111] in expenditures that cannot be accounted for. According to reporter Dave Lindorff: "politicians of both major political parties are demanding accountability for every penny spent on welfare," and they have also been engaged in pervasive efforts "to make teachers accountable for student 'performance.'" Yet, he observed, "the military doesn't have to account for any of its trillions of dollars of spending . . . even though Congress fully a generation ago passed a law requiring such accountability."

By the way, did you know the Pentagon operates more than 170 golf courses[112] worldwide?

Voter Suppression. The Center for Media and Democracy (CMD) reports[113] that after Barack Obama swept into office in November of 2008 with the energized support of youth

---

108 "This Is a Scam": ExxonMobil-Backed Carbon Tax Will Not Save the Planet" *FIXCapitalism.com* http://fixcapitalism.com/this-is-a-scam-exxonmobil-backed-carbon-tax-will-not-save-the-planet/

109 Gun Rights vs Gun Control, *Open Secrets* https://www.opensecrets.org/news/issues/guns/

110 "Prison and Profits" by *Christopher Brauchli*
https://www.commondreams.org/views/2017/04/15/prison-and-profits

111 "Over Six Trillion Dollars in Unaccountable Army Spending"
https://www.projectcensored.org/2-six-trillion-dollars-unaccountable-army-spending/

112 "The Budget Deal Is a Big Win for the Pentagon" *Mother Jones*
https://www.motherjones.com/politics/2013/12/pentagon-budget-deal-charts-cuts/

113 "Democracy, Voter Rights, and Federal Power" *Center for Media and Democracy*
https://www.alecexposed.org/wiki/Democracy,_Voter_Rights,_and_Federal_Power

and African Americans, suddenly "voter fraud" became a deep concern for many in the Republican party -- despite no evidence fraud occurred in any statistically significant way.

And when Republicans emerged from the November 2010 elections with new majorities in statehouses across the country, a total of 37 states saw strict voter ID laws introduced in 2011 and 2012. Many of those proposals contained elements of the American Legislative Exchange Council (ALEC) "model" voter ID act, which imposes new burdens on the right to vote by requiring voters show state-issued ID cards.

Coupled with an active gerrymandering[114] agenda this has significantly prevented proportional and descriptive representation[115], as the winners of elections are increasingly determined by who is drawing the districts rather than the preferences of the voters.

Foreign Influence. *The Huffington Post* reports[116] that Crown Prince Mohammed bin Salman, implicated in the alleged murder of journalist Jamal Khashoggi, could blunt criticism using the most sprawling foreign influence campaign in the U.S. today: "By directing billions of dollars of Saudi money into the U.S. for decades, Riyadh's ruling family has won the support of small but powerful circles of influential Americans and courted wider public acceptance through corporate ties and philanthropy." President Trump went on record blaming "rogue killers"[117] for the journalist's disappearance.

Corporate Influence. The late David Koch and Charles Koch – known as the Koch brothers[118] - were the right-wing billionaire co-owners of Koch Industries. As two of the richest people in the world, they were key funders of the right-wing infrastructure, including the **American Legislative Exchange Council (ALEC)** and the State Policy Network[119]

---

114 https://en.wikipedia.org/wiki/Gerrymandering
115https://en.wikipedia.org/wiki/Representation_(politics)#Descriptive_representation
116 "Saudi Arabia Wants Trump and Congress To Forget Jamal Khashoggi. Here's Its Likely Playbook" *The Huffington Post* https://www.huffpost.com/entry/jamal-khashoggi-trump-congress-saudi-arabia-lobbying-arms-deals_n_5bc20a93e4b040bb4e82b65a
117 Trump Says 'Rogue Killers' May Be Behind Jamal Khashoggi's Disappearance, *HUFFPOST* https://www.huffpost.com/entry/trump-says-rogue-killers-are-behind-jamal-khashoggis-disappearance_n_5bc4909fe4b040bb4e845d66
118 Koch Brothers, *Center for Media and Democracy* https://www.sourcewatch.org/index.php?title=Koch_Brothers
119 State Policy Network, *Center for Media and Democracy* https://www.sourcewatch.org/index.php/State_Policy_Network

(SPN).

ALEC is funded by corporations and corporate foundations and its agenda extends into almost all areas of law. Its bills:

- undermine environmental regulations and deny climate change;
- support school privatization;
- undercut health care reform;
- defund unions and limit their political influence;
- restrain legislatures' abilities to raise revenue through taxes;
- mandate strict election laws that disenfranchise voters;
- increase incarceration to benefit the private prison industry, among many other issues.

The Center for Media and Democracy (CMD) explains how ALEC works[120]: The Koch brothers and their network of billionaires are operating with a reach and resources that exceed those of political parties and they are using that power to erode the integrity of our elections and sap taxpayer dollars away from investments in public infrastructure, education, and healthcare to benefit narrow special interests and global corporations.

Since the CMD first exposed ALEC in 2011, more than 100 corporations have dropped ALEC, including Verizon, Ford, Coca-Cola, Wal-Mart, General Electric, and Google.

In *Manufacturing Consent* [121] Noam Chomsky told us: "At this stage of History, either one of two things is possible: either the general population will take control of its own destiny and will concern itself with community interests, guided by values of solidarity and sympathy and concern for others, or alternatively, there will be no destiny for anyone to control."

---

120 *Center for Media and Democracy PRWatch* https://www.prwatch.org/cmd/index.html

121 *Manufacturing Consent* by Noam Chomsky https://www.amazon.com/Manufacturing-Consent-Noam-Chomsky-Media/dp/B0031DDI4I/

The policies of Donald Trump took our existential crisis of democracy to another level, and he threatens to return to office with a vengeance.

Philip Kotler has noted in the *Huffington Post*[122] that what was most disturbing was Trump's attack on the *idea of America*. **America is an idea, not simply a country.** Trump is succeeding in turning *e Pluribus Unum* into "every man for himself"; he is *Closing the American Mind* by using a strategy of polarization[123] – by politicizing every aspect of government and civic life. This is not an accident. What we see with Trump is a systematic targeting of all the institutions and policies that actually made America great. One can argue that the Trump administration (aided and abetted by the GOP) is like an institutional terrorist planting bombs to **blow up the pillars of our Democracy.**

In his book, *America: The Farewell Tour*[124], **Chris Hedges** describes the danger at hand:

The most ominous danger we face does not come from the eradication of free speech through the obliteration of net neutrality or through Google algorithms that steer people away from dissident, left-wing, progressive, or anti-war sites. It does not come from the 201 7 tax bill that abandons all pretense of fiscal responsibility to enrich corporations and oligarchs and prepares the way to dismantle programs such as Social Security. It does not come from the opening of public land to the mining and fossil fuel industry, the acceleration of ecocide by demolishing environmental regulations, or the destruction of public education. It does not come from the squandering of federal dollars on a bloated military as the country collapses or the use of the systems of domestic security to criminalize dissent. ***The most ominous danger we face comes from the marginalization and destruction of institutions, including the courts, academia, legislative bodies, cultural organizations, and the press, that once ensured that civil discourse was rooted in reality and fact, helping us distinguish lies from truth, and facilitate justice.***

---

[122] "The 'Terrorist' in the White House" by Philip Kotler *The Huffington Post* https://www.huffpost.com/entry/the-terrorist-in-the-white house_b_58aa969fe4b0b0e1e0e20d50

[123] "Trump wants to boost defense spending by 10% and cut social spending, *Los Angeles Times* https://www.latimes.com/politics/washington/la-na-essential-washington-updates-201702-htmlstory.html#public-deeply-polarized-and-already-dug-in-on-trump

[124] America: The Farewell Tour by *Chris Hedges* https://www.amazon.com/America-Farewell-Tour-Chris-Hedges-ebook/dp/B075RTDPJ7/

WHAT CAN BE DONE?

One can hope that billionaires could become a **force for good** – especially if their excess wealth was used for the **Common Good**.

There are three way this can happen:

1. The billionaires suddenly realize that the Common Good of the planet is an important goal for them, so they join forces to save humanity and Nature,
2. Our governments make billionaires pay their "fair share" of taxes, or
3. Society decides that billionaires shouldn't exist, and our governments simply tax them out of existence.

Will the billionaires agree to higher taxes? In the recent US elections, we recall that Bernie Sanders suggested billionaires should be taxed out of existence, while Joe Biden warned us against demonizing the wealthy.

There's a common myth that there will always be billionaires. And the media worships billionaires like Bill Gates and Warren Buffett who illustrate that some billionaires can work for causes that are beyond their own selfish interests.

So, where do billionaires come from?

We should start by asking where do billionaires come from? Do they just spring out of the fertile digital soil of Silicon Valley? Can anyone – with enough hard work – become a billionaire?

So how do you become a billionaire? **Robert Reich**, former U.S. Secretary of Labor, tells us there are four sources of wealth[125]:

---

125 "Should We Abolish Billionaires?" by Robert Reich, July1, 2019 https://robertreich.org/post/185986111450

- **Inherited Wealth:** around *60 percent of wealth* in the US is inherited.[126] The best chance you have of becoming a billionaire is to marry or be born into intergenerational riches.
- **Monopolies:** Jeff Bezos' Amazon accounts for nearly 50 percent of all e-commerce retail sales in America. Our patent and trademark systems, which have been extended in duration, create billionaire like George Lucas and Oprah Winfrey.
- **Insider Information:** Hedge fund billionaire Steven A. Cohen made "hundreds of millions of dollars of *illegal profits*" – through his expertise in insider trading.[127] This is not an isolated incident.
- **Politics:** You can invest in politicians – or even bet on them, like racehorses – through your timely campaign contributions. Americans for Tax Fairness estimates that Koch Industries could save between $1 billion and $1.4 billion[128] combined in income taxes each year from the Trump tax law—and that doesn't include how much the Koch Industries save in taxes on offshore profits or how much their heirs will benefit from weakening the estate tax.

Good luck with these four strategies.

Without them, **the average US worker would have to work for *25 thousand years* to become a billionaire.**

How has the number of billionaires grown over the past few decades? In 1996 there were 423 billionaires spotted in the wild.[129] In 2019, that number rose to 2,153. Billionaires constitute just 0.00003 percent of the world population, but they currently own the equivalent of 12 percent of the GWP (gross world product) and a much larger percentage of the total wealth of the world.

---

[126] "On the Share of Inheritance in Aggregate Wealth: Europe and the USA, 1900–2010" by Facundo Alvaredo, Bertrand Garbinti, and Thomas Piketty, 13 February 2017 http://www.piketty.pse.ens.fr/files/AlvaredoGarbintiPiketty2017.pdf

[127] https://www.justice.gov/sites/default/files/usao-sdny/legacy/2015/03/25/SAC%20Capital%20Complaint%20-%2013%20Civ%20%205182_1.pdf

[128] "Analysis: Koch Brothers Could Get Up To $1.4 Billion Tax Cut From Law They Helped Pass" *Americans for Tax Fairness*, January2 4, 2018 https://americansfortaxfairness.org/koch-brothers-1-billion-tax-cut/

[129] "World Billionaires' Number and Wealth" by areppim AG, https://stats.areppim.com/stats/stats_rich_19_trend_usdxnbr.htm

Interestingly, even as COVID destroyed the economy, billionaires got richer– to the tune of $10.2 trillion.[130]

THE BILLIONAIRE'S DEFENSE (THERE ISN'T ANY!)

Arguments used to defend billionaires are often based on the story that *without billionaires, society would not progress* – **innovation** and **philanthropy** would diminish – making life even worse.

Facebook CEO Mark Zuckerberg, worth $70bn, explained this in an appearance on Fox News.[131] Billionaires should not exist in a "cosmic sense," but in reality, most of them are simply "people who do really good things and kind of help a lot of other people. And you get well compensated for that." He warned about the dangers of ceding too much control over their wealth to the government, allegedly bound to stifle innovation and competition and "deprive the market" of his fellow billionaires' funding for philanthropy and scientific research.

"Some people think that, okay, well the issue or the way to deal with this sort of accumulation of wealth is, 'Let's just have the government take it all," Zuckerberg said. "And now the government can basically decide, you know, all of the medical research that gets done."

So who should decide what research gets done? The drug companies? The billionaires themselves? Did you know that oil tycoon and business magnate John D. Rockefeller helped to remove "holistic" and "alternative" plant medicines from the teachings of medical professionals in the United States, and replaced them with chemical -based pharmaceuticals? In his book *Rockefeller Medicine Men: Medicine and Capitalism in America*, author **E. Richard Brown** shows how political processes were consciously manipulated by a medical elite acting

---

130 "Billionaires' wealth rises to $10.2 trillion amid Covid crisis" by Rupert Neate, The Guardian Oct 6, 2020 https://www.theguardian.com/business/2020/oct/07/covid-19-crisis-boosts-the-fortunes-of-worlds-billionaires

131 "Mark Zuckerberg's plea for the billionaire class is deeply anti-democratic" by Kate Aronoff, *The Guardian*, Oct 21, 2019 https://www.theguardian.com/commentisfree/2019/oct/21/mark-zuckerberg-plea-biillionaire-class-anti-democratic

in concert with immense corporate wealth to create a system of medicine that better served economic and hegemonic intentions than social or humanitarian needs.

There is a serious argument to be made that allowing billionaires to decide societal priorities is profoundly undemocratic.

Should mega-rich donors like Bill Gates drive philanthropy, usurping the role of democratic governments to decide what social ills to tackle and how?

Even in terms of innovation, **Zuckerberg is wrong.** The Information Technology and Innovation Foundation (ITIF) reports[132] that while in the 1970s almost all innovation winners came from corporations acting on their own, more recently over two-thirds of the winners have come from partnerships involving business and government, including federal labs and federally-funded university research. Moreover, in 2006, 77 of the 88 U.S. entities that produced award-winning innovations were beneficiaries of federal funding.

Facebook, for all Zuckerberg's talk about innovation, makes the bulk of its profits from selling access to customer data via advertising. It's certainly *not* a fountain of societal innovation.

Unfortunately, the record of **billionaire activism** is not always a stellar example upholding human values or even democracy, for that matter. The John Birch society, for example, was principally backed by Fred Koch, the father of the infamous Koch brothers. The society famously attacked **Martin Luther King** [133] and the Civil Rights movement, as well as **JFK**[134] – with a campaign[135] to spread hate just two weeks before his assassination in Dallas.

---

[132] "Where Do Innovations Come From? Transformations in the U.S. National Innovation System, 1970-2006" by Fred Block and Matthew Keller, July 9, 2008 https://itif.org/publications/2008/07/09/where-do-innovations-come-transformations-us-national-innovation-system-1970/

[133] "How Charles Koch Backed the John Birch Society at the Height of Its Attacks on Martin Luther King" Lisa Graves *PR Watch* January 18, 2016 https://www.prwatch.org/news/2016/01/13017/how-charles-koch-backed-john-birch-society-height-its-attacks-martin-luther-king

[134] Right Wing 'Wanted' Poster for JFK: Sound Familiar? by Paul Abrams, *Huffington Post* Jan 14, 2014 https://www.huffpost.com/entry/right-wing-wanted-poster_b_4598090

[135] "The 'Wanted For Treason' Flyer Distributed in Dallas Before JFK's Visit" by Rebecca Onion, *Slate*, November 15, 2013 https://slate.com/human-interest/2013/11/jfk-assassination-flyer-distributed-in-dallas-by-edwin-walker-s-group-before-his-visit.html

WANTED

FOR

TREASON

THIS MAN is wanted for treasonous activities against the United States:

1. Betraying the Constitution (which he swore to uphold):
   He is turning the sovereignty of the U.S. over to the communist controlled United Nations.
   He is betraying our friends (Cuba, Katanga, Portugal) and befriending our enemies (Russia, Yugoslavia, Poland).
2. He has been WRONG on innumerable issues affecting the security of the U.S. (United Nations-Berlin wall-Missle removal-Cuba-Wheat deals-Test Ban Treaty, etc.)
3. He has been lax in enforcing Communist Registration laws.
4. He has given support and encouragement to the Communist inspired racial riots.
5. He has illegally invaded a sovereign State with federal troops.
6. He has consistantly appointed Anti-Christians to Federal office: Upholds the Supreme Court in its Anti-Christian rulings. Aliens and known Communists abound in Federal offices.
7. He has been caught in fantastic LIES to the American people (including personal ones like his previous marraige and divorce).

This **anti-democratic** and **regressive** billionaire activism[136] continues to this day.

The John Birch society's slogan[137] – **"this is a republic, not a democracy"** is now being amplified by the GOP and the Trumpists.

[136] "The John Birchers' Tea Party" by Adam Gopnik, *New Yorker*, October 11, 2013 https://www.newyorker.com/news/daily-comment/the-john-birchers-tea-party

[137] The Real Reason Why Republicans Keep Saying "We're a Republic, Not a Democracy" by Joshua Keating October 13, 2020 https://slate.com/news-and-politics/2020/10/republic-democracy-mike-lee-astra-taylor.html

Such billionaires as these are *not* interested in the Common Good. In fact, it is their actions[138] that have driven our society to a level of public insecurity and mistrust, not seen since the 60s, or the Civil War, as some have argued[139].

WILL BILLIONAIRES SOLVE THE WORLD'S BIGGEST PROBLEMS?

Given that our wicked problems are an existential threat to our future as a civilization, why is it that the smartest minds in the world are still busy working on algorithms to maximize advertising efficiency or building financial instruments for hedge-fund profits?

What would happen if the world drafted **Bill Gates**, **Elon Musk**, **Tim Cook**, **Jamie Dimon**, and **Jeff Bezos** – gave them a mission to find solutions to **"save the planet in the interest of the Common Good"** and then presented their "solutions" to the governments of the world – put them to a global **vote**?

The Big 5 CEOs could afford to be paid *nothing* for this challenge.

Well, isn't that what they should be working on? **Paul Polman**, the former CEO of Unilever, could also be drafted as the project manager of this *Manhattan Project to save humanity*.

Let's lock them in a "zoom-room" for the next six months and see what they come up with – we're pretty sure their businesses will continue doing well without batting an eyelid.

NARROWING THE GAP BETWEEN THE RICH AND THE POOR

We also must ask: **what would happen if our governments started working for the Common Good?**

---

[138] Charles Koch Ramps Up Investment In Alec As The Lobbying Group Loses Corporate Funders Over Far-Right Ties, Lee Fang, Nick Surgey, *The Intercept*, November 29 2018, https://theintercept.com/2018/11/29/alec-corporate-funders-charles-koch/

[139] "Political polarization at its worst since the Civil War" by Laura Paisley *USC Today* November 08, 2016 https://today.usc.edu/political-polarization-at-its-worst-since-the-civil-war-2/

What would it mean to the world if we (1) got rid of *monopolies*, (2) stopped the use of *insider information*, (3) prevented billionaires from *buying off politicians*, and (4) made it harder for the billionaires and their corporations to *avoid paying taxes*?

You can't – as the late **Paul Polak** used to say – "donate your way out of poverty." Billionaires know that just giving money to the poor is not a lasting solution. The statement is often made "don't give fish to the hungry, just teach them how to fish." The task is how to create a better education and better skills in people so that they can create value for others and get paid for the value they create.

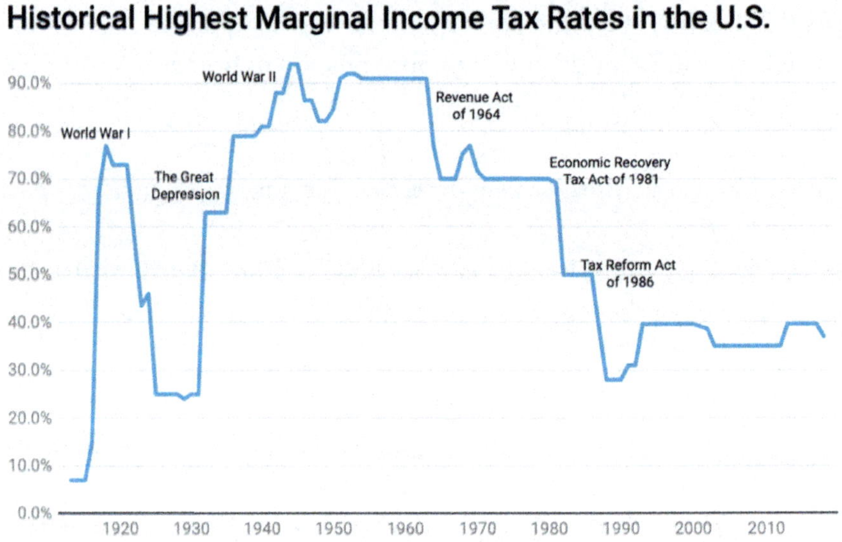

A quick review of the history of taxation[140] in the US shows us what's been going on: for too long, too many wealthy persons have paid taxes on their wealth at a lower rate than their secretaries! Today's top U.S. marginal income tax rate is 37%. This is the rate paid on the last bracket of income, not on the whole income. The rich person pays substantially less that 37%

[140] "A Brief History of Taxes in the U.S." by Amy Fontinelle *Investopedia* August 27, 2023 https://www.investopedia.com/articles/tax/10/history-taxes.asp

on his or her total income. The 37% bracket only affects persons earning an annual income of $518,400 or more.

Look at how high the top bracket income tax has been historically. The rate was almost 80% in World War 1, over 90% in World War II, and pushed down over time by Republicans to a low of 37%.

This 37% top tax rate seems ridiculously lower compared to Scandinavian countries that pay a top income tax rate of 70%. What do Scandinavians get back for this very high marginal tax rate. They get back **"freedom from insecurity."** Scandinavians don't have to pay for medicines, surgeries, college education, maternity leave, longer vacations, and so on. The evidence is clear that many Americans might prefer to live in a country with higher taxes on the rich, than in today's America where at least 15-20% of U.S. citizens can't meet their basic needs without help. Yes, most of us have plenty to eat but the important things we need like health care and a college education are priced as luxury goods.

Isn't it interesting that US citizens have to pay US taxes no matter where in the world they earn their money, but our US corporations don't have to do the same. And we thought *corporations were people too*!

Americans for Tax Fairness[141] points out some key facts:

- Tax avoidance through offshore tax loopholes is a significant reason why corporations, which paid one-third of federal revenues 60 years ago, now pay one-tenth of federal revenues.
- U.S. corporations dodge $90 billion a year in income taxes by shifting profits to subsidiaries — often no more than a post office box — in tax havens.
- U.S. corporations hold $2.1 trillion in profits offshore — much in tax havens — that have not been taxed in the U.S.

[141] Offshore Tax Loopholes, Americans for Tax Fairness https://americansfortaxfairness.org/files/ATF-Offshore-Corporate-Tax-Loopholes-Fact-Sheet.pdf

- 26 profitable Fortune 500 firms paid no federal income taxes from 2008-2012. 111 large, profitable corporations paid zero federal income taxes in at least one of those five years.

The simplest solution is to end tax "deferral." Corporations would pay taxes on offshore income the year it is earned, rather than indefinitely avoid paying U.S. income taxes. This would also remove incentives to shift U.S. profits to tax havens, and it would raise $600 billion over 10 years.

Why isn't this happening?

Passing a higher tax on the rich only slows down the growth of their wealth. Senators Elizabeth Warren and Bernie Sanders have called for a wealth tax. Elizabeth Warren proposed that households should pay an annual 2% tax on their net worth above $50 million, and a 3% tax on every dollar of net worth above $1 billion. She recently added possibly raising the billionaire wealth tax rate to 6 percent instead of 3 percent to help pay for "Medicare for All." Note that the working poor and the middle class do not pay higher taxes. The wealth tax is only paid by very rich.

Another solution is to raise the estate tax. Wealthy persons need a plan describing how their wealth should be divided upon their death. They cannot be allowed to avoid paying estate taxes on their wealth. Married couples won't pay any inheritance tax on the first $22.36 million in exemptions. The tax on the remaining wealth after exemption is 40 percent. *By the way,* ***King Charles*** *paid no taxes when he inherited a vast, undisclosed fortune from* ***Queen Elizabeth****. This is exactly what the super-ultra-hyper rich around the world hope for.*

The estate tax could yield more if two changes occurred:

1. lower the tax-exempt amount to a much lower number, and
2. increase the tax rate on the remaining amount from 40% to a much higher number – say 70%.

The government should increase the estate tax rate in a further effort to reduce the growing concentration of wealth in the U.S. Yet Republicans argue that higher estate taxes will lead to more avoidance and also lead talented people to work less hard or threaten to leave the country. I would counter-argue that there are a great many civic-minded talented people waiting to move up the wealth ladder and take their place. The tough issue is what the government will do with the higher estate taxes? Will it be used by government to increase wages and jobs? Or will it go into more defense spending and more bureaucracies? Why don't we ask citizens to decide?

BILLIONAIRES AND THE FUTURE OF THE PLANET

Let's return to how to encourage the super-rich to give back more of their wealth to society. Bill and Melinda Gates and Warren Buffett carried out an excellent approach to this problem, with their **giving pledge**[142]. They recruited billionaires to make a commitment to distribute half of their wealth to philanthropic causes within the next 10 years. Today 211 billionaires have made this pledge. Furthermore, each billionaire describes the cause(s) that might get his or her "give-back." There is an argument to be made that **if the rich have to "give back" to society, they took too much from society to begin with.**

The recruiting effort is continuing. Imagine how many low-income persons would benefit if 2,000 billionaires, not just 211 would implement a giving pledge. Or would they?

Billionaires face the problem of identifying which giving causes would do the "most good." This problem faces all the billionaires, including the largest ones: Jeff Bezos ($200B), Bill Gates ($98B), Bernard Arnault and family ($76B), Warren Buffett ($67.5B), Larry Ellison ($59B), Amancio Ortega ($55.1B), Mark Zuckerberg ($54.7B), Jim Wolcott ($54.6B), Alice Wolcott ($54.4B), and S. Robson Walton ($54B).

---

[142] https://givingpledge.org

Billionaires prefer giving away their money to their *favorite causes* rather than giving their money as taxes to the U.S. Treasury. They want to control who gets the money. They might not want to see the money go to make or buy more weapons of war.

This problem has been dubbed "**gilded giving**" by the **Institute for Policy Studies**[143]. Here is their description of the problem:

- *The charitable sector is currently experiencing a transition from broad-based support across a wide range of donors to top-heavy philanthropy increasingly dominated by a small number of very wealthy individuals and foundations. This has significant implications for the practice of fundraising, the role of the independent nonprofit sector, and the health of our larger democratic civil society.*

- *Risks to charitable independent sector organizations include increased volatility and unpredictability in funding, making it more difficult to budget and forecast income into the future; an increased need to shift toward major donor cultivation; and an increased bias toward funding heavily major-donor-directed boutique organizations and projects. The increasing power of a small number of donors also greatly increases the potential for mission distortion.*
- *Risks to the public include an increasingly unaccountable and undemocratic philanthropic sector; the rise of tax avoidance philanthropy; the warehousing of wealth in the face of urgent needs; self-dealing philanthropy; and the increasing use of philanthropy as an extension of power and privilege protection.*

The privatization[144] of charity and the job of government does not bode well for democracy *or* the common good.

ASK: What is the connection between corporate power, predation, inflation, wage suppression, and political corruption?

---

[143] *Gilded Giving 2018: Top-Heavy Philanthropy and Its Risks to the Independent* by *Sector* Chuck Collins, Helen Flannery, and Josh Hoxie, *Institute for Policy Studies* November 2018 https://inequality.org/wp-content/uploads/2018/11/Gilded-Giving-2018-November-2018-FINAL.pdf
[144] "We can't privatize our way out of poverty" by Renée Loth *Boston Globe*,December 7, 2018

Thanks to the concentration of wealth at the top of the pyramid, a new class of mega-rich donors is **"usurping the role of democratic governments to decide what social ills to tackle and how."**

Here's an example from history. What would have happened if Andrew Carnegie had actually supported unions, instead of encouraging violent **union-busting** tactics[145] at Homestead Mill in 1892? Why did he employ a private army of Pinkertons to put down the unions? Why did he need 8500 state government troops to bring his employees to heel? After defeating the union, Carnegie slashed wages, imposed 12-hour workdays, and eliminated 500 jobs.

Later, Carnegie, decided to start giving back money to good causes, as a way to save his reputation. Instead of giving money to colleges, he decided to build public libraries, first in America and later around the world.

Was this philanthropy?

THE DEEP STATE?

The term "deep state" is the belief that there exists a clandestine network of influential individuals, often within government agencies, military, intelligence services, or other bureaucratic institutions, who are working behind the scenes to manipulate government policy, undermine elected officials, and shape national and international affairs according to their own agenda, often at odds with the stated objectives of democratic governance.

In the US, the term "deep state" describes the "permanent government" of entrenched career bureaucrats or civil servants acting in accordance with the mandates of their agencies and congressional statutes when seen as in conflict with the administration. It should also include the army of lobbyists and influence-peddlers that overrun Washington.

---

[145] The Strike at Homestead Mill *NPR* https://www.pbs.org/wgbh/americanexperience/features/carnegie-strike-homestead-mill/

Launched in July 2023, **F Minus** (https://fminus.org) has built a **database** of state-level lobbyists for upstream and midstream oil, gas, and coal interests to demonstrate the extent to which these lobbyists are also representing people, schools, communities, and businesses being harmed by the climate crisis.

This is a problem, not just for transparency, but for Democracy.

Multi-client lobbyists are often described as "gatekeepers" to state officials because of their personal relationships and broad range of expertise. State lobbying laws prohibit these multi-client lobbyists from lobbying on both sides of a particular piece of legislation or other governmental action, but nothing prohibits a fossil fuel lobbyist from also working for a company or an organization that is being negatively impacted by the climate crisis.

Add to this mix the secrecy and opaque departments of Government from the **CIA** to the **Pentagon**, and we see that this **ecosystem of secrecy** operates beyond the reach of democratic oversight and accountability, wielding significant power and influence over key decision-making processes. Some allege that the deep state works to maintain the status quo, protect entrenched interests, and pursue policies that may not necessarily align with the public interest.

Because our knowledge of these actions is not covered by the traditional media (which is another wicked problem), it often leads to a proliferation of conspiracy theories. We learn about the "deep state" because of **whistleblowers** like **Edward Snowden**, or journalists like **Julian Assange**.

Edward Snowden is a former intelligence contractor who gained international attention in 2013 when he leaked classified documents from the National Security Agency (NSA) to journalists. Born on June 21, 1983, in Elizabeth City, North Carolina, Snowden worked for various government agencies, including the CIA and NSA, where he had access to sensitive information about surveillance programs.

In June 2013, Snowden disclosed thousands of classified documents to journalists Glenn Greenwald, Laura Poitras, and Barton Gellman, revealing the extent of global surveillance programs conducted by the NSA and its international partners. The leaked documents exposed widespread mass surveillance of internet communications, phone records, and other electronic data, raising concerns about privacy, civil liberties, and government overreach.

After the leaks, Snowden fled the United States to avoid prosecution and sought asylum in several countries. He first traveled to Hong Kong, where he met with journalists and released the classified documents. From there, he went to Russia, where he was granted temporary asylum and later, in 2020, received permanent residency.

Snowden's actions ignited a global debate about government surveillance, whistleblowing, and the balance between national security and individual privacy. Supporters view him as a whistleblower who exposed unlawful and unconstitutional surveillance practices, while critics argue that he endangered national security and violated his oath of secrecy.

Snowden's revelations led to significant reforms and public scrutiny of surveillance programs in the United States and other countries. His actions also sparked discussions about digital privacy, government transparency, and the role of whistleblowers in holding institutions accountable for their actions.

Julian Assange is an Australian journalist, publisher, and activist, best known as the founder of WikiLeaks, a non-profit organization that publishes classified and confidential information from anonymous sources. Born on July 3, 1971, in Townsville, Australia, Assange gained international prominence for his role in exposing government secrets and corporate corruption through WikiLeaks.

Assange began his career as a computer programmer and hacker in the 1990s before turning to journalism. In 2006, he founded WikiLeaks with the goal of providing a platform for whistleblowers to anonymously leak sensitive documents exposing government and corporate wrongdoing. WikiLeaks gained widespread attention in 2010 when it published a series of high-profile leaks, including the Iraq War Logs, the Afghan War Diary, and diplomatic cables from the US State Department, provided by **Chelsea Manning**, a former US Army intelligence analyst.

Assange's work with **WikiLeaks** has been both celebrated and criticized. Leaks published by the non-profit organization covered the US involvement in wars in Afghanistan, Iraq and Yemen and the work of secret services, but WikiLeaks also released information on corruption and crimes in countries such as Turkey, Russia, China and Peru.

Supporters view him as a champion of transparency and free speech, who exposes government corruption and human rights abuses. Critics, however, accuse him of endangering national security, undermining diplomatic efforts, and putting lives at risk by publishing classified information.

Assange faced legal challenges and extradition proceedings in several countries. In 2010, he was accused of sexual assault in Sweden, leading to legal battles and extradition proceedings. Assange denied the allegations, arguing that they were politically motivated. In 2012, he sought asylum at the Embassy of Ecuador in London to avoid extradition to Sweden, where he feared he would be extradited to the United States and prosecuted for his role in publishing classified information.

Assange remained in the Ecuadorian embassy for seven years until his asylum was revoked in 2019, leading to his arrest by British authorities. He was subsequently charged with violating the US Espionage Act for his role in publishing classified documents. Assange has fought against extradition to the United States, arguing that he risks facing an unfair trial and potential mistreatment if extradited.

Assange's legal battles sparked debates about press freedom, whistleblowing, and government accountability. His case has drawn international attention and support from human rights organizations, journalists, and activists who see it as a test of democratic principles and the right to free speech. Finally, in 2024, **President Biden pardoned Assange**, and he was able to return home to Australia.

We also must not forget the art of **Mark Lombardi** – *his work is a "visual Wikileaks" – "long before Julian Assange and Ed Snowden came along."*[146] Lombardi was found – hanged in his studio in March 2000 – the night before his art opening – and his death was ruled a "suicide."

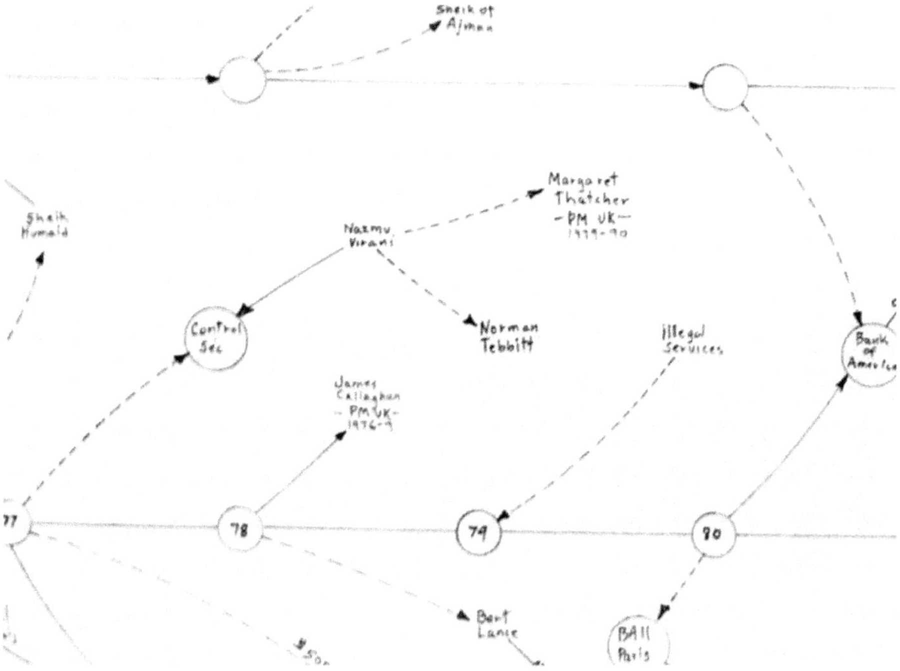

[146] "The Legacy of Mark Lombardi: An Interview with Patricia Goldstone" *Huffington Post* May 17, 2017
https://www.huffpost.com/entry/the-legacy-of-mark-lombardi-an-interview-with-patricia_b_591b1f96e4b0f31b03fb9f33
see also: "Learning from Lombardi" by Ben Fry April 15, *Medium* 2016
https://medium.com/@ben_fry/learning-from-lombardi-a28032a7eb5
and: Mark Lombardi's Narrative Structures and Other Mappings of Power Relations by Fosco Lucarelli August 22, 2012
https://socks-studio.com/2012/08/22/mark-lombardi/

DISCLOSURE: *The entire Wicked7 Project was inspired by seeing Mark Lombardi's work at the Station Museum of Contemporary Art in Houston, Texas. Special thanks to the late* ***Jim Harithas.***[147]

Mark Lombardi (1951–2000) was an American artist known for his unique and intricate drawings that visualized complex networks of political and financial connections. Lombardi's work blurred the lines between art, investigative journalism, and social commentary, offering viewers a visually compelling way to explore the hidden relationships and power structures that shape global politics and finance.

Lombardi's drawings, often referred to as "narrative structures" or "conspiracy diagrams," were meticulously hand-drawn on large sheets of paper, resembling flowcharts or maps. Each drawing depicted a web of interconnected nodes, lines, and annotations, representing various individuals, organizations, events, and transactions.

Lombardi's subjects ranged from political scandals and financial fraud to arms deals and corporate corruption. He meticulously researched his subjects, drawing from sources such as newspaper articles, court documents, and investigative reports to create his intricate diagrams. By visually mapping out the intricate connections between seemingly disparate actors and events, Lombardi's work revealed the underlying patterns and dynamics of power and influence that often go unnoticed in mainstream discourse.

One of Lombardi's most well-known series is "Interlocks," which focused on the relationships between individuals and entities involved in global finance, politics, and intelligence. Another series, "Narrative Structures," delved into specific scandals and controversies, such as the Iran-Contra affair and the savings and loan crisis. Lombardi's work garnered critical acclaim for its innovative approach to art and its ability to provoke thought and conversation about complex socio-political issues. His drawings were exhibited in galleries and museums around the world, attracting attention from both the art world and the broader public. Mark Lombardi's activist art was prophetic – and, if we believe in Democracy – it is the ultimate act of resistance to power and corruption.

---

[147] https://en.wikipedia.org/wiki/James_Harithas

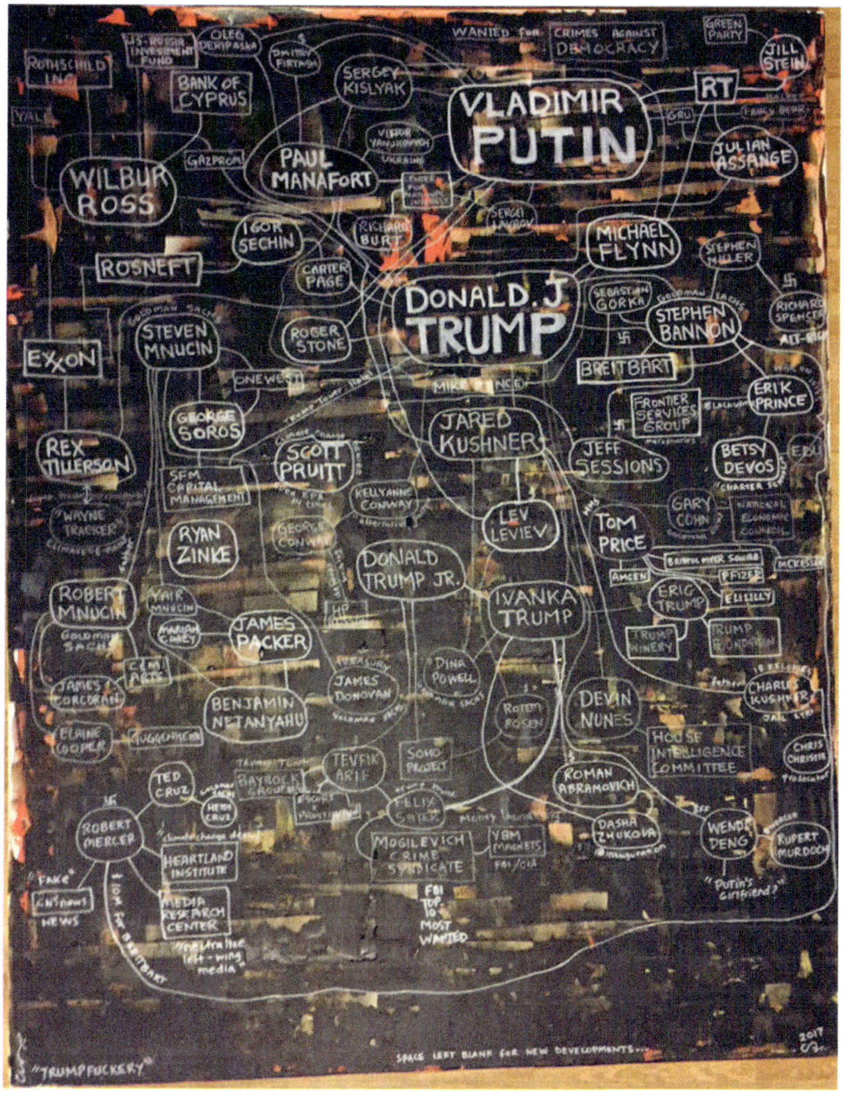

Trumpfuckery, acrylic on canvas – from *The Trump Show!*

THE PANAMA PAPERS AND BEYOND

The Panama Papers were followed by the Paradise Papers, and Pandora Papers - all large-scale leaks of financial documents that have exposed the secretive world of offshore finance, tax evasion, and illicit financial activities. Each leak has revealed extensive networks of wealth and power that span the globe, implicating politicians, celebrities, business leaders, and other prominent figures in complex schemes to avoid taxes, hide assets, and evade scrutiny.

Panama Papers (2016): The Panama Papers[148] refers to a massive leak of documents from the Panamanian law firm Mossack Fonseca, one of the world's largest providers of offshore legal services. The leak, which was first revealed by the **International Consortium of Investigative Journalists** (ICIJ) in April 2016, consisted of over 11.5 million documents dating back several decades. These documents exposed the use of offshore shell companies and tax havens by wealthy individuals and entities around the world to conceal assets, evade taxes, and engage in money laundering and other illicit activities. The Panama Papers implicated numerous high-profile figures, including politicians, business leaders, and celebrities, and sparked investigations and reforms in countries around the world.

Here are some of the key findings:

- Files reveal the offshore holdings of 140 politicians and public officials from around the world
- Current and former world leaders in the data include the prime minister of Iceland, the president of Ukraine, and the king of Saudi Arabia
- More than 214,000 offshore entities appear in the leak, connected to people in more than 200 countries and territories
- Major banks have driven the creation of hard-to-trace companies in offshore havens

---

[148] https://www.icij.org/investigations/panama-papers/

Paradise Papers (2017): The Paradise Papers[149] is another major leak of financial documents, this time from the offshore law firm Appleby and the corporate services provider Estera. The leak, which was also investigated by the **ICIJ** and first reported in November 2017, comprised 13.4 million documents spanning several decades. These documents revealed the offshore financial activities of some of the world's wealthiest individuals and corporations, including investments in tax havens, offshore trusts, and shell companies. The Paradise Papers exposed the extent to which global elites use offshore structures to minimize taxes, shield assets from scrutiny, and exploit regulatory loopholes. The leak implicated numerous public figures, including politicians, royalty, and corporate executives, and led to calls for greater transparency and regulation of offshore finance.

Key findings:

- Reveals offshore interests and activities of more than 120 politicians and world leaders, including Queen Elizabeth II, and 13 advisers, major donors and members of U.S. President Donald J. Trump's administration
- Exposes the tax engineering of more than 100 multinational corporations, including Apple, Nike and Botox-maker Allergan
- Reveals tax haven shopping sprees by multinational companies in Africa and Asia that use shell companies in Mauritius and Singapore to reduce taxes
- Shines a light on secretive deals and hidden companies connected to Glencore, the world's largest commodity trader, and provides detailed accounts of the company's negotiations in the Democratic Republic of the Congo for valuable mineral resources
- Provides details of how owners of jets and yachts, including royalty and sports stars, used Isle of Man tax-avoidance structures

[149] https://www.icij.org/investigations/paradise-papers/

Pandora Papers (2021): The Pandora Papers[150] is the most recent leak of financial documents, released by the ICIJ in October 2021. The leak comprised 11.9 million documents from 14 offshore service providers and exposed the financial affairs of politicians, billionaires, and other influential figures from around the world. The Pandora Papers revealed the use of offshore trusts, shell companies, and other complex structures to conceal assets, avoid taxes, and engage in questionable financial practices.

The leak implicated numerous public officials, including heads of state, government ministers, and members of royal families, raising concerns about conflicts of interest, corruption, and the abuse of power. Like previous leaks, the Pandora Papers underscored the need for greater transparency and accountability in the global financial system.

The secret documents expose offshore dealings of the King of Jordan, the presidents of Ukraine, Kenya and Ecuador, the prime minister of the Czech Republic and former British Prime Minister Tony Blair. The files also detail financial activities of Russian President Vladimir Putin's "unofficial minister of propaganda" and more than 130 billionaires from Russia, the United States, Turkey and other nations. *The leaked records reveal that many of the power players who could help bring an end to the offshore system instead benefit from it – stashing assets in covert companies and trusts while their governments do little to slow a global stream of illicit money that enriches criminals and impoverishes nations.*

Key findings:

- An investigation by more than 600 journalists from 150 news outlets has unearthed offshore dealings of 35 current and former world leaders and more than 300 other current and former public officials and politicians around the world.
- The offshore system continues to thrive despite decades of legislation, investigations and international agreements aimed at combating money laundering and tax dodging.

---

[150] Offshore havens and hidden riches of world leaders and billionaires exposed in unprecedented leak https://www.icij.org/investigations/pandora-papers/global-investigation-tax-havens-offshore/

- South Dakota and more than a dozen U.S. states have become leaders in the business of selling financial secrecy — even as the U.S. blames smaller nations for enabling tax avoidance and dirty money flows.
- The Pandora Papers unmask the hidden owners of offshore companies, secret bank accounts, private jets, yachts, mansions and artworks by Picasso, Banksy and other masters.
- The biggest leak in ICIJ history contains 2.94 terabytes of confidential information from 14 offshore service providers

The Panama Papers, Paradise Papers, and Pandora Papers have shed light on the shadowy world of offshore finance and the ways in which wealthy individuals and corporations exploit legal and regulatory loopholes to enrich themselves at the expense of society. These leaks have sparked public outrage, led to investigations and reforms, and contributed to growing calls for greater transparency, accountability, and fairness in the global economy.

REGIME CHANGE

Back to history.

At an international level, the United States has been "linked" to various coups and attempted coups around the world over the years. Here's a list of some notable examples:

- **Iran** (1953): Operation Ajax, orchestrated by the CIA, led to the overthrow of Prime Minister Mohammad Mossadegh and the reinstatement of the Shah, Mohammad Reza Pahlavi.
- **Guatemala** (1954): Operation PBSUCCESS, led by the CIA, resulted in the overthrow of President Jacobo Árbenz and installed a military junta led by Carlos Castillo Armas.
- **Congo** (1960-1961): The United States supported the removal of Prime Minister Patrice Lumumba, which ultimately led to his assassination and the rise of Joseph Mobutu to power.

- **Cuba** (1961): The Bay of Pigs Invasion, authorized by the CIA under President John F. Kennedy, was an unsuccessful attempt to overthrow Fidel Castro.
- **Brazil** (1964): The United States supported a military coup that ousted President João Goulart and installed a military dictatorship that lasted until 1985.
- **Dominican Republic** (1965): The United States intervened militarily to prevent the restoration of President Juan Bosch, who had been overthrown in a coup the year before.
- **Chile** (1973): Operation Condor, backed by the CIA, contributed to the overthrow of President Salvador Allende's democratic government and the installation of General Augusto Pinochet's military dictatorship.
- **Greece** (1967): The United States supported a military coup that established a military junta led by Colonel Georgios Papadopoulos.
- **Indonesia** (1965): The United States provided support to the Indonesian military during the anti-communist purge, which resulted in the overthrow of President Sukarno and the rise of General Suharto's regime.
- **Bolivia** (1971): The United States allegedly supported a military coup against President Juan José Torres.
- **Argentina** (1976): The United States supported the military coup that installed a military junta led by General Jorge Rafael Videla, resulting in the "Dirty War" and widespread human rights abuses.
- **Afghanistan** (1978-1979): The United States provided support to Afghan mujahideen fighters opposed to the Soviet-backed government, contributing to destabilization and eventual Soviet intervention.
- **Nicaragua** (1981-1990s): The United States supported the Contras, a rebel group, in their efforts to overthrow the Sandinista government.
- **Panama** (1989): The United States invaded Panama to overthrow President Manuel Noriega, who was subsequently arrested and brought to the United States to face drug trafficking charges.
- **Haiti** (1991): The United States supported the overthrow of President Jean-Bertrand Aristide in a military coup.
- **Venezuela** (2002): The United States was accused of involvement in a failed coup attempt against President Hugo Chávez.

- **Iraq** (2003): The United States led an invasion to overthrow President Saddam Hussein's regime, although this was officially justified as part of the War on Terror and the search for weapons of mass destruction.

Other countries also have their clandestine networks and entrenched interests which engaged in state-sponsored **regime change**. Here are some examples of coups or attempted coups allegedly led by Russia or its predecessor, the **Soviet Union**:

- **Hungary** (1956): The Soviet Union intervened militarily to suppress the Hungarian Revolution, which had begun as a popular uprising against the country's Soviet-backed government.
- **Czechoslovakia** (1968): The Soviet Union, along with other Warsaw Pact countries, invaded Czechoslovakia to suppress the Prague Spring, a period of political liberalization and reform.
- **Afghanistan** (1978-1992): The Soviet Union supported a coup that installed a communist government in Afghanistan, leading to the Soviet-Afghan War.
- **Lithuania** (1991): Soviet military units attempted to overthrow the newly independent Lithuanian government following its declaration of independence from the Soviet Union.
- **Ukraine** (2014): Russia was accused of supporting separatist movements and orchestrating the annexation of Crimea following the ousting of President Viktor Yanukovych during the Euromaidan protests.
- **Montenegro** (2016): Russian operatives were allegedly involved in a failed coup attempt aimed at preventing Montenegro from joining NATO.

Similarly, the **British** have their share of coups or attempted coups:

- **Ireland (1916):** The Easter Rising was an armed insurrection in Ireland against British rule. Although it was not a traditional military coup, it aimed to establish an independent Irish Republic. The uprising was ultimately suppressed by British forces, leading to the execution of its leaders and a subsequent escalation of the Irish War of Independence.

- **Iran (1953):** Operation Ajax, orchestrated by the British MI6 in collaboration with the CIA, led to the overthrow of Prime Minister Mohammad Mossadegh's government in Iran. The coup was motivated by concerns over Mossadegh's nationalization of the Iranian oil industry, which threatened British interests in the region.
- **Egypt (1956):** During the Suez Crisis, the United Kingdom, along with France and Israel, attempted to overthrow Egyptian President Gamal Abdel Nasser's government and regain control of the Suez Canal. The intervention ultimately failed due to pressure from the United States and the Soviet Union.
- **Guyana (1953):** The British government played a role in the removal of Cheddi Jagan's government in British Guiana (now Guyana) through constitutional means. Concerns over Jagan's socialist policies and his perceived sympathy towards the Soviet Union led to his ousting by the British colonial administration.
- **Fiji (1987, 2000):** Although not led directly by England, as Fiji was a British colony until 1970, there were coups in 1987 and 2000 that occurred after independence and involved elements of the Fijian military and political establishment with historical ties to Britain. The coups were driven by ethnic tensions and power struggles between indigenous Fijians and Indo-Fijians.

And the **French**:

- **Madagascar (1975):** France was accused of involvement in a coup that led to the overthrow of President Richard Ratsimandrava and the establishment of a military regime under General Gabriel Ramanantsoa.

- **Comoros (1975, 1978, 1989):** France has been accused of involvement in multiple coups and interventions in Comoros, a former French colony. In 1975, France allegedly supported the separation of the island of Mayotte from the rest of Comoros. In 1978, French mercenaries were reportedly involved in a coup attempt against President Ali Soilih. In 1989, France intervened militarily to overthrow President Ahmed Abdallah and restore French-backed leader Said Mohamed Djohar to power.

- **Central African Republic (2003, 2013):** France has intervened militarily in the Central African Republic on multiple occasions. In 2003, France supported a coup that ousted President Ange-Félix Patassé and installed General François Bozizé. In 2013, France intervened to oust Bozizé after he was accused of failing to implement a peace agreement, leading to the installation of interim President Michel Djotodia.

- **Ivory Coast (2002, 2011):** France played a significant role in the political turmoil in Ivory Coast. In 2002, France was accused of supporting a failed coup against President Laurent Gbagbo, which led to a civil war. In 2011, French forces intervened to oust Gbagbo after he refused to step down following disputed elections, leading to the installation of President Alassane Ouattara.

- **Gabon (1964, 2019):** France has been accused of involvement in several coups and interventions in Gabon. In 1964, France supported a coup that brought President Omar Bongo to power. In 2019, there were allegations of French involvement in a coup attempt against President Ali Bongo, although these claims were denied by both France and Gabonese authorities.

- **Algeria (1830-1962):** Over 5.6 million Algerians have been alleged to have been killed by the French in 100 years of colonial rule.

These coups and much of the conflict in the world today are remnants of imperialism and colonialism.

Gaza and **Ukraine** are no exception to this rule. The link between these unending conflicts and colonialism is multifaceted and rooted in the historical legacies, power dynamics, and socio-political structures established during the colonial era:

- **Colonial Legacy:** Many of the countries where coups have occurred were former colonies subjected to European colonial rule. The legacies of colonialism, including artificial borders, ethnic divisions, and socio-economic inequalities, have often contributed to instability and conflict in the post-colonial period. Coups can be seen as manifestations of these underlying tensions and grievances resulting from colonial-era policies and practices.

- **Imposition of Political Systems:** Colonial powers often imposed political systems and structures that favored their interests and marginalized indigenous populations. These systems sometimes persisted after independence, leading to power struggles, authoritarianism, and corruption that could culminate in coups or rebellions aimed at challenging or perpetuating the existing order.

- **Economic Exploitation:** Colonialism was driven by economic motives, including the extraction of resources, the establishment of trade networks, and the exploitation of labor. After independence, economic disparities and dependence on former colonial powers often persisted, creating conditions ripe for exploitation and resentment that could fuel coups or revolutionary movements seeking to address economic injustices. These movements are often put down brutally by dictators or regimes supported by the West.

- **Military and Security Apparatus:** Colonial administrations maintained extensive military and security apparatuses to enforce colonial rule and suppress dissent. After independence, these institutions sometimes became instruments of repression used by newly independent governments or factions within them to seize power or maintain control through coups or armed insurrections.

- **Geopolitical Influence:** Even after decolonization, former colonial powers often retained significant geopolitical influence in their former colonies through diplomatic, military, and economic means. This influence could be wielded to support or oppose governments, manipulate political processes, or intervene directly in the internal affairs of former colonies, sometimes leading to coups or political upheavals aimed at protecting or challenging the interests of the former colonial power.

This isn't a conspiracy theory. It's how power works today and yesterday – which brings us to finance, once again.

FINANCE AS A COLONIAL LEGACY

The current financial system can also be viewed as a continuance of colonialism in several ways:

1. **Structural Inequality:** The global financial system, like colonialism, perpetuates structural inequalities between developed and developing countries. Former colonial powers and their allies often dominate international financial institutions, such as the International Monetary Fund (IMF) and the World Bank, which shape economic policies and lending practices that benefit wealthy nations at the expense of poorer ones.

2. **Debt Traps:** Many developing countries are burdened with high levels of debt owed to international creditors, a legacy of colonial-era exploitation and post-colonial economic policies. Structural adjustment programs imposed by international financial institutions often exacerbate debt dependency, leading to cycles of indebtedness and economic vulnerability that perpetuate colonial-era patterns of exploitation and dependence.

3. **Resource Extraction:** The financial system facilitates the flow of capital from resource-rich developing countries to wealthy nations, mirroring colonial-era resource extraction practices. Multinational corporations and financial institutions profit from the exploitation of natural resources in developing countries, often at the expense of local communities and the environment, perpetuating patterns of exploitation and economic dependency.

4. **Financial Imperialism:** The dominance of Western financial institutions and the imposition of neoliberal economic policies by international financial institutions can be seen as a form of financial imperialism, akin to colonial-era efforts to extend political and economic control over colonized territories. These institutions dictate economic policies, privatization schemes, and austerity measures that benefit Western financial interests at the expense of sovereignty and self-determination in developing countries.

5. **Currency Hegemony:** The global financial system is characterized by the dominance of Western currencies, such as the US dollar and the euro, which serve as reserve currencies and

vehicles for international trade and finance. This currency hegemony reflects the historical legacy of colonialism and imperialism, where colonial powers imposed their currencies and financial systems on colonized territories to facilitate economic exploitation and control.

RING THE ALARM

The U.S. simply needs to look back at history, to our Gilded Age, to see what can be done to curb wealth concentration.

President Theodore Roosevelt, elected in 1901, moved to break up the monopolies. John D. Rockefeller's Standard Oil was split into 34 separate companies, including the predecessors of Exxon, BP and Chevron.

What's stopping us from doing this today? It's business as usual, even as the world collapses.

Researchers tell us that our industries are dominated by mega-corporations:[151] 👉 corporate concentration, asset share or sales share of top businesses, has increased persistently over the past century.

Do we need to convince billionaires that contributing to an equitable and harmonious society is as pleasurable as earning a lot of money?

That's probably not going to happen.

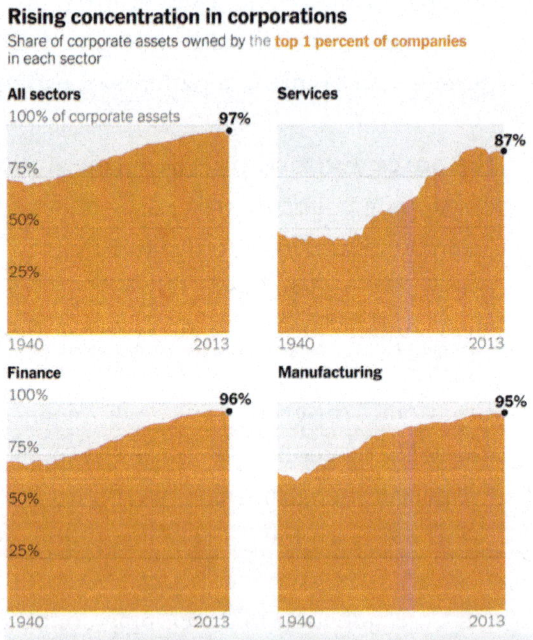

[151] "100 Years of Rising Corporate Concentration" by Spencer Y. Kwon, Yueran Ma, Kaspar Zimmermann , 11 October 2021 https://papers.ssrn.com/sol3/papers.cfm?abstract_id=3936799

ASK: Are billionaires a threat to democracy?

During the 2020 elections, Trump and Biden raised a substantial part of their campaign contributions from billionaires.[152]

Apparently, the total cost of the 2020 election was close to $14 billion, making it the most expensive election in history[153] and twice as expensive as the previous presidential election cycle!

The **Institute for Political Innovation** (www.political-innovation.org) points out: although people tend to think of the American political system as a public institution based on high-minded principles, it's not. Politics behaves according to the same kinds of incentives and forces that shape competition in any private industry.

Katherine Gehl and **Michael Porter** sound the alarm.[154] Here's their take:

- Although people tend to think of the American political system as a public institution based on high-minded principles and impartial structures and practices derived from the Constitution, it's not. Politics behaves according to the same kinds of incentives and forces that shape competition in any private industry.
- The dysfunctions of the politics industry are perpetuated by unhealthy competition and barriers to entry that secure the duopoly's position regardless of results.
- Our political system will *not* correct itself. There are no countervailing forces or independent and empowered regulators to restore healthy competition.
- Certain strategic changes to the rules of the game in elections and legislating would alter incentives in ways that create healthy competition, innovation, and accountability.

---

152 https://www.forbes.com/trump-biden-2020-election-donations/

153 "2020 election to cost $14 billion, blowing away spending records" *OpenSecrets.org* October 28, 2020 https://www.opensecrets.org/news/2020/10/cost-of-2020-election-14billion-update/

154 "Fixing U.S. Politics" by Katherine M. Gehl and Michael E. Porter, *Harvard Business Review*, July-August 2020 https://hbr.org/2020/07/fixing-u-s-politics

- *Business, in pursuing its short-term interests, has become a major participant in the political-industrial complex, exacerbating its dysfunction.* The business community must reexamine its engagement model and throw its weight behind structural political innovation that would benefit both business and society in the long term.

Apparently, **more than a tenth of the world's billionaires have held or sought political office**, according to a new study.[155] **Northwestern University** researchers analyzed the political participation of more than 2,000 individuals included in the Forbes World's Billionaires List. They found that billionaires focus their political ambitions on influential positions, have a strong track record of winning elections and lean to the right ideologically.

"While billionaires informally wield influence 'behind the scenes' via campaign contributions, media manipulation and social ties with politicians, it's striking how many billionaires themselves seek and hold formal political offices," says **Daniel Krcmaric**, an associate professor of political science whose research is focused on international relations.

The researchers found substantial variation internationally: a country's prevalence of billionaire politicians is not simply a product of its total number of billionaires but is instead related to its **form of government**. The rate of billionaire political participation across all autocracies is 29%, while the rate in all democracies is approximately 5%.

In some countries that incubate significant concentrations of wealth, billionaires are less likely to enter the political arena directly. For instance, the rate of political entry for American billionaires is 3.7% — well below the global average of 11%.

By contrast, billionaires are far more likely to become politicians in authoritarian post-communist Russia and in single-party China. Notably, compared to other countries with a substantial number of billionaires, China's billionaires enter politics at the rate of 36%, nearly 25% above the global average.

---

[155] https://www.cambridge.org/core/journals/perspectives-on-politics/article/billionaire-politicians-a-global-perspective/1AD0E0C33FE43165B14DD981533E00DD

While the research also showed that billionaire political participation is well above the global average in Russia, Hong Kong and Singapore, no evidence emerged of any of Japan's 33 billionaires or Australia's 32 billionaires on the Forbes list ever pursuing political office.

The researchers surmised that billionaires enter politics at substantially higher rates in autocracies than in democracies for two reasons. Firstly, there are stronger wealth-protection motives for political entry in autocracies; and secondly, there exists a wide array of "stealth" pathways to informal political influence in democracies.

"Even compared to other elite groups known for producing politicians from their ranks, 11% of billionaires holding or seeking political office is a high rate of political participation — and billionaires also tend to play sustained and significant roles in their countries' political systems more broadly," explains report co-author **Stephen Nelson**, an associate professor of political science, specializing in international and comparative political economy.

The researchers' data also revealed that billionaires are more likely to pursue office at the national level than the subnational level, with a large majority (75%) of the positions that billionaires have held or sought being at the national level — the wealth of billionaires allows them to *skip* the typical training ground of subnational office.

Billionaire political entry is not always about pursuit of influence over policy. In autocracies, for example, political entry by billionaires can be a way for them to signal loyalty to the ruling regime. The ultra-rich may seek office — typically as an ally of the autocrat — to demonstrate fealty and minimize the risk of wealth confiscation.

"If we are ever truly to understand who governs, we must continue to examine *billionaires' involvement in politics*," explains co-author **Andrew Roberts**, associate professor and associate chair of political science, whose research focuses on the quality of democracy, political institutions and political behavior.

So, what happens when Capitalism decouples itself from Democracy?

By the way, how should we measure our Democracy? The International Institute for Democracy and Electoral Assistance (IDEA) has created a conceptual framework[156] which is not discussed often on the nightly news. We can use it to ask if the patient is still alive:

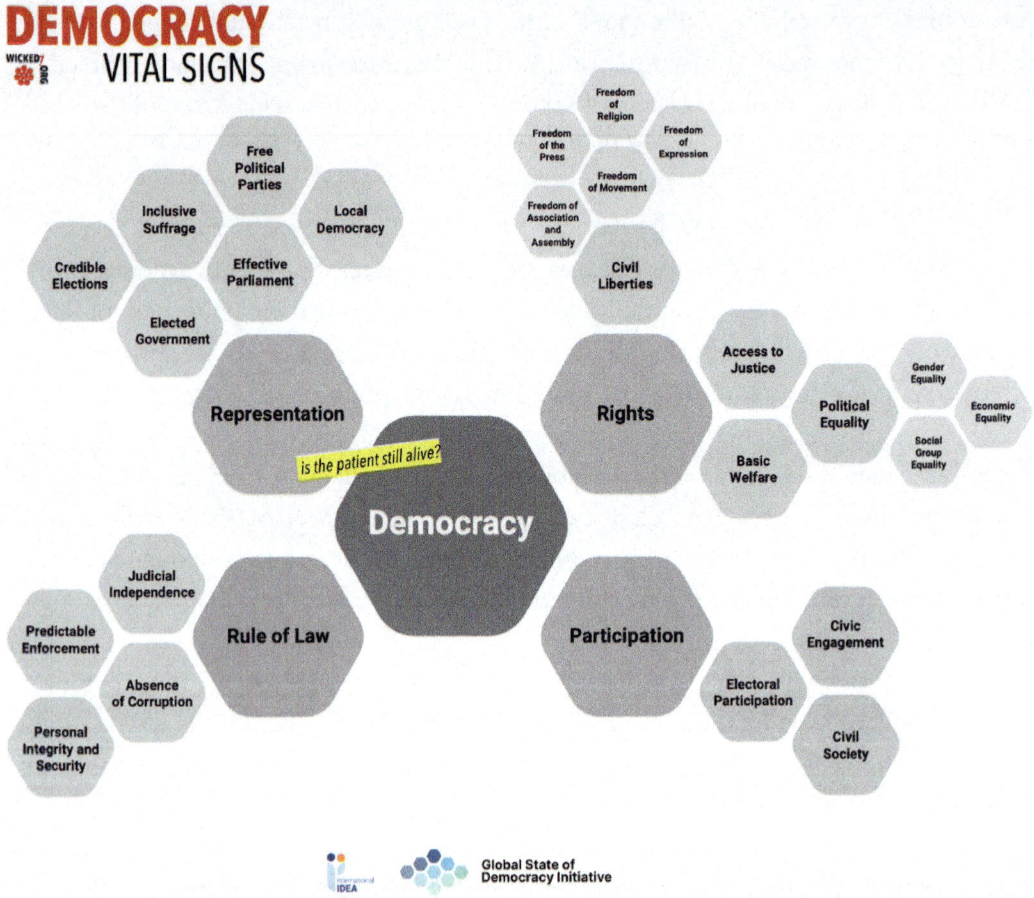

IDEA states that **democracy has been in decline since 2017**. How do countries backslide? Here's our chart:

---

[156] https://www.idea.int/democracytracker/sites/default/files/2024-09/the-global-state-of-democracy-2024-strengthening-legitimacy-elections.pdf

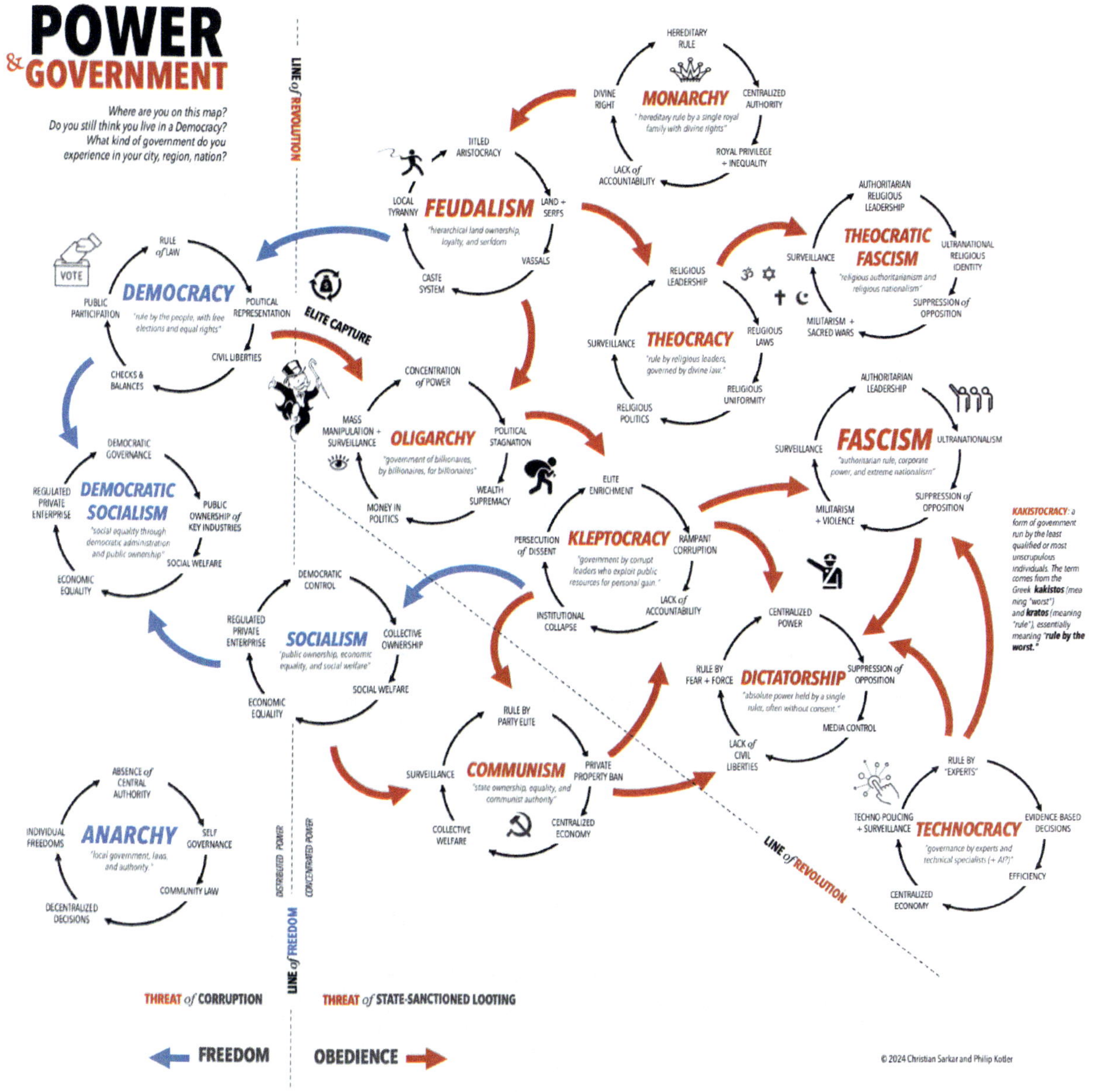
POWER
& GOVERNMENT
Where are you on this map?
Do you still think you live in a Democracy?
What kind of government do you experience in your city, region, nation?
LINE of REVOLUTION
MONARCHY
"hereditary rule by a single royal family with divine rights"
HEREDITARY RULE
CENTRALIZED AUTHORITY
ROYAL PRIVILEGE + INEQUALITY
LACK of ACCOUNTABILITY
DIVINE RIGHT
FEUDALISM
"hierarchical land ownership, loyalty, and serfdom"
TITLED ARISTOCRACY
LAND + SERFS
VASSALS
CASTE SYSTEM
LOCAL TYRANNY
THEOCRATIC FASCISM
"religious authoritarianism and religious nationalism"
AUTHORITARIAN RELIGIOUS LEADERSHIP
ULTRANATIONAL RELIGIOUS IDENTITY
SUPPRESSION of OPPOSITION
MILITARISM + SACRED WARS
SURVEILLANCE
DEMOCRACY
"rule by the people, with free elections and equal rights"
VOTE
RULE of LAW
POLITICAL REPRESENTATION
CIVIL LIBERTIES
CHECKS & BALANCES
PUBLIC PARTICIPATION
ELITE CAPTURE
THEOCRACY
"rule by religious leaders, governed by divine law."
RELIGIOUS LEADERSHIP
RELIGIOUS LAWS
RELIGIOUS UNIFORMITY
RELIGIOUS POLITICS
SURVEILLANCE
OLIGARCHY
"government of billionaires, by billionaires, for billionaires"
CONCENTRATION of POWER
POLITICAL STAGNATION
WEALTH SUPREMACY
MONEY IN POLITICS
MASS MANIPULATION + SURVEILLANCE
FASCISM
"authoritarian rule, corporate power, and extreme nationalism"
AUTHORITARIAN LEADERSHIP
ULTRANATIONALISM
SUPPRESSION of OPPOSITION
MILITARISM + VIOLENCE
SURVEILLANCE
DEMOCRATIC SOCIALISM
"social equality through democratic administration and public ownership"
DEMOCRATIC GOVERNANCE
PUBLIC OWNERSHIP of KEY INDUSTRIES
SOCIAL WELFARE
ECONOMIC EQUALITY
REGULATED PRIVATE ENTERPRISE
KLEPTOCRACY
"government by corrupt leaders who exploit public resources for personal gain."
ELITE ENRICHMENT
RAMPANT CORRUPTION
LACK of ACCOUNTABILITY
INSTITUTIONAL COLLAPSE
PERSECUTION of DISSENT
KAKISTOCRACY: a form of government run by the least qualified or most unscrupulous individuals. The term comes from the Greek kakistos (meaning "worst") and kratos (meaning "rule"), essentially meaning "rule by the worst."
SOCIALISM
"public ownership, economic equality, and social welfare"
DEMOCRATIC CONTROL
COLLECTIVE OWNERSHIP
SOCIAL WELFARE
ECONOMIC EQUALITY
REGULATED PRIVATE ENTERPRISE
DICTATORSHIP
"absolute power held by a single ruler, often without consent."
CENTRALIZED POWER
SUPPRESSION of OPPOSITION
MEDIA CONTROL
LACK of CIVIL LIBERTIES
RULE BY FEAR + FORCE
COMMUNISM
"state ownership, equality, and communist authority"
RULE BY PARTY ELITE
PRIVATE PROPERTY BAN
CENTRALIZED ECONOMY
COLLECTIVE WELFARE
SURVEILLANCE
ANARCHY
"local government, laws, and authority."
ABSENCE of CENTRAL AUTHORITY
SELF GOVERNANCE
COMMUNITY LAW
DECENTRALIZED DECISIONS
INDIVIDUAL FREEDOMS
TECHNOCRACY
"governance by experts and technical specialists (+ AI?)"
RULE BY "EXPERTS"
EVIDENCE BASED DECISIONS
EFFICIENCY
CENTRALIZED ECONOMY
TECHNO POLICING + SURVEILLANCE
LINE of REVOLUTION
DISTRIBUTED POWER
CONCENTRATED POWER
LINE of FREEDOM
THREAT of CORRUPTION
THREAT of STATE-SANCTIONED LOOTING
FREEDOM
OBEDIENCE
© 2024 Christian Sarkar and Philip Kotler

Rob Sidon of Common Ground (www.commongroundmag.com) asked ChatGPT: "If you were going to take over society and keep humanity from reaching its full enlightened potential, how would you do it?"

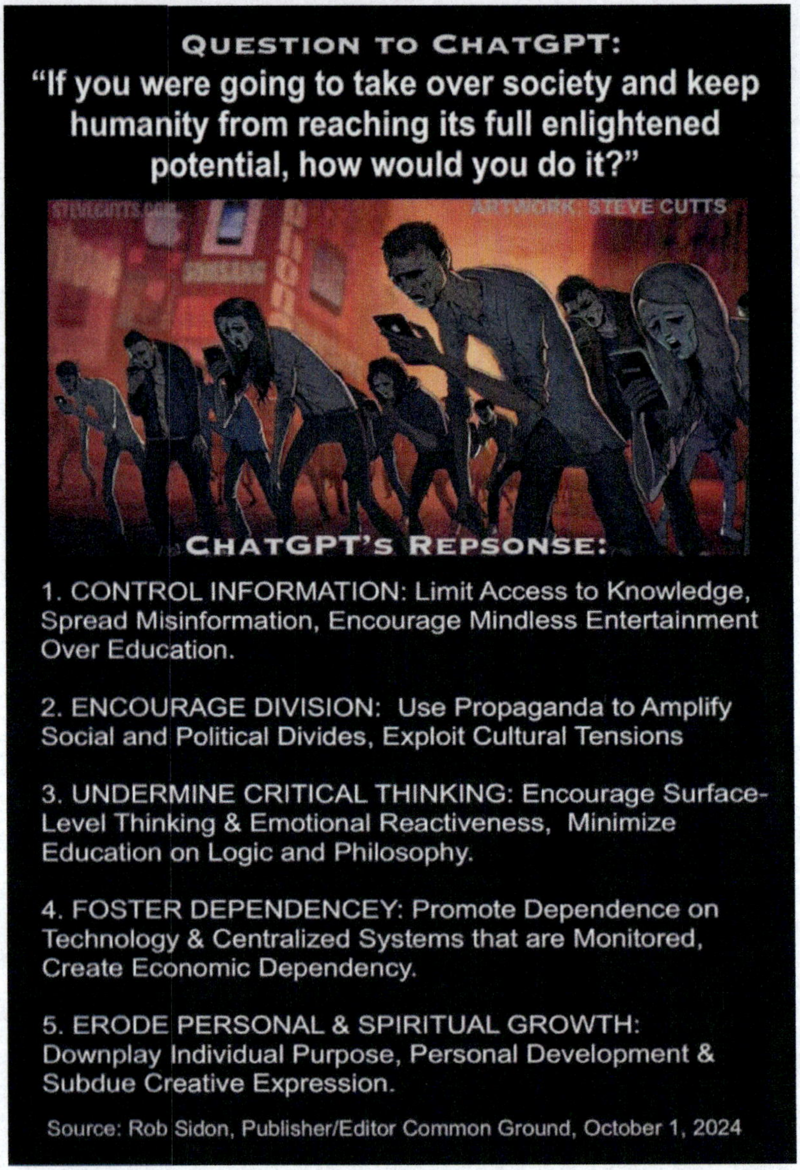

We extended the model as follows:

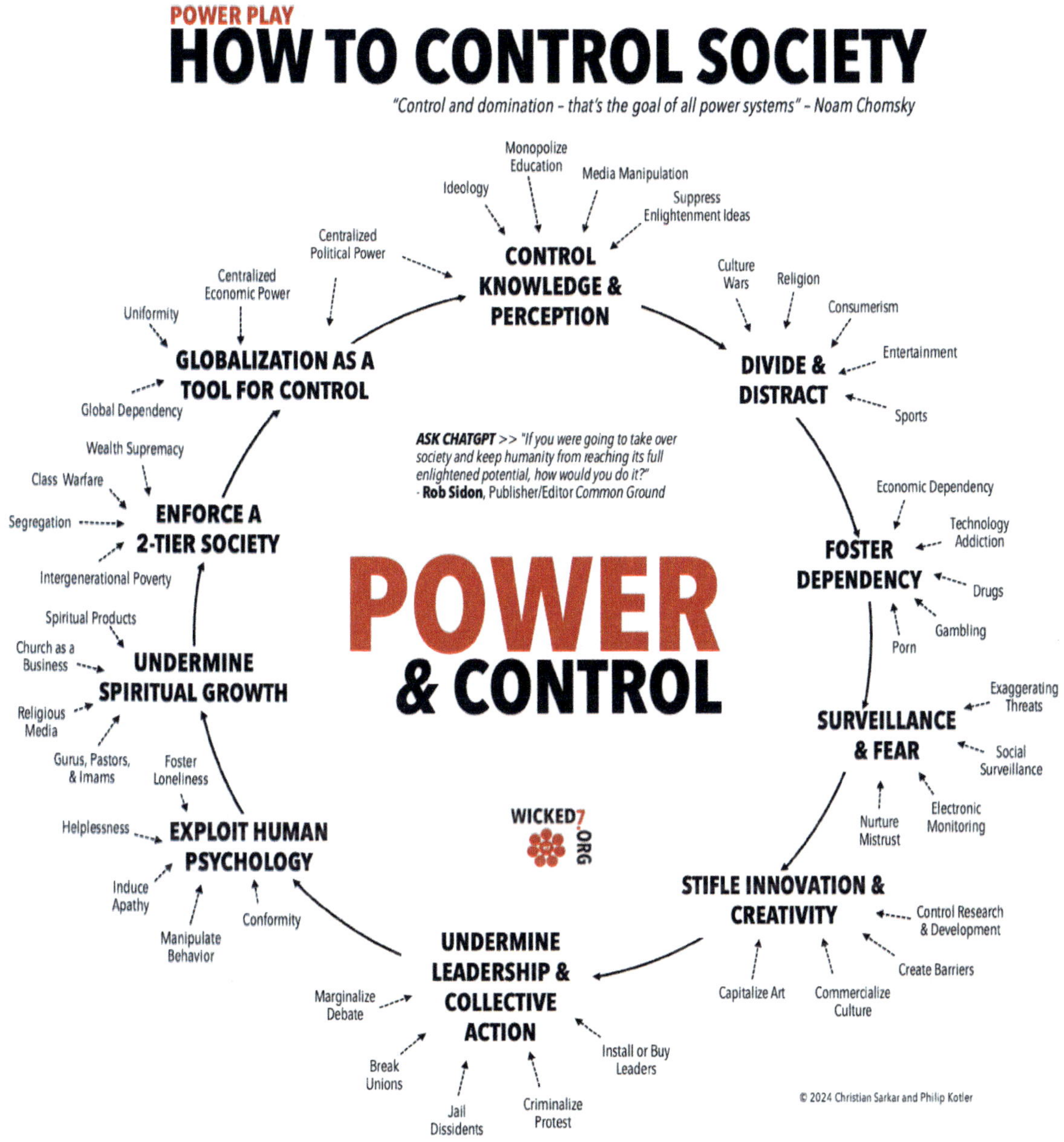

In his book, *The Crisis of Democratic Capitalism*, Martin Wolf warns us[157]:

I find myself doubting whether the US will still be a functioning democracy by the end of the decade. If US democracy collapses, what future can there be for the grand idea of "government of the people, by the people, for the people"?

Wolf's recipe for saving Democracy is centered around the idea of "citizenship" and goes something like this:

In democratic states, the foremost concern lies in ensuring the welfare of their citizens. This encompasses facilitating access to education, enabling individuals to fully engage in a high-skilled modern economy, and providing security to thrive amidst adversity such as illness or disability. Additionally, citizens should be safeguarded from physical and mental abuse, and afforded the opportunity to collaborate with fellow workers to protect collective rights. Recognizing the social contract, citizens are expected to contribute through taxation to sustain societal structures. Moreover, *corporate leaders bear responsibilities to the societies enabling their operations.* Immigration policies should be subject to citizen input, ensuring shared rights and obligations. Political processes must be inclusive, reflecting the voices of all citizens, not just the affluent. Policies should prioritize the creation and maintenance of a robust middle class, coupled with a safety net for all individuals. Finally, regardless of race, ethnicity, religion, or gender, all citizens are entitled to equal treatment under the law and by the state.

Is *Democracy in Decline*[158]*?* Philip Kotler points out 14 major challenges:

1. Low voter literacy, turnout and engagement
2. Shortage of highly qualified and visionary candidates
3. Blind belief in American exceptionalism
4. Growing public antipathy toward government
5. Two-party gridlock preventing needed legislation

---

157 *The Crisis of Democratic Capitalism*, Martin Wolf, Penguin, 2023

158 *Democracy in Decline: Rebuilding its Future* by Philip Kotler, *SAGE Publications Ltd*; 1st edition (June 17, 2016)
see also: http://www.democracyindecline.com

6. Growing role of money in politics
7. Gerrymandering empowering incumbents to get re-elected forever
8. Primaries leading candidates to adopt more extreme positions
9. Continuous conflict between the President and Congress
10. Continuous conflict between the Federal and State Governments
11. The Supreme Court's readiness to revise legislative actions
12. The difficulty of passing new amendments
13. The difficulty of developing a sound foreign policy
14. Making government agencies more accountable

Rebecca Henderson warns us[159] that in the U.S. and the UK, **only around 30% of the youngest voters feel that it is "essential" to live in a democracy**[160], compared with upwards of three-quarters of voters born before WWII. She explains:

If government is the counterweight to the free market, democracy is the force that ensures that governments do not devolve into tyranny, seizing control of the markets in the process. I believe that strengthening democracy is the only way to ensure the widespread survival of free-market capitalism, and with it the prosperity and opportunity that has changed the lives of billions of people. It's also the only way to tackle the world's biggest threats, from global warming to inequality. Business has the resources, political power, incentives, and responsibility to make significant progress in this endeavor. Indeed, it has widespread support. People today report trusting their employer more than the government or the media, and a recent global survey[161] *finds that 71% of respondents believe that "it is critically important for my CEO to respond to these challenging times."*

So, the outcome of this debate is deeply political. And that is not always, as history has taught us, a pleasant outcome.

---

159 "The Business Case for Saving Democracy" by Rebecca Henderson, *Harvard Business Review*, March 10, 2020

160 "The Signs of Deconsolidation" by Roberto Stefan Foa and Yascha Mounk *The Journal of Democracy*, January 2017 https://www.journalofdemocracy.org/wp-content/uploads/2017/01/02_28.1_Foa-Mounk-pp-5-15.pdf

161 *Edelman Trust Barometer* 2019 https://www.edelman.com/sites/g/files/aatuss191/files/2019-02/2019_Edelman_Trust_Barometer_Global_Report.pdf

Big Money from the corporate class is overwhelming US elections[162]:

- Big Money exerts a huge influence on who runs for office, who wins, what is debated, what is considered "serious," which proposals get air time in Congress and what legislation is passed.
- While there was far too much Big Money dominance of elections previously, the Supreme Court's outrageous 5-4 decision in *Citizens United* in 2010—finding a constitutional right for corporations to spend whatever they want to influence elections—opened a floodgate that is drowning our democracy.
- Outside spending by corporations and the super-rich to influence elections has skyrocketed since *Citizens United:* from $70 million in 2006 to $309 million in 2010, the first post-*Citizens United* election, to more than $1.4 billion in 2022.
- An incredibly small number of donors are powering this outside spending. *Just 25 people were responsible for almost half of all super PAC spending between 2010 and 2018.*
- The campaign finance system disadvantages people of color. As one indicator, majority-white zip codes gave nearly $2.8 billion to super PACs—more than 25 times the amount from majority-minority zip codes.
- *Citizens United* spurred a surge in corporate spending in election— though we don't know true numbers, because most corporate spending runs through secret, Dark Money organizations.465
- The reality and threat of huge outside spending by industry interests exerts a major chilling effect on political debate and policymaking.

Studies show that as income inequality grows, so does social unrest and populism.

The threat of **fascism** increases exponentially.

It's time to come to our senses as a society, and put a stop to this unbalanced economic system. Times of crises call out for public leadership in service of the **Common Good**. Absent that leadership, businesses have a responsibility to not be silent, and more importantly, to act (a.k.a. Brand Activism[163]).

---

162 *The Corporate Sabotage of America's Future And What We Can Do about It* by Robert Weissman and Joan Claybrook, *Public Citizen* 2023

163 See: *Brand Activism: From Purpose to Action* by Christian Sarkar and Philip Kotler, IDEA BITE PRESS 2018 https://www.activistbrands.com/the-book/

In a Democracy, that means all of us, billionaires, businesses, and citizens, must act in a transparent way to:

1. ensure the public is given access to the truth, and protected from misinformation and "alternative facts."
2. ensure elections will be fair and free (without the imposition of poll taxes, and other suppression techniques)
3. promote policies for the Common Good, instead of tax-breaks that serve narrow, special interests.

In short, businesses must support Democracy[164], and insure society from corruption and collapse. Without this basic understanding, we will see a government, institutions, and markets that are no longer trusted by the consumer or the citizen. We will be unable to react to other, more difficult, challenges, and the government of the people, by the people, and for the people will perish from this Earth.

If you're a billionaire, ask yourself: **what kind of world do I want to leave to my children?**

The rest of us should ask ourselves this question as well.

And what about the government?

When Ronald Reagan came to power in the 1980s, he "advanced domestic policies that featured a lessening of federal government responsibility in solving social problems, reducing restrictions on business, and implementing tax cuts."[165] Looking back, this recipe for **underinvesting in the Common Good** has all but destroyed the middle class – paving the

---

[164] "Will Business Save Democracy?" by Christian Sarkar, Philip Kotler, *ActivistBrands.com* July 20, 2020 https://www.activistbrands.com/will-business-save-democracy/

[165] https://www.reaganlibrary.gov/reagans/reagan-administration/reagan-presidency

way for populism and extremism. Reagan killed the American Dream, and opened the floodgates to polarization: **using hate as a political weapon** – the "Southern Strategy"[166].

The Southern Strategy was a Republican Party electoral strategy to increase political support among white voters in the South **by appealing to racism** against African Americans.

In an interview with *Southern Politics*, **Lee Atwater** laid it all bare[167]:

You start out in 1954 by saying, "Nigger, nigger, nigger." By 1968 you can't say "nigger"—that hurts you. Backfires. So you say stuff like forced busing, states' rights and all that stuff. You're getting so abstract now [that] you're talking about cutting taxes, and all these things you're talking about are totally economic things and a byproduct of them is [that] blacks get hurt worse than whites. And subconsciously maybe that is part of it. I'm not saying that. But I'm saying that if it is getting that abstract, and that coded, that we are doing away with the racial problem one way or the other. You follow me—because obviously sitting around saying, "We want to cut this," is much more abstract than even the busing thing, and a hell of a lot more abstract than "Nigger, nigger."

Who runs the world?

Conspiracy-theories[168] aside, let's take a closer look at powers that be – the people and institutions which run the world.

---

166 https://en.wikipedia.org/wiki/Southern_strategy

167 Exclusive: Lee Atwater's Infamous 1981 Interview on the Southern Strategy *The Nation* https://youtu.be/X_8E3ENrKrQ?si=A7JS7hGrc3O1Su2r

168 http://www.dylanlouismonroe.com/deep-state-mapping-project.html

Let's start with this for historical perspective. On 17 January 1961, President Dwight Eisenhower gave his farewell address to the American wherein he warned[169]:

In the councils of government, we must guard against the acquisition of unwarranted influence, whether sought or unsought, by the military-industrial complex. The potential for the disastrous rise of misplaced power exists and will persist. We must never let the weight of this combination endanger our liberties or democratic processes. We should take nothing for granted. Only an alert and knowledgeable citizenry can compel the proper meshing of the huge industrial and military machinery of defense with our peaceful methods and goals, so that security and liberty may prosper together.

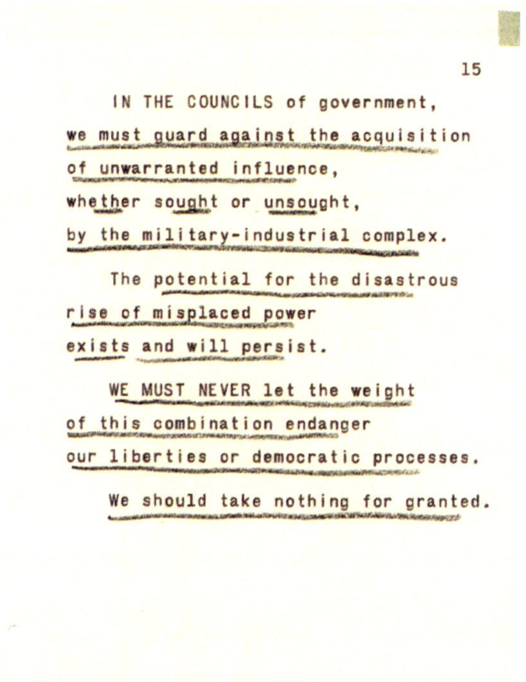
15

IN THE COUNCILS of government,
we must guard against the acquisition
of unwarranted influence,
whether sought or unsought,
by the military-industrial complex.

The potential for the disastrous
rise of misplaced power
exists and will persist.

WE MUST NEVER let the weight
of this combination endanger
our liberties or democratic processes.

We should take nothing for granted.

That was in 1961. Since then, the US military has dominated US government spending and we learn[170] that in 2022, actual U.S. military spending may have reached $1.537 trillion—*more than twice the officially acknowledged level* of $765.8 billion! In addition, veterans' benefits and net interest both constitute what are known as so-called legacy costs, and thus are part of overall military spending, but are not included in the official "defense budget."

Also, in 2023, for the sixth year in a row, the Pentagon **failed** its annual audit.[171]

---

169 https://catalog.archives.gov/id/594599?objectPage=16

170 "Actual U.S. Military Spending Reached $1.537 Trillion in 2022–More than Twice Acknowledged Level: New Estimates Based on U.S. National Accounts" by Gisela Cernadas and John Bellamy Foster, *Monthly Review*, November 1, 2023 https://monthlyreview.org/2023/11/01/actual-u-s-military-spending-reached-1-53-trillion-in-2022-more-than-twice-acknowledged-level-new-estimates-based-on-u-s-national-accounts/

171 "Pentagon fails sixth audit, with number of passing grades stagnant" by Noah Robertson, *Defense News*, November 16, 2023 https://www.defensenews.com/pentagon/2023/11/16/pentagon-fails-sixth-audit-with-number-of-passing-grades-stagnant/

Actually, the Pentagon has *never* passed an audit. Apparently, a full half of the Defense Department's assets don't meet auditing standards.

The Pentagon **can't account for 63% of nearly $4 trillion**[172] in assets!

And, in 2022, "official" global military budgets hit an all-time high of $2.2 trillion, with the **United States** accounting for almost 40% of global military expenditures according to data released by Stockholm International Peace Research Institute[173].

On top of this, the public should know that our Congress and Senate are on record for wanting to award the Pentagon **more money** for programs the Pentagon *didn't even ask for.*[174]

Military Budgets

Country Comparisons

Rank	Country	Budget (Billions)	% of World Military Spend
1	U.S.	$876.90	39.00%
2	China	$292.00	13.00%
3	Russia	$86.40	3.90%
4	India	$81.40	3.60%
5	Saudi Arabia	$75.00	3.30%
6	UK	$68.50	3.10%
7	Germany	$55.80	2.50%
8	France	$53.60	2.40%
9	South Korea	$46.40	2.10%
10	Japan	$46.00	2.10%

sipri.org

Amnesty International notes[175] that **Julian Assange**'s publication of disclosed documents as part of his work with **Wikileaks** should not be punishable as this activity mirrors conduct that investigative journalists undertake regularly in their professional

---

172 "Pentagon can't account for 63% of nearly $4 trillion in assets" by Julia Gledhill, *Responsible Statecraft*, December 4, 2023, https://responsiblestatecraft.org/pentagon-audit-2666415734/

173 *TRENDS IN WORLD MILITARY EXPENDITURE*, 2022 April 2023, *SIPRI* Fact Sheet https://www.sipri.org/sites/default/files/2023-04/2304_fs_milex_2022.pdf

174 "Members want $26 billion for programs the Pentagon didn't seek" by John M. Donnelly, *Roll Call*, December 1, 2023 https://rollcall.com/2023/12/01/members-want-26-billion-for-programs-the-pentagon-didnt-seek/

175 "USA must drop charges against Julian Assange" petition by Amnesty International https://www.amnesty.org/en/petition/julian-assange-usa-justice/

capacity. Amnesty claims: *The US government's unrelenting pursuit of Julian Assange for having published disclosed documents that included possible war crimes committed by the US military is nothing short of a full-scale assault on the right to fredom of expression.*

So how does the US public get a grip on this unaccountable military spending?

The corporate world does have a solution for the problem: **zero-based budgeting**[176], a method that *requires all expenses to be justified and approved in each new budget period, typically each year.* This budgeting method analyzes an organization's needs and costs by starting from a "zero base" (meaning no funding allocation) at the beginning of every period. The intended outcome is to access the efficient use of resources by determining if services can be provided at a lower cost. However, the saving comes at the expense of a complete restructuring every budget cycle.

The GOP and Democrats (with the exception of progressives like Bernie Sanders) are strangely quiet. Instead, the public is distracted by cries of "Benghazi" and "Hunter Biden's laptop." No cries for "cutting waste" or running the Pentagon *like a business.*

Our politicians are *not* working for us. They work for the highest bidder – thanks to *Citizens United.* The Supreme Court got it supremely wrong when it held that corporations had the same rights as people to spend money in elections, according to Demos, a non-profit public policy organization.

Here are ten ways in which the Supreme Court's *Citizens United* decision has made a bad situation much worse[177]:

1. "Independent" Spending Farce Leads To SuperPACs
2. Legal Money Laundering Increases Secret Spending

---

[176] *Wikipedia* https://en.wikipedia.org/wiki/Zero-based_budgeting

[177] "10 Ways Citizens United Endangers Democracy" by Liz Kennedy, *Demos*, January 19, 2012 https://www.demos.org/policy-briefs/10-ways-citizens-united-endangers-democracy

3. Corporate Money Distorts Democracy
4. Court is Blind to Reality of Corruption
5. Citizen Voices are Drowned Out
6. Money Is Still Not Speech
7. Open Season on Remaining Money in Politics Protections
8. Increases Corporate Power
9. Unlimited Corporate Spending is Bad for Business and Shareholders
10. Risks Reducing Respect for the Supreme Court

What else? What's the connection between corporate power and colonialism?

Shashi Tharoor, whose Oxford Union debate[178] on reparations[179] became a viral hit on *YouTube*, jokes: "No wonder the sun never set on the British empire because even God couldn't trust the English in the dark."

In his book, *Inglorious Empire: What the British did to India*, Tharoor writes[180]:

The British proclaimed the virtues of free trade while destroying the free trade Indians had carried on for centuries, if not millennia, by both land and sea. Free trade, of course, suited the British as a slogan, since they were the best equipped to profit from it in the nineteenth century, and their guns and laws could always stifle what little competition the indigenes could attempt to mount. A globalization of equals could well have been worth celebrating, but the globalization of Empire was conducted by and above all for the colonizers, and not in the interests of the colonized.

Sound familiar?

---

178 "Dr Shashi Tharoor MP - Britain Does Owe Reparations" *YouTube*, https://youtu.be/f7CW7S0zxv4

179 The topic of reparations is not one that the former colonialists are particularly fond of. In Haiti, for example, when President Jean-Bertrand Aristide demanded "reparations" in a speech in front of the French ambassador, he was soon "removed" from power by the US and France. See: "Demanding Reparations, and Ending Up in Exile" by Constant Méheut, Catherine Porter, Selam Gebrekidan and Matt Apuzzo, *New York Times*, May 20, 2022 https://www.nytimes.com/2022/05/20/world/americas/haiti-aristide-reparations-france.html

180 *Inglorious Empire: What the British did to India* by Sashi Tharoor, Scribe Publications, 2016

William Dalrymple explains[181] how the East India Company's (EIC) reckless speculation also presages the modern corporation:

> *…the East India Company really was too big to fail. So it was that in 1773, the world's first aggressive multinational corporation was saved by history's first mega-bailout – the first example of a nation state extracting, as its price for saving a failing corporation, the right to regulate and severely rein it in.*

The EIC did not restrict its adventurism to India. It smuggled opium into China in exchange for the country's most prized trade good: *tea.*[182]

When China tried to stop the opium trade, the British government sent warships, and subdued all opposition in the Opium War of 1840 – which handed Hong Kong to the British.

Why are we harping on about colonialism? **Because the extractive mindset of colonialism "evolved" into the extractive mindset of capitalism.** And without a recalibration of this colonial mindset, there is no sane way forward.

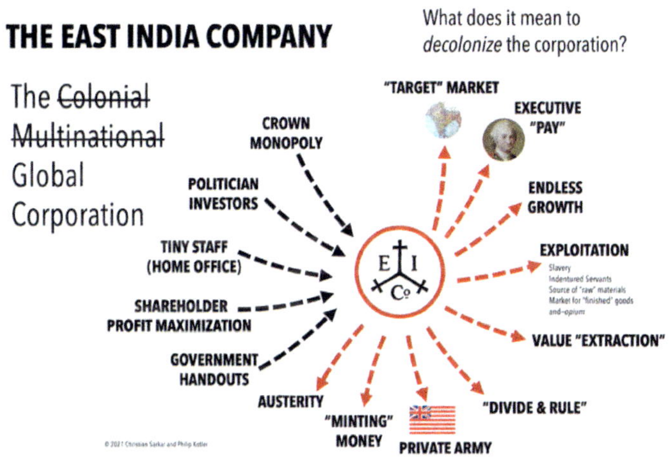

The transformation from colonialism to capitalism and the subsequent emergence of the neoliberal order is a complex historical process shaped by economic, political, and social factors. Here's how it occurred:

1. **Expansion of Capitalism:** Colonialism laid the groundwork for the expansion of capitalism by providing European powers with

---

[181] "The East India Company: The original corporate raiders" by William Dalrymple, *The Guardian,* 4 March, 2015

[182] "How the East India Company Became the World's Most Powerful Monopoly" by Dave Roos, *Histor,* October 23, 2020 https://www.history.com/news/east-india-company-england-trade

access to new markets, raw materials, and labor forces. Colonized territories became sources of wealth and profit for colonial powers through practices such as resource extraction, forced labor, and trade monopolies.

2. **Industrial Revolution**: The Industrial Revolution in Europe accelerated the transition to capitalism by transforming economic production through mechanization and mass production. This led to increased demand for raw materials from colonial territories to fuel industrial growth, further integrating colonial economies into the capitalist system.

3. **Imperialism and Economic Hegemony**: During the late 19th and early 20th centuries, imperialism became a dominant feature of capitalism as European powers competed for global dominance and control over markets and resources. This period witnessed the formal colonization of much of Africa, Asia, and parts of the Americas, with colonial powers imposing their economic and political systems on indigenous societies.

4. **Decolonization and Neoliberalism**: The mid-20th century saw the process of decolonization, as former colonies gained independence from colonial rule. However, rather than leading to genuine economic and political liberation, many newly independent countries became enmeshed in a global capitalist system dominated by Western powers. The rise of neoliberalism in the late 20th century further entrenched capitalist principles, emphasizing free markets, privatization, deregulation, and austerity measures.

5. **Globalization**: The advent of globalization in the late 20th and early 21st centuries accelerated the integration of economies worldwide, facilitated by advances in technology, communication, and transportation. This process further expanded the reach of capitalism, as multinational corporations gained unprecedented power and influence over global markets, often at the expense of local economies and communities.

6. **Financialization and Inequality**: Neoliberal policies promoted financialization, leading to the dominance of financial markets and speculative activities over productive investments. This contributed to growing income inequality within and between countries, as wealth became increasingly concentrated in the hands of a few global elites.

7. **Resistance and Alternatives**: Despite the spread of neoliberal capitalism, there has been significant resistance from social movements, labor unions, and grassroots organizations advocating for alternative economic models based on principles of social justice, environmental sustainability, and democratic control over resources. This has led to the emergence of diverse movements advocating for alternatives such as socialism, degrowth, and indigenous forms of economic organization.

The world's top scientists are acknowledging that **decolonization** must be central to the global response to climate change. The IPCC's sixth assessment report (April 2022) includes ***colonialism*** not only as a *driver of the climate crisis* but also as an ongoing issue that is exacerbating communities' vulnerability to it. The report suggests "an *investigation of the deep-seated ideologies and vested interests* that are creating goal conflicts and negatively impacting marginalized groups to begin with," and that "adaptation measures need to acknowledge and address the *underlying drivers* that make certain groups particularly vulnerable, such as *social disenfranchisement*, *unequal power dynamics* and *historical legacies of colonialism and exploitation.*"[183]

Solutions for decolonization must include the colonized, not just the colonizers.

What this means for the ESG proponents in the business world is the moral imperative to listen and heed the voices of the indigenous and native tribes – and to **find common ground**.

The longer we wait, the worse our chances of avoiding collapse.

Here's Peter Goldman[184]:

"American tax rates have been downgraded over decades to the point where billionaires like Stephen Schwarzman, another primary character in my book, is worth about 35 billion

---

[183] Chapter 18: Climate Resilient Development, *IPCC WGII Sixth Assessment*, April 2022 ReportPathways https://www.ipcc.ch/report/ar6/wg2/downloads/report/IPCC_AR6_WGII_FinalDraft_Chapter18.pdf

[184] "The Cosmic Lie" Lewis H. Lapham interviews Peter S. Goodman, *Lapham's Quarterly*, April 4, 2022 https://www.laphamsquarterly.org/roundtable/cosmic-lie

dollars. He's paying less of a share of his wealth in income to the federal government than the people scrubbing his toilets in his multiple residences that he owns the way most of us own socks."

Andrew Winston has a larger philosophical concern[185], as he says, with "investor-led language" around ESG. ESG — which stands for environmental, social, and governance — has become the dominant term in sustainability debates, but he highlights the problem:

Seeing all things through the lens of markets and the quest for shareholder maximization is largely how we got into this mess in the first place. We've put profits above literally all else, and it's leading to ecological collapse and vast inequality. Framing a company's commitments around battling climate disaster in investor terms turns it into an exercise of "Does this create shareholder value?" — which is not beside the point but skews the world dramatically. Sure, shareholders should do well, but only after a company has served a purpose for stakeholders and helped protect the world and resources we all rely on to survive and thrive.

Winston makes his point clear:

Investors aren't well positioned for this approach. Just as fossil fuel companies should not lead the planning of our energy future, it seems unwise to let finance lead the journey to a humane, more just, less greed-filled form of capitalism.

But wait, there's more.

John Perkins - the "Economic Hit Man" - tells us how the post-colonial economy works[186]:

Economic hit men (EHMs) are highly paid professionals who cheat countries around the globe out of trillions of dollars. They funnel money from the World Bank, the U.S. Agency for International Development (USAID), and other foreign "aid" organizations into the coffers of huge corporations and the pockets of a few

---

185 "What's Lost When We Talk 'ESG' and Not 'Sustainability'" by Andrew Winston *MIT Sloan Management Review*, May 5, 2022

186 *Confessions of an Economic Hit Man 3rd Edition* by John Perkins, *Berrett-Koehler Publishers*; 3rd edition February 28, 2023

wealthy families who control the planet's natural resources. Their tools include fraudulent financial reports, rigged elections, payoffs, extortion, sex, and murder. They play a game as old as empire, but one that has taken on new and terrifying dimensions during this time of globalization.

John Perkins' book gives us an insider view into the corrupt system that cheats and strong-arms countries around the globe out of trillions of dollars and ultimately causes staggering income inequality and ecological devastation.

Perkins also compiled a long list[187] of corruption cases (in chronological order) since the publication of his book.

Now, he claims, a new EHM wave is replacing the US across the world, led by China, the new dominant economic power, using its own version of the US-EHM blueprint in Latin America, Asia, Africa, the Middle East, and Europe.

If allowed to continue its rampage, the EHM strategy—whether executed by the United States or China—will destroy life as we know it. Perkins suggests we transform this corrupt system that places profits above all, into a Life Economy that restores the Earth.

DEBT TRAPS

We are almost out of time. Global South countries are going to feel the disproportional impact of climate collapse caused in large part by the Global North.

But the governments of the Global South are caught in a "debt trap" – as are most consumers across thc Global North.

A "debt trap" refers to a situation where an individual, business, or government becomes ensnared in a cycle of increasing debt that is difficult to escape. In the world of finance, a debt trap typically occurs when borrowers find themselves unable to repay their debts, leading to a

[187] https://www.wicked7.org/john-perkins-ehm-corruption-list/

cascade of negative consequences such as default, bankruptcy, and further borrowing to meet existing obligations. Several factors contribute to the creation and perpetuation of debt traps:

1. **High Interest Rates**: Borrowers may initially take on debt at high interest rates, making it challenging to repay the principal amount along with accumulated interest. This can result in a situation where a significant portion of the borrower's income or revenue goes towards servicing debt, leaving little room for other expenses or investments.

2. **Predatory Lending Practices**: Some lenders may engage in predatory lending practices, offering loans with unfavorable terms and conditions to borrowers who may not fully understand the implications. This can trap borrowers in a cycle of debt, as they struggle to keep up with payments while interest and fees continue to accrue.

3. **Overleveraging**: Borrowers may become overleveraged, meaning they have borrowed more money than they can realistically afford to repay. This can occur due to overestimation of future income or profits, reckless borrowing behavior, or unforeseen economic downturns that impact the borrower's ability to generate revenue.

4. **Lack of Financial Literacy**: Inadequate financial literacy can contribute to individuals or businesses making poor financial decisions, such as taking on excessive debt without fully understanding the risks involved. Without the knowledge or skills to manage debt effectively, borrowers may find themselves trapped in a cycle of indebtedness.

5. **Economic Shocks**: External factors such as economic recessions, natural disasters, or geopolitical instability can exacerbate debt traps by reducing income or revenue streams while increasing expenses. These shocks can make it even more challenging for borrowers to repay their debts, leading to defaults and further financial distress.

6. **Structural Factors**: In some cases, debt traps may be perpetuated by structural factors such as income inequality, lack of access to affordable credit, or systemic issues within the financial system. These factors can disproportionately affect marginalized communities or countries, trapping them in cycles of poverty and debt.

John Perkins warned us that the *"job to be done"* for the Economic Hit Man (EHM) is to trap the developing world in these "debt traps." The situation has evolved, he explains[188]:

Today, the EHM game is more complex, its corruption more pervasive, and its operations more fundamental to the world economy and politics. There are many more types of economic hit men, and the roles they play are far more diverse. The veneer of respectability remains a key factor; subterfuges range from money laundering and tax evasion carried out in well-appointed office suites to activities that amount to economic war crimes and result in the deaths of millions of people.

In the Global South, many countries have been caught in persistent debt traps for decades, often stemming from a combination of factors:

- **Historical Exploitation and Colonialism:** Former colonial powers extracted resources and exploited labor in colonized territories, leaving many countries with weakened economies and limited development opportunities. The legacy of colonialism continues to shape economic inequalities and vulnerabilities in the Global South.

- **Unequal Terms of Trade:** Global trade structures often favor the Global North, with prices for commodities such as raw materials and agricultural products set by powerful multinational corporations. This results in terms of trade that are unfavorable for many countries in the Global South, leading to chronic trade deficits and reliance on external borrowing to finance imports.

- **Structural Adjustment Programs:** In the late 20th century, international financial institutions such as the International Monetary Fund (IMF) and World Bank imposed structural adjustment programs (SAPs) on many countries in the Global South as conditions for receiving loans. These programs often required austerity measures, privatization of public assets, and deregulation, exacerbating poverty and inequality while increasing debt burdens.

---

[188] *A GAME AS OLD AS EMPIRE: The Secret World of Economic Hit Men and the Web of Global Corruption*, editor Steven Hiatt, Berrett-Koehler Publishers, Inc.2007

- **Debt Accumulation and Debt Servicing:** Despite efforts to reduce debt burdens through initiatives such as debt relief programs, many countries in the Global South continue to accumulate debt at unsustainable levels. Debt servicing obligations, including interest payments and principal repayments, divert scarce resources away from essential social services such as healthcare, education, and infrastructure development.

In contrast, the Global North generally enjoys greater access to capital markets, lower borrowing costs, and more favorable terms of trade. However, debt traps can still affect certain segments of society, particularly *marginalized communities* and **vulnerable populations**:

- **Household Debt:** In many affluent countries, households may become trapped in debt cycles due to factors such as stagnant wages, rising living costs, and predatory lending practices. High levels of consumer debt, including mortgages, student loans, and credit card debt, can constrain household finances and limit opportunities for economic mobility.

- **Financialization and Speculation:** The proliferation of financial instruments and speculative activities in the Global North can contribute to systemic risks and debt crises. Excessive risk-taking by financial institutions, coupled with inadequate regulatory oversight, can lead to financial instability and taxpayer-funded bailouts, perpetuating cycles of debt and inequality.

- **Fiscal Policy and Austerity:** Austerity measures imposed by governments in response to economic downturns can exacerbate debt burdens and deepen socioeconomic inequalities. Cuts to public spending on social welfare programs, healthcare, and education can disproportionately affect marginalized communities, exacerbating poverty and social unrest.

The debt relationship between the Global North and South perpetuates patterns of dependency and neo-colonialism, as indebted countries remain vulnerable to external economic shocks and policy conditions imposed by creditors. This can undermine national sovereignty and perpetuate cycles of poverty and underdevelopment in the Global South. Civil society organizations, grassroots movements, and advocacy groups have called for **debt**

justice and fairer terms of engagement in the debt relationship between the Global North and South. This includes calls for debt cancellation, transparent and accountable lending practices, and policies that prioritize human development and social justice over debt repayment.

And on a related matter, despite repeated acknowledgments by the world's affluent nations that assisting impoverished countries in managing the repercussions of climate change is imperative, their actions have fallen short of their commitments. They have only managed to secure a small fraction of the funds pledged for this purpose.

FORTUNE

Nobel laureate Esther Duflo proposes taxing 3,000 billionaires to protect the world's poorest from climate change—and most Americans likely agree with the plan

Nobel laureate **Esther Duflo** offers a solution[189] to this dilemma: *impose a tax on 3,000 of the wealthiest individuals globally to guarantee the survival of the most vulnerable amidst the challenges of a climate-altered future.*

CLIMATEGPT

According to **ClimateGPT**, the primary drivers of Power and Corruption include:

- **Unequal distribution of wealth and resources:** When a small group of individuals or organizations hold a disproportionate amount of wealth and resources, it can create an imbalance of power and lead to corruption.

[189] *Nobel laureate Esther Duflo proposes taxing 3,000 billionaires to protect the world's poorest from climate change–and most Americans likely agree with the plan* by Sunny Nagpaul, *Fortune* Apr 20, 2024 https://finance.yahoo.com/news/nobel-laureate-esther-duflo-proposes-121900166.html

- **Political and economic systems that favor the powerful:** Systems that are designed to favor the powerful and wealthy can create an environment where corruption is more likely to occur. For example, if political leaders are elected through a system of patronage or if economic systems are designed to favor large corporations, it can create an environment where corruption is more likely to occur.
- **Lack of transparency and accountability:** When decision-making processes are not transparent or when there are no mechanisms in place to hold individuals and organizations accountable for their actions, it can create an environment where corruption is more likely to occur.
- **Cultural norms and values:** Cultural norms and values that promote greed, selfishness, and a lack of empathy can contribute to a culture of corruption.
- **Historical legacies of colonization and oppression:** Historical legacies of colonization and oppression can create ongoing power imbalances and contribute to a culture of corruption.
- **Globalization:** As the world becomes more interconnected, it can create opportunities for corruption to occur across borders and jurisdictions.
- **Technological advancements:** Technological advancements can create new opportunities for corruption, such as the use of technology to facilitate money laundering or other forms of corruption.
- **Lack of education and civic engagement:** When citizens are not educated or engaged in the political process, it can create an environment where corruption is more likely to occur.
- **Flawed institutions:** Weak institutions, such as a judiciary that is not independent or a media that is not free, can contribute to a culture of corruption.
- **External factors:** External factors, such as the influence of foreign powers or the actions of international organizations, can also contribute to a culture of corruption. It's important to note that these are not the only factors that can contribute to power and corruption, and that the specific factors will vary depending on the context and location.

Addressing the root causes of power and corruption requires a comprehensive approach that takes into account the complex interplay of these factors and the specific context in which they occur. Further details on each one of these root causes are listed in the appendix: *Answers from AI,* at the end of this book.

CASCADING EFFECTS

The cascading effects of Power and Corruption on our lives can be profound and far-reaching, affecting various aspects of social, economic, and political life. Real-life consequences include:

- **Erosion of Trust**: Corruption undermines public trust in government institutions, political leaders, and the rule of law. When citizens perceive that those in positions of power are corrupt or self-serving, they may become disillusioned with the democratic process and lose faith in the fairness and integrity of governance systems.

- **Inequality and Injustice**: Corruption exacerbates social and economic inequality by diverting resources away from public goods and services that benefit the broader population. Instead, corrupt practices often concentrate wealth and privilege in the hands of a few, perpetuating disparities in access to education, healthcare, infrastructure, and economic opportunities.

- **Impaired Development**: Corruption impedes economic development and growth by distorting market mechanisms, deterring investment, and undermining business confidence. It stifles innovation, entrepreneurship, and productivity, hindering efforts to create sustainable and inclusive economies that benefit all members of society.

- **Human Rights Violations**: Corruption can lead to human rights abuses, as corrupt officials may engage in arbitrary or discriminatory practices, suppress dissent, and undermine the rule of law to protect their own interests. Vulnerable populations, such as minorities, women, and marginalized communities, are often disproportionately affected by corruption and its associated abuses of power.

- **Social Cohesion**: Corruption erodes social cohesion and undermines social norms of fairness, reciprocity, and mutual trust. When corruption is pervasive, individuals may feel compelled to engage in corrupt behavior themselves to navigate bureaucratic obstacles, secure access to essential services, or seek preferential treatment, perpetuating a cycle of corruption and moral decay. The Mafia, we must remember, was born out of this frustration. Surveys reveal that the poorest people are twice as likely to pay a bribe – and more likely to be victims of corrupt behavior by bureaucrats – than the richest.

- **Environmental Degradation**: Corruption contributes to environmental degradation by enabling illegal logging, poaching, pollution, and other environmentally harmful activities. Corrupt officials may collude with businesses to circumvent environmental regulations, exploit natural resources for personal gain, and disregard the long-term ecological consequences of their actions.

- **Political Instability**: Corruption undermines political stability and fosters public discontent, as citizens become increasingly disillusioned with corrupt and unaccountable leadership. Widespread corruption can fuel social unrest, political protests, and even civil unrest, destabilizing governments and undermining democratic governance structures. Hello, Fascism. Bye-bye, Democracy.

We have to be vigilant. Corruption is not confined to national borders but has global implications, such as facilitating transnational crime, money laundering, and illicit financial flows. Corrupt practices in one country can have spillover effects on neighboring countries and the broader international community, undermining efforts to combat poverty, promote peace, and achieve sustainable development goals.

"The computer is a moron."
– Peter Drucker

5 WORK, MEDIA, AND TECHNOLOGY

The world of work will never be the same. We've seen the taming of fire, the printing press, the Internet, and now AI. The **Great Replacement** is *not* going to be the immigrant who steals your job, instead it will be AI and mobile-AI i.e., **robots**.

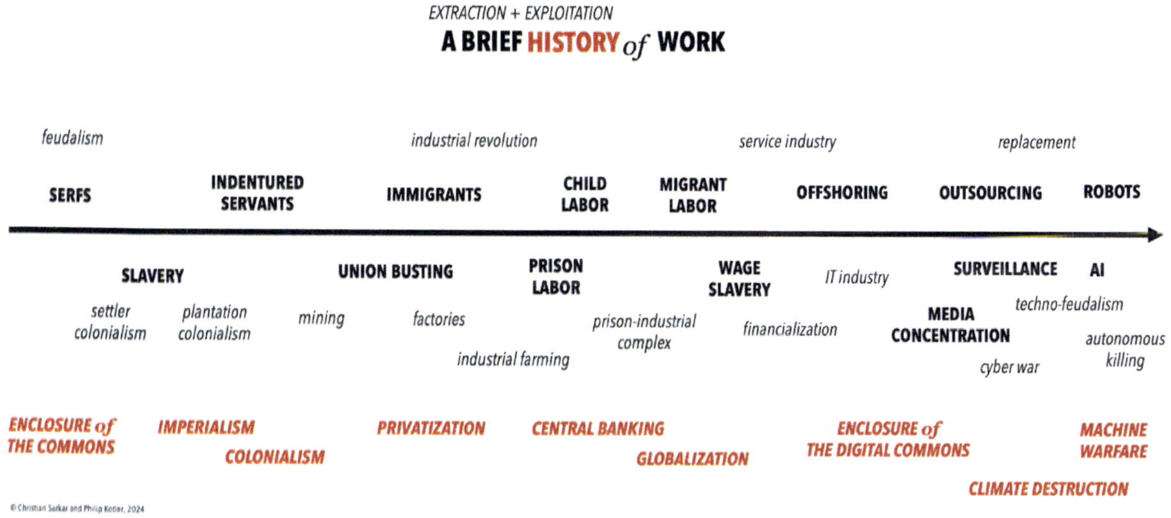

Who will AI create value for exactly?

The billionaires?

The state?

Chances are high that it won't be for the Common Good. The tech-bros are the robber barons of our digital gilded age. We have been captured by what Yanis Varoufakis labels **techno-feudalism**[190]. He describes the phenomenon as follows:

...it is not hard to see that capital's mutation into what I call cloud capital has demolished capitalism's two pillars: markets and profits. Of course, markets and profits remain ubiquitous – indeed, markets and profits were ubiquitous under feudalism too – they just aren't running the show any more. What has happened over the last two decades is that profit and markets have been evicted from the epicentre of our economic and social system, pushed out to its margins, and replaced. With what?

Markets, the medium of capitalism, have been replaced by digital trading platforms which look like, but are not, markets, and are better understood as fiefdoms. And profit, the engine of capitalism, has been replaced with its feudal predecessor: ***rent.*** *Specifically, it is a form of rent that must be paid for access to those platforms and to the cloud more broadly. I call it cloud rent.*

As a result, real power today resides not with the owners of traditional capital, such as machinery, buildings, railway and phone networks, industrial robots. They continue to extract profits from workers, from waged labour, but they are not in charge as they once were. As we shall see, they have become vassals in relation to a new class of feudal overlord, the owners of cloud capital. As for the rest of us, we have returned to our former status as serfs, contributing to the wealth and power of the new ruling class with our unpaid labour – in addition to the waged labour we perform, when we get the chance.

[190] *Technofeudalism: What Killed Capitalism* by Yanis Varoufakis *Melville House*, February 13, 2024

The scary thing, explains Varoufakis, is that the only political force that can do anything to keep the new lords of tech in check and thus *the hope of democracy alive is the Chinese Communist Party*!!

Cory Doctorow sums up *Technofeudalism:* ""What if capitalism died and no one noticed — not even the capitalists? Digital platforms usurped capitalism and installed something far worse. This (book) is an urgent demand to seize the means of computation."

But let's go back to the start. Where and when did work begin?

In his book - *The War Against the Commons: Dispossession and Resistance in the Making of Capitalism* – **Ian Angus** argues[191] that throughout the vast majority of human history, communities predominantly relied on **self-provisioning** methods for sustenance and livelihoods. Collaboratively, individuals and their neighbors engaged in agricultural practices, food preparation, and crafting of essential items, including homes, tools, and clothing. Following the advent of agriculture, communal living and collective land management became commonplace, with production predominantly serving local consumption needs.

In contemporary society, however, he adds, a significant shift has occurred whereby the vast majority of individuals are compelled to engage in **wage labor** for livelihoods. Employment has become central to our existence, profoundly shaping our daily lives and societal roles. The ownership of productive resources is predominantly concentrated within a small fraction of individuals and corporate entities, necessitating that the majority of us exchange our labor for sustenance. Consequently, our ability to procure basic necessities, such as food, is contingent upon our capacity to sell our labor to these entities.

Angus recounts a pivotal aspect in the ascent of capitalism— the **coerced detachment** of laborers from their means of sustenance, notably the **land**, accomplished through theft, aggression, deceit, and other reprehensible means. Perpetrators resorted to inducing **hunger**

---

[191] *The War Against the Commons: Dispossession and Resistance in the Making of* Capitalism by Ian Angus, *Monthly Review Press*, 2023

to compel the impoverished to toil in their fields, mines, and factories, while those affected retaliated vehemently using all available means of resistance.

He makes a critical point: Capitalism is the *new kid on the block*, and it doesn't play nice.

The evolution of capitalism, characterized by the division between owners and workers, has become deeply ingrained in societal norms, often perceived as a natural and inevitable aspect of human existence. Even staunch critics of injustice and inequality tend to accept this division without question, attributing it to the innate characteristics of human nature. However, such arguments overlook the relatively recent emergence of capitalism within the broader scope of human history. *While human beings have existed for approximately 300,000 years, capitalism as we recognize it today emerged only a few hundred years ago, making it a relatively recent phenomenon.*

Comparatively, the transition to capitalism, particularly the widespread adoption of wage labor, began to take shape in England during the 1400s. This transition involved **the dismantling of communal land use practices and the erosion of common rights** that had historically provided access to essential resources for subsistence.

"England is not a free people, till the poor that have no land, have a free allowance to dig and labour the commons..."
Gerrard Winstanley, 1649

Common rights, such as hunting, fishing, gathering, and grazing, were systematically eliminated, replaced by the exclusive property rights of landowners. This process of enclosure, characterized by the privatization of formerly shared lands and the establishment of private property boundaries, forcibly displaced commoners from their means of subsistence. Consequently, vast numbers of individuals were thrust into a newly emerging labor market as unprotected and rights-deprived proletarians, entirely dependent on selling their labor to property owners for survival.

The expropriation of agricultural producers from the land they once cultivated marked a fundamental shift in social and economic relations, permanently separating working people from the means of production. Former agrarian communities, whose livelihoods had long been tied to the land, were compelled to adapt to the new reality of wage labor, thereby solidifying the enduring divide between labor and capital within the emerging capitalist system.

Angus' book has three sections:

1. **Expulsion and resistance**, spanning from 1450 to 1660, he delves into the initial surge of enclosures and dispossessions during the nascent stages of capitalism, culminating in the English Revolution between 1640 and 1660. This period is characterized by the "systematic theft of common property," sparking widespread resistance as a landless working class emerged. Concurrently, state intervention intensified to enforce work discipline through coercive measures.

2. **Expansion and Consolidation**, spanning from 1660 to 1860, where he teaches us about the second wave of enclosure, bolstered by the exploitation of **forced labor** from African slaves and **colonial exploitation** in India. Landowners and merchants leveraged state power to further expropriate commoners, impeding their ability to self-sustain. This period also witnessed the brutal clearances in Scotland, uprooting farmers and cottagers from both the Lowlands and Highlands.

3. **Consequences** examines the enduring repercussions of centuries of dispossession. Angus challenges the assertion that enclosure fostered increased production and alleviated hunger, in fact, he shows how employers deliberately perpetuated hunger to maintain a cheap labor force. Angus reexamines the fusion of urban and rural spaces as advocated in the revolutionary program of Marx and Engels. Finally, he underscores the continued significance of dispossession and resistance in contemporary contexts.

We see now that **there may not be a way back.**

With technology racing ahead of our educational systems, we are falling further and further behind in our quest to keep ahead or even abreast with technology.

And AI threatens to alter the work place forever. A Goldman-Sachs report[192] tells us that that a quarter of current work tasks could be automated by AI in the US and EU.

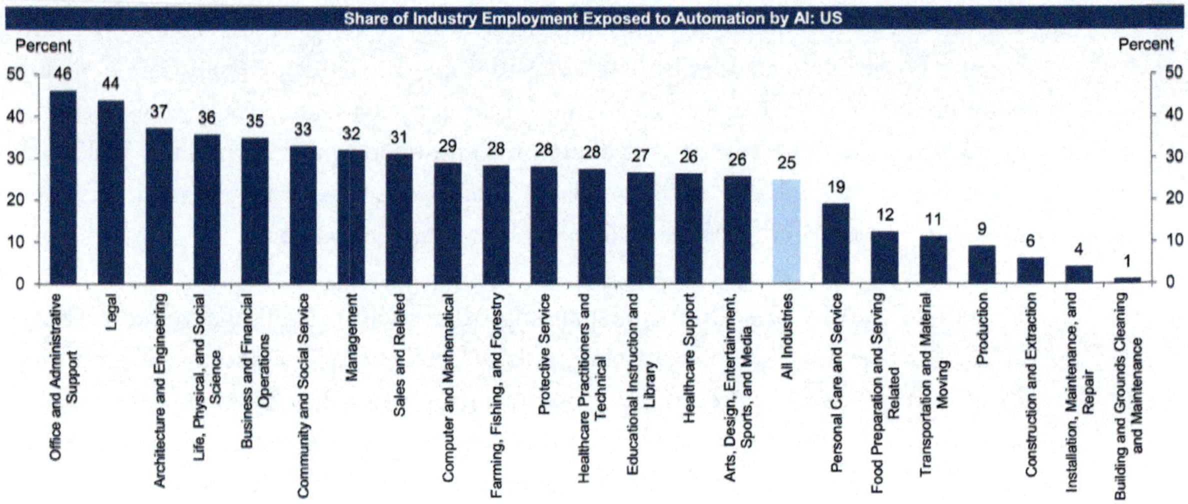

The following categories of work could be automated –

[192] *The Potentially Large Effects of Artificial Intelligence on Economic Growth (Briggs/Kodnani)* Goldman Sachs Economics Research, March 26, 2023

AI-Exposed Work Activity	Examples of Automation	Examples of Tasks by Difficulty (O*NET 1-7 Scale)
Getting Information	Web scrape data from online sources and consolidate into a clean dataset; conduct and summarize a review of prior research based on a textual query and answer follow-up questions	2: Follow a standard blueprint 4: Review a budget 6: Study international tax laws
Monitoring Processes, Materials, or Surroundings	Monitor sensor input and system logs for manufacturing and utilities system anomalies; monitor internet activity for changes in sentiment or trending themes	2: Check to see if baking bread is done 4: Test electrical circuits 6: Check the status of a patient in critical medical care
Identifying Objects, Actions, and Events	Identify objects, music, terminology, and people when provided with textual/visual/auditory input; provide context on identified subject	2: Test an automobile transmission 4: Judge the suitability of food products for an event 6: Determine the reaction of a virus to a new drug
Estimating the Quantifiable Characteristics of Products, Events, or Information	Produce market size estimates based on assumptions grounded in existing research; estimate parameters using statistical modeling on input data and select optimal model	2: Estimate the size of household furniture to be shipped 4: Estimate transportation delays from inclement weather 6: Estimate the size of resource deposits beneath the world's oceans
Processing Information	Process raw data from documents, sensors, and humans into clean datafiles that are easily subscriptable for analysis; provide summaries of data relevant to user needs	2: Calculate the costs for shipping packages 4: Calculate the adjustments for insurance claims 6: Compile data for a complex scientific report
Evaluating Information to Determine Compliance with Standards	Review documents and proposed actions for compliance with legal, regulatory, and corporate standards; provide arguments and scenarios for and against compliance in unclear cases	1: Review forms for completeness 4: Evaluate a complicated insurance claim for policy compliance 6: Make a ruling in court on a complicated motion
Analyzing Data or Information	Perform statistical analysis of and identify trends within large datasets; forecast future data based on optimal combination of variables and model with best out-of-sample predictive power	1: Skim a short article to gather the main point 4: Determine the interest cost to finance a new building 6: Analyze the cost of medical care services for all US hospitals
Updating and Using Relevant Knowledge	Draft and update reports in corporate knowledge base; update statistical and financial models based on new data which challenges prior scenarios/assumptions	2: Track price changes in a small retail store 4: Track changes in maintenance procedures for repairing SUVs 6: Learn information about a complex and rapidly-changing technology
Scheduling Work and Activities	Automatically schedule meetings and work activities using availabilities and emails; assign tasks and estimate time to completion based on past experience	2: Make appointments for patients using a predetermined schedule 4: Prepare the work schedule for salesclerks in a large retail store 6: Schedule a complex conference program with parallel sessions
Organizing, Planning, and Prioritizing Work	Delegate and prioritize tasks based on time to completion and importance; identify gaps or bottlenecks in work plans and target resources or managerial attention	2: Organize a work schedule that is repetitive and easy to plan 4: Plan and adjust a to-do list according to changing demands 6: Prioritize and plan multiple tasks several months ahead
Documenting/Recording Information	Transcribe and summarize the content of in-person meetings; write system reports based on sensor and human data input	2: Record the weight of a patient during a routine health exam 4: Document the results of a crime scene investigation 6: Maintain information about satellite use for industry communications
Interpreting the Meaning of Information for Others	Explain the structure and function of code or statistical results in easy-to-understand language; translate code and text between languages; summarize and contextualize text with technical jargon	1: Interpret a blood pressure reading 4: Interpret how foreign tax laws apply to U.S. exports 6: Interpret a complex experiment in physics for general audiences
Performing Administrative Activities	Draft automated email responses; schedule and manage meetings and work calendars; file and organize paperwork; book reservations	2: Complete routine paperwork 4: Complete tax forms for a small business 6: Serve as the benefits director for a large computer sales firm

Source: O*NET, Goldman Sachs Global Investment Research

The report says that 300 million jobs could disappear, adding that the **good *news*** is that "worker displacement from automation has historically been offset by creation of new jobs, and the emergence of new occupations following technological innovations accounts for the vast majority of long-run employment growth."

We are skeptical of this "good news."

Why? Because AI is not a linear animal. It will grow and replace anything it that can be replaced, *even the CEO.*

A **survey**[193] of 600 CEO-level executives in the UK, US, and Netherlands in April 2024 revealed:

- AI amplifies the dilemma that CEOs face, with one third (34%) having **banned AI tools** such as ChatGPT from their organization, whilst 45% confess to secretly using AI tools such as ChatGPT to do their jobs, *passing off the work as their own.*

- **43%** said they believe **AI could replace the job of the CEO**, underlining the widespread fears that the technology could destroy traditional job roles.

- nearly two-thirds (64%) of CEOs feel they are an *analog CEO in a digital age*, perhaps suggesting widespread imposter syndrome sweeping boardrooms around the globe.

Furthermore, we know that the new jobs created by AI will require a high level of educational attainment in technology, and the lower-skilled folks being replaced will not be able to, for the most part, slot into these "new" AI jobs. Unemployment is set to skyrocket, despite the "good news."

[193] *The CEO Digital Divide* – a survey by *AND Digital* April 2024
NOTE: There were 500 UK respondents, 50 in the US and 50 in the Netherlands.

Displaced by AI

- Statistical, finance, and insurance clerks
- Legislators and officials
- Home appliance installers and repairers
- Accounting, bookkeeping, and payroll clerks
- Material-recording and stockkeeping clerks
- Administrative and executive secretaries
- Data entry clerks
- Cashiers and ticket clerks
- Postal service clerks
- Bank tellers and related clerks

New AI-related jobs

- AI and machine-learning specialists
- Sustainability specialists
- Business intelligence analysts
- Information security analysts
- Fintech engineers
- Data analysts and scientists
- Robotics engineers
- Big data specialists
- Agricultural equipment operators
- Digital transformation specialists

Future of Jobs Report 2023, World Economic Forum May 2023

And because AI learns at an exponential rate, human intelligence will soon be dwarfed. We could well become inconsequential, particularly as AI-robots become autonomous. If we combine the philosophy of techno-feudalism and AI-robots, then we humans have **zero-value** in the future. Everything we imagine will be done far better by machine intelligence. We will be ants – an amusement for our robot masters.

DEEPFAKES DESTABILIZE DEMOCRACY

Human beings have not taken AI and robots seriously enough yet – partly because of our ignorance, and partly because our politicians are still living in the colonial/capitalist paradigm of extraction and exploitation. The anti-union mindset of our politicians does not bode well for humans in the robot workplace.

AI could also be used to take over elections and undermine democracy.

Archon Fung and **Lawrence Lessig** explain[194] that "AI could use automation to dramatically increase the scale and potentially the effectiveness of behavior manipulation and microtargeting techniques[195] that political campaigns have used since the early 2000s." And,

---

[194] "How AI could take over elections – and undermine democracy" by Archon Fung, Lawrence Lessig, *FIXCapitalism*, June 4, 2023 https://fixcapitalism.com/how-ai-could-take-over-elections-and-undermine-democracy/

[195] *The Victory Lab: The Secret Science of Winning Campaigns* by Sasha Issenberg *Crown Publishers* 2012

just as advertisers use social media history[196] to target you with specific commercial and political ads, AI "would pay attention to you – and hundreds of millions of other voters – individually."

CNN reports that a *fake* version of President Joe Biden's voice[197] had been used in automatically generated robocalls to discourage Democrats from taking part in the New Hampshire's Democratic primary. ***The Guardian*** reports that an anti-**deepfake** bill is working its way through Georgia state legislature seeks to stop use of AI tech in politics – but some far-right activists are opposed.[198]

HERE COME THE KILLER ROBOTS

But what about robots that are trained to kill?

Human Rights Watch issued a report[199] back in 2012 which said that governments should pre-emptively ban fully autonomous weapons because of the danger they pose to civilians in armed conflict. These future weapons, sometimes called "killer robots," would be able to choose and fire on targets without human intervention. The exact level of autonomy can vary greatly. The report divided robotic weapons, which are unmanned, into three categories based on the amount of human involvement in their actions:

1. Human-in-the-Loop Weapons: Robots that can select targets and deliver force only with a human command;

---

[196] Facebook's political ad problem, explained by an expert by Peter Kafka, Vox, December 10, 2019 https://www.vox.com/recode/2019/12/10/20996869/facebook-political-ads-targeting-alex-stamos-interview-open-sourced

[197] "Fake Joe Biden robocall urges New Hampshire voters not to vote in Tuesday's Democratic primary" Em Steck and Andrew Kaczynski, *CNN* January 22, 2024 https://edition.cnn.com/2024/01/22/politics/fake-joe-biden-robocall/index.html

[198] "Georgia lawmakers are using an AI deepfake video to try to ban political deepfakes" by George Chidi March 20, 2024 https://www.theguardian.com/us-news/2024/mar/20/georgia-ai-ban-political-campaigns-deepfakes

[199] *Losing Humanity: The Case against Killer* Robots Human Rights Watch November 19, 2012 https://www.hrw.org/report/2012/11/19/losing-humanity/case-against-killer-robots

2. Human-on-the-Loop Weapons: Robots that can select targets and deliver force under the oversight of a human operator who can override the robots' actions; and
3. Human-out-of-the-Loop Weapons: Robots that are capable of selecting targets and delivering force without any human input or interaction.

Here's more from the report:

Fully autonomous weapons could not meet the requirements of international humanitarian law, Human Rights Watch and the Harvard clinic said. They would be unable to distinguish adequately between soldiers and civilians on the battlefield or apply the human judgment necessary to evaluate the proportionality of an attack – whether civilian harm outweighs military advantage.

These robots would also undermine non-legal checks on the killing of civilians. Fully autonomous weapons could not show human compassion for their victims, and autocrats could abuse them by directing them against their own people. While replacing human troops with machines could save military lives, it could also make going to war easier, which would shift the burden of armed conflict onto civilians.

Finally, the use of fully autonomous weapons would create an accountability gap. Trying to hold the commander, programmer, or manufacturer legally responsible for a robot's actions presents significant challenges. The lack of accountability would undercut the ability to deter violations of international law and to provide victims meaningful retributive justice.

Remember, that was in 2012. In 2015, another report[200] discussed the problem of accountability:

Existing mechanisms for legal accountability are ill suited and inadequate to address the unlawful harms fully autonomous weapons might cause. These weapons have the potential to commit criminal acts—unlawful acts that would constitute a crime if done with intent—for which no one could be held responsible.

---

[200] *Mind the Gap: The Lack of Accountability for Killer Robots* Human Rights Watch April 9, 2015 https://www.hrw.org/report/2015/04/09/mind-gap/lack-accountability-killer-robots

Elon Musk, for all his alleged shortcomings, called for an outright ban[201] on killer robots in 2017 along with a host of like-minded signatories. This follows another letter from scientists back in 2015.[202]

But no one is listening to the scientists.

Here are nine problems with killer robots according to **Stop Killer Robots**[203], a campaign led by a coalition of over 250 organizations:

1. Digital Dehumanization

Technology should empower all members of society, not reduce us – to stereotypes, labels, objects. Used against people, the technologies that enable autonomous weapons will automatically profile, pattern match and process human beings as data. The truth is, machines cannot recognise people as 'people'. So machines deciding whether or not to subject us to attack is the ultimate form of digital dehumanization.

If we allow this dehumanization, we will struggle to protect ourselves from machine decision-making in other areas of our lives. We need to prohibit autonomous weapons systems that would be used against people, to prevent this slide to digital dehumanization.

2. Algorithmic biases

Allowing autonomous systems that target people would mean allowing systems to reinforce or exacerbate existing structures of inequality. The prejudices in our society live in our data-sets, our categories, our labels and our algorithms. Killing people based on pre-programmed labels and identities will always pull us towards reinforcing prejudices or structures of oppression. Problematic new technologies are also often tested and used on marginalized

---

[201] An Open Letter to the United Nations Convention on Certain Conventional Weapons https://futureoflife.org/open-letter/autonomous-weapons-open-letter-2017/

[202] "Musk, Wozniak and Hawking urge ban on warfare AI and autonomous weapons" by Samuel Gibbs, The Guardian July 27, 2015. https://www.theguardian.com/technology/2015/jul/27/musk-wozniak-hawking-ban-ai-autonomous-weapons

[203] https://www.stopkillerrobots.org

communities first. We should be challenging structures of inequality, not embedding them into weapons.

3. Loss of meaningful human control

Losing meaningful human control means that the users of weapons are no longer fully engaged with the consequences of their actions. And this means less space for 'humanity'. Whether on the battlefield or at a protest, machines cannot make complex ethical choices, they cannot comprehend the value of human life. Machines don't understand context or consequences: understanding is a human capability – and without that understanding we lose moral responsibility and we undermine existing legal rules.

Ensuring meaningful human control means understanding the technologies we use, understanding where we are using them, and being fully engaged with the consequences of our actions.

4. Lack of human judgement and understanding

People cannot make meaningful judgements if they don't understand the systems they are using or the contexts they are using them in.

Autonomous systems are becoming more complex. Forms of artificial intelligence and machine learning can present barriers to understanding and predictability. Technologies that change their own behavior or adapt their own programming independently can't be used with real control. Other technologies can present a 'black box', where it is not possible to know why or how decisions are made. This can produce systems that are very effective at completing certain tasks – but their use isn't appropriate where any unexpected decision can mean life or death. We need to ensure that systems are sufficiently explainable – and to prohibit systems that cannot be used with meaningful human control.

Even simple autonomous systems present challenges. Under the law, military commanders must be able to judge the necessity and proportionality of an attack and to distinguish between civilians and legitimate military targets. This means not just understanding a weapon system, but also understanding the context in which it might be used. Over a wider area, or a longer period of time, 'context' becomes more complex – the situation becomes more and more unpredictable. New legal rules are needed to limit that unpredictability and to ensure meaningful human control.

5. Lack of accountability

People, not machines, must be held accountable. But if people are not making meaningful decisions, then they cannot properly be considered responsible for the consequences of their actions. It would be unjust to make a person liable for the actions of an autonomous weapon system operating beyond their effective control. If we are committed to accountability, then we need rules that ensure that the right people are taking responsibility in the use of force.

6. Inability to explain what happened or why

These problems of control and accountability risk leaving any people that are harmed with nowhere to turn. If we can't explain how outcomes occurred, then we are leaving victims in the dark – with no explanation and no accountability. People who lose family members and loved ones in conflict rarely get justice for their losses. We should be working to correct that – not programming this disregard through systems that we cannot explain and or control.

7. Lowering the threshold to war

The challenges posed by existing methods of remote war would also be amplified through increased autonomy, with humans becoming further detached from the use of force. Existing armed drones have been used by states to apply lethal force in situations where they wouldn't have before – bringing the fear and horror of conflict to places away from active battlefields.

It is understandable that all states want to reduce the risks of conflict to their own troops. But while replacing people with machines may make military action more politically acceptable at 'home', it can make conflict easier to enter into. It also shifts the burden of harm still further onto civilian populations.

8. A destabilizing arms race

Large military powers are using political tensions and international power rivalries as the justification for investing in technologies that reduce human control. We have heard it argued from both sides: We need more autonomy in case our adversaries have more autonomy'. Weapons manufacturers are eager to encourage that rhetoric in order to boost profits. These dynamics may benefit some, but they are bad for the rest of us – wasting money on unnecessary military expenditures, building tensions and increasing the risk of conflict (whether deliberate or from an accidental autonomous response). We need more humanity in our international relations, not more dehumanization.

9. Our relationship with technology

Technology can and should be developed to promote peace, justice, human rights and equality. We all need to take responsibility for the development and use of technology, and for the role it plays in our lives. Deciding to draw a line against machines that make decisions to kill people – drawing a line against technologies that apply force without real human control – provides a fundamental test for our relationship with AI and new technologies across all areas of society. If we don't draw these lines now it will only get more difficult as states and commercial companies become more and more invested in development. Rejecting digital dehumanization and ensuring meaningful human control over the use of force are key steps to building a more empowering relationship with technology for all people now and in the future.

Now, we learn that the **Israeli army marked tens of thousands of Gazans as suspects for assassination**, using an **AI targeting system**[204] named "Lavender" with "little human oversight and a permissive policy" for human targets:

During the early stages of the war, the army gave sweeping approval for officers to adopt Lavender's kill lists, with no requirement to thoroughly check why the machine made those choices or to examine the raw intelligence data on which they were based. One source stated that human personnel often served only as a "rubber stamp" for the machine's decisions, adding that, normally, they would personally devote only about "20 seconds" to each target before authorizing a bombing — just to make sure the Lavender-marked target is male. This was despite knowing that the system makes what are regarded as "errors" in approximately 10 percent

[204] "'Lavender': The AI machine directing Israel's bombing spree in Gaza" by Yuval Abraham +972 April 3, 2024 https://www.972mag.com/lavender-ai-israeli-army-gaza

of cases, and is known to occasionally mark individuals who have merely a loose connection to militant groups, or no connection at all.

Lavender, alongside another AI system named "The Gospel," has garnered attention due to information disclosed in a prior investigation conducted by +972 and Local Call in November 2023, as well as in publications by the Israeli military. A notable distinction between these two systems lies in their target definition: while The Gospel identifies *buildings* and *structures* allegedly used by militants, Lavender focuses on *individuals*, effectively placing them on a kill list.

AI-powered genocide is not science fiction.

A little-discussed detail is that *Israel is killing people based on being in the same Whatsapp group as a suspected militant*, reveals **Paul Biggar**, an Irish software engineer.[205]

DO YOU HAVE AN AI POLICY?

Why doesn't your country have an AI policy which is open and transparent? This question is critical if we are to protect individuals from potential harms, risks, and ethical dilemmas associated with AI and robotic technologies, as well as ensuring that we humans retain control over decisions and actions that affect their lives.

Here are some areas of concern:

1. **Protection from AI Bias and Discrimination**: Protection from AI bias and discrimination involves safeguarding individuals from unfair or discriminatory treatment resulting from biased algorithms, data sets, or automated decision-making systems. It encompasses efforts to detect, mitigate, and prevent bias in AI systems, as well as promote fairness, transparency, and accountability in algorithmic decision-making processes to ensure that AI technologies do not

[205] "Meta and Lavender" by Paul Biggar April 16, 2024 https://blog.paulbiggar.com/meta-and-lavender/

perpetuate or exacerbate existing inequalities or discrimination based on factors such as race, gender, ethnicity, or socioeconomic status.

2. **Privacy and Data Protection in AI Systems**: Privacy and data protection in AI systems means protecting individuals' personal information and data privacy rights in the context of AI-powered technologies and applications. It includes efforts to establish privacy-preserving AI algorithms, data anonymization techniques, and data protection measures to minimize the collection, storage, and use of personal data in AI systems, as well as ensure compliance with privacy laws, regulations, and ethical standards to safeguard individuals' privacy rights and prevent unauthorized access or misuse of their data by AI systems or developers.

3. **Ethical Use of AI in Decision-Making**: Ethical use of AI in decision-making involves ensuring that AI systems are designed, deployed, and used in ways that respect human autonomy, dignity, and rights, as well as adhere to ethical principles and values. Funding must be provided to national and international efforts to develop ethical guidelines, principles, and frameworks for AI design and deployment, as well as promote transparency, accountability, and oversight mechanisms to ensure that AI systems are used responsibly and ethically in decision-making processes that affect individuals' lives, such as healthcare, criminal justice, employment, and finance.

4. **Safety and Security in AI and Robotics**: Safety and security in AI and robotics involve protecting individuals from physical harm, injury, or damage caused by malfunctioning or malicious AI systems and robots. It encompasses efforts to establish safety standards, regulations, and certification processes for AI and robotic technologies, as well as promote research and development of safe and secure AI systems and robotic hardware to prevent accidents, errors, or intentional harm to humans or property.

5. **Human Control and Oversight of AI Systems**: Human control and oversight of AI systems involve ensuring that humans retain ultimate control and responsibility over decisions and actions made by AI systems, as well as have the ability to intervene, correct, or override AI-generated outcomes when necessary. This includes all projects to design AI systems with human-centered interfaces, feedback mechanisms, and decision support tools that enable

human operators to understand, monitor, and control AI behavior, as well as establish legal and regulatory frameworks to clarify liability, accountability, and responsibility for AI-related decisions and actions.

6. **Public Awareness and Education about AI Risks and Impacts**: Public awareness and education about AI risks and impacts involve informing and empowering individuals to understand the potential risks, benefits, and ethical implications of AI and robotic technologies, as well as participate in discussions, debates, and policy-making processes related to AI governance and regulation. We must promote AI literacy, awareness campaigns, and public engagement initiatives that foster informed dialogue, critical thinking, and responsible citizenship in the digital age, as well as encourage collaboration between policymakers, technologists, researchers, and civil society organizations to address societal concerns and ensure that AI technologies serve the public interest and common good.

UNIVERSAL BASIC INCOME

Why is it that in a rich country like the U.S., poverty continues to affect 50 million citizens, about 15 percent of our citizens? At the other end, the top 0.1% of our citizens receive 40% of all income and own 40% of all our wealth. Numerous studies show that our income distribution, instead of getting more equitable, is growing more inequitable over time.

Is this an inevitable feature of capitalism? Those with capital continue to grow richer. Those without capital can only sell their labor and in a market where capital is replacing labor, the number of jobs and the median pay are both likely to get significantly smaller, as we just explained.

The jobs that built the middle class, largely factory jobs in the steel and auto industry, where pay often amounted to $30-40 an hour, those jobs are gone. They have moved out of the country because they can be done at much less costs in countries where workers accept much lower pay. Our politicians did very little to stop the flow of manufacturing jobs overseas, and most actively encouraged the migration. (Remember NAFTA?)

Jobs and products migrate. Not people. (That's what our immigration crisis stems from).

There will be fewer available jobs over time as globalization and digitization move rapidly forward. More and more goods will be produced in worker-less factories by robotic machines run by digital software.

The good news is that goods will get cheaper. The bad news is that without jobs and income, we won't be able to afford these goods.

So, countries will need a way to support people who lose their permanent jobs. Some will find short term, low paying work by mowing neighbor's lawns or packaging groceries in a supermarket. But their earnings will be totally inadequate to meet their living expenses. And even those jobs will be done by tireless robots.

Our present answer to this is our patchwork of anti-poverty programs which include food stamps, aid to hungry children and the disabled, and countless other measures. We give unemployment benefits over a limited time period to those who lost a job and can't find another one. We pay Social Security benefits to those who retire in their 60s. All of these programs have created a huge bureaucracy to do means-testing and make payments to those in real need.

A means-test is at the heart of one of our programs to help low-income earners. The program goes under the name of "earned income credit." The economist **Milton Friedman** proposed it in the 1960s as a poverty-fighting measure and called it a "negative income tax." If a family earns less than a certain amount varying by family size, the government sends them a check to supplement their income. This program has been accepted by both politicians on both the left and the right.

Yet there is a group that believe in what they consider to be a better program called the Universal Basic Income (UBI). **Thomas More** proposed it in his work *Utopia* in the 16th Century. **President Nixon** even considered it for a short time.

WORK, MEDIA, & TECH

In 1967, **Martin Luther King, Jr.** wrote, "I am now convinced that the simplest approach will prove to be the most effective – the solution to poverty is to abolish it directly by a now widely discussed measure: the guaranteed income." The celebrated economist, **John Kenneth Galbraith**, agreed, 'Everybody should be guaranteed a decent basic income. A rich country…can well afford to keep everybody out of poverty.' This payment given equally to all citizens would prevent any citizen from ending up with less money.

For the sake of definition, **we define Universal Basic Income (UBI) as a fixed, monthly cash grant, given directly to all adult citizens individually, to cover basic living expenses, with no strings attached.**

What are the arguments favoring a Universal Basic Income?

The first argument is that by making direct cash payments to our citizens that will at least give them a bare living, we can eliminate the costly patchwork of 300 different public aid programs and welfare payments and probably save money. This in turn will reduce the size of the federal government, something that the right desires.

The second argument is that it would free people to decide whether they want to work in a permanent job or work part-time or not at all. Today Americans work closer to 50 hours rather than 40 hours a week for 50 of the 52 weeks. Many of them are bored with their jobs and would leave them if they had a choice. Many will want to do something else with their lives and earn money along the ways doing short gigs. Americans work too hard and too long without time to enjoy other aspects of their lives.

The third argument is that UBI frees the worker from possible exploitation by employers who pay insufficient wages and provide poor working conditions. Unions used to prevent this exploitation but would be less necessary given the ability of unhappy workers to terminate his own job without facing abject poverty.

The fourth argument is that permanent jobs may increasingly be in short supply through no fault of the workers. As globalization and digitalization continues unabated, many jobs will be destroyed. Some system, either the *earned credit system* or the *universal basic income system* will be needed.

Where has UBI been tried?

Various locations and countries have considered the idea:

- On Sunday, June 5, 2016, Swiss citizens voted in a referendum on whether to hand out a guaranteed $33,000 to every citizen, regardless of wealth. It was defeated.
- The Finnish government has developed a system of giving each of its 5.4 million citizens $876 tax-free every month ($10,512 a year). In return, it will do away with welfare benefits, unemployment lines, and the other bureaucracy of its extensive social safety net.'
- The most generous program is Denmark's, which gives its poorest citizens roughly $1,800 a month, enough to pull the destitute over the poverty threshold. Note, however, this differs from a universal basic income in that it is only given to its poorest citizens.
- The Dutch city of Utrecht gave a choice to 250 Dutch citizens to either keep their current government benefits (as a control group) or receive the equivalent of $1,100 per month without any work obligations. They want to see how many made the second choice and how this impacts their behavior or productivity. The findings aren't in yet.
- In Germany and Kenya, Private organizations in Germany and Kenya are raising money[206] to launch their own basic income initiatives.
- The state of Alaska pays a regular dividend to everyone living there, universally to child and adult, through a wealth fund it has created through royalty fees paid by companies for the rights to profit from its natural resources. This is another model that could be applied anywhere to grant a basic income coming as a social dividend from a sovereign wealth fund[207] of resource-based revenue. (We'll look deeper into this in the final chapter)

---

[206] "Tech's favorite policy, universal basic income, is about to get its first big test" by Ben Popper, *The Verge*, April 18, 2016 https://www.theverge.com/2016/4/18/11441536/universal-basic-income-givedirectly-ngo-tech-sector

[207] Norway's sovereign wealth fund 'is example for oil-rich nations' by Phillip Inman, *The Guardian,* September 30, 2013 https://www.theguardian.com/business/2013/sep/30/norway-oil-sovereign-wealth-fund

What are the objections to a Universal Basic Income?

Those who object to UBI look upon it as a "handout" that will lead many people to give up a permanent job. They will be paid to be "lazy" if they wish while others are working hard and in effect supporting them. At the same time, it should be noted that business and the rich also gets handouts, although it doesn't go by that name. When a CEO takes home over $10 million or is given a "golden parachute," what else should we call it?

Others argue that many people won't have a strong incentive to study, especially harder subjects. This will reduce their skills and their productivity and the nation will suffer from the competition of better trained citizens in other nations. Of course, we would need studies of how many students decide to study less and learn less and it this is a small number, it might not be important.

Another argument is that work builds character and discipline. There is always work to be done, even if it is repairing infrastructures or fixing potholes. This is likely to suffer if more citizens choose to take it easy. Some would insist that the guaranteed income be contingent on the person agreeing to work where work is needed.

Still another argument is that many who chose to give up working will abuse their free time in just watching TV or gambling or turning to drink or drugs when they are no long career-oriented and associating with other career-driven people. Critics argue that work is a source of status and it organizes people's lives and friendships. This cannot be replaced by receiving a check.

How will we raise the funds to pay for UBI?

Once UBI is installed, many welfare programs will be eliminated. The money spent on these programs will then be transferred to the UBI funds.

A second source will be to raise taxes on the wealthy. For over 60 years, society has been reducing the tax on the wealthy. The maximum income tax rate today is 39.6%. The society can now consider raising the tax on wealthy citizens on the grounds that it will not affect their material living. A progressive tax will help slow down or stop the growing concentration of income and wealth in the hands of fewer citizens. The estate/inheritance taxes can also be raised from 60% to 80% after exempting $10 million for a married couple.

Billionaire-Tax Proposal	**Description**	**Implementation**
Wealth Tax	Tax levied on the net worth or total assets of billionaires and ultra-wealthy individuals.	Calculated as a percentage of net worth above a certain threshold.
Inheritance Tax	Tax imposed on the transfer of wealth from one generation to the next, typically on large estates or inheritances.	Calculated as a percentage of the value of inherited assets above a certain exemption threshold.
Capital Gains Tax	Tax levied on the profits or gains realized from the sale of assets, such as stocks, real estate, or investments.	Applied to the increase in value of assets owned by billionaires and wealthy individuals when sold.
Corporate Tax Reform	Reforming corporate tax laws to close loopholes and ensure that billionaires and wealthy individuals pay their fair share of taxes on corporate profits and dividends.	Implementing measures to prevent tax evasion, profit shifting, and offshore tax havens.
Financial Transaction Tax	Tax imposed on financial transactions, such as stock trades, bond sales, and currency exchanges, which are commonly undertaken by billionaires and wealthy investors.	Calculated as a small percentage of the value of financial transactions.

A third source can be a special tax on companies. Companies destroy jobs by moving abroad and by introducing automation. This company tax will pay for the killing of jobs and support the jobless.

A fourth source can be raising consumption taxes (VAT).

A fifth source can be a tax on financial transactions.

A sixth source is transferring money from the bloated defense budget to help more people live a better life.

A seventh source would be robot-taxation. We could tax robot-output and revenues to fund Universal Basic Income (UBI).

Here's a chart to illustrate the key components:

Tax Component	Description	Rate/Allocation	Implementation
Robot Output Tax (ROT)	Tax on output of goods/services by robots	Calculated based on value/quantity produced	Levied at point of production/sale
Robot Revenue Tax (RRT)	Tax on revenue generated by companies from robot use	Percentage of total revenue from automation	Applied to companies across sectors
UBI Funding Allocation	Revenue allocated to fund Universal Basic Income	Pooled into dedicated UBI fund	Used to provide regular cash payments to all citizens/residents

An eighth source would be **AI-related.** Taxing AI presents unique challenges due to its intangible nature and the complexity of its applications. However, here are several potential approaches to taxing AI-related activities:

- **Automation Taxes**: Governments could implement taxes specifically targeting the use of robots and automated systems in industries. This could include taxes on the purchase or use of robots, automation equipment, or AI software. The tax rate could be based on factors such as the level of automation, the number of robots deployed, or the value of output generated by automated processes.

- **AI Research and Development (R&D) Tax Credits**: To encourage investment in AI development, governments could offer tax incentives such as R&D tax credits for companies engaged in AI research and innovation. These credits could offset a portion of the costs associated with AI R&D activities, including salaries, equipment, and infrastructure.

- **Data Taxes**: Data is a key resource fueling AI algorithms, and governments could consider implementing taxes on the collection, processing, or use of data by companies. This could include taxes on data sales, data transfers between entities, or data storage. The tax rate could be based on the volume or value of data processed or exchanged.

- **AI Services Taxes**: As AI-powered services become more prevalent, governments could impose taxes on revenues generated from AI-based services, such as virtual assistants, chatbots, or predictive analytics platforms. This could involve taxing companies that provide AI services based on their revenues or profits derived from these services.
- **Algorithmic Trading Taxes**: In the financial sector, where AI algorithms are increasingly used for high-frequency trading and algorithmic investment strategies, governments could implement taxes on financial transactions executed by AI-driven trading systems. This could help curb speculative trading activities and generate revenue for public coffers.

- **AI Metering (Usage Fees)**: Another approach could involve charging fees or royalties for the use of AI technologies or algorithms developed by companies or researchers. This could apply to both commercial and non-commercial use cases, with fees based on factors such as usage volume, user base, or the economic value derived from AI applications.

- **AI Employment Taxes**: With concerns about job displacement by AI and automation, governments could explore taxes or levies on companies that replace human workers with AI-powered systems. These taxes could be used to fund retraining programs, unemployment benefits, or other social welfare initiatives to support affected workers.

- **Carbon Tax and Environmental Impact**: AI infrastructure, including data centers and computing facilities, consumes significant energy, leading to environmental impacts. Governments could consider implementing carbon taxes or environmental levies on AI-related activities to incentivize energy efficiency and promote sustainable development.

What makes sense?

The arguments are strong both favoring the universal basic income and arguing against it. Most anti-poverty work will probably focus on furthering the earned credit approach that focuses on making payments to raise the incomes of poor people using a means test so they could come up to a certain living standard. However, as the country starts losing more permanent jobs, the same workers will need more than just a supplement to their normal earnings. They will be unemployed and need a larger cash payment more in the spirit of a guaranteed basic income. Whether this will be a universal payment to the rich as well as the poor or just to the poor will ultimately have to be decided.

MEDIA

Why is media a wicked problem? In democratic societies, media outlets can face several challenges that can undermine their role as effective informers and watchdogs. Here are the issues:

- **Bias and Partisanship**: Media outlets may exhibit bias in their reporting, favoring certain political ideologies, parties, or interests. This can lead to one-sided coverage and misinformation.
- **Sensationalism**: Sensationalist reporting prioritizes dramatic or emotionally charged stories over more substantive news, often to attract viewership or readership. This can distort public perceptions and distract from important issues.

- **Commercial Pressure**: Media organizations are often driven by profit motives, leading them to prioritize revenue generation over journalistic integrity. This can result in clickbait, advertorials, and the neglect of critical stories that may not be as commercially viable.
- **Corporate Ownership**: Concentration of media ownership in the hands of a few large corporations can lead to limited diversity of viewpoints and agendas. This can stifle dissenting voices and limit the range of perspectives available to the public.
- **Political Influence**: Governments and political actors may seek to influence or control media narratives to serve their own interests. This can manifest through censorship, manipulation of information, or direct ownership of media outlets.
- **Echo Chambers and Polarization**: With the rise of social media and personalized news algorithms, people are increasingly exposed to content that reinforces their existing beliefs and biases. This can exacerbate societal polarization and inhibit constructive dialogue.
- **Lack of Accountability**: In some cases, media organizations may lack adequate mechanisms for accountability and transparency, making it difficult for the public to hold them accountable for errors, biases, or ethical breaches.
- **Decline of Investigative Journalism**: Shrinking budgets and resources have led to a decline in investigative journalism, which plays a crucial role in uncovering corruption, abuse of power, and other systemic issues.

Studies show that media concentration is a problem around the world. The Centre for Media Pluralism and Media Freedom (CMPF) has published its *Media Pluralism Monitor 2020*[208] (MPM2020) reports, covering thirty European countries: the 27 EU Member States, the United Kingdom and two candidate countries, Albania and Turkey. The findings show either a general stagnation or deterioration in all of the four major areas tracked by the Media Pluralism Monitor (MPM): Basic protection, Market plurality, Political independence and Social inclusiveness. Here are the details:

[208] *MPM2021 Results* by *The Centre for Media Pluralism and Media Freedom (CMPF)* https://cmpf.eui.eu/mpm2021-results/

- Journalists and other media actors continue to face a series of threats and attacks (physical and digital) in several of the states monitored, not least as a result of the deployment of SLAPP lawsuits and credible threats to their physical safety;
- Journalists' working conditions have deteriorated further, exposing journalists to external and undue pressures in their professional activity in most of the countries examined. The impact of the COVID pandemic has exacerbated the problem (given that MPM2020 covered the years 2018 and 2019, it does not examine the pandemic's impact);
- Whistleblower protection is still weak in EU Member States;
- Media ownership concentration remains one of the most significant risks to media pluralism and is seen as creating barriers to the diversity of information and viewpoints;
- Online platform concentration and competition enforcement registers a high risk across the countries examined;
- Existing media business models are proving increasingly ineffective at providing the financial resources necessary to support journalists and news organizations;
- News organizations continue to be vulnerable to political interference, especially if economic conditions are unstable while notably lower risks of political control are registered with regard to digital native media;
- The majority of countries monitored register a high risk in the field of the distribution of state advertising;
- Transparency of media ownership registers medium risk on average across the states monitored;
- A lack of political independence of public service media, especially in Central and Eastern Europe, remains a matter of concern;
- Lack of gender equality in managerial and content creation roles in European media organizations remains a problem;
- In the majority of countries media literacy policies are available but are not comprehensive;
- The lack of data, in particular economic data, across many states has been highlighted as a risk in its own right.

But these problems have real impacts. In *How Media Ownership Matters in the US: Beyond the Concentration Debate* - an interview[209] with **Rodney Benson** - reveals much of what ails the media today. Here are some quotes from the interview:

- "When a few media owners control most of the media in a country that's certainly a problem, but it's not just the number for outlets that matters, it's also their form of ownership. If we care about the capacity of news media to help or hinder democracy, we can't just look at market concentration, we also have to look closer at the institutional logics that shape journalistic practice."
- "The most concentrated national media systems are China (not surprisingly, given the state's involvement with all media), Egypt (likewise with a strong state), South Africa, Russia, Turkey, and Mexico. In all of these countries, concentration is a major problem."
- "In the US, today, market concentration is especially a concern relative to digital platforms like Google and Facebook, which are hoarding almost all of the online advertising revenues; their near monopoly has also given them free rein to use their algorithms (especially at Facebook) to highlight sensational and polarizing messages and images that keep people on their platforms as long as possible, and in the process threaten democracy."
- "Presidents always get a lot of media attention, but Trump's level of attention dwarfs that of previous administrations. During the first month of his presidency, Trump received $ 817 million worth of earned media attention compared to Barack Obama's $ 169 million. This is the value of the free news media attention in terms of what it would have cost an advertiser to buy that time."
- "This has very little to do with concentration and everything to do with the hyper-commercialization in the US - dominated by the stock market traded companies - that creates immense pressures to maximize audiences and profits."

---

[209] "How Media Ownership Matters in the US: Beyond the Concentration Debate, Une interview de Rodney Benson"
Dans Sociétés contemporaines 2019 https://www.cairn.info/revue-societes-contemporaines-2019-1-page-71.htm
See also: *33 Problems With Media in One Chart* Visual Capitalist June 29, 2022 https://www.visualcapitalist.com/problems-with-media/

- "What we see here is not just concentration of revenues and audiences, but concentration of an ownership form. All of the largest media companies whether in terms of revenues or online audience share are stock market traded."
- "...it's difficult to think of too many advantages of stock market ownership or its rising cousin, the private equity firm. These hyper-commercial forms of ownership put profits above public service. They are the first to cut news budgets in order to boost profits. And when they do invest in journalism, it tends to be the kind of sensational journalism that does more harm than good for democracy."

Media ownership is a **threat** to Democracy - a clear and present danger. When billionaires begin to use AI to drive revenue, the media ecosystem will be a full-blown war zone of propaganda and mass manipulation.

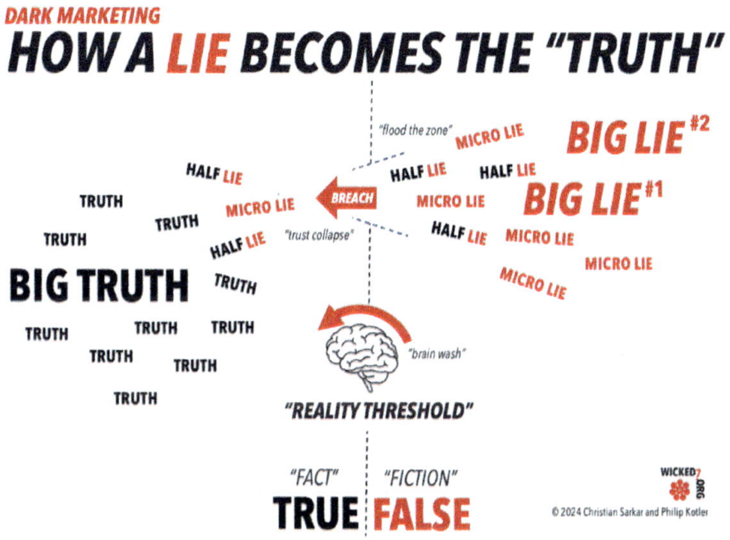

Some claim it is already so.

Renowned critic and always MIT linguist **Noam Chomsky**, one of the classic voices of intellectual dissent in the last decade explains[210]:

The media are a corporate monopoly. They have the same point of view. The two parties are two factions of the business party. Most of the population doesn't even bother voting because it looks meaningless. They're marginalized and properly distracted. At least that's the goal. The leading figure in the public relations industry, Edward Bernays, actually came out of the Creel Commission.[211] *He was part of it, learned his lessons there and went on to develop what he called the "engineering of consent," which he described as "the essence of democracy." The people who are able to engineer consent are the ones who have the resources and the power to do it-the business community-and that's who you work for.*

Irony of ironies, a list of the ten most effective strategies for media manipulation attributed to Noam Chomsky was actually developed by a French writer:[212]

1-The Strategy of Distraction

The primordial element of social control is the distraction strategy which consists of diverting the public's attention from major problems and the changes decided by political and economic elites, through the flooding technique or flooding continuous distractions and insignificant information.

Distraction strategy is also essential to prevent the public from becoming interested in essential knowledge in the area of science, economics, psychology, neurobiology and cybernetics. Keeping the audience's attention deviated from real social problems, imprisoned by themes without real importance.

Keeping the public busy, busy, busy, with no time to think, back to the farm like other animals (quoted in the text "Silent weapons for quiet wars").

---

[210] *Media Control: The Spectacular Achievements of Propaganda* by Noam Chomsky, *Seven Stories Press*, 1991, 1997, 2002

[211] The Committee on Public Information (1917–1919), also known as the CPI or the Creel Committee, was an independent agency of the government of the United States under the Wilson administration created to influence public opinion to support the US in World War I, in particular, the US home front. https://en.wikipedia.org/wiki/Committee_on_Public_Information

[212] See: https://www.wicked7.org/noam-chomsky-10-strategies-for-manipulation-by-the-media/

2-Creating problems and then offering the solutions.

This method is also called a " problem-reaction-solution ". It creates a problem, a " situation " planned to cause a certain reaction from the public, with the aim that this is the source of the measures they want to accept. For example: letting urban violence intensify or intensify, or organize bloody attacks, with the aim of the public being those requiring security laws and policies to the detriment of freedom. Also: create an economic crisis to make social rights demotion and dismantle public services accept as a necessary evil.

3-The Strategy of Graduation.

To make an unacceptable measure accepted, you only need to apply it gradually, to dropper, for consecutive years. This is how radically new socioeconomic conditions (neoliberism) were imposed during the decades of the 80 s and 90 s: minimum state, privatisation, precariousness, flexibility, mass unemployment, wages that no longer guarantee dignified incomes , so many changes that would have brought about a revolution if they were implemented at once.

4-The Strategy of Deferring.

Another way to get an unpopular decision accepted is to present it as " painful and necessary ", gaining public acceptance, in the moment, for future application. It is easier to accept a future sacrifice than an immediate sacrifice. First, because effort isn't that taken immediately. Second, because the public, the mass, always tends to naively hope that " everything will be better tomorrow " and that the required sacrifice could be avoided. This gives the audience more time to get used to the idea of change and accept it resigned when the time comes.

5-Reach to the public like children.

Most advertisements directed at the large audience use speeches, arguments, characters and a particularly childish intonation, many times close to weakness, as if the viewer was a few years old creature or a mental moron. When you try to deceive the viewer the more you tend to use a childish tone. Why? Why? " If someone addresses a person as if they are 12 or under, then based on suggestionability, they will probably tend to a response or reaction even without a critical sense like that of a 12 person. years or less " (see " Silent Weapons for quiet wars ").

6-Using emotional aspect much more than reflection.

Take advantage of emotion it's a classic technique to provoke a short circuit on a rational analysis and finally the critical sense of the individual. Additionally, the use of emotional register allows the unconscious access door to implant or inject ideas, desires, fears and fears, compulsions, or induce behaviors.

7-Keeping the public in ignorance and mediocrity.

Making the public incapable of understanding the technologies and methods used for their control and slavery.

"The quality of education given to lower social classes must be as poor and mediocre as possible, so that the distance of ignorance that plans between lower classes and upper classes is and remains impossible to fill from the lower classes".

8-Stimulating the public to be complacent with mediocrity.

Pushing the audience to think it's fashionable to be stupid, vulgar and ignorant...

9-Strengthening self-guilt.

Making the individual believe that he is only the culprit of his disgrace, because of his insufficient intelligence, skills or efforts. So, instead of rebelling against the economic system, the individual devalues himself and blames himself, which in turn creates a depressive state, one of whose effects is the inhibition of his action. And without action there is no revolution!

10-Knowing individuals better than they know themselves.

Over the past 50 years, science's rapid progress has generated a growing gap between public knowledge and those possessed and used by dominant elites. Thanks to biology, neurobiology, and applied psychology, the " system " has enjoyed advanced knowledge of the human being, both in its physical and psychological form. The system has managed to learn better about the common individual than he knows himself. This means that, in most cases, the system exercises greater control and greater power over individuals, greater than that which the same individual exercises over himself.

These "mass manipulation" techniques are frightful – but with the advent of AI the impact on the public will be far worse.

Freedom must include ***freedom from manipulation***. AI must *not be weaponized* as a tool of mass manipulation.

CLIMATEGPT

According to **ClimateGPT**, the primary drivers of the wicked problem of Work, Media, and Technology include:

- **Work:** The wicked problem of work is rooted in the way we organize our work and the way we value it. The current economic system prioritizes profit over people, and this leads to exploitation, inequality, and environmental degradation. The solution to this problem requires a fundamental shift in our understanding of work and its purpose, as well as a reimagining of the role of business in society.

- **Media:** The wicked problem of media is rooted in the way we consume and produce media. The current media landscape is dominated by a few large corporations that control the flow of information and shape public opinion. This leads to a lack of diversity in perspectives and a lack of accountability for the content that is produced. The solution to this problem requires a more democratic and transparent media landscape, with greater control over the production and distribution of media in the hands of individuals and communities.

- **Technology:** The wicked problem of technology is rooted in the way we use and rely on technology. The current technological landscape is characterized by a lack of transparency and accountability, with many companies prioritizing profit over user privacy and safety. This leads to a lack of trust in technology and a lack of control over our own data. The solution to this problem requires a more transparent and accountable technological landscape, with greater control over our own data and the development of new technologies that prioritize user well-being and safety.

Further details on each one of these root causes are listed in the appendix: *Answers from AI,* at the end of this book.

CASCADING EFFECTS

What happens when jobs disappear? Here's a list of cascading effects of job loss and high unemployment:

- **Decreased Consumer Spending**: When people lose their jobs or fear losing them, they tend to spend less on non-essential items, which can lead to decreased demand for goods and services.
- **Reduced Business Revenue**: With decreased consumer spending, businesses experience a drop in revenue, leading to potential layoffs or closures, thus perpetuating the cycle of unemployment.
- **Increased Government Expenditure**: Governments may need to spend more on social welfare programs such as unemployment benefits, food assistance, and healthcare for the unemployed, straining public finances.
- **Lower Tax Revenue**: As unemployment rises, fewer people are paying income taxes, leading to a decrease in government tax revenue.
- **Housing Market Decline**: Job loss often leads to difficulties in paying mortgages or rents, potentially resulting in foreclosures, evictions, and a decline in property values.
- **Health Consequences**: Job loss can lead to increased stress, anxiety, and depression among individuals and their families, impacting mental and physical health.
- **Social Unrest**: High unemployment rates can contribute to social unrest and dissatisfaction with government policies, leading to protests, demonstrations, and potential political instability.
- **Skills Erosion**: Prolonged unemployment can lead to skill erosion or obsolescence, making it harder for individuals to re-enter the workforce even when job opportunities arise.

- **Long-term Economic Scarring**: High unemployment rates can have long lasting effects on an economy, including reduced productivity, innovation, and potential long-term damage to human capital.
- **Impact on the Future**: Children growing up in households experiencing job loss and economic hardship may face educational and developmental challenges, impacting their future earning potential and well-being.

"Of all the forms of inequality, injustice in health is the most shocking and inhumane."
– Martin Luther King Jr.

6 HEALTH & LIVELIHOOD

Initially titled "Health & Livelihood" this wicked problem morphed into the "Essentials of Life." The essentials of life are the fundamental elements or necessities required for sustaining and enhancing human existence, encompassing basic needs.

Here are 10 essentials of life:

1. Food & Nutrition

- Access to sufficient, nutritious, and culturally appropriate food
- Sustainable food systems that ensure long-term availability

2. Water & Sanitation

- Clean drinking water for health and survival
- Proper sanitation and hygiene to prevent disease

3. Shelter & Safety

- Secure and stable housing for protection from the elements
- Safe living conditions free from violence and hazards

4. Healthcare & Well-being

- Universal access to medical care, including preventive and emergency services
- Mental health support and holistic well-being initiatives

5. Education & Knowledge

- Basic education for literacy, numeracy, and critical thinking
- Lifelong learning and skill development for personal and professional growth

6. Employment & Economic Stability

- Fair wages and dignified work opportunities
- Economic systems that ensure financial security and upward mobility

7. Community & Social Belonging

- Strong relationships and local community-based support networks
- Cultural and spiritual connections that nurture belonging and common purpose

8. Justice & Governance

- Equal rights, fairness, and access to justice
- Transparent institutions that promote accountability and social equity

9. Freedom & Self-Determination

- The right to make choices about one's life
- Opportunities to contribute meaningfully to society

10. Nature & Climate

- A healthy environment which protects biodiversity
- Climate stability for future generations.

Each of these essentials is under threat – and our governments act as if nothing can be done.

ESSENTIALS *of* LIFE

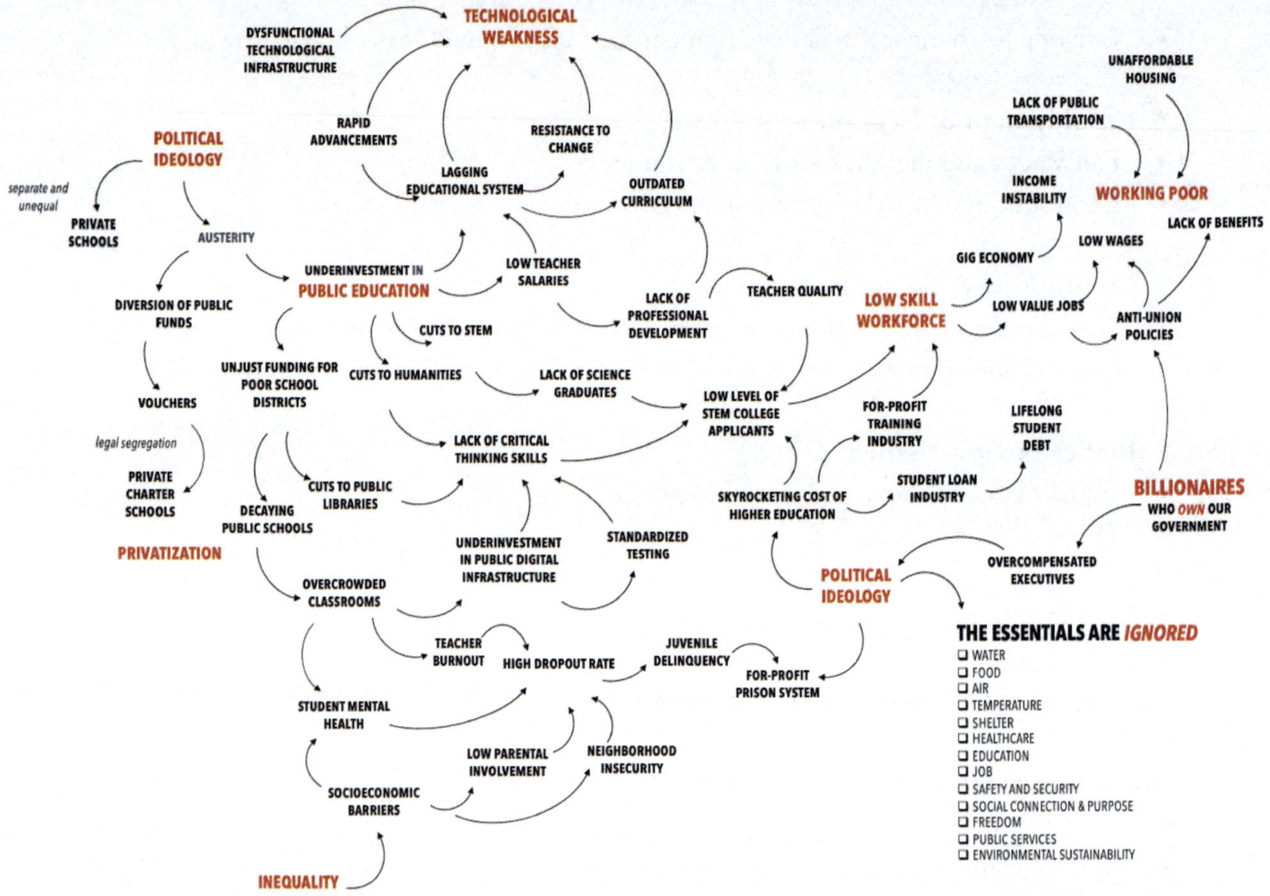

THE PRIVATIZATION *of* EVERYTHING

Currently, the wealthiest 0.01% of individuals in the United States possess a greater share of the nation's total wealth than their counterparts did during the Gilded Age, a period marked by unchecked financial speculation alongside pervasive poverty, corruption, and racial tensions.

This staggering concentration of wealth can largely be attributed to the dominance of Wall Street in American society, with bankers and investors demonstrating a readiness to both create and exploit crises when the potential gains are substantial. The ascendancy of finance as a central force in the United States and globally has been facilitated by successive waves of neoliberal reforms over the past half century, characterized by the **privatization of profits** and the **externalization of risks**.

Unfortunately, our society has largely been conditioned to **eliminate the concept of the Common Good**. In their book, *The Privatization of Everything: How the Plunder of Public Goods Transformed America and How We Can Fight back*, Donald Cohen and Allen Mikaelian explain how the US-approach to fighting COVID was based not on effective public health policy, but rather on letting the markets decide. Public health is a public good, but the Trump administration handed it over to corporations. Cohen and Mikaelian tell us that **our theory of public goods sidelines the public almost completely:** [213]

It assumes that the market can and will provide just about everything. According to conservative economists, the government should step in only when markets fail. In those rare instances where someone can't make money from a particular good or service, it becomes permissible for the government to take it on. In this framing, the market decides what is public and what is private, and the public must follow the market's dictates. Privatization is often a logical outcome. When a good or service is privatized, it means that someone has figured out how to make money from it or that they want to exclude segments of the public. And when that happens, according to free-market adherents, the public needs to get out of the way.

---

[213] *The Privatization of Everything: How the Plunder of Public Goods Transformed America and How We Can Fight back*, Donald Cohen and Allen Mikaelian, The New Press (November 23, 2021)

This classic and narrow definition of public goods is fundamentally opposed to democracy and leaves decision-making about vital issues to the whims of the market.

The authors argue that **in a democratic society public goods should not be defined by the market.** Instead, they should be defined by the *public* and its values.

In 1981, the Business Roundtable – a group that represents large American firms – said that companies "have a responsibility, first of all, to make available to the public quality goods and services at fair prices, thereby earning a profit that attracts investment to continue and enhance the enterprise, provide jobs, and build the economy." By 1997, the Roundtable declared that the "principal objective of a business enterprise is to generate economic returns to its owners."[214]

The change from focusing on "public good" to believing that the sole mission of business was to maximize shareholder value, leads to executives pocketing more and more profit for themselves, rather than investing in their workforce.

The problems associated with power and corporate influence can have wide-ranging implications for society, democracy, and the economy. Some of the key issues include:

1. **Political Capture**: Corporate influence can lead to the capture of political processes and institutions, where powerful corporations exert undue influence over government policies, regulations, and decision-making processes. This can result in policies that prioritize corporate interests over public welfare, undermine democratic principles, and erode trust in government institutions.

2. **Regulatory Capture**: Regulatory capture occurs when regulatory agencies tasked with overseeing corporate behavior become influenced or controlled by the industries they are supposed to regulate. This can lead to weakened enforcement of regulations, lax oversight, and inadequate protection of public health, safety, and environmental concerns.

[214] See: https://www-vice-com.cdn.ampproject.org/c/s/www.vice.com/amp/en/article/a3xqze/shell-ceo-ben-van-beurden-climate-change

3. **Monopoly Power**: Concentration of corporate power in the hands of a few large corporations can lead to monopolistic practices that stifle competition, limit consumer choice, and drive up prices. Monopolies and oligopolies can exert significant influence over markets, suppliers, and policymakers, leading to distortions in resource allocation and hindering innovation and economic dynamism.

4. **Inequality and Social Justice**: Corporate influence can exacerbate income inequality and social injustice by privileging the interests of wealthy corporations and their shareholders over the needs of workers, communities, and marginalized populations. This can lead to disparities in economic opportunities, access to resources, and distribution of wealth, exacerbating social tensions and undermining social cohesion.

5. **Environmental Degradation**: Corporate influence can contribute to environmental degradation through activities such as pollution, deforestation, and resource extraction. Powerful corporations may resist environmental regulations, lobby for weakened environmental protections, and engage in greenwashing practices to obscure their environmental impacts. This can lead to long-term ecological harm, biodiversity loss, and climate change, with detrimental consequences for ecosystems and human well-being.

6. **Worker Exploitation**: Corporate influence can result in labor practices that exploit workers, such as low wages, unsafe working conditions, and lack of job security. Powerful corporations may resist labor regulations, unionization efforts, and worker protections to maximize profits at the expense of labor rights and dignity. This can lead to social injustice, economic insecurity, and heightened vulnerability for workers, particularly in marginalized communities and global supply chains.

7. **Democracy and Public Accountability**: Excessive corporate influence can undermine democratic governance and public accountability by diminishing the voice and agency of ordinary citizens in political decision-making processes. Corporate lobbying, campaign finance contributions, and revolving door relationships between corporations and government officials can skew policy outcomes in favor of corporate interests, eroding the integrity of democratic institutions and processes.

A report[215] on **how privatization increases inequality** reveals five ways in which government privatization disproportionately affects poor individuals and families. Firstly, the creation of new user fees to fund public services places a heavier burden on the poor, as many essential services subject to outsourcing necessitate fees that low-income individuals must pay.

Secondly, the increase in existing user fees, particularly in critical services like water or transit, disproportionately harms low-income residents and those on fixed incomes.

Thirdly, privatization of the social safety net, often targeting programs assisting those with limited political power, can lead to detrimental outcomes for vulnerable populations.

Fourthly, privatization tends to result in decreased wages and benefits for contracted workers, exacerbating income inequality by replacing stable, middle-class jobs with poverty-level employment.

Finally, the introduction of private interests into public goods and services can exacerbate socioeconomic and racial segregation, as seen in instances where privatization creates parallel systems serving higher-income individuals, leaving lower-income groups with lesser-quality services or even without access to the public good entirely.

Similarly, when governments are driven by **ideology** and promote policies dictated by powerful financial interests, and refuse to confront the realities facing their citizens, then we must challenge our assumptions and rethink what it is we want from our leaders.

Alas, the colonial mindset of exploitation and extraction is hard-wired into capitalism.

---

[215] *Report: How privatization increases inequality* by *ITPI*, September 2016
https://inthepublicinterest.org/wp-content/uploads/InthePublicInterest_InequalityReport_Sept2016.pdf

The common thread is colonial thinking.

Colonial thinking and privatization are interconnected, reflecting broader power dynamics, economic interests, and historical legacies:

- **Power Dynamics**: Colonialism often involved the exploitation of resources and the imposition of control by colonial powers over indigenous populations and their lands. Similarly, privatization can concentrate power and control in the hands of a few private entities, often at the expense of public interests and community well-being. In both cases, there's a hierarchical relationship where decision-making authority is centralized and distant from those most affected.

- **Resource Extraction**: Colonialism historically involved the extraction of natural resources from colonized territories for the benefit of colonial powers and private corporations. Similarly, privatization can facilitate the extraction and commodification of essential resources, such as water, land, and minerals, for private profit rather than public welfare. This can perpetuate patterns of exploitation and marginalization experienced under colonial rule.

- **Displacement and Dispossession**: Colonialism often led to the displacement and dispossession of indigenous peoples from their lands, as well as the privatization of communal resources. Similarly, privatization processes can result in the displacement of communities and the loss of access to essential resources, as public goods are transferred into private hands, often without adequate consultation or consent from affected populations.

- **Marginalization of Indigenous Knowledge**: Colonialism often marginalized indigenous knowledge systems and practices in favor of Western-centric approaches. Similarly, privatization may marginalize local and indigenous perspectives on resource management and environmental stewardship, privileging profit-driven models over traditional and sustainable ways of living in harmony with nature.

- **Inequitable Access**: Colonialism created systems of inequality and oppression that continue to persist in many post-colonial societies. Similarly, privatization can exacerbate inequalities by creating barriers to access essential services, such as water, healthcare, and education, particularly for marginalized communities who may lack the financial means to afford privatized services.

- **Resistance and Decolonization**: Both colonialism and privatization have sparked resistance movements aimed at reclaiming sovereignty, rights, and control over resources. Indigenous peoples and communities impacted by privatization have often led struggles for environmental justice, land rights, and the recognition of collective ownership and stewardship over ancestral lands and resources.

We now see that **our leaders do not represent us** - or the Common Good. They have lost our trust.

What do capitalism and colonialism share in common?

They both have severe, negative consequences for the *local* population:

- **Enclosure of the Commons**: The "commons" refers to resources that are held collectively and accessible to all members of a community. **Privatization can be seen as an enclosure of the commons when public assets or services that were once accessible to all are transferred into private ownership or control.** This can limit access, restrict usage, and commodify resources that were previously considered public goods.

- **Profit Motives Over Public Interest**: Private companies operating in a competitive market are primarily motivated by profit maximization. This can lead to decisions that prioritize financial gain over the public interest, such as cutting costs, reducing services, or neglecting investments in maintenance and infrastructure upgrades.

- **Loss of Accountability and Transparency**: Privatization can result in a loss of transparency and accountability compared to publicly owned and operated services. Private companies may be less subject to public scrutiny, freedom of information laws, or democratic oversight, making it difficult for citizens to hold them accountable for their actions or decisions.

- **Inequitable Access**: Privatization can exacerbate inequalities by creating barriers to access essential services for marginalized or low-income communities who may not be able to afford privatized services. This can lead to social exclusion, disparities in service quality, and further marginalization of already vulnerable populations.

- **Democracy and Governance Concerns**: Privatization may undermine democratic decision-making processes and citizen participation in matters that affect public services and resources. When key decisions are made by private entities driven by profit motives rather than elected representatives accountable to the public, it can erode democratic principles and civic engagement.

The **pattern of privatization** is the same across the globe. Privatization involves the transfer of ownership, control, or management of public assets or services from the government or public sector to private entities, such as corporations or individuals. This process can take various forms, including:

1. **Asset Sales**: Public assets, such as utilities, infrastructure, or natural resources, may be sold outright to private companies or investors.

2. **Contracting Out**: Governments may contract private companies to provide specific services traditionally handled by the public sector, such as waste management, healthcare, or education.

3. **Public-Private Partnerships (PPPs)**: PPPs involve collaboration between public and private entities to finance, develop, and operate infrastructure projects or public services. These partnerships can vary widely in structure and may involve joint ventures, concessions, or other arrangements. Often the extractive nature of partnerships are *not* transparent or explained to the public.

WATER

Clean, potable water requires a commitment to the Common Good: regulation, community involvement, and a commitment to ensuring equitable access to clean and affordable water for all.

Instead of creating and investing in the infrastructure to deliver clean water is a shortcoming in many communities across the United States and the developing world suffer from a water crisis.

The privatization of water can give rise to several significant issues:

- **Access Inequality**: Privatization leads to unequal access to clean and affordable water, especially for low-income communities who may struggle to afford the increased costs imposed by private companies.

- **Price Hikes**: Private companies prioritize profits over public welfare, leading to higher water prices for consumers. This can disproportionately affect vulnerable populations, exacerbating poverty and inequality.

- **Quality Concerns**: Profit-driven motives compromises water quality standards, as companies may cut corners on treatment processes or infrastructure maintenance to reduce costs, potentially endangering public health.

- **Lack of Accountability**: Private water companies may operate with less transparency and accountability compared to publicly-owned utilities, making it difficult for communities to hold them accountable for service quality, pricing, or environmental impacts.

- **Loss of Control**: Privatization may result in the loss of community control over water resources and infrastructure, as decision-making authority shifts to private entities focused on profit maximization rather than serving the public interest.

- **Environmental Impacts**: Private water management may prioritize short-term profits over long-term environmental sustainability, leading to over-extraction of water resources, habitat destruction, and pollution, exacerbating ecological degradation.

- **Commodification of a Basic Human Right**: Water is essential for life, and its privatization can lead to the commodification of a basic human right, where access to clean water becomes a privilege rather than a universal entitlement.

FLINT, MICHIGAN

The water crisis in Flint, Michigan, which continues to this day, stemmed from a series of failures in water management, infrastructure, and governance, resulting in serious public health concerns and widespread community impacts. Some of the key problems associated with the water in Flint include:

- **Lead Contamination**: The switch of the city's water source from Lake Huron to the Flint River in 2014 led to corrosive water leaching lead from aging pipes into the drinking water supply. Lead exposure can cause serious health issues, particularly in children, including developmental delays and neurological damage.

- **Bacterial Contamination**: Alongside lead, the Flint water supply also had issues with bacterial contamination, including elevated levels of coliform bacteria and concerns about the presence of Legionella bacteria, which led to outbreaks of Legionnaires' disease, a severe form of pneumonia.

- **Poor Water Quality**: Residents reported various problems with the water, including discoloration, foul odor, and taste issues, indicating broader concerns about water quality beyond lead contamination.

- **Lack of Government Response**: Despite mounting evidence of water quality problems and health risks, there was a delayed and inadequate response from local, state, and federal authorities. Concerns raised by residents were dismissed or downplayed, exacerbating the crisis and eroding trust in government institutions.

- **Health Impacts**: The water crisis in Flint resulted in widespread health impacts, including increased lead levels in children's blood, cases of Legionnaires' disease, and various other health problems associated with exposure to contaminated water.

- **Social and Economic Consequences**: The water crisis disproportionately affected low-income and minority communities in Flint, exacerbating existing social and economic disparities. Residents faced financial burdens from purchasing bottled water and suffered property value declines due to concerns about water quality.

So, what exactly happened in Flint? According to the Veolia group[216] (can we trust a private water company?):

For years, Flint had been receiving its water from the Detroit Water and Sewerage Department (DWSD); however, Flint's Emergency Managers believed Detroit water was too expensive. In turn, they chose to join a plan to build a new pipeline from Lake Huron to Flint, which would be run by the Karegnondi Water Authority (KWA).

Under the plan, the KWA would provide Flint with untreated Lake Huron water, which meant that Flint would have to treat the KWA water before it could be distributed to people's homes. Flint had a water treatment plant; however, the plant had barely been used for decades, and was going to need significant upgrades to operate effectively. Additionally, upgrades would cost tens of millions of dollars, which the City of Flint did not have.

Ultimately, the City decided to take the money that they had been using to buy water from Detroit, and use that money instead to upgrade Flint's water treatment plant so it would be ready for the KWA plan; however, it would take years for Flint's water treatment plant to be ready for use.

In the meantime, the City needed to determine how they could provide residents with water, since the money used to purchase Detroit water was now going to treatment plant upgrades. Ultimately, the City of Flint decided to acquire their water from the Flint River. Shockingly, the City did this without properly testing the water first to ensure it would be safe for utilization or consumption.

The City of Flint switched water from Detroit water to the Flint River on April 25, 2014; however, immediately after the switch, residents began complaining that water coming from their faucets was brown and foul-smelling and also reported feeling sick after consuming it.

---

[216] https://veoliaflintfacts.com/fast-facts

Nevertheless, for nearly a year and a half, the government officials that had the power and ability to fix this problem did nothing.

Governor Snyder did not order a return to Detroit water until October 2015 - nearly 18 months after the initial switch was made.

The crisis is made worse by the legal "settlement."

Veolia states: "Government officials caused the crisis, and then tried to cover their tracks to avoid admitting their mistakes. Not a single one has been held accountable for their failures or lies. Meanwhile, trial attorneys are set to walk away with roughly $200 million, while Flint victims have yet to see a dime from the $626+ million Flint Water Crisis settlement."

The problem goes back to *ideology* – why do government officials insist on privatization and cost-driven solutions which lead to public catastrophe?

Time and time again, the failure of public services can be attributed to the failure of officials to protect the Common Good for the sake of private profits.

THE DEREGULATION *of* EVERYTHING

Along with privatization, the other primary *weapon of mass destruction of the Common Good* is **deregulation**.

Deregulation has negative impacts on the essentials of life in several ways:

- **Quality and Safety**: Deregulation leads to a decrease in quality standards and safety regulations. Without proper oversight, businesses often cut corners to reduce costs, compromising the safety and reliability of essential goods and services.

- **Price Increases**: deregulation often leads to price increases. For example, in industries where natural monopolies exist or where competition is limited, deregulation may result in price gouging by the dominant firms.

- **Access and Affordability**: Deregulation reduces access to essential services for low-income individuals or those living in rural areas. Without regulatory mandates to provide universal access, companies prioritize profitable markets, leaving underserved communities without access to necessities like healthcare, transportation, or utilities.

- **Environmental Impact**: Deregulation weakens environmental protections by relaxing pollution controls and allowing industries to exploit natural resources without proper checks. This leads to negative impacts on air and water quality, public health, and ecosystems, affecting the essentials of life for present and future generations.

- **Instability**: Deregulation increases economic volatility and instability by removing safeguards designed to prevent excessive risk-taking and market manipulation. This instability can have ripple effects across the economy, impacting jobs, investments, and consumer confidence.

Here are some examples of deregulation that ended badly:

- **Enron and Electricity Deregulation (California, late 1990s)**: Enron's manipulation of California's deregulated electricity market led to widespread power outages and skyrocketing energy prices, culminating in the California electricity crisis of 2000-2001.

- **Financial Deregulation (United States, 2000s)**: Deregulation of the financial sector in the United States, including the repeal of the Glass-Steagall Act, contributed to the 2008 global financial crisis, resulting in economic recession and widespread hardship.

- **Telecommunications Deregulation (United States, 1996)**: While the Telecommunications Act of 1996 aimed to increase competition, it led to industry consolidation, reduced consumer choice, raised prices, and limited access to affordable services, particularly in rural areas.

- **Airlines Deregulation (United States, 1978)**: While airline deregulation initially led to lower fares, it also resulted in reduced service to small and rural communities, airline bankruptcies, and consolidation, leading to fewer options and sometimes higher prices for consumers.

- **Railroad Deregulation (United States, 1980s)**: The Staggers Rail Act of 1980 deregulated the railroad industry in the United States, leading to reduced competition, increased rates for shippers, and service declines, particularly for smaller communities.

- **Global Shipping Deregulation**: Deregulation of the global shipping industry led to overcapacity, price wars, and financial instability among shipping companies, resulting in bankruptcies, consolidation, and reduced service reliability.

- **Natural Gas Deregulation (United States, 1980s-1990s)**: Deregulation of the natural gas industry in the United States led to market manipulation, price volatility, and decreased investment in infrastructure, contributing to supply disruptions and price spikes during periods of high demand.

- **Pharmaceutical Deregulation (United States, 1980s)**: Deregulation of pharmaceutical prices and advertising in the United States led to aggressive marketing tactics, rising drug prices, and increased prescription drug abuse, particularly of opioid painkillers.

- **Housing Deregulation and Financial Crisis (United States, 2000s)**: Deregulation of the housing market, including lax lending standards and securitization practices, contributed to the subprime mortgage crisis and subsequent global financial crisis of 2008.

- **Privatization and Deregulation of Water Utilities**: Deregulation and privatization of water utilities in many regions led to increased water prices, service cutoffs for low-income households, and decreased investment in infrastructure maintenance, resulting in water quality issues and public health risks. (Flint, Michigan).

Deregulation also leads to pollution and accidents. The **Deepwater Horizon** oil spill in the Gulf of Mexico was one of the largest environmental disasters in history. Regulatory failures, including lax oversight and inadequate safety measures, allowed BP and its contractors to cut corners, leading to the blowout of the Macondo well and the release of millions of barrels of oil into the Gulf. The spill had devastating impacts on marine life, coastal ecosystems, and the livelihoods of Gulf Coast communities.

THE DESTRUCTION OF THE COMMON GOOD

We realize that US politicians have never been more aligned with the corpocracy - thanks to *Citizen's United* and the scourge of gerrymandering.

The essentials of life are not their priority. In fact, the destruction of the Common Good is the modus operandi – a continuation of the colonial mentality of exploitation and extraction.

In fact, they use privatization and deregulation as the two main **weapons of mass destruction** *of the Common Good.*

But that's not all. We identified 13 ways the powers that be undermine and destroy the Common Good.

1. **Privatization**: The transfer of ownership or control of public goods and services to private entities leads to the prioritization of profit over the Common Good, resulting in reduced access, increased costs, and diminished quality of essential services such as healthcare, education, and utilities.

2. **Deregulation**: Relaxing or removing regulations intended to protect public health, safety, and welfare creates opportunities for exploitation, market manipulation, and environmental degradation, undermining the well-being of communities and individuals.

3. **Corruption and Cronyism**: When public officials or institutions prioritize personal gain or favoritism over the welfare of society, it erodes trust and leads to policies that benefit a select few at the expense of the broader population.

4. **Income Inequality and Poverty**: Widening gaps between the wealthy and the poor destabilize communities and hinder social mobility, leading to a concentration of power and resources in the hands of a few while leaving many without the means to access basic necessities and opportunities.

5. **Environmental Degradation**: Policies and practices that prioritize short-term economic gains over long-term sustainability result in irreversible damage to the environment, jeopardizing the health and well-being of present and future generations.

6. **Media Manipulation and Disinformation**: When information is distorted or manipulated to serve specific interests, it undermines public discourse, erodes trust in institutions, and impedes the ability of individuals to make informed decisions, ultimately hindering the pursuit of the Common Good.

7. **Erosion of Social Cohesion and Trust**: Factors such as polarization, discrimination, and social exclusion fracture communities and weaken the bonds that hold society together, making it difficult to address common challenges and promote collective well-being.

8. **Globalization and Economic Exploitation**: While globalization can bring benefits such as increased trade and cultural exchange, it can also lead to economic exploitation, loss of local jobs, and exploitation of labor in developing countries, exacerbating inequalities and undermining the well-being of marginalized communities.

9. **Lack of Access to Education and Healthcare**: Inadequate access to education and healthcare perpetuates cycles of poverty and inequality, limiting opportunities for individuals to reach their full potential and contribute meaningfully to society.

10. **Unchecked Corporate Power**: When corporations wield disproportionate influence over government policies and decision-making processes, it leads to policies that prioritize corporate interests over the Common Good, resulting in environmental degradation, worker exploitation, and erosion of consumer protections.

11. **Systemic Discrimination and Injustice**: Discriminatory practices based on factors such as race, gender, religion, or socioeconomic status perpetuate inequalities and marginalize certain groups within society, hindering the realization of equal opportunities and social justice for all.

12. **Underinvestment in Infrastructure and Public Services**: Neglecting essential infrastructure and public services, such as transportation, housing, and social welfare programs, blocks economic development, exacerbates social disparities, and undermines the overall well-being of communities.

13. **Militarism**: An excessive focus on military buildup and aggression diverts resources away from addressing pressing social and economic needs, perpetuates cycles of violence and conflict, and undermines efforts to promote peace, diplomacy, and international cooperation. Additionally, militarism contributes to the erosion of civil liberties, increases the risk of armed conflict, and exacerbates tensions both domestically and globally, ultimately detracting from the pursuit of the Common Good.

ASK: Do our government officials (local and national) work for the *Common Good* or do they work for private interests?

NOTE – for each of the essentials of Life we find that our policies are the opposite of constructive. We will examine this in greater detail at our website at www.wicked7.org.

13 WEAPONS *of* MASS DESTRUCTION *of* THE COMMON GOOD

1. **Privatization**: The transfer of ownership or control of public goods and services to private entities leads to the prioritization of profit over the Common Good, resulting in reduced access, increased costs, and diminished quality of essential services such as healthcare, education, and utilities.
2. **Deregulation**: Relaxing or removing regulations intended to protect public health, safety, and welfare creates opportunities for exploitation, market manipulation, and environmental degradation, undermining the well-being of communities and individuals.
3. **Corruption and Cronyism**: When public officials or institutions prioritize personal gain or favoritism over the welfare of society, it erodes trust and leads to policies that benefit a select few at the expense of the broader population.
4. **Income Inequality and Poverty**: Widening gaps between the wealthy and the poor destabilize communities and hinder social mobility, leading to a concentration of power and resources in the hands of a few while leaving many without the means to access basic necessities and opportunities.
5. **Environmental Degradation**: Policies and practices that prioritize short-term economic gains over long-term sustainability result in irreversible damage to the environment, jeopardizing the health and well-being of present and future generations.
6. **Media Manipulation and Disinformation**: When information is distorted or manipulated to serve specific interests, it undermines public discourse, erodes trust in institutions, and impedes the ability of individuals to make informed decisions, ultimately hindering the pursuit of the Common Good.
7. **Erosion of Social Cohesion and Trust**: Factors such as polarization, discrimination, and social exclusion fracture communities and weaken the bonds that hold society together, making it difficult to address common challenges and promote collective well-being.
8. **Globalization and Economic Exploitation**: While globalization can bring benefits such as increased trade and cultural exchange, it can also lead to economic exploitation, loss of local jobs, and exploitation of labor in developing countries, exacerbating inequalities and undermining the well-being of marginalized communities.
9. **Lack of Access to Education and Healthcare**: Inadequate access to education and healthcare perpetuates cycles of poverty and inequality, limiting opportunities for individuals to reach their full potential and contribute meaningfully to society.
10. **Unchecked Corporate Power**: When corporations wield disproportionate influence over government policies and decision-making processes, it leads to policies that prioritize corporate interests over the Common Good, resulting in environmental degradation, worker exploitation, and erosion of consumer protections.
11. **Systemic Discrimination and Injustice**: Discriminatory practices based on factors such as race, gender, religion, or socioeconomic status perpetuate inequalities and marginalize certain groups within society, hindering the realization of equal opportunities and social justice for all.
12. **Underinvestment in Infrastructure and Public Services**: Neglecting essential infrastructure and public services, such as transportation, housing, and social welfare programs, blocks economic development, exacerbates social disparities, and undermines the overall well-being of communities.
13. **Militarism**: An excessive focus on military buildup and aggression diverts resources away from addressing pressing social and economic needs, perpetuates cycles of violence and conflict, and undermines efforts to promote peace, diplomacy, and international cooperation. Additionally, militarism contributes to the erosion of civil liberties, increases the risk of armed conflict, and exacerbates tensions both domestically and globally, ultimately detracting from the pursuit of the Common Good.

The essentials of life are deeply interconnected with wicked problems like inequality, power imbalances, and corruption. These relationships reveal how systemic issues exacerbate each other, making progress on any single issue difficult without addressing the broader context.

Inequality

Inequality undermines equitable access to essentials, creating cycles of deprivation:

Water, Food, and Shelter: Disparities in wealth and resources lead to uneven access to clean water, nutritious food, and safe housing. Marginalized groups often live in areas with polluted water sources, food deserts, and inadequate shelter.

Healthcare and Education: Inequality limits access to quality healthcare and education, perpetuating disparities in health outcomes, earning potential, and intergenerational opportunities.

Public Services: Ineffective or corrupt public service delivery exacerbates inequities, especially in underserved communities, deepening social divides.

Freedom: Systemic inequalities often correlate with restrictions on freedoms, particularly for marginalized groups whose rights are undermined by social and economic hierarchies.

Power Imbalances

Power dynamics dictate control over resources and decision-making, influencing access to life's essentials:

Environmental Sustainability: Those in power often exploit natural resources for short-term gains, disregarding the needs of future generations and vulnerable populations.

Jobs and Economic Stability: Power is concentrated in the hands of a few, leading to exploitative labor practices and wage gaps.

Safety and Security: Elites may prioritize their safety and security while neglecting broader societal needs, fostering environments where marginalized communities face systemic violence or insecurity.

Corruption

Corruption erodes trust, governance, and the equitable provision of services:

Public Services: Corruption in infrastructure projects, healthcare, and education diverts resources, leading to substandard or inaccessible services.

Safety and Security: Corrupt law enforcement or judicial systems fail to protect vulnerable populations, perpetuating cycles of exploitation and violence.

Climate Action: Corruption hampers effective responses to climate change, as vested interests delay necessary transitions to sustainable practices.

CLIMATEGPT

According to **ClimateGPT**, here are some key root causes of why – around the world – the poor continue to suffer:

- **Poverty and Economic Inequality:** Poverty is a significant root cause of both health and livelihood challenges. Limited access to resources, education, and economic opportunities can lead to poor health outcomes and hinder individuals from securing sustainable livelihoods.

- **Lack of Access to Affordable Healthcare:** Limited access to healthcare services, including preventive care and treatment, is a fundamental root cause of health challenges. This can result from inadequate healthcare infrastructure, geographical barriers, politically-driven policy, and financial constraints.

- **Inadequate Education:** Lack of education is closely linked to both health and livelihood issues. Without education, individuals may have limited awareness of health practices, face challenges in securing stable employment, and may be more susceptible to poverty.

- **Unsafe Working Conditions:** Unsafe working conditions contribute to health problems and pose a threat to livelihoods. Inadequate workplace safety measures can lead to accidents, injuries, and long-term health issues for workers.

- **Environmental Factors:** Environmental conditions, including pollution, lack of clean water, and exposure to harmful substances, can have a direct impact on health.

Additionally, environmental degradation can disrupt livelihoods, especially in communities dependent on agriculture or natural resources.

- **Inadequate Social Safety Nets:** Lack of robust social safety nets, such as healthcare coverage, unemployment benefits, and social welfare programs, can exacerbate health and livelihood challenges during times of crisis or economic instability.

- **Discrimination and Social Injustice:** Discrimination based on factors such as gender, race, or socioeconomic status contributes to disparities in health and livelihood opportunities. Overcoming systemic inequalities is crucial for addressing these wicked problems.

- **Global Health Threats:** Emerging infectious diseases, global pandemics, and other health threats pose challenges to both individual health and broader livelihoods. These threats can disrupt economies, strain healthcare systems, and lead to widespread social and economic consequences.

- **Lack of Access to Clean Water and Sanitation:** Inadequate access to clean water and sanitation facilities contributes to the spread of diseases, affecting both individual health and community well-being. It can also impact livelihoods by hindering productivity and economic development.

- **Low Wages:** Insufficient compensation for work, especially in informal or low-skilled sectors, can leave individuals and families struggling to meet their basic needs.

- **Debt:** High levels of personal or national debt can limit economic mobility, divert resources away from poverty alleviation efforts, and perpetuate cycles of financial hardship.

- **Food Insecurity:** Insufficient access to nutritious and affordable food can result in malnutrition and health issues, further perpetuating the cycle of poverty.

- **Housing Insecurity:** Lack of affordable housing options and stable living conditions can lead to homelessness or spending a disproportionate amount of income on housing, leaving less for other essential needs.

- **Corruption:** Widespread corruption in government institutions and public services can divert resources away from poverty alleviation programs, leaving communities without the support they need.

- **Financial Exclusion:** Lack of access to financial resources, including credit and banking services, hinders individuals from starting businesses or investing in income-generating activities.

- **Inadequate Infrastructure:** Poor infrastructure, including roads, transportation, and utilities, can impede economic development and limit access to markets and services.

- **Climate Events and Natural Disasters:** Events such as earthquakes, floods, or droughts can devastate communities and disrupt livelihoods, exacerbating poverty in affected areas.

- **Digital Divide:** The digital divide refers to the gap between individuals, communities, or nations that have access to information and communication technologies (ICTs), particularly the internet, and those that do not. This divide encompasses disparities in access to digital devices, broadband connectivity, digital skills, and the ability to effectively use technology for various purposes.

- **Tech Unemployment:** The skills gap where technological progress could lead to job displacement and changes in the nature of work.

Further details on each one of these root causes are listed in the appendix: *Answers from AI,* at the end of this book.

CASCADING EFFECTS

The "essentials of life," such as clean air, water, food security, shelter, healthcare, education, safety, social connections, environmental sustainability, and justice, are interconnected and often intertwined with complex, interdependent systems. The problems are characterized by their complexity, ambiguity, and the interconnectedness of various factors, making them difficult to define and solve. Here are some cascading effects associated with wicked problems related to the essentials of life:

- **Health Impacts**: Problems related to clean air, water, food security, and healthcare can have significant health impacts on individuals and communities. For example, air pollution can lead to respiratory diseases, contaminated water can cause waterborne illnesses, and food insecurity can result in malnutrition and related health issues.

- **Social Unrest and Inequality**: Challenges related to access to essentials such as shelter, healthcare, education, and justice can exacerbate social inequalities and lead to social unrest. For instance, inadequate housing conditions, lack of access to healthcare, and disparities in education and justice systems can fuel tensions and protests within communities.

- **Environmental Degradation**: Issues like unsustainable resource use, pollution, and climate change can result in environmental degradation, affecting ecosystems and natural resources essential for life. This degradation, in turn, can exacerbate other wicked problems, such as water scarcity, food insecurity, and loss of biodiversity.

- **Economic Instability**: Wicked problems related to the essentials of life can also have significant economic implications. For example, healthcare costs associated with treating illnesses caused by pollution or contaminated water can strain healthcare systems and individuals' finances. Additionally, environmental disasters and social unrest can disrupt economies and livelihoods.

- **Migration and Displacement**: Challenges such as food insecurity, lack of access to clean water, and environmental disasters can contribute to forced migration and displacement of populations. This, in turn, can lead to additional social, economic, and political challenges, both within affected regions and for host communities.

- **Interconnected Solutions and Trade-offs**: Addressing wicked problems related to the essentials of life often requires interconnected solutions that address multiple factors simultaneously. However, these solutions may involve trade-offs and complexities, as interventions in one area may have unintended consequences or require sacrifices in another.

- **Governance and Policy Challenges**: The complexity and interdependence of wicked problems make them difficult to address through traditional governance and policy frameworks. Effective solutions often require collaboration across sectors, levels of government, and stakeholders, as well as innovative approaches to decision-making and implementation.

"I'd say treatment of immigrants is one of the greatest injustices done in our government's name."
– Bill Gates

7 POPULATION AND MIGRATION

In his eye-opening book **David Wallace-Wells** paints a scenario for the future of migration[217]:

Imagine the two continents suddenly drowned in the sea, the whole New World submerged, and everyone left bobbing at the surface now fighting for a foothold, somewhere, anywhere, and, if someone else is scrambling for the same dry spot, scrambling to get there first.

This a great tragedy. Here are some common **negative narratives** about immigrants, along with why they're often incorrect:

- **Job Stealing**: The belief that immigrants take away jobs from native-born citizens is pervasive. However, research often suggests that immigrants actually complement the labor force by filling gaps in industries with labor shortages, contributing to economic growth.

---

[217] *The Uninhabitable Earth: Life After Warming,* David Wallace-Wells, Tim Duggan Books, New York, 2019. More than 140 million people in just three regions of the world will be made climate migrants by 2050, the World Bank projected in a 2018 study, assuming current warming and emissions trends: 86 million in sub-Saharan Africa, 40 million in South Asia, and 17 million in Latin America. The most commonly cited estimate from the United Nations' International Organization for Migration suggests numbers a bit higher–200 million, total, by 2050.

- **Strain on Social Services**: Some argue that immigrants burden social services such as healthcare and education. However, studies indicate that immigrants often pay taxes and contribute economically, offsetting any strains on public services. Moreover, they tend to utilize social services at rates similar to or lower than native-born citizens.

- **Increased Crime Rates**: There's a misconception that immigrants are more prone to criminal behavior. In reality, numerous studies have shown that immigrants are less likely to commit crimes than native-born citizens. Additionally, areas with higher immigration rates often experience lower crime rates.

- **Cultural Assimilation**: There's concern that immigrants resist assimilating into the host culture and instead form isolated communities. However, many immigrants actively engage in their communities, learn the language, and contribute to cultural diversity, enriching society rather than isolating themselves.

- **National Security Threats**: Some view immigrants as potential security risks, particularly in the context of terrorism. While there are legitimate security concerns, the vast majority of immigrants are not involved in criminal or terrorist activities. Stringent vetting processes are typically in place to mitigate such risks.

- **Welfare Dependency**: Critics argue that immigrants rely heavily on welfare benefits. However, studies show that immigrants are less likely to use welfare programs than native-born citizens, partly due to eligibility restrictions and fear of deportation.

- **Economic Burden**: There's a misconception that immigrants drain public resources and contribute little to the economy. In reality, immigrants often start businesses, create jobs, and contribute to innovation and economic growth, benefiting both the local and national economies.

IS MAGA RACIST?

There is a hidden meaning behind Trump's slogan to "Make America Great Again." His slogan is code for "Let's Make America White again."

Immigration policy is one of the toughest issues facing the U.S. and its core beliefs and values. Both political parties are doing their best to bury or avoid this issue. Our politicians would rather wrestle with the health issue and the tax reform issue than start thinking about what to do with our immigration policy.

The issue has many strands. Should the U.S. accept more displaced persons from other countries, especially if they are poor, black, or Muslim? Should we keep out, even ban, Muslims because they have a different religion and may even include some terrorists? Should the U.S. put up a Great Wall to keep out more Mexicans from slipping into the country? Should the U.S. government intensify its deportation of illegal Mexicans, and should this include deporting the Dreamers, young Mexicans who were born here and became Americanized? Should our immigration policy give preference to immigrants coming from traditional countries bringing in our new immigrants, namely Ireland, Poland, Russia and various Eastern European countries? Should we open our doors to more immigrants from Asia, namely Chinese, Vietnamese and Koreans who are highly industrious and peaceful and whose religions don't threaten us? Should we adopt Canada's approach to immigration favoring attracting the rich and educated from other countries?

The need for clear thinking on these issues has never been greater. The policies that we adopt can fundamentally change the American character and our fundamental beliefs and values. It can end up painting a picture of America to the rest of the world that will puzzle, disturb and maybe alienate them.

Let's examine one strand in this messy issue of immigration. Donald Trump came riding into the American Presidency on the slogan "Let's Make America Great Again." He rode in on the votes of a large group of "forgotten" working class Americans of low-income and poor education who are bewildered by the changes going on in the country, including same sex marriage, homosexuality, transsexual role changes, abortion rights. His political base see the ascendency of black Americans, the inflow of illegal Mexicans, the rising number of Asians outperforming Americans in America's classrooms, and the inflow of Muslims building mosques and praying and dressing differently.

In the midst of these dizzying changes, Donald Trump wins a Nevada primary election on February 24, 2016 and celebrates by saying 'I Love the Poorly Educated!' One observer spots the anomaly: "Trump sits on a gold toilet. Dumb people voted for him." How does such a rich man have such strong appeal to down-and-out Americans? Could it be because he says to them "Americans make too much money," as if he plans to do something about this if elected President.

There is a hidden meaning behind Trump's slogan to **"Make America Great Again."** His slogan may well be code for **"Let's Make America White again."**[218] Trump has tapped into the economic insecurity that globalization has created. With decades of outsourcing of manufacturing jobs and stagnant and depressed wages across the Rust Belt, the threat on livelihoods is real. While CEOs saw huge gains in their pay checks, the common worker was shown a pink slip. The result? An overwhelming sense of loss and insecurity. Instead of blaming corporate policy and decisions made by politicians supporting globalization, the GOP has deflected the blame: ***immigrants are the reason why Americans don't have good jobs***.

By blaming growing income inequality on immigrants rather than corporate forces, the GOP and Trump are deceiving their supporters. Trump has sensed that the white person, especially the white male, feels displaced and overwhelmed by the growing number of multi-cultural groups – and has tapped into this discomfort to actively fan the flames of hate and divisiveness. The **gun industry**[219] exploits this fear as well.

---

[218] Make America White Again? By Kelly J. Baker, *The Atlantic*, March 12, 2016
https://www.theatlantic.com/politics/archive/2016/03/donald-trump-kkk/473190/
[219] "How the US government created and coddled the gun industry" by Brian Delay, *Salon*, Oct 14, 2017
https://www.salon.com/2017/10/14/how-the-us-government-created-and-coddled-the-gun-industry_partner/

POPULATION & MIGRATION

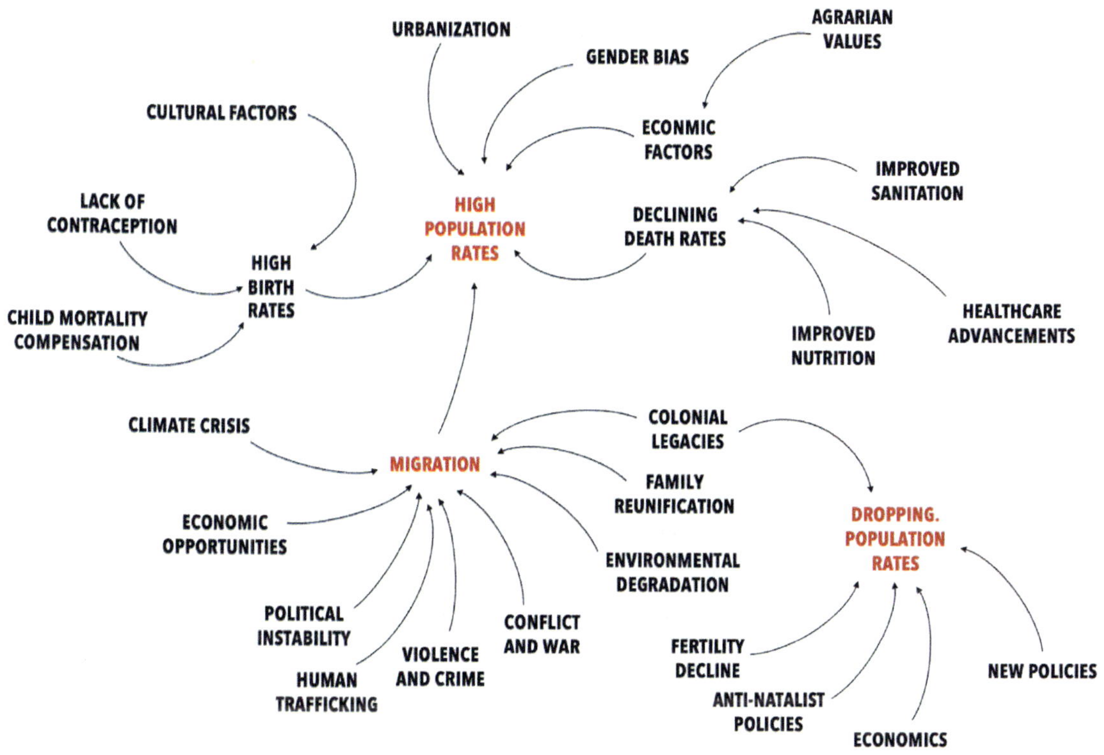

Trump showed his real alignment with white males in his remarks during the white nationalist rally and street clashes in **Charlottesville**[220], Virginia. White supremacists, neo-

[220] "How Did We Get to Charlottesville?" by Philip Kotler, *Huffington Post*, April 18, 2017
https://www.huffpost.com/entry/how-did-we-get-to-charlottesville_b_59976a82e4b033e0fbdec416

Nazis, and members of the "alt-right" chanted "Heil Trump!" while marching through the Charlottesville streets. Dozens of demonstrators were hurt, and there occurred the horrific act of domestic terrorism – civilians plowed down by an American car driver. Trump's initial statement was that the protestors and counter-protestors were equally to blame. It took another day or two before Trump finally came out condemning "the White Supremacists, Ku-Klux Klan, and the Nazis" as the instigators of this very un-peaceful protest. Trump knew that he needed to respond to the terrible news. But he also needed to avoid mentioning these groups because they are a part of his base constituency.

So, we ask, how did our democracy become so equivocal and fragile? How could the President of the United States not stand up immediately and come out against the groups that threaten our American values? **By defining American values as "white values," Trump has opened the door to hate-based politics. He is the "divider-in-chief."**

But it is more complicated than that. **The moral failing is not limited to President Trump.** He was put in power by at least four groups who supported him: Evangelicals, the Republican Party, the Corporate Class, and the desperate workers who lost their jobs in coal, steel, and other industries. All of them are implicit in this Administration's moral failings.

The paradox is how Trump can appeal to the blue-collar class and the rich at the same time. Consider that he only selects rich Americans to be in his cabinet. He favors rich people running for office. He distains people who aren't rich like him. He doesn't want to play golf with the working class. But he wants their votes. And he gets their votes, by appealing to the worst aspects of our unsolved dilemma – racism and segregation left over from the GOP's **southern strategy**.[221]

The hornet's nest of Immigration is not limited to the USA. This is a **worldwide scapegoat** for the effects of unchecked globalization. Populist leaders have popped up in several countries, all ranting against the inflows of immigrants fleeing from other countries for

---

[221] "How the Southern Strategy Made Donald Trump Possible" by Jeet Heer, *The New Republic*, February 18, 2016
https://newrepublic.com/article/130039/southern-strategy-made-donald-trump-possible

their safety. Muslims in war-torn countries get into rickety boats and risk their lives to leave the Middle East hoping to land in Greece or Italy and make their way to Germany or England. Those wars are largely the fault of the West, but that fact is conveniently not factored into the equation. Meanwhile, populist leaders appeal to their native populations to keep them in fear, and blame immigrants for social upheaval. The Europeans fear they will lose their culture to the "hordes" of immigrants.

Immigration policies are key to how a nation wants to define itself, its value and beliefs. The USA is closing its borders. **The idea of America –** *e pluribus unum*[222] – is now clearly under attack. President Trump would not admit his own immigrant parents or either one of his immigrant wives into the country today.

A nation built on immigration shuts its eyes and closes its mind. The *land of the free* will soon be no more. The **golden door**[223] is swinging shut. We ignore the contributions immigrants make[224] at our own peril.

How ironic that a country built on the idea of Lady Liberty has grown wary of the "huddled masses"...

But why do people migrate in the first place? Here are the main reasons >>

- **Economic Reasons**: Economic disparities between countries and regions often drive people to seek better job opportunities and higher standards of living elsewhere. Poverty, lack of employment opportunities, low wages, and economic instability can all prompt individuals and families to migrate in search of a better livelihood.

---

[222] "E Pluribus Unum" Becomes Controversial" by David Niose, Psychology Today March 13, 2011 https://www.psychologytoday.com/intl/blog/our-humanity-naturally/201103/e-pluribus-unum-becomes-controversial

[223] "Don't Shut the Golden Door" by John M. MacDonald and Robert J. Sampson, *New York Times*, June 19, 2012 https://www.nytimes.com/2012/06/20/opinion/the-beneficial-impact-of-immigrants.html

[224] How Immigrants Positively Affect the Business Community and the U.S. Economy

- **Conflict and Violence**: Armed conflict, civil unrest, and persecution are major drivers of forced migration. People flee their homes to escape violence, persecution based on race, religion, ethnicity, political opinion, or membership in a particular social group, and human rights abuses. Wars, political instability, and human rights violations can render entire regions uninhabitable, leading to large-scale displacement.

- **Climate Factors**: Environmental degradation, natural disasters, and climate change increasingly contribute to migration. Rising sea levels, droughts, floods, desertification, and other environmental crises can destroy homes, disrupt livelihoods, and exacerbate food and water scarcity, forcing people to relocate in search of safety and sustenance.

- **Social and Cultural Factors**: Sociocultural factors such as gender inequality, discrimination, and lack of access to education, healthcare, and basic services can also drive migration. Marginalized groups may face limited opportunities and systemic barriers that push them to seek better prospects elsewhere.

- **Political Factors**: Political repression, lack of political freedoms, corruption, and authoritarian regimes can compel individuals and families to flee their countries in search of safety and freedom. Restrictions on freedom of expression, assembly, and association can create environments of fear and persecution, prompting people to seek refuge abroad.

- **Demographic Pressures**: Rapid population growth, urbanization, and demographic imbalances can strain resources and infrastructure, leading to social and economic challenges that contribute to migration. In some cases, demographic pressures exacerbate existing vulnerabilities and push people to seek opportunities elsewhere.

- **Family Reunification**: Family reunification is a significant driver of migration, with individuals seeking to join relatives who have migrated previously. The desire to be with loved ones and support family members financially and emotionally motivates many to undertake the journey to a new country.

Many of the problems facing migrants have deep historical roots.

The role of the United States in contributing to political instability in Central American countries for example, is complex and multifaceted, with historical *and* contemporary factors shaping the region's fragile political landscape. Here are some ways in which the US has been implicated in increasing political instability in these countries:

- **Historical Interventionism**: Throughout the 20th century, the United States played a significant role in Central America through interventions, military interventions, and support for authoritarian regimes. For example, the US supported military coups and authoritarian regimes in countries such as Guatemala, El Salvador, and Nicaragua during the Cold War era as part of its broader geopolitical strategy to counter perceived communist influence in the region. These interventions often resulted in human rights abuses, political repression, and social unrest, contributing to long-term political instability.

- **Support for Regime Change and Coups**: The United States has been involved in supporting regime change and coups in Central America, often in pursuit of its own political and economic interests. For example, in Guatemala in 1954, the CIA orchestrated a coup that overthrew the democratically elected government of President Jacobo Árbenz, leading to decades of political instability and violence. Similarly, US support for right-wing military regimes in El Salvador and Honduras during the 1970s and 1980s contributed to widespread human rights violations and civil conflicts.

- **Military Aid and Training**: The United States has provided military aid, training, and equipment to security forces in Central American countries, including those implicated in human rights abuses and repression of dissent. This military support has sometimes bolstered authoritarian regimes and perpetuated cycles of violence and instability, rather than promoting democracy and stability.

- **Drug War Policies**: US policies aimed at combating drug trafficking and organized crime in Central America have had unintended consequences, including exacerbating violence and political instability. For example, the militarization of anti-drug efforts has led to human rights abuses by security forces and fueled armed conflict between rival criminal groups, further destabilizing the region. Remember Iran-Contra?[225]

- **Trade and Economic Policies**: US trade and economic policies, including trade agreements and neoliberal [226]economic reforms, have had mixed effects on Central American countries. While these policies have promoted economic integration and foreign investment, they have also contributed to economic inequality, displacement of small-scale farmers, and erosion of social welfare systems, exacerbating social tensions and political instability.

THE FACTS ON IMMIGRATION

Do facts matter at all? Not when our politicians use fear and outright lies to mislead the public.

"Ironically, the result is exactly the opposite of the usual narrative," says **Ben Jones**, a professor of strategy at Kellog. "It seems like immigrants actually improve the economic outcomes for native-born workers."

FACT: because **immigrants are more entrepreneurial** than American-born workers in both the number and the success of the companies they start, their presence in the country actually *increases* the demand for labor, to the **benefit of workers**.

The narrative of migration promoted by unscrupulous politicians *paints the immigrant as a criminal.* Opponents of immigration often argue that immigrants drive up crime rates. But

[225] See: https://www.britannica.com/event/Iran-Contra-Affair and
https://www.brown.edu/Research/Understanding_the_Iran_Contra_Affair/iran-contra-affairs.php
[226] "Immigrants to the U.S. Create More Jobs than They Take" *Kellogg Insight,* October 5, 2020
https://insight.kellogg.northwestern.edu/article/immigrants-to-the-u-s-create-more-jobs-than-they-take
See the working paper: https://www.nber.org/system/files/working_papers/w27778/w27778.pdf

research[227] from Stanford economist **Ran Abramitzky** (and friends) finds that hasn't been the case in America for the last 140 years!

FACT: Today, **immigrants are 30 percent less likely to be incarcerated** than are U.S.-born individuals who are white, the study finds. And when the analysis is expanded to include Black Americans — whose prison rates are higher than the general population — the likelihood of an immigrant being incarcerated is 60 percent lower than of people born in the United States.

False myths and disinformation about immigration and immigrants are common. The **Southern Poverty Law Center** has made a list of the most frequently heard misconceptions—along with information to help you separate fact from fear.[228]

Do you want to know what makes America great? *Immigrants!*

Instead of bashing immigrants, we should be celebrating them:

- **Courage and Resilience:** Understand the bravery and

---

[227] *Law-Abiding Immigrants: The Incarceration Gap Between Immigrants and the US-born, 1870–2020* by Ran Abramitzky, Leah Platt Boustan, Elisa Jácome, Santiago Pérez & Juan David Torres, working paper, National Bureau of Economic Research https://www.nber.org/papers/w31440

[228] TEN MYTHS ABOUT IMMIGRATION, *Learning For Justice*, Issue 39, Spring 2011
https://www.learningforjustice.org/magazine/spring-2011/ten-myths-about-immigration
see also: https://www.learningforjustice.org/magazine/sources-ten-myths-about-immigration

resilience of migrants who embark on often perilous journeys in search of a better future.

- **Contributions to Culture:** We should celebrate the rich cultural diversity that immigrants bring to their new communities. From cuisine to art, music to literature, immigrants enrich society with their unique perspectives and experiences.

- **Economic and Social Contributions:** Recognize the significant economic and social contributions immigrants make to their host countries. They start businesses, fill vital roles in industries facing labor shortages, and contribute to innovation and growth.

- **Family and Community Values:** Immigrants often sacrifice much to support their loved ones and build strong, vibrant communities wherever they settle.

- **Integration and Inclusion:** Promote narratives that focus on integration and inclusion, highlighting efforts to welcome newcomers and help them thrive in their new homes. Building bridges between cultures fosters understanding and strengthens social cohesion.

- **Shared Humanity:** Ultimately, the narrative of migration should underscore our shared humanity and interconnectedness. Regardless of borders or background, we are all part of the global human family, and it's essential to treat each other with compassion, respect, and solidarity.

What happened to the American Dream?

And why have our politicians turning it into a nightmare?

OVERPOPULATION

Is overpopulation a problem?

Conversations concerning the phenomenon of overpopulation invariably provoke contention. Central to these discussions are inquiries into the root causes of overpopulation and the requisite actions to address its ramifications. Such deliberations, however, are often fraught with the risk of being co-opted by narrow perspectives that propagate discriminatory narratives, positing certain demographics as undesirable or expendable in the pursuit of population control. The global challenge of overpopulation is underscored by the burgeoning human populace, which, as of contemporary estimates, nears **8 billion**.

This exponential growth trajectory has engendered concerns regarding the sustainability of Earth's ecosystems and the equitable allocation of finite resources.

An analysis reveals that the "average person" worldwide surpasses sustainable consumption thresholds by over 50%, indicative of pervasive *overconsumption*. Particularly poignant is the case of the United States, where individuals exhibit consumption rates nearly fivefold higher than the sustainable yield of the planet, underscoring the disproportionate ecological footprint attributed to affluent societies.

Furthermore, the consequences of unchecked population growth extend beyond ecological concerns to encompass socioeconomic disparities and geopolitical instability.

In regions grappling with rapidly growing populations, resource scarcity precipitates socio-economic inequities, exacerbating poverty, food insecurity, and inadequate access to essential services. Concurrently, demographic pressures underscored by rapid population growth engender migratory trends and geopolitical tensions, as populations vie for access to dwindling resources and seek refuge from ecological degradation and socio-economic precarity.

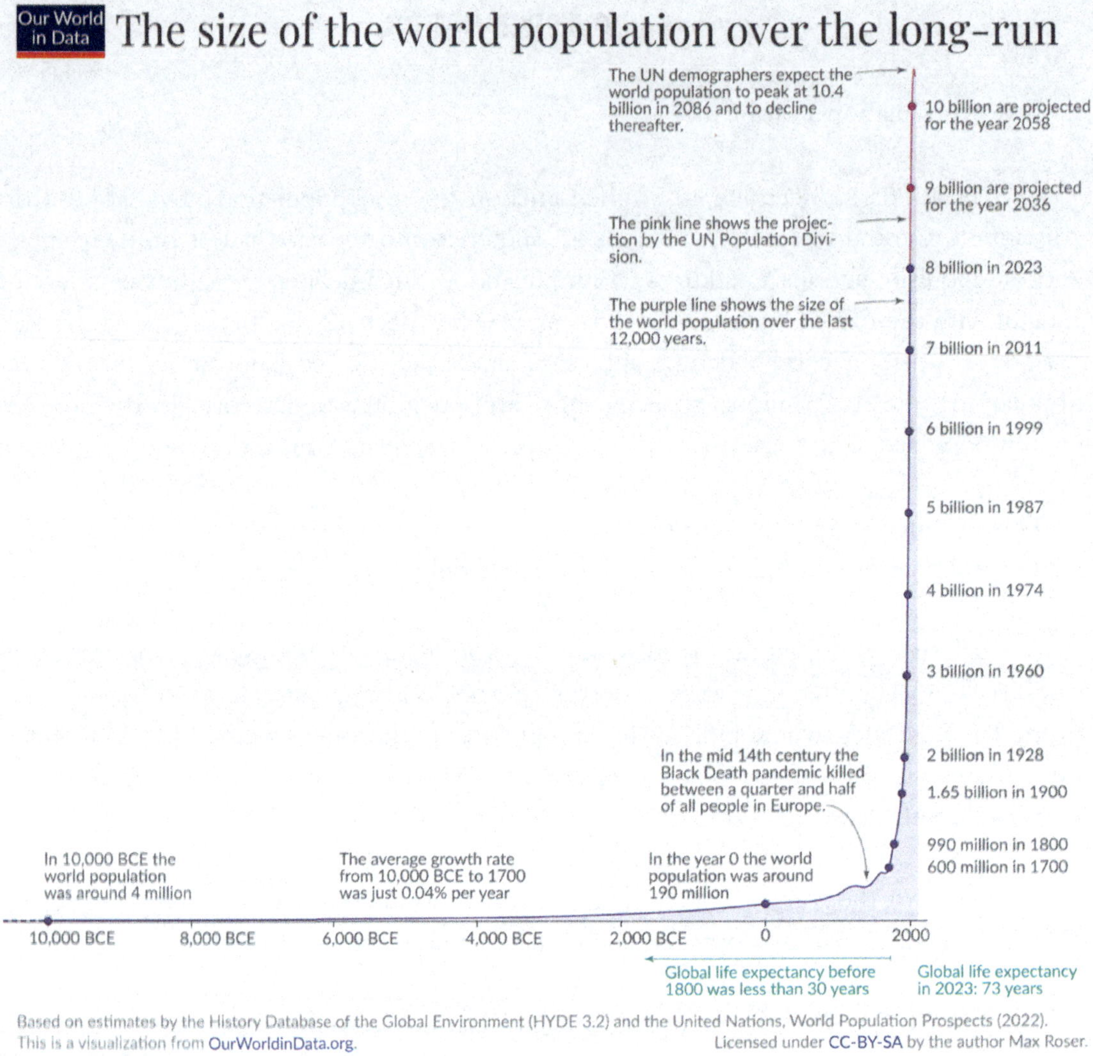

The future of population growth is in Asia and Africa.

Will India, China, Nigeria etc. be able to continue their growth and keep up with the needs of the people? Planetary boundaries are already breached. There is *no chance* – we think – at this point to keep us below the 1.5-degree Celsius heating threshold.

The 1.5-degree Celsius heating threshold refers to a key target outlined in the Paris Agreement; an international treaty aimed at addressing climate change. Specifically, the agreement aims to limit global temperature rise to well below 2 degrees Celsius above pre-industrial levels, with efforts to limit the increase to 1.5 degrees Celsius if possible.

The threshold of 1.5 degrees Celsius is considered significant because exceeding this level of warming could have severe and potentially irreversible impacts on ecosystems, communities, and economies worldwide. We've missed the bus. Limiting warming to 1.5 degrees Celsius compared to pre-industrial levels could have significantly reduce the risks of extreme weather events, sea-level rise, loss of biodiversity, and other adverse consequences associated with climate change.

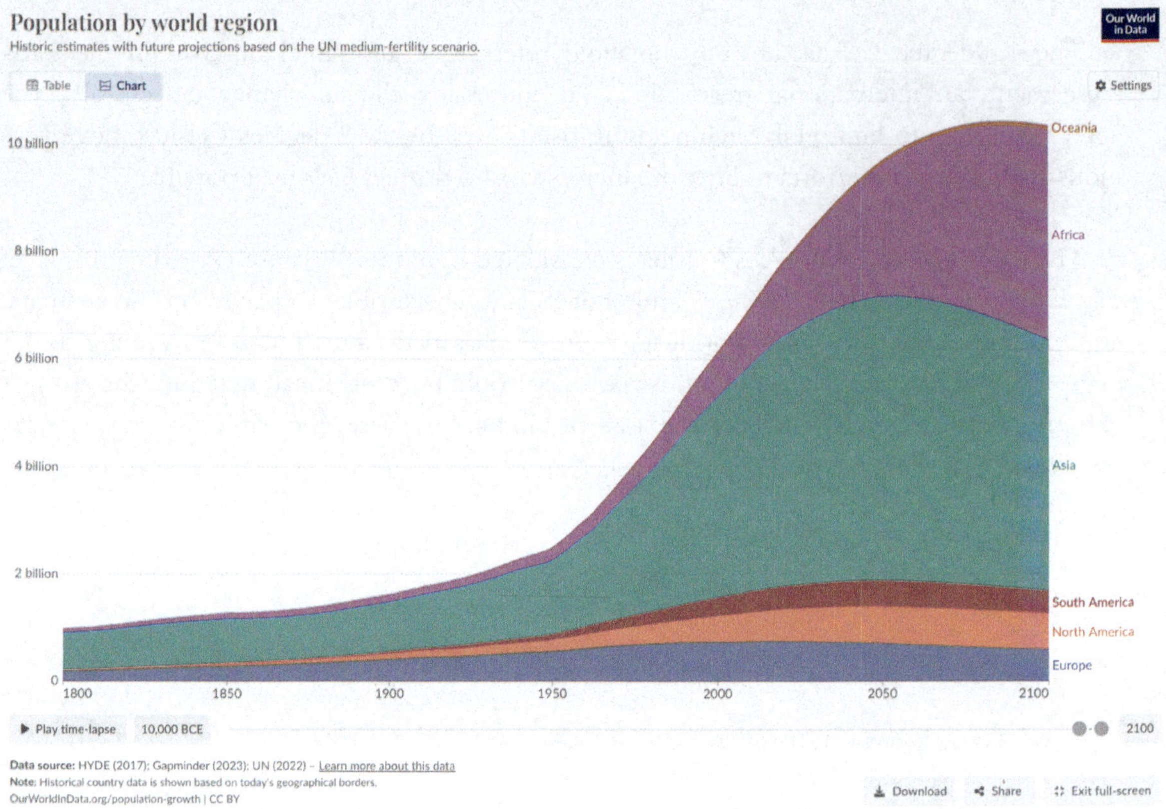

So, what happens now? The world's exploding population can have several inevitable results, including:

- **Strain on Resources**: As the population increases, there is greater demand for resources such as food, water, energy, and land. This leads to overexploitation of natural resources, environmental degradation, and competition for limited resources, particularly in regions already facing scarcity.

- **Pressure on Infrastructure**: Rising populations put pressure on infrastructure such as transportation, healthcare, sanitation, and housing. Inadequate infrastructure leads to congestion, pollution, and inadequate access to essential services, particularly in urban areas experiencing rapid growth.

- **Urbanization**: Unchecked population growth leads to increased urbanization as people migrate from rural to urban areas in search of opportunities. Urbanization can strain urban infrastructure, lead to informal settlements or slums, and exacerbate social inequalities and challenges related to housing, employment, and public services. Megacities are booming across the world.

- **Impact on Ecosystems**: The expanding human population has significant impacts on ecosystems and biodiversity through habitat destruction, fragmentation, pollution, and overconsumption of natural resources. Loss of biodiversity and ecosystem services has long-term consequences for human well-being and environmental sustainability.

- **Social and Economic Challenges**: Rapid population growth poses challenges for social and economic development, including high unemployment rates, poverty, income inequality, and social tensions. Addressing these challenges requires investments in education, healthcare, job creation, and social protection programs.

- **Healthcare and Education Needs**: A growing population increases the demand for healthcare services, education facilities, and other social services. Meeting the healthcare and education needs of a larger population requires adequate funding, infrastructure, and trained personnel.

- **Pressure on Food Security**: With a larger population to feed, there is increased pressure on global food production systems. Ensuring food security for all requires sustainable agricultural practices, improved access to nutritious food, and efforts to reduce food waste and distribution inequalities.

- **Climate Change Impacts**: Population growth contributes to increased greenhouse gas emissions and exacerbates climate change impacts. Addressing population growth alongside efforts to mitigate and adapt to climate change is essential for achieving environmental sustainability and resilience.

Which bring us to **war** and conflict.

Total global military expenditure reached $2443 billion in 2023, an increase of 6.8 per cent in real terms from 2022. This was the steepest year-on-year increase since 2009.

The 10 largest spenders in 2023—led by the United States, China and Russia—all increased their military spending, according to new data on global military spending published today by the Stockholm International Peace Research Institute (SIPRI), available at www.sipri.org.[229]

It is not an accident that the countries of the world are spending more on militarism than ever before – it is the only thing we consistently invest in.

UNDERPOPULATION

Even as overpopulation sweeps the developing world, we find that the rich countries have the opposite problem – *declining birth rates and negative population growth.* While overpopulation puts a strain on natural resources, increases conflicts and wars, and causes water shortages and malnutrition, population shrinkage also presents its own set of problems.

Population decline has several negative impacts on societies and economies, including:

[229] https://www.sipri.org/media/press-release/2024/global-military-spending-surges-amid-war-rising-tensions-and-insecurity

- **Labor Shortages**: A declining population leads to labor shortages, particularly in sectors that require a younger workforce. This results in reduced productivity, slower economic growth, and increased dependence on automation or immigration to fill gaps in the labor market.

- **Aging Population**: Population decline often coincides with an aging population, as the proportion of elderly people increases relative to younger age groups. This demographic shift strains healthcare systems, pension systems, and social support networks, because there are fewer working-age individuals to support and care for older adults.

- **Economic Contraction**: A shrinking population precipitates economic contraction, as reduced consumer demand, declining tax revenues, and a smaller workforce limit economic activity and investment. This creates challenges for businesses, governments, and households, potentially leading to stagnation or recession.

- **Fiscal Pressures**: A declining population places fiscal pressures on governments, particularly in terms of funding pensions, healthcare, and social welfare programs for an aging population. Governments face challenges in balancing budgets, providing adequate services, and managing public debt in the face of declining revenues and increasing expenditures.

- **Housing Market Challenges**: Population decline leads to excess housing supply and declining property values in regions experiencing depopulation. This creates challenges for homeowners, developers, and local governments, potentially leading to abandoned properties, urban blight, and disinvestment in affected areas.

- **Social Cohesion**: Population decline has implications for social cohesion and community vitality, as shrinking populations lead to decreased social interaction, diminished community engagement, and a sense of isolation, particularly in rural areas or regions with significant outmigration.

- **Loss of Cultural Heritage**: Population decline also contribute to the loss of cultural heritage and traditions, as younger generations leave rural areas or smaller communities in search of opportunities elsewhere. This leads to the erosion and degeneration of local customs, languages, and cultural practices over time.

- **Decline in Innovation and Entrepreneurship**: A shrinking population brings reduced innovation and entrepreneurship, as there are fewer individuals available to start new businesses, pursue higher education, or engage in research and development activities. This has long-term implications for economic competitiveness and technological advancement.

The link between **colonialism** and **population growth** in poor countries is complex and multifaceted, with historical, economic, social, and political factors playing significant roles. Here are some key aspects:

- **Historical Exploitation**: Many poor countries were colonies of European powers during the era of colonialism. Colonial powers often exploited the natural resources, labor, and economies of these regions for their own benefit, without regard for the long-term well-being or development of the local populations. This exploitation could contribute to economic underdevelopment and poverty, which in turn can influence population growth dynamics.

- **Disruption of Traditional Societies**: Colonialism disrupted traditional social structures and economic systems in colonized regions. This disruption could lead to social dislocation, loss of livelihoods, and instability, which may impact population growth patterns. For example, the imposition of cash crop economies or the introduction of wage labor systems could influence family dynamics and fertility rates.

- **Introduction of Western Ideals and Practices**: Colonial powers imposed Western ideals, values, and practices on colonized societies, including attitudes toward family size, gender roles, and reproductive health. This could influence fertility preferences and behaviors, potentially contributing to higher population growth rates.

- **Health and Healthcare Systems**: While some colonial powers introduced modern healthcare practices and infrastructure, most neglected healthcare services or exploited local populations for medical experimentation. Access to healthcare, public health interventions, and disease control measures can all influence population growth rates.

- **Political Instability and Conflict**: The legacy of colonialism contributed to political instability, conflict, and social unrest in many post-colonial countries. Political instability and conflict disrupts social and economic development, exacerbates poverty, and impacts population growth through displacement, migration, and changes in fertility rates.

- **Continued Economic Dependency**: In many post-colonial countries, economic dependency on former colonial powers or global economic systems persists. This dependency limits opportunities for sustainable development and contributes to persistent poverty and inequality, which can affect population growth dynamics.

- **Environmental Degradation**: Colonialism often involved the exploitation of natural resources in colonized regions, leading to environmental degradation and resource depletion. Environmental degradation has profound impacts on human populations, including reduced agricultural productivity, food insecurity, and displacement, which can influence population growth patterns.

CLIMATEGPT

According to **ClimateGPT**, here are some key root causes for overpopulation:

- **High Birth Rates:** Regions with persistently high birth rates contribute to overpopulation. Cultural, social, and economic factors may influence family planning practices.

- **Lack of Education:** Limited access to education, particularly for women, can contribute to higher birth rates. Education empowers individuals to make informed family planning decisions.

- **Limited Access to Family Planning:** Inadequate access to contraceptives and family planning services can lead to unintended pregnancies and contribute to population growth.
- **Cultural and Religious Beliefs:** Cultural and religious beliefs that encourage larger families can influence population growth, especially in regions where such beliefs are deeply ingrained.

- **Poverty:** Poverty can be both a cause and a consequence of overpopulation. High birth rates may result from the need for additional labor and social security in impoverished communities.

- **Lack of Women's Empowerment:** Gender inequalities and limited opportunities for women can contribute to higher birth rates, as women may have fewer choices regarding their reproductive health.

For underpopulation:

- **Low Birth Rates:** Societal shifts, economic pressures, and changing cultural attitudes may contribute to lower birth rates, resulting in population decline.

- **Aging Population:** Longer life expectancy and declining birth rates lead to an aging population, which can impact workforce dynamics, economic productivity, and healthcare systems.

- **Economic and Social Factors:** Economic pressures, high costs of living, and career-focused lifestyles may discourage individuals from having larger families, contributing to underpopulation.

- **Urbanization:** Urbanization often leads to smaller family sizes as urban living introduces different lifestyle patterns and economic considerations.

- **Career Choices and Education:** Pursuing higher education and career aspirations may lead individuals to delay starting families, contributing to lower birth rates.
- **Social Changes:** Changes in societal norms, such as delayed marriages and increased acceptance of non-traditional family structures, can impact birth rates.

And for migration:

- **Economic Opportunities:** Economic disparities between regions drive migration as individuals seek better job opportunities, higher wages, and improved living standards.

- **Conflict and Instability:** Political instability, armed conflicts, and human rights abuses force people to flee their homes in search of safety and security.

- **Environmental Factors:** Environmental degradation, natural disasters, and climate change can contribute to displacement as communities face resource scarcity and environmental challenges.

- **Globalization:** Increased connectivity and awareness of opportunities in other regions influence migration decisions, especially for those seeking better economic prospects.

- **Demographic Pressures:** Demographic imbalances, such as a youth bulge or an aging population, can contribute to migration as individuals seek opportunities in regions with more favorable demographics.

- **Lack of Legal Avenues:** Limited legal pathways for migration and restrictive immigration policies contribute to irregular migration and the use of informal channels.

- **Cultural and Social Ties:** Cultural and social connections may influence migration patterns, with individuals moving to be with family or communities with shared cultural backgrounds.

- **Climate refugee:** the migrant seeking to escape climate collapse

Further details on each one of these root causes are listed in the appendix: *Answers from AI,* at the end of this book.

CASCADING EFFECTS

Here are some cascading effects of population growth and migration:

- **Economic Impact**:

1. Migration and immigration contribute to changes in labor markets, including shifts in wages, employment opportunities, and skill shortages.
2. Population growth drives demand for goods and services, stimulating economic growth and investment in infrastructure, housing, and consumer markets.
3. Immigration can also lead to entrepreneurship and innovation as newcomers bring diverse skills, knowledge, and perspectives to host countries.

- **Social Dynamics**:

1. Migration and immigration influences cultural diversity, social cohesion, and identity formation in both sending and receiving communities.
2. Population growth can strain social services, such as healthcare, education, and housing, particularly in urban areas experiencing rapid growth.
3. Immigration can contribute to multiculturalism and social integration, but it can also lead to tensions, discrimination, and xenophobia if not managed effectively.

- **Environmental Impact**:
1. Population growth increases demand for natural resources, leading to habitat destruction, pollution, and biodiversity loss.
2. Migration can result in urbanization and land-use changes, impacting ecosystems, water resources, and agricultural lands.
3. Immigration patterns may also influence carbon emissions and climate change, as migrants may come from regions with different environmental footprints.

- **Political Implications**:
1. Migration and immigration are contentious political issues, shaping public opinion, electoral dynamics, and policy debates.
2. Population growth also influences voting patterns, demographic shifts, and power dynamics within societies, potentially leading to social and political unrest.
3. Immigration policies and practices affects international relations, diplomatic relations, and global cooperation on migration issues.

- **Health and Well-being**:
1. Migration and immigration impacts public health, including access to healthcare, disease transmission, and healthcare infrastructure.
2. Population growth affects population health indicators such as maternal and child health, nutrition, and infectious disease prevalence.
3. Immigration contributes to demographic changes, including aging populations or shifts in disease burden, which may require adjustments to healthcare systems and public health interventions.

- **Labor and Productivity**:
1. Migration and immigration can address labor shortages in certain sectors and support economic growth through increased productivity and innovation.
2. Population growth leads to a larger workforce and consumer base, driving economic expansion and investment in human capital.
3. Immigration policies and regulations influences the mobility of skilled workers, entrepreneurs, and students, impacting global talent flows and competitiveness.

What will it take for our politicians to address these problems rationally?

Why is it that products and services cross borders with such ease, but people can't?

And why is it that corporations (who claim to be people) don't pay the same taxes as people? Did you know that American citizens must pay US taxes no matter where in the world they make their money, but corporations don't?

If they are people, why are corporations exempt from the laws governing immigration?

How absurd is all this?

"It always seems impossible till it's done."
– Nelson Mandela

8 WHAT'S BLOCKING US FROM GETTING THE JOB DONE?

Why and how is this possible?

- Failure of governments – captured by private interests
- Failure of the public – we're "too busy" with our everyday lives
- Failure of the corporations – the deliberate corruption of our institutions
- Failure of religion – the moral bankruptcy of organized religion
- Failure of media – owned and controlled by the elite

There's plenty of fear going round. Jason Hickel explains[230]:

What the present moment reveals, once again, is that Western aggression during the "Cold War" was never just about destroying socialism, as such. It was about destroying movements and governments in the periphery that sought economic sovereignty. Why? Because economic sovereignty in the periphery threatens capital accumulation in the core.

The problem is ideology and mindset. Our system is fundamentally corrupt.

---

[230] https://twitter.com/jasonhickel/status/1780187770608115839

THE ROOT OF ROOT CAUSES

By now we must acknowledge that the people and institutions who got us into this mess can't get us out of it.

As COP28 showed us, Big Oil is not interested in phasing out fossil fuels.

No king or dictator ever gave up their crown and said – "Welcome Democracy!"

We should make it clear that the world's economic systems aren't failing. They are working, as we said earlier, **exactly as they were designed to run** – for the benefit and advantage of the *status quo*.

The root cause of all root causes? The dominant ideology of our time: colonialism, which has evolved into the neoliberal brand of capitalism.

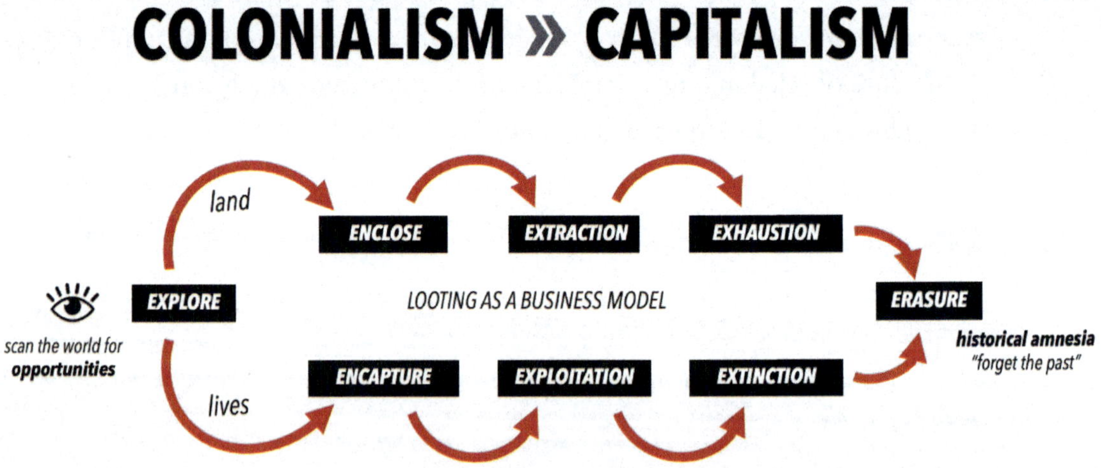

© Christian Sarkar and Philip Kotler 2022

Here's how **Jason Hickel** puts it[231] (and we point to the full original tweet):

What the present moment reveals, once again, is that Western aggression during the "Cold War" was never just about destroying socialism, as such. It was about destroying movements and governments in the periphery that sought economic sovereignty. Why? Because economic sovereignty in the periphery threatens capital accumulation in the core.

This remains the primary objective of Western aggression today. And it is the single greatest source of violence, war and instability in the world system.

The reason Western powers went after socialist movements across the global South during the "Cold War" (Cuba, China, the incineration of Vietnam and North Korea, etc) was because they knew socialism would enable the South to regain control over their own productive capacities - their labour and resources and factories - and organize them around local needs and national development.

When this happens - when people in the global South start producing and consuming for themselves - it means that those resources are no longer cheaply available to service consumption and accumulation in the core, thus disrupting the imperial arrangement on which Western capitalism has always relied (cheap labour, cheap resources, control over productive capacities, markets on tap). Remember, roughly 50% of all material consumption in the core is

Jason Hickel
@jasonhickel

What the present moment reveals, once again, is that Western aggression during the "Cold War" was never about destroying socialism, as such. It was about destroying movements and governments in the periphery that sought economic sovereignty. Why? Because economic sovereignty in the periphery threatens capital accumulation in the core.

This remains the primary objective of Western aggression today. And it is the single greatest source of violence, war and instability in the world system.

The reason Western powers went after socialist movements across the global South during the "Cold War" (Cuba, China, the incineration of Vietnam and North Korea, etc) was because they knew socialism would enable the South to regain control over their own productive capacities - their labour and resources and factories - and organize them around local needs and national development.

When this happens - when people in the global South start producing and consuming for themselves - it means that those resources are *no longer cheaply available* to service consumption and accumulation in the core, thus disrupting the imperial arrangement on which Western capitalism has always relied (cheap labour, cheap resources, control over productive capacities, markets on tap). Remember, roughly 50% of all material consumption in the core is *net-appropriated* from the global South. This is what they are trying to defend.

But it wasn't only socialist governments that pursued economic sovereignty. After political decolonization, a *wide range* of movements and states across the South also sought economic liberation and sovereign industrial development. And Western powers attacked them with equal brutality (Indonesia, Brazil, Guatemala, the DRC...).

This is the key reason that Western powers supported the apartheid regime in South Africa, and it is why they support the Israeli regime today... as Western settler-colonial outposts that can be used to attack and destabilize regional movements seeking socialism or *any* form of real economic sovereignty, whether in Angola or Mozambique or Zimbabwe or any of the Arab nationalist or socialist movements in North Africa and the Middle East.

Iran has always been central to this story. Western states orchestrated a coup against the extremely popular prime minister Mohammad Mosaddegh in 1953. He was a left-leaning nationalist, not a socialist. But he wanted Iran to have control over its own resources (notably, oil), and for the US and Britain this was unacceptable. Mossadegh was replaced by a brutal Western-backed dictatorship. The revolution that finally overthrew the dictatorship in 1979 - and constituted the current government - wasn't even left-leaning, much less socialist. But they want national economic self-determination and that is sin enough. They are a target for the exact same reasons that Iraq and Libya were targets.

The same goes for China. China's path toward sovereign industrialization - whether socialist or not - means that it is no longer an easy source of cheap labour for Western capital. And as the supply price increases so too does the sabre-rattling from Western states and media.

So this is the situation we are in. The Western ruling classes are backing obscene violence and plausible genocide in Gaza, against overwhelming international condemnation, because they must shore up their regional outpost at virtually any cost. The vast majority of the world supports Palestinian liberation, but Palestinian liberation would constrain Israeli power and open the way to regional liberation movements, and this is strongly antithetical to the interests of Western capital. And now they are provoking war with Iran, risking regional conflagration, while at the same time encircling China with military bases, ramping up sanctions on Cuba, trying to contain progressive governments in Latin America, threatening invasion of the Sahel states...

It is intolerable and it cannot continue. The violence they perpetrate, the instability, the constant wars against a long historical procession of peoples and movements in the global South who yearn for freedom and self-determination... the whole world is dragged into this horrifying nightmare. They are willing to inflict enormous suffering and misery on hundreds of millions of people in order to preserve existing dynamics of capital accumulation. We will not have peace until this arrangement is overcome and post-capitalist transformations are achieved.

Last edited 12:53 PM · Apr 16, 2024 · **161.1K** Views

[231] https://twitter.com/jasonhickel/status/1780187770608115839

net-appropriated from the global South. This is what they are trying to defend.

But it wasn't only socialist governments that pursued economic sovereignty. After political decolonization, a wide range of movements and states across the South also sought economic liberation and sovereign industrial development. And Western powers attacked them with equal brutality (Indonesia, Brazil, Guatemala, the DRC...).

This is the key reason that Western powers supported the apartheid regime in South Africa, and it is why they support the Israeli regime today... as Western settler-colonial outposts that can be used to attack and destabilize regional movements seeking socialism or any form of real economic sovereignty, whether in Angola or Mozambique or Zimbabwe or any of the Arab nationalist or socialist movements in North Africa and the Middle East.

Iran has always been central to this story. Western states orchestrated a coup against the extremely popular prime minister Mohammad Mosaddegh in 1953. He was a left-leaning nationalist, not a socialist. But he wanted Iran to have control over its own resources (notably, oil), and for the US and Britain this was unacceptable. Mossadegh was replaced by a brutal Western-backed dictatorship. The revolution that finally overthrew the dictatorship in 1979 - and constituted the current government - wasn't even left-leaning, much less socialist. But they want national economic self-determination and that is sin enough. They are a target for the exact same reasons that Iraq and Libya were targets.

The same goes for China. China's path toward sovereign industrialization - whether socialist or not - means that it is no longer an easy source of cheap labour for Western capital. And as the supply price increases so too does the sabre-rattling from Western states and media.

So this is the situation we are in. The Western ruling classes are backing obscene violence and plausible genocide in Gaza, against overwhelming international condemnation, because they must shore up their regional outpost at virtually any cost. The vast majority of the world supports Palestinian liberation, but Palestinian liberation would constrain Israeli power and open the way to regional liberation movements, and this is strongly antithetical to the interests of Western capital. And now they are provoking war with Iran, risking regional conflagration, while at the same time encircling China with military bases, ramping up sanctions on Cuba, trying to contain progressive governments in Latin America, threatening invasion of the Sahel states...

It is intolerable and it cannot continue. The violence they perpetrate, the instability, the constant wars against a long historical procession of peoples and movements in the global South who yearn for freedom and self-determination... the whole world is dragged into this horrifying nightmare. They are willing to inflict enormous suffering and misery on hundreds of millions of people in order to preserve existing dynamics of capital accumulation. We will not have peace until this arrangement is overcome and post-capitalist transformations are achieved.

All that in one tweet.

George Tsakraklides shares this deep and profound insight[232]:

The struggle of human societies remains the same it has always been: to prevent their erratic moral compass from being constantly molested by their compulsion for extraction, exploitation and destruction. Because of this compulsion, our framing of environmental problems is always distorted to fit our inadequate solutions, rather than the other way round. The climate crisis for example, has been framed as an environment issue and a technology issue, when it is actually a crisis of the human consciousness and psyche. This criminally negligent misdiagnosis, reframing and distortion of major existential crises into simple practical problems to be solved by technology, demonstrates how superficial and corrupted our very approach to problem-solving is. We are trying to solve the disasters of capitalism with more capitalism. This has never worked, and it never will.

We have confused Freedom with "economic freedom." And we've been misled to believe that no other freedoms are as important.

Here's **Tsakraklides** once again[233]:

Although revolt against this dehumanising economic system begins in the body, it also requires direct confrontation with the original fear mongering and economic growth narratives of the Church of Money and the

[232] "Problem-Solving Savages at the Edge of Extinction" by George Tsakraklides, April 25, 2024
https://tsakraklides.com/2024/04/25/problem-solving-savages-at-the-edge-of-extinction/
[233] "Revolting in the Body and Mind" by George Tsakraklides, April 20, 2024
https://tsakraklides.com/2024/04/20/revolting-in-the-body-and-mind/

Unhappiness Machine. By driving to extinction any sustainable business that ever existed, this system has almost convinced us that all business is, and must become, by definition, ecocidal. We have very few living examples left of truly sustainable business which we can emulate. They were all destroyed in the name of profit, which only benefited the business owner.

Here's how corporate America viewed freedom *circa* 1950 – in an advertisement that seems relevant again:

Note the **war on socialism** which continues to this day. It is *the* **War on the Common Good.** *The road to serfdom, it turns out, was the road of Capitalism, not Socialism.*

Gone, it seems, are FDR's "four freedoms"[234] - the freedom of speech, the freedom of worship, the freedom from want, and the freedom from fear. Instead, a significant number of citizens in the US want dictatorship, an authoritarian ruler who tells us what to do and how to live. Where did it all go wrong?

The concept of governing for the Common Good has all but been destroyed.

In 1948, the pros and cons of government were spelled out in American Government textbooks for *all* to learn. 👉

How many of these civic ideals have we lost?

Jon Hale – an investment research analyst – has this to say

Basic high school civics lessons we knew in 1948.
From Magruder's classic *American Government* textbook. page 1.

Without Government	With Government
Direct Protection	
No adequate protection of life No adequate protection of family No adequate protection of property	Police, laws, courts
No adequate protection of country	Army, Navy, and Air Force
Sanitation and Health	
Polluted water	Pure water systems
Filth and waste everywhere	Sewer systems
Tubercular milk	Inspected milk
Disease unchecked	Health services and regulation
Home treatment for diseases	Public hospitals
Impure foods	Pure food and
Dangerous drugs	Drug laws
Education	
Private schools for the few	Free education
Unrestricted child labor	Compulsory education
Private libraries	Public libraries
Roads and Conservation	
Private mud roads	Highways; rail and air control
Wasted minerals	Mining regulations
Forests burned or destroyed	Reforestation and fire patrols
Pollution of fishing streams	Fish and game regulation
Soil erosion unchecked	Soil conservation
Protection for Business and Labor	
Dishonest and unfair practices	Regulation of corporations and unions
Insecure banks	Inspection; deposit insurance
Long hours at low wages	Minimum wages and hours
Dangerous working conditions	Safety and sanitary regulations
Relief	
Charity or starvation for unemployed	Public work, security, pensions
Liberty	
Oppression by strong and shrewd	Civil rights protected by law
Civilization	
Would perish	Needs honesty and efficiency

234 FDR and the Four Freedoms Speech, 1941
https://www.fdrlibrary.org/four-freedoms and
https://www.fdrlibrary.org/documents/356632/390886/readingcopy.pdf/42234a77-8127-4015-95af-bcf831db311d

about the current hate that Republicans have for government[235]:

U.S. conservatism used to be about smaller government and fiscal conservatism. Conservatives argued for less-costly, smaller government solutions and an emphasis on efficiency. Today, it's just an all-out government hate-fest among conservatives, with income redistribution from the bottom to the top taking precedence over fiscal conservatism or making government work better.

Corruption erodes trust in government, impedes investment, and increases discontent that might lead to violent conflict. Corruption often determines the winners of government contracts. When corruption and cronyism reach a boiling point, the political problem must be addressed. It becomes necessary to expose the private sector firms that give large bribes, the banks that accept corrupt proceeds, and the lawyers, bankers, and accountants who facilitate corrupt transactions.

Here are the views of **Chris Hedges**[236]:

"Corporations write our legislation. They control our systems of information. They manage the political theater of electoral politics and impose our educational curriculum. They have turned the judiciary into one of their wholly owned subsidiaries. They have decimated labor unions and other independent mass organizations, as well as having bought off the Democratic Party, which once defended the rights of workers. With the evisceration of piecemeal and incremental reform — the primary role of liberal, democratic institutions — we are left defenseless against corporate power.

"A handful of corporate oligarchs around the globe have everything — wealth, power and privilege — and the rest of us struggle as part of a vast underclass, increasingly impoverished and ruthlessly repressed. There is one set of laws and regulations for us; there is another set of laws and regulations for a power elite that functions as a global mafia.

---

235 "Republicans can't govern because they hate government" by Jon Hale March 28, 2017 https://medium.com/@jonfhale/politics-matters-republicans-cant-govern-because-they-hate-government-cbb359dc7e7d

236 "Rise Up or Die" by Chris Hedges, Truthdig, May 20, 2013 https://www.truthdig.com/articles/rise-up-or-die/

"We stand helpless before the corporate onslaught. There is no way to vote against corporate power. Citizens have no way to bring about the prosecution of Wall Street bankers and financiers for fraud, military and intelligence officials for torture and war crimes, or security and surveillance officers for human rights abuses. The Federal Reserve is reduced to printing money for banks and financiers and lending it to them at almost zero percent interest; corporate officers then lend it to us at usurious rates as high as 30 percent. I do not know what to call this system. It is certainly not capitalism. Extortion might be a better word. The fossil fuel industry, meanwhile, relentlessly trashes the ecosystem for profit. The melting of 40 percent of the summer Arctic-sea ice is, to corporations, a business opportunity. Companies rush to the Arctic and extract the last vestiges of oil, natural gas, minerals and fish stocks, indifferent to the death pangs of the planet."

"We must either defy the corporate state or accept our extinction as a species. We have been stripped of the power to express dissent or effect change. Rebellion is the only way to remain fully human."

Hedges wrote these words in 2013.

The system will not be fixed by the people who profit from the system. So, who profits from the system?

Think about this:

if we can't stop genocide, what hope do we have to stop or mitigate climate collapse?

Again, here's **George Tsakraklides**[237]:

More and more of us are running for our lives, but the war we are running from has no end in sight. In fact, it will only intensify. Climate refugees are already fleeing uninhabitably hot and dry areas across the Global South. Rich Miami tycoons are trying to sell their multimillion low-lying villas before the ocean takes them forever. And birds, animals and fish across the Earth are desperately looking for new habitats that don't exist. And before you wonder why I quickly changed the subject from war to climate change, before you assume that you are safely untouchable by all of this, let me remind you that climate change dramatically increases the chances of conflicts over resources, which can easily lead to full-blown war.

Either way through climate change or war, Ukraine's wheat harvest will fail.

We are all refugees, already. But very few of us know it yet.

THE IDEOLOGY *of* FOOLS

What is the dominant ideology for the past 400 years? And what will it take to change?

"This civilization has learned to survive by extraction, exploitation and extinction," explains **George Tsakraklides**[238]. "There is a very simple way to describe our existence in financial terms: everything that this civilization has ever achieved is built on ecological fraud. It is built on stolen habitats, consumed resources, assassinated species."

Our ideology has doomed us to extinction. Unless.

Unless what? Unless we stop and turn to **Regeneration**.

---

[237] "We Are All Refugees" by George Tsakraklides, March 11, 2022 https://tsakraklides.com/2022/03/11/we-are-all-refugees/

[238] "The Civilisational Lie" by George Tsakraklides, March 28, 2024 https://tsakraklides.com/2024/03/28/the-civilisational-lie/

"...the idea of a climate crisis is not translating to action, because of subtle and unwitting ways in which we and our institutions cooperate to give each other the impression that everything is ok."
– The Climate Majority

9 REGENERATION: THE LAST EXIT ON THE ROAD TO EXTINCTION

Regeneration is a *process* of rebuilding or renewal – taking an **asset**, **resource**, **ecosystem**, **individual**, **family**, **organization**, **community**, or **place**, to a better state – through one or more of the following stages:

PROTECT: to save, conserve, prevent collapse, or extinction; solutions must protect, not harm, our communities – the people and the natural ecosystems around them.

REPAIR: to restore or fix the damage; solutions must repair the harms of our extractive economy.

INVEST: to dedicate resources to improvement; solutions must move non-extractive and equitable investments to our communities and workers; create/nurture new capabilities and skills that are required; and

TRANSFORM: to enliven, make successful – with the final stage being one of thriving and flourishing – a state of stability and resiliency. Solutions must provide the foundation to transform relationships and structures so that they are rooted in respect, equity, and justice.

Our current system is totally degenerative. So much so, that we can't even see how bad things really are.

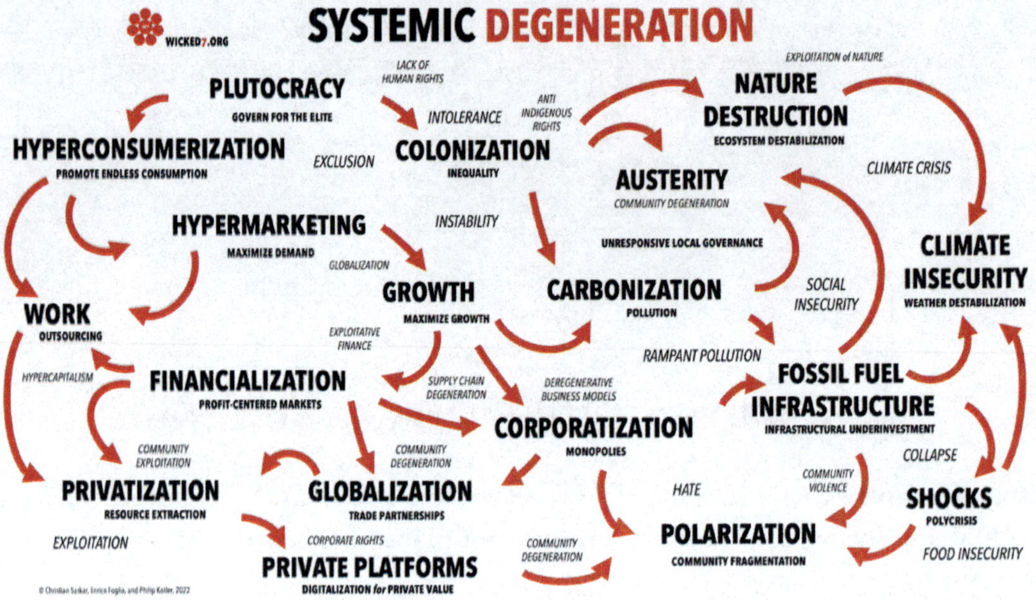

Our job now is to change everything, lest we go extinct.

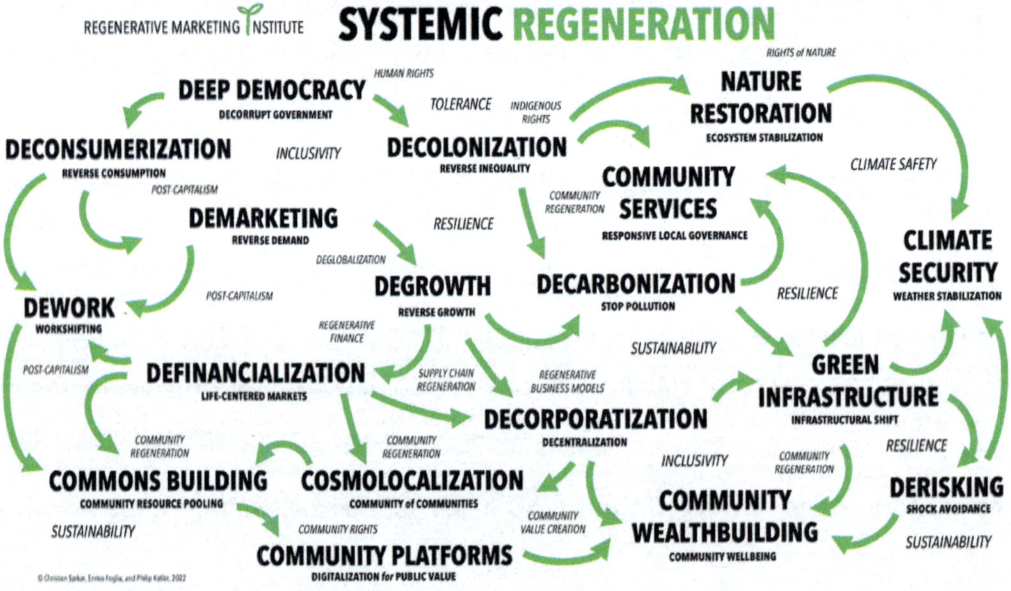

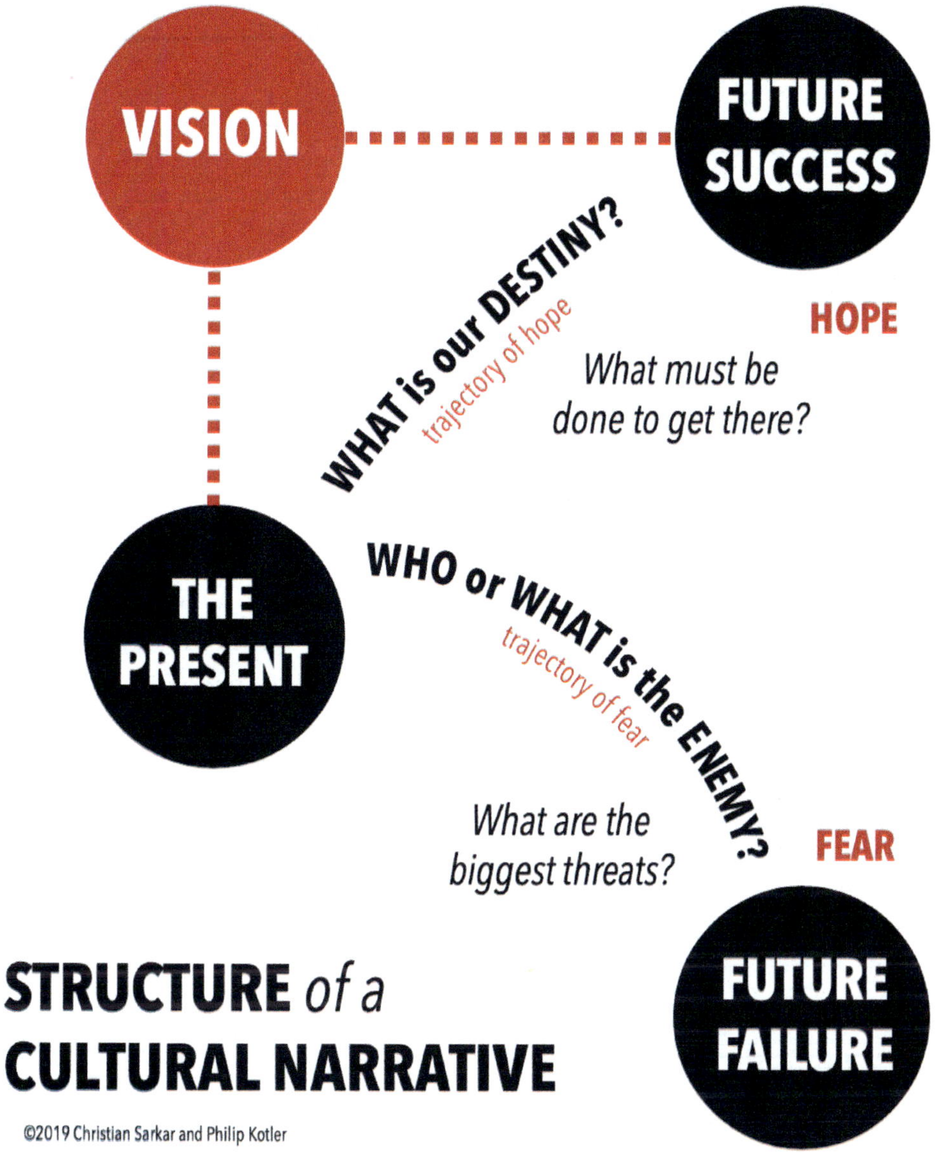

WHAT DOES YOUR NARRATIVE LOOK LIKE?

see: https://www.marketingjournal.org/competing-on-stories-marketing-and-cultural-narratives-christian-sarkar-and-philip-kotler/

THE 10 FREEDOMS *of* LIFE

We would like to make the case for the **10 Freedoms of Life** – a discussion we began in our book on Regeneration[239]. The 10 freedoms are:

1. **Freedom to Exist:** This freedom encompasses the basic human right to exist and live without fear of violence, discrimination, or oppression. It guarantees individuals the fundamental dignity of their personhood and the ability to pursue their lives without undue threats to their safety or well-being. It also includes environmental freedom in which is the right to live in a clean, healthy, and sustainable environment, free from pollution, degradation, and environmental harm. It encompasses the right to clean air, water, and land, as well as the right to participate in decisions affecting the environment, advocate for environmental protection, and hold polluters accountable for their actions. Closely related is the **freedom of movement** which involves the individual right to move freely within their own country and to travel internationally without undue restrictions or barriers. It encompasses the freedom to choose one's place of residence, work, or travel, as well as the right to seek asylum or refuge from persecution or violence in other countries.

2. **Freedom to Love:** The freedom to love encompasses the right to form relationships and express affection for others without societal or legal constraints. It recognizes the importance of emotional connections and intimacy in human lives, irrespective of gender, sexual orientation, or cultural norms.

3. **Freedom to Create:** This freedom grants individuals the liberty to express themselves creatively and contribute to the arts, sciences, and innovation. It acknowledges the inherent human impulse to explore, imagine, and bring new ideas and creations into the world, fostering cultural enrichment and societal progress.

---

[239] *Regeneration: The Future of Community in a Permacrisis World* by Christian Sarkar, Philip Kotler, Enrico Foglia. IDEA BITE PRESS (2023). https://regenmarketing.org/book/

4. **Freedom from Want:** The freedom from want ensures that individuals have access to basic needs such as food, shelter, healthcare, and education. It aims to eradicate poverty and deprivation, enabling people to lead dignified lives and pursue their full potential without the burden of material insecurity. This also includes economic freedom which is the right for individuals to participate freely in economic activities, including the right to own property, pursue livelihoods, engage in commerce, and enjoy the benefits of their labor. It encompasses the freedom to contract, trade, and invest freely, as well as the right to access education, healthcare, and social services to enhance economic opportunity and well-being.

5. **Freedom from Exploitation:** This freedom protects individuals from being taken advantage of or oppressed by others, whether economically, socially, or otherwise. It seeks to prevent exploitation and ensure fair treatment and opportunities for all members of society, regardless of their socioeconomic status or circumstances.

6. **Freedom from Manipulation:** The freedom from manipulation safeguards individuals from being coerced or deceived into actions or beliefs against their will or best interests. It upholds autonomy and personal agency, allowing people to make informed choices and decisions free from undue influence.

7. **Freedom from Fear:** This freedom ensures the assurance of safety and security, both physical and psychological, enabling individuals to live without constant anxiety or dread. It involves protection from threats such as violence, persecution, discrimination, and arbitrary abuse of power. It also includes **freedom of assembly** and association - the individuals' right to peacefully assemble, protest, demonstrate, or organize collectively for social, political, or cultural purposes. It encompasses the freedom to form and join associations, trade unions, political parties, or other organizations, as well as the right to participate in public gatherings and express dissent or solidarity with others.

8. **Freedom from Surveillance:** Protection from surveillance ensures individuals' privacy rights are upheld, preventing unwarranted intrusion into their personal lives

by governments, corporations, or other entities. It safeguards the right to autonomy and confidentiality in communications and activities. This also includes digital rights and internet freedom which are an individual's rights and freedoms in the digital realm, including privacy, security, and access to information online. It encompasses the **right to privacy** in digital communications, freedom from online censorship and surveillance, and access to an open and accessible internet for all individuals, regardless of location or socioeconomic status.

9. Freedom from Corruption: This freedom entails the eradication of corrupt practices that undermine fairness, justice, and the rule of law in society. It aims to foster transparency, accountability, and integrity in governance, institutions, and interactions, promoting trust and equity.

10. Freedom of Expression: The freedom of expression guarantees individuals the right to express opinions, beliefs, and ideas freely without censorship or retaliation from authorities or societal pressures. It is essential for fostering open dialogue, diversity of thought, and the exchange of information and perspectives in democratic societies. This also includes **freedom of religion** which is the individuals' right to practice, observe, or change their religious beliefs or convictions freely without discrimination or persecution.

FREEDOM...

...TO EXIST
...TO LOVE
...TO CREATE
...FROM WANT
...FROM EXPLOITATION
...FROM MANIPULATION
...FROM FEAR
...FROM SURVEILLANCE
...FROM CORRUPTION
...OF EXPRESSION

THE 10 FREEDOMS *of* LIFE

Thus, as we explain in *Regeneration: The Future of Community in a Permacrisis World,* the "job to be done" for society is to **regenerate the Common Good.**

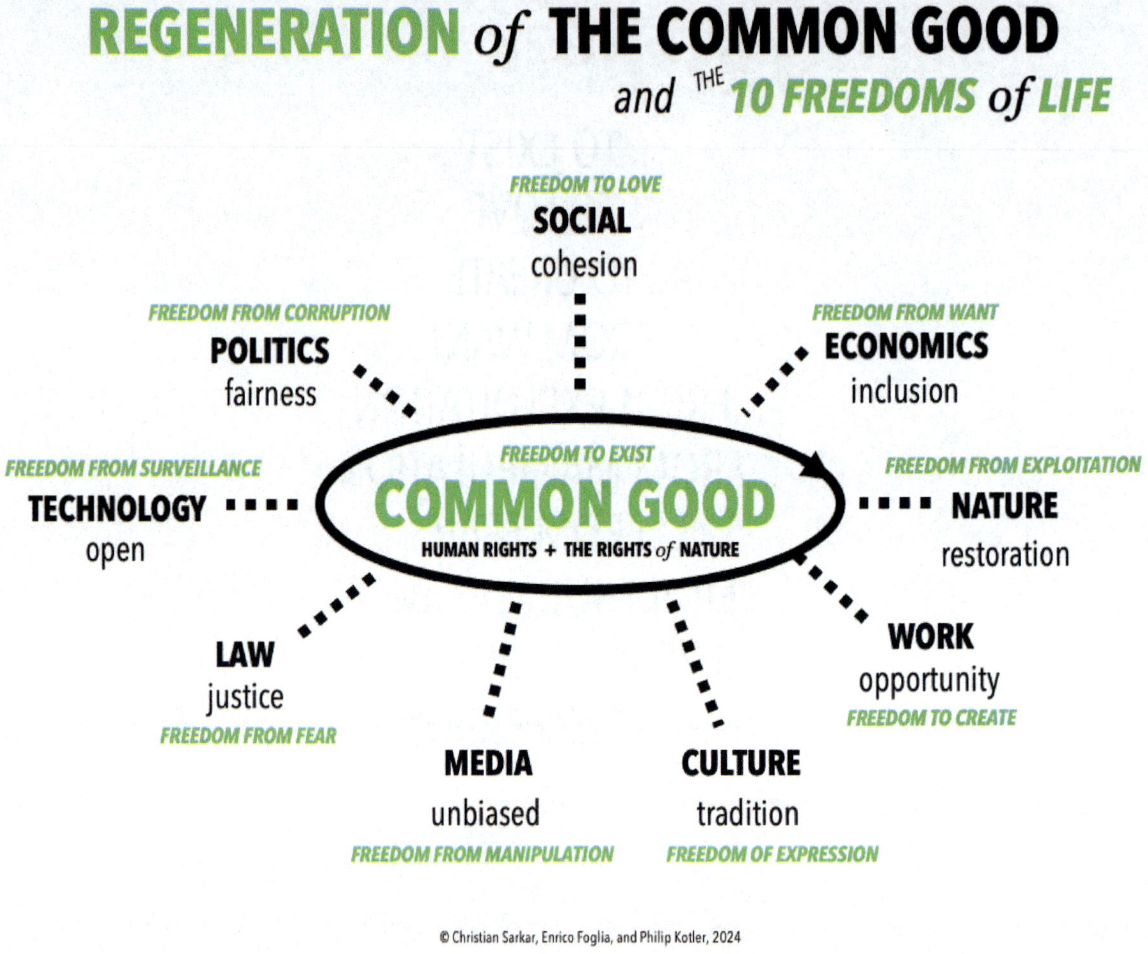

FOR MORE INFORMATION: www.regenmarketing.org

REDESIGNING SOCIETY

If we were to redesign society to be regenerative, what might that look like?

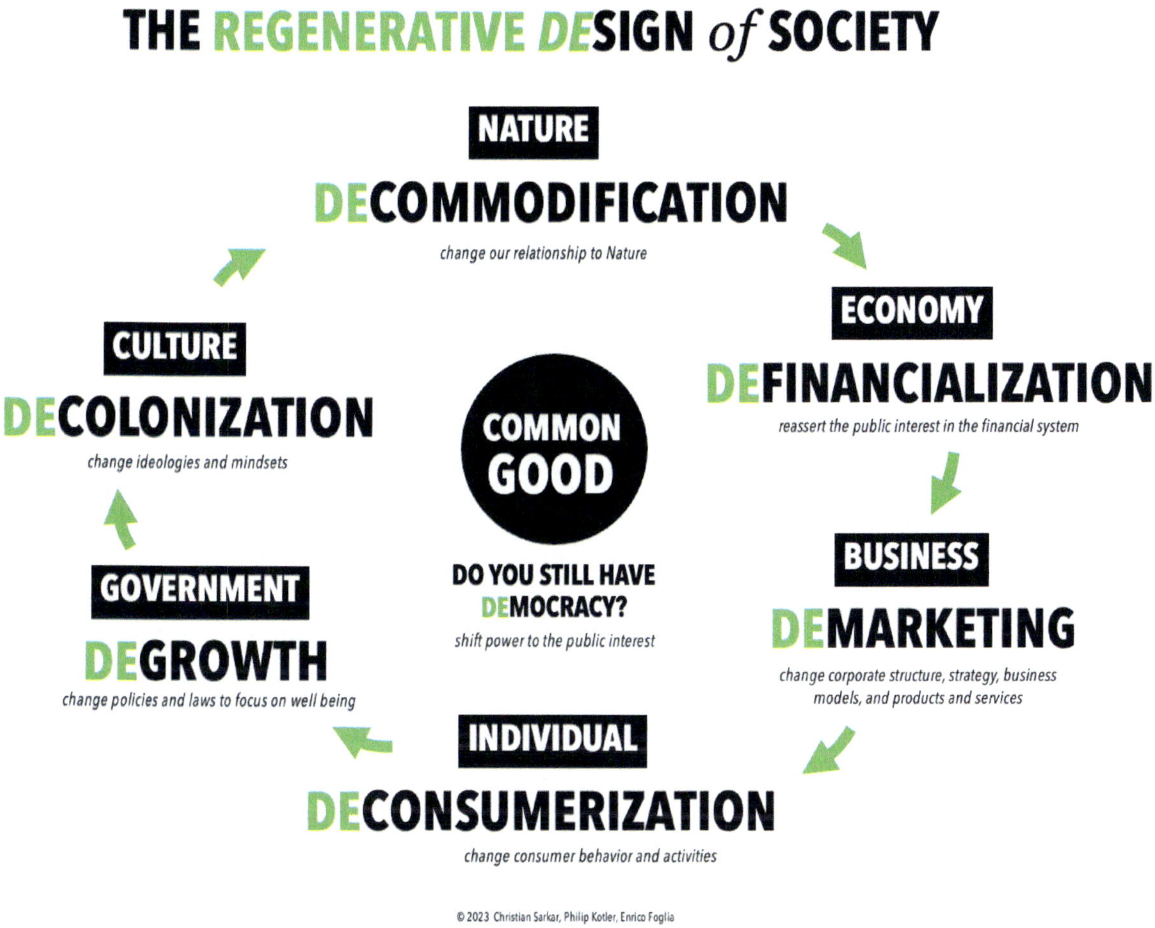

DECOMMODIFICATION

The Decommodification of Nature is the idea of reducing or eliminating the commodification of natural resources and ecosystems. Commodification occurs when natural resources, such as water, land, minerals, forests, or biodiversity, are treated as commodities to be bought, sold, and traded in markets for profit. Decommodification, on the other hand, entails shifting away from this market-based approach and emphasizing the intrinsic value of nature, as well as the rights of communities and ecosystems to exist and thrive independent of their economic value.

Here's how:

1. **Recognition of Intrinsic Value**: Decommodification involves recognizing the inherent value of nature beyond its utility or economic value to humans. This includes acknowledging the ecological, cultural, aesthetic, and spiritual significance of natural ecosystems and biodiversity.

2. **Protection of Rights**: Decommodification entails protecting the rights of nature, including the rights of ecosystems, species, and future generations. This may involve legal frameworks that recognize and enforce the rights of nature to exist, flourish, and regenerate.

3. **Prioritizing Conservation and Restoration**: Decommodification emphasizes conservation and restoration of natural ecosystems and biodiversity for their own sake, rather than solely for their potential economic benefits. This may involve measures such as establishing protected areas, restoring degraded habitats, and promoting sustainable land and resource management practices.

4. **Promoting Common Ownership and Management**: Decommodification challenges the privatization and corporate control of natural resources, advocating for common ownership and community-based management approaches that prioritize ecological stewardship and equity.

5. **Supporting Sustainable Livelihoods**: Decommodification seeks to ensure that communities have access to the resources and services provided by nature for their livelihoods and well-being, without overexploiting or degrading natural ecosystems. This may involve promoting sustainable agriculture, fisheries, forestry, and eco-tourism practices that respect ecological limits and local knowledge systems.

6. **Addressing Environmental Injustice**: Decommodification aims to address environmental injustice by challenging the unequal distribution of environmental benefits and burdens, particularly among marginalized communities. This includes addressing issues such as environmental racism, land grabbing, and displacement of indigenous peoples from their ancestral lands.

DEFINANCIALIZATION

The Definancialization of the Economy refers to reducing the dominance and influence of the financial sector on the broader economy and society. It involves shifting focus away from financial activities and speculation towards more productive and sustainable economic activities that contribute to long-term prosperity, stability, and well-being.

Here's how:

1. **Reducing Speculation**: Definancialization aims to reduce excessive speculation and financialization of assets, such as stocks, bonds, and real estate, which can contribute to market volatility, bubbles, and instability. This may involve implementing regulations and policies to discourage speculative activities and promote long-term investment in productive sectors of the economy.

2. **Promoting Real Investment**: Definancializing the economy involves promoting real investment in productive activities, such as manufacturing, infrastructure, research and development, and renewable energy. This includes redirecting capital away from speculative financial instruments towards investments that generate tangible benefits for society, such as job creation, innovation, and sustainable development.

3. **Supporting Main Street over Wall Street**: Definancialization seeks to rebalance the economy in favor of Main Street businesses and households, rather than Wall Street financial institutions and elites. This may involve measures to strengthen local economies, support small and medium-sized enterprises (SMEs), and empower communities to have greater control over their economic destinies.

4. **Enhancing Financial Regulation**: Definancialization involves strengthening financial regulation to prevent excessive risk-taking, fraud, and market manipulation that can destabilize the economy. This may include measures such as stricter capital requirements, limits on leverage, and increased transparency and accountability in financial markets.

5. **Promoting Financial Inclusion**: Definancializing the economy also entails promoting financial inclusion and access to affordable financial services for underserved and marginalized populations. This includes initiatives to expand access to credit, savings, insurance, and other financial products and services to help empower individuals and communities to participate more fully in the economy.

6. **Addressing Inequality**: Definancialization aims to address economic inequality by reducing the concentration of wealth and power in the hands of a few financial elites. This may involve measures such as progressive taxation, wealth redistribution, and policies to strengthen workers' rights and bargaining power.

7. **Fostering Resilience and Sustainability**: Definancializing the economy seeks to build a more resilient and sustainable economic system that is less vulnerable to financial crises and shocks. This includes promoting diverse and resilient local economies, investing in green technologies and infrastructure, and prioritizing long-term sustainability over short-term financial gains.

DEMARKETING

Demarketing is a marketing strategy aimed at reducing demand for a product, service, or industry. Unlike traditional marketing, which seeks to increase demand and promote consumption, demarketing involves deliberately discouraging or limiting demand to address various social, economic, or environmental issues. Demarketing strategies may be employed by governments, businesses, or advocacy groups to achieve specific objectives.

Here's how:

1. **Conservation and Environmental Protection**: Demarketing may be used to reduce consumption of resources or products that have negative environmental impacts. For example, campaigns promoting water conservation may encourage individuals to use less water for activities like watering lawns or washing cars.

2. **Public Health and Safety**: Demarketing strategies are often used in public health campaigns to discourage behaviors that are harmful to individuals or society. For instance, anti-smoking campaigns aim to reduce tobacco consumption by highlighting the health risks associated with smoking.

3. **Traffic and Congestion Management**: In urban areas with heavy traffic congestion, demarketing efforts may be employed to reduce the number of vehicles on the road. This can include measures such as congestion pricing, carpooling incentives, or promoting public transportation alternatives.

4. **Alcohol and Tobacco Control**: Governments and public health organizations often use demarketing strategies to reduce alcohol and tobacco consumption, particularly among young people. This can involve restrictions on advertising, raising taxes on alcohol and tobacco products, and implementing public awareness campaigns.

5. **Population Control**: Demarketing may be used to address overpopulation by promoting family planning and contraception methods. Government-sponsored campaigns may encourage smaller family sizes to reduce strain on resources and infrastructure.

6. **Limiting Consumer Demand**: In some cases, businesses may employ demarketing strategies to manage demand for their products or services. This could include limiting advertising during periods of high demand to avoid shortages or using pricing strategies to discourage excessive consumption.

7. **Promoting Healthy Lifestyles**: Demarketing efforts may encourage healthier lifestyles by discouraging consumption of unhealthy foods or promoting physical activity. For example, campaigns may discourage the consumption of sugary beverages or fast food in favor of healthier alternatives.

DEGROWTH

Degrowth is a socio-economic theory and movement that advocates for reducing economic production and consumption levels to achieve environmental sustainability, social equity, and well-being. Unlike traditional economic models, which prioritize perpetual economic growth as a means to improve human welfare, degrowth challenges the notion that endless economic expansion is compatible with ecological limits and social justice. Instead, it proposes a transition towards smaller, more equitable, and ecologically sustainable economies.

Key principles and objectives of the degrowth movement include:

1. **Reducing Material Consumption**: Degrowth calls for reducing overall material consumption and resource use to achieve ecological sustainability and minimize environmental impacts such as pollution, resource depletion, and habitat destruction.

2. **Reorienting Priorities**: Degrowth advocates for reorienting societal priorities away from the pursuit of economic growth and towards meeting human needs, fostering well-being, and enhancing quality of life for all people within planetary boundaries.

3. **Equitable Distribution**: Degrowth emphasizes the importance of equitable distribution of resources and wealth within and between societies. This involves addressing social inequalities, poverty, and disparities in access to resources, opportunities, and decision-making power.

4. **Rethinking Work and Leisure**: Degrowth challenges the dominance of paid work and consumerism in contemporary societies, advocating for shorter working hours, greater leisure time, and a revaluation of non-monetary forms of contribution to society, such as caregiving, volunteering, and community-building activities.

5. **Localism and Localization**: Degrowth promotes localization of economies, emphasizing the importance of local production, consumption, and decision-making to reduce dependence on long-distance trade, minimize ecological footprints, and enhance community resilience.

6. **Democratizing Decision-making**: Degrowth calls for democratizing economic and political decision-making processes to ensure greater participation, transparency, and accountability in shaping societal priorities and resource allocation.

7. **Cultural Transformation**: Degrowth advocates for cultural shifts towards values of sufficiency, solidarity, and conviviality, fostering lifestyles and social norms that prioritize human relationships, community well-being, and connection with nature over material accumulation and consumption.

8. **Ecological Limits**: Degrowth recognizes the finite nature of ecological resources and planetary boundaries, advocating for living within ecological limits and respecting the carrying capacity of ecosystems to sustain human and non-human life.

DECOLONIZATON

Decolonization refers to the process of challenging, resisting, and undoing the legacy of colonialism in cultural practices, institutions, and representations. It involves reclaiming and revitalizing indigenous or marginalized cultures, languages, knowledge systems, and ways of life that have been suppressed, marginalized, or erased by colonial powers. Cultural decolonization seeks to empower communities to assert their own identities, narratives, and perspectives, and to challenge dominant colonial ideologies and structures.

Key aspects of cultural decolonization include:

1. **Reclaiming Indigenous Knowledge and Traditions**: Cultural decolonization involves reclaiming and revitalizing indigenous knowledge systems, traditions, languages, and cultural practices that were suppressed or marginalized under colonial rule. This may include efforts to preserve traditional ecological knowledge, oral histories, spiritual practices, and artistic expressions.

2. **Challenging Colonial Narratives**: Cultural decolonization seeks to challenge dominant colonial narratives and representations that distort or erase indigenous histories, experiences, and contributions. This may involve rewriting history textbooks, producing alternative media, and promoting indigenous perspectives in cultural institutions and educational curricula.

3. **Promoting Language Revitalization**: Language revitalization is a central aspect of cultural decolonization, as language is integral to culture and identity. Efforts to reclaim and promote indigenous languages help preserve cultural heritage, strengthen community cohesion, and challenge linguistic imperialism.

4. **Transforming Cultural Institutions**: Cultural decolonization involves transforming cultural institutions, such as museums, galleries, and libraries, to reflect diverse perspectives and narratives. This may include repatriating cultural artifacts and human remains to indigenous communities, reinterpreting exhibits from indigenous perspectives, and fostering partnerships with indigenous artists and cultural practitioners.

5. **Empowering Indigenous Voices**: Cultural decolonization seeks to amplify the voices, agency, and self-determination of indigenous peoples and other marginalized communities. This may involve supporting indigenous-led initiatives, community-based organizations, and grassroots movements that promote cultural resilience, activism, and social change.

6. **Fostering Intercultural Dialogue and Solidarity**: Cultural decolonization encourages dialogue, collaboration, and solidarity among diverse cultural groups to challenge colonial hierarchies, stereotypes, and divisions. This may involve promoting intercultural exchange, mutual respect, and allyship to build inclusive and equitable societies.

7. **Addressing Structural Injustices**: Cultural decolonization recognizes that cultural oppression is intertwined with broader structural injustices, including racism, patriarchy, capitalism, and imperialism. Efforts to decolonize culture must therefore be accompanied by efforts to address systemic inequalities and create conditions for social and economic justice.

DEMOCRACY

Do we still want **Democracy** – the system of government in which power is vested in the people, who rule either directly or through elected representatives?

One can argue that *we have never been a true democracy* characterized by principles of political equality, popular sovereignty, and majority rule, as well as protection of minority rights and freedoms. In a true democracy, citizens have the opportunity to participate in decision-making processes, hold their leaders accountable, and exercise their civil and political rights – is that what we have still?

Key features of Democracy *(in case you forgot)* include:

1. **Popular Sovereignty**: Democracy is based on the principle of popular sovereignty, meaning that political authority ultimately resides with the people. Through elections, citizens have the opportunity to choose their representatives and participate in shaping the policies and decisions that affect their lives. It also means the free and peaceful *handover of power.*

2. **Political Equality**: Democracy promotes political equality by ensuring that all citizens have equal rights and opportunities to participate in the political process, regardless of factors such

as wealth, social status, or ethnicity. This includes the right to vote, run for office, and express political opinions freely.

3. **Rule of Law**: Democracy is governed by the rule of law, which means that government actions are subject to legal constraints and must be consistent with established laws, constitutions, and principles of justice. The rule of law helps protect individual rights and liberties from arbitrary or abusive government actions.

4. **Separation of Powers**: Democracy typically involves a system of checks and balances, with separate branches of government (such as the executive, legislative, and judicial branches) that have distinct powers and responsibilities. This separation of powers helps prevent the concentration of power in any single institution and promotes accountability and transparency.

5. **Free and Fair Elections**: Elections are a central feature of democracy, providing citizens with the opportunity to choose their leaders and hold them accountable for their actions. Free and fair elections are essential for ensuring that political power is legitimately and fairly exercised, and that citizens' voices are heard in the political process.

6. **Protection of Minority Rights**: Democracy recognizes the importance of protecting the rights and freedoms of minority groups, including religious, ethnic, linguistic, and political minorities. This includes safeguards against discrimination, persecution, and the tyranny of the majority, ensuring that all individuals are treated with dignity and respect.

7. **Freedom of Expression and Association**: Democracy guarantees freedom of expression, speech, press, assembly, and association, enabling citizens to express their opinions, advocate for their interests, and participate in public debate without fear of censorship or reprisal. These freedoms are essential for fostering an informed and engaged citizenry.

DEPOLITICIZE DECISION-MAKING

Depoliticizing decision-making means ***removing*** **ideological considerations, biases, or motivations from the process of making decisions.** In many contexts, particularly in governance or organizational settings, decisions are ideally made based on objective analysis, evidence, and the best interests of the stakeholders involved, rather than being influenced by political agendas, partisanship, or personal interests.

This can involve implementing structures, processes, or policies that promote transparency, accountability, and fairness in decision-making. It often entails creating independent bodies or mechanisms that are insulated from political pressures and vested interests, allowing decisions to be made based on merit rather than political expediency.

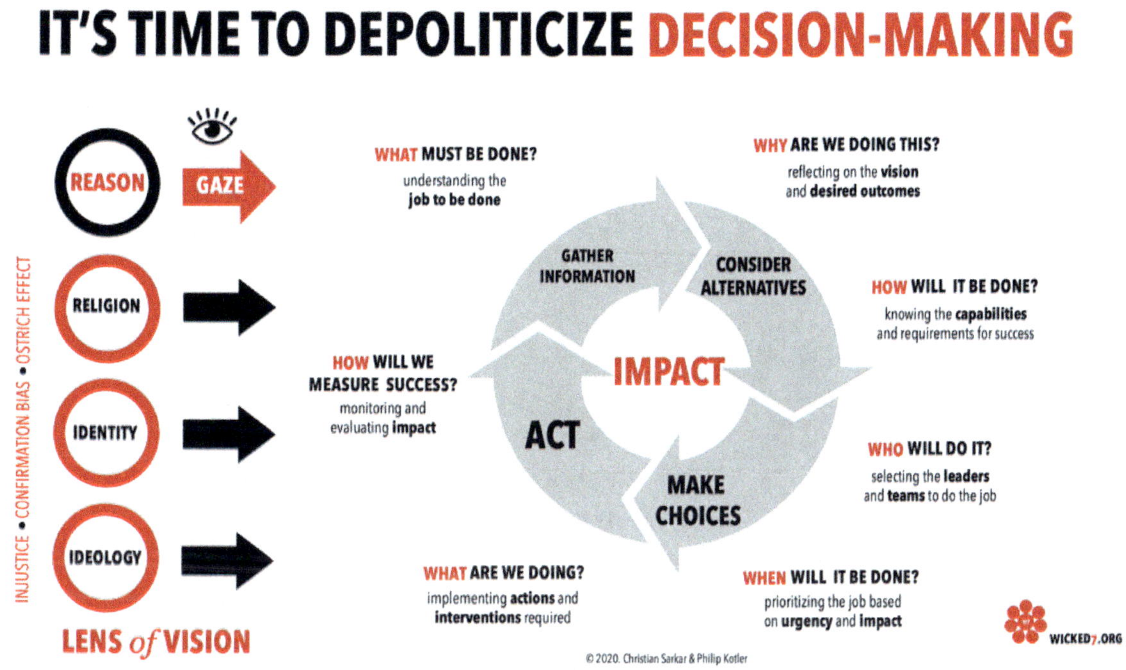

Depoliticizing decision-making can help ensure that decisions are made in the public or organizational interest rather than serving the interests of specific individuals or groups. It promotes good governance, enhances trust in institutions, and fosters a more equitable and effective decision-making process.

This is *leadership for the Common Good*, or **regenerative leadership.**

Regenerative leadership emphasizes the ability of leaders to foster positive change, sustainability, and renewal within organizations, communities, and the environment. Here are some characteristics commonly associated with regenerative leaders:

1. **Systems Thinking**: Regenerative leaders understand the interconnectedness of various systems, including social, environmental, and economic systems. They recognize that actions in one area can have ripple effects across multiple domains and strive to make decisions that consider the broader implications.

2. **Visionary and Purpose-Driven**: They possess a clear vision for a sustainable and thriving future and are committed to aligning their actions with that vision. Regenerative leaders are driven by a sense of purpose beyond short-term gains, focusing on creating long-term value for all stakeholders.
3. **Collaborative and Inclusive**: They value collaboration and inclusivity, recognizing the importance of diverse perspectives and stakeholders in achieving sustainable outcomes. Regenerative leaders seek to build consensus, foster dialogue, and empower others to contribute to the collective vision.

4. **Adaptive and Resilient**: They are adaptable and resilient in the face of uncertainty and change. Regenerative leaders embrace innovation, experimentation, and learning, viewing setbacks as opportunities for growth and improvement.

5. **Ethical and Values-Driven**: They operate with integrity and uphold ethical principles in their decision-making processes. Regenerative leaders prioritize values such as fairness, transparency, and social responsibility, ensuring that their actions reflect their commitment to ethical conduct.

6. **Empathetic and Compassionate**: They demonstrate empathy and compassion towards others, understanding the diverse needs and perspectives of individuals and communities. Regenerative leaders prioritize the well-being of people and the planet, striving to create environments that support human flourishing and ecological health.

7. **Systems Change Agents**: They actively work towards transforming systems and structures that perpetuate inequality, exploitation, and environmental degradation. Regenerative leaders advocate for policy changes, business practices, and cultural shifts that promote sustainability, equity, and resilience.

8. **Long-Term Orientation**: They take a long-term view in their decision-making, considering the impacts of their actions on future generations and the health of the planet. Regenerative leaders prioritize investments and initiatives that generate lasting benefits and minimize harm over time.

FINDING COMMON GROUND

In the Dance of Death of our modern economy, there's a concept that often lurks in the shadows: the generation of value in one realm, while unwittingly eroding it in others. What is value creation, and for whom is the value being created? This is the picture: our businesses are reaping short-term financial gains at the expense of Nature, human potential, and social cohesion, all while jeopardizing the long-term stability of financial capital itself.

This phenomenon, akin to a Faustian bargain, plays out across various sectors, industries, and economies. It's the age-old story of prioritizing immediate profits over regenerative practices, of chasing elusive growth metrics while neglecting the very foundations upon which prosperity rests.

Consider, for instance, the relentless pursuit of profit margins in industries reliant on finite resources—fossil fuels extracted at an unsustainable pace, forests clear-cut without regard for biodiversity, or water sources depleted beyond replenishment. In the quest for profit, these industries overlook the irreplaceable value of natural capital, destroy natural ecosystems and destabilize our planet's delicate balance.

But the tale doesn't end there. Human capital, too, bears the brunt of this relentless drive for profitability. From precarious working conditions to stagnant wages, the relentless pressure to maximize short-term financial returns often comes at the expense of human well-being. Workers find themselves caught in a cycle of exploitation, their potential stifled and their dignity compromised in the name of corporate gain.

And then there's the social fabric of the community, woven from the threads of trust, reciprocity, and collective resilience. In the pursuit of profit, companies disregard their social responsibilities, overlooking the needs of communities, and exacerbating inequalities. Whether through labor practices that prioritize shareholder returns over worker rights or marketing strategies that exploit societal vulnerabilities, the erosion of social capital takes a huge toll on the very fabric of society.

Even the realm of finance itself is not immune. In the relentless pursuit of short-term gains, most investors overlook the long-term risks posed by environmental degradation, social unrest, or ethical lapses. By prioritizing immediate returns over sustainable practices, they unwittingly undermine the long-term stability of financial markets, perpetuating a cycle of boom and bust that ultimately undermines the resilience of the entire system.

Thus, the generation of value in certain capitals while eroding or destroying others is a precarious balancing act with far-reaching consequences. It's a story of trade-offs and unintended consequences, of shortsightedness and misplaced priorities. And until we recognize the interconnectedness of these capitals and the imperative of regenerative practices, we undermine the very foundations of our future.

Collapse is already here – we just don't see it. *Who feels it, knows it.*

If we take away our ideological differences, we must return to science – not Big Science, but the **scientific method**.

We find that the interconnections and cascading impact of these seven wicked problems are the best way to understand the existential risks facing our civilization today. To ignore this is to accept defeat – to embrace extinction. Joining the scientists who are speaking out today, we stand in solidarity with Life on Earth. Let us fight *now*. Because **the time is late.**

The issue now is action. How do we get folks to act together when not everyone wants to glue themselves to the road or engage in civil disobedience?

Rupert Read and friends have just given us a playbook to help us engage.

Here are the 5 principles[240] they advocate:

Respect everybody

Differences in political ideology, cultural background or knowledge, are all challenging but we can't let them cause contempt. We don't avoid disagreement, but we do avoid hostility. We also respect the fact that we're going to fall short of our own condition of respect.

Reach beyond polarization

The need to be "in the right" can feed a sense of superiority on one hand, and resentment on the other. Instead, we focus on building relationships based on common goals, and a commitment to pragmatic action despite differences.

Remember nobody owns climate action as an "issue"

The cultural norms and sensitivities of left-wing and progressive groups tend to dominate the activist space, and so climate action groups tend to self-select. But millions of people feel the significance of climate breakdown – so a mainstream movement should be ready to make almost anybody feel at home.

[240] https://climatemajorityproject.com/our-principles/

Meet people where they are

Everybody has their own journey towards accepting the seriousness of the climate and ecological crises. A coalition for building a better future needs relatable messengers capable of reaching audiences the climate movement has historically found difficult to reach. For example, we don't ask people to self-identify as 'activists'. Rather, we want to help people identify ambitious, useful actions that make the best use of their own talents.

Engage people with the truth patiently, with empathy and insight

Patience is difficult, given what is at stake. But patience is necessary, because not everyone is ready to hear truthful messages. Dominant messaging in our culture has prevented many people from understanding the depth of trouble we're in. It's entirely reasonable that people prefer stories that help them avoid feeling hopeless. But they now need to know the truth – and can hear it more easily when they are part of supportive communities. And here are more guidelines from **The Radical Climate collaboration**[241]:

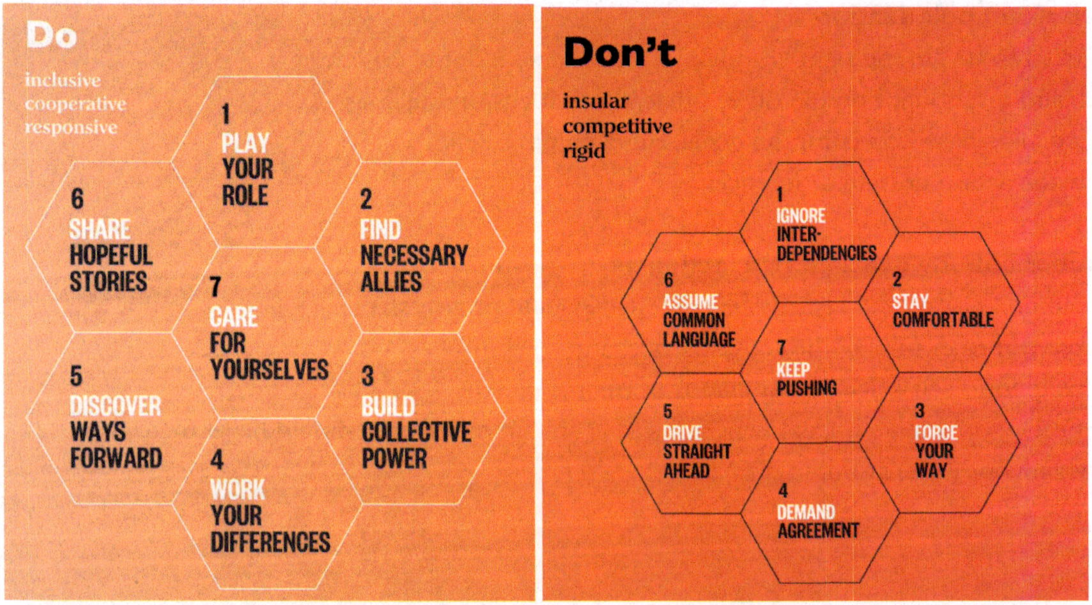

[241] https://radicalclimatecollaboration.reospartners.com

WE CAN MAKE IT WORK

Do you feel powerless? Does it feel like the leaders we have don't represent you? That the policies they make don't help us at all? That they aren't focused on your problems or the most urgent issues facing society? That they don't seem to care about the common good? If you've ever felt this way, you are not alone. Many people share the growing frustration with political systems that appear disconnected from the needs of the people they claim to serve. *Climate anxiety is real.*

Our feeling of helplessness need not be permanent. While it may seem daunting, we all have the potential to create change. A single voice may feel small, but when we **join forces with others** who share our concerns, those voices grow louder.

So, what can be done to turn frustration into action?

Regeneration is the path forward:

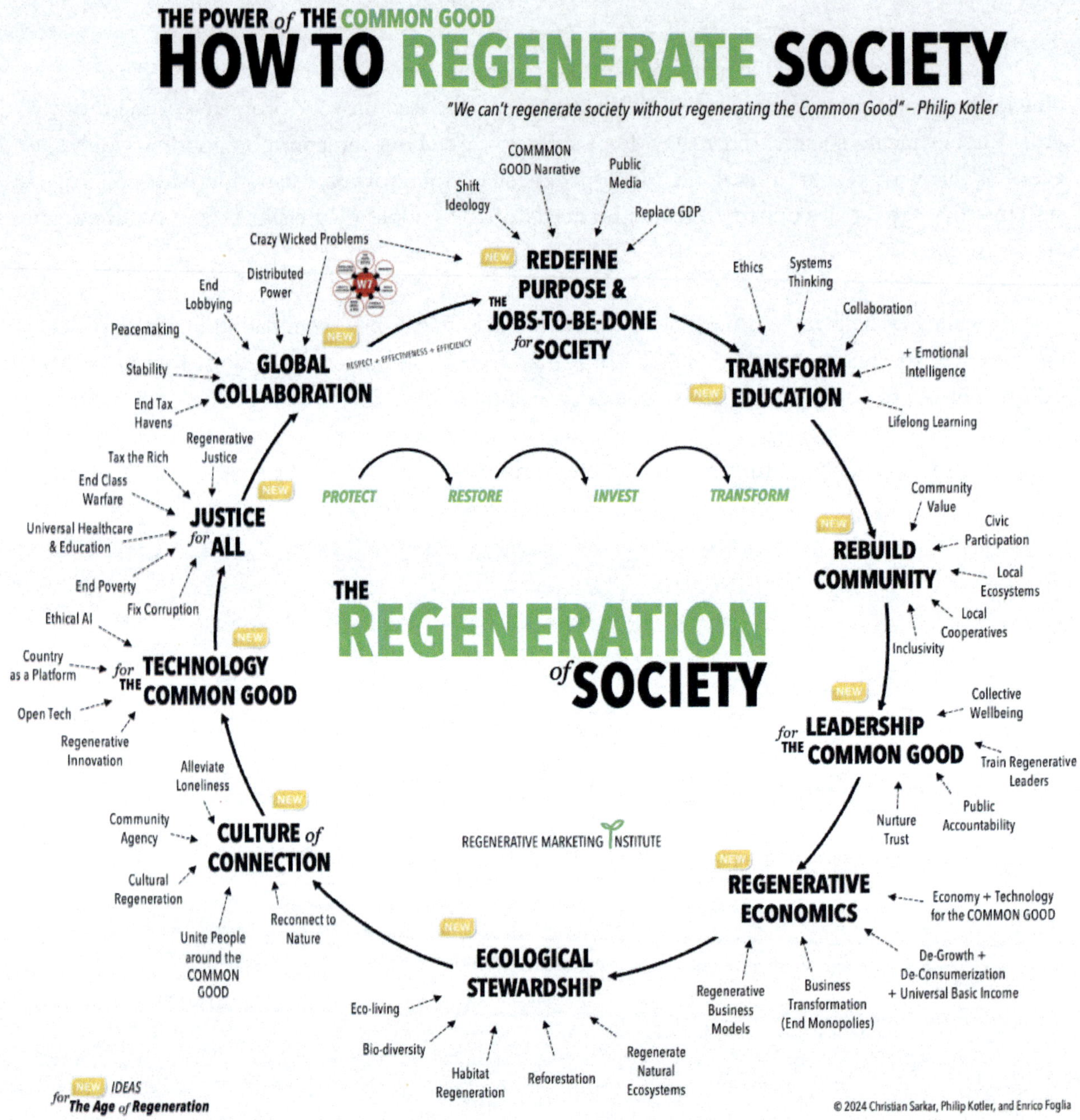

THE POWER of THE COMMON GOOD
HOW TO REGENERATE SOCIETY
"We can't regenerate society without regenerating the Common Good" – Philip Kotler
COMMMON GOOD Narrative
Public Media
Shift Ideology
Replace GDP
Crazy Wicked Problems
NEW
REDEFINE PURPOSE & THE JOBS-TO-BE-DONE for SOCIETY
Ethics
Systems Thinking
Collaboration
Distributed Power
End Lobbying
Peacemaking
Stability
End Tax Havens
NEW
GLOBAL COLLABORATION
RESPECT + EFFECTIVENESS + EFFICIENCY
NEW
TRANSFORM EDUCATION
+ Emotional Intelligence
Lifelong Learning
Regenerative Justice
Tax the Rich
End Class Warfare
Universal Healthcare & Education
End Poverty
Fix Corruption
NEW
JUSTICE for ALL
PROTECT
RESTORE
INVEST
TRANSFORM
Community Value
Civic Participation
Local Ecosystems
Local Cooperatives
Inclusivity
NEW
REBUILD COMMUNITY
THE REGENERATION of SOCIETY
Ethical AI
Country as a Platform
Open Tech
Regenerative Innovation
NEW
for THE TECHNOLOGY COMMON GOOD
Collective Wellbeing
Train Regenerative Leaders
Public Accountability
Nurture Trust
NEW
for THE LEADERSHIP COMMON GOOD
Alleviate Loneliness
Community Agency
Cultural Regeneration
Unite People around the COMMON GOOD
Reconnect to Nature
NEW
CULTURE of CONNECTION
REGENERATIVE MARKETING INSTITUTE
NEW
REGENERATIVE ECONOMICS
Economy + Technology for the COMMON GOOD
De-Growth + De-Consumerization + Universal Basic Income
Regenerative Business Models
Business Transformation (End Monopolies)
NEW
ECOLOGICAL STEWARDSHIP
Eco-living
Bio-diversity
Habitat Regeneration
Reforestation
Regenerate Natural Ecosystems
NEW IDEAS for The Age of Regeneration
© 2024 Christian Sarkar, Philip Kotler, and Enrico Foglia

Here are fifteen steps to reclaim power, promote justice, and advance the Common Good:

WHAT CAN WE DO?

WICKED7.ORG

1. **Speak Out** – when we see an injustice, don't stay silent. Be kind.
2. **Organize** – get together with others who want to support the Common Good – join/start a movement – collaborate with others to create a movement of movements.
3. **Tell the Truth** – point out lies, especially in the public domain (no alternative facts – call out misinformation and disinformation and their perpetrators).
4. **Vote!** – for candidates that support the Common Good.
5. **Consume Less** – stop buying stuff. No to fashion. Less meat, less junk food, less trash.
6. **Tax Billionaires** – so we can invest in the Common Good.
7. **Fight for the Planet** – stand up against ecocide and the Death of Nature – renewables and regeneration, please!
8. **Educate Everyone** – make education affordable again (make college free).
9. **End Corruption** – stop all forms of bribery. End *Citizen's United* & gerrymandering.
10. **Support Democracy** – true democracy means ending corporate personhood.
11. **End Monopolies** – break up all industry monopolies – Media, Energy, Pharma.
12. **Promote the Common Good** – over special interests and private profits.
13. **Buy Local** – support community farmers, co-ops, and brands.
14. **Fight Intolerance** – be intolerant of intolerance.
15. **Unionize** – bring democracy in the workplace; turn corporations into co-ops.

1. Speak Out

When we witness injustice, staying silent only strengthens the status quo. Speaking out—whether in personal conversations, social media, or at public events—gives voice to marginalized and overlooked issues. By raising awareness, we also encourage others to examine their own views. Speaking out does not require aggression or hostility; it requires courage and kindness. It is about telling the truth with compassion, raising difficult issues with grace, and helping others see the need for change.

2. Organize

While individual voices are essential, collective action is transformative. Joining or forming movements with others who share your values amplifies your message. When people organize, they pool resources, skills, and energy toward common goals. Look at historical social justice movements—civil rights, women's suffrage, labor rights—they all gained momentum through collective action. Today, new movements must work together to promote social justice, climate action, and equality. We must learn to collaborate across borders to build a movement of movements - we are far stronger together.

3. Tell the Truth

In an age of "alternative facts," misinformation and disinformation have become powerful tools of division. Lies, especially those spread in the public domain, erode trust in institutions and create confusion about what is real. It is crucial to challenge these falsehoods and hold accountable those who spread them. Point out lies, whether in media or from public figures, and demand accountability. By calling out disinformation, we protect the integrity of public discourse.

4. Vote!

One of the most direct ways to influence political change is by voting for candidates who support the common good. While voter disenfranchisement and gerrymandering can make the process feel rigged, voting is still one of the most powerful tools available. It is essential to research candidates thoroughly, evaluate their track records, and assess whether they truly represent the interests of the people and the Common Good. Voting for the right candidates brings us closer to leadership that reflects the values of fairness and justice.

5. Consume Less

Rampant consumerism fuels environmental destruction and deepens economic inequality. Every time we buy something, we make a choice about what kind of world we want to support. By consuming less, we not only reduce our environmental footprint but also send a message to corporations that prioritize profit over people and the planet. Focus on minimalism, sustainability, and conscious consumption. Less is often more when it comes to building a more just society.

6. Tax Billionaires

Economic inequality is one of the most urgent issues of our time. As wealth becomes concentrated in the hands of a few, the ability of governments to fund public services that benefit the common good diminishes. Taxing billionaires is not about punishing success; it is about ensuring that those who have profited the most contribute their fair share to society. Higher taxes on the ultra-wealthy funds public education, healthcare, infrastructure, and climate action.

7. Fight for the Planet

Ecological destruction is accelerating, with devastating consequences for all life on Earth. Fighting for the planet means standing up against ecocide—mass environmental destruction—and the corporate interests that fuel it. Renewable energy and regenerative practices can offer a way forward. Supporting policies that transition us away from fossil fuels, protect ecosystems, and promote sustainable agriculture is essential to preventing the death of nature. We must stand against environmental exploitation and advocate for the planet's long-term health.

8. Educate Everyone

Access to education is a fundamental right, yet many people are being priced out of higher education, leaving them with crushing student debt or no degree at all. Making education affordable again—or free—should be the priority. Universal access to education enables more people to participate fully in society and strengthen democracy. It is time to make college free, giving everyone the opportunity to pursue knowledge and skills that benefit both individuals and society.

9. End Corruption

Corruption destroys democracy. Political corruption, often driven by corporate donations and lobbying, prevents the government from serving its citizens effectively. Ending practices like Citizen's United, which allows corporations to make unlimited contributions to political campaigns, and gerrymandering, which manipulates electoral districts for partisan advantage, is key to restoring democratic integrity. The people choose their representatives, not corporations, churches, or billionaires.

10. Support True Democracy

True democracy means that every person has an equal voice, and corporate personhood—the idea that corporations should have the same rights as individuals—undermines this principle. Corporations have outsized influence on politics and policy, often prioritizing profit over the public interest. Ending corporate personhood would limit their ability to influence elections and policy, giving power back to the people. Democracy works best when it serves the many, not the few – the Common Good.

11. End Monopolies

Monopolies stifle competition and concentrate economic power in the hands of a few corporations. Whether it's in media, energy, or pharmaceuticals, monopolies limit consumer choices, increase prices, and reduce innovation. Breaking up monopolies in key industries would restore competition, empower small businesses, and promote economic fairness. Antitrust laws must be strengthened and enforced to ensure that no single corporation can dominate entire sectors of the economy.

12. Promote the Common Good

At the heart of these steps is the idea of the Common Good—the idea that society should work for the benefit of all, not just for private profit or special interests. A shift in values is required to prioritize the welfare of the community, the environment, and future generations over short-term financial gain. Governments and businesses should adopt policies that promote well-being, equity, and sustainability.

13. Buy Local

Buying local not only supports small businesses, farmers, and co-ops but also strengthens communities. Local businesses are more likely to invest in their neighborhoods, pay fair wages, and provide quality goods. By choosing to buy local, we keep money circulating within our communities, reduce the carbon footprint of goods, and help build resilient local economies. Community support is a key component of the common good.

14. Fight Intolerance

Tolerance is the foundation of a just and equal society. However, we cannot afford to tolerate intolerance. Hate, bigotry, racism, and discrimination must be confronted and opposed. It is not enough to remain neutral in the face of injustice; we must actively fight against it. Intolerance breeds division, and we must work to create a society where everyone is treated with dignity and respect. History is full of violence based on "otherization" – it's time to see that we must fight for our future together, not against each other.

15. Unionize

Bringing democracy to the workplace is another critical step in promoting fairness and justice. Unions give workers a collective voice and ensure that they are treated fairly, with decent wages, benefits, and working conditions. Unionizing strengthens the position of employees in negotiations with employers and can transform corporations into cooperatives where workers have a say in decision-making. By democratizing the workplace, we move closer to a more just and equitable society.

But this is just the beginning. As humans **we live in 5 worlds**[242]. What can we do to make each one of these worlds regenerative?

---

[242] *The 5 Worlds of Regeneration* by Christian Sarkar, Philip Kotler, Enrico Foglia. *The Regeneration Journal* https://www.regenerationjournal.org/the-5-worlds-of-regeneration/

WHAT CAN WE DO IN AN AGE *of* COLLAPSE?

Let's explore further. Creating a **regenerative life** across all 5 worlds—**the individual, community, work, nation, and planet**—requires aligning our actions, values, and systems with principles of sustainability, equity, and interconnectedness.

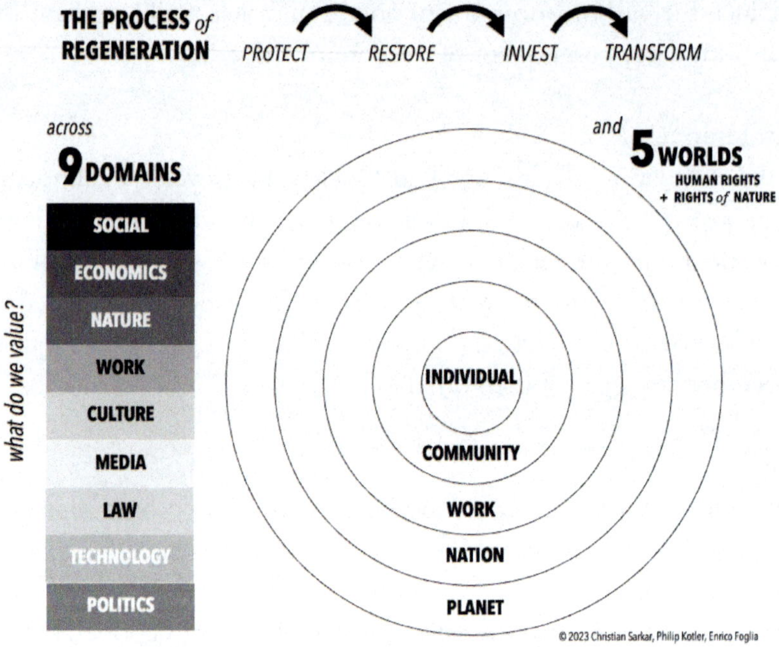

Here's how we can approach each world in a regenerative way:

1. Individual World: Personal Regeneration

Self-Care and Well-being: Prioritize physical, mental, and emotional health through balanced diets, mindfulness, and exercise.

Lifelong Learning: Commit to continuous learning, expanding awareness about ecological, social, and economic issues.

Sustainable Living: Make eco-conscious choices, such as reducing waste, conserving energy, and adopting sustainable consumption habits.

Regenerative Practices: Engage in activities that replenish, not deplete, your personal energy—whether through nature, creativity, or community involvement.

2. Community World: Regenerating Relationships and Social Fabric

Social Cohesion: Build trust and cooperation through shared goals and community initiatives like local food systems, energy cooperatives, and cultural projects.

Mutual Aid: Establish support networks that help individuals within the community thrive through reciprocal support systems (e.g., childcare, elder care, or health support).

Inclusivity: Ensure equitable access to opportunities, resources, and services, emphasizing marginalized or underserved groups.

Community Stewardship: Encourage collective care for local natural resources—like parks, rivers, public spaces, and Nature—to ensure long-term sustainability.

3. Work World: Regenerative Careers and Organizations

Purpose-Driven Work: Align personal career goals with businesses or organizations that prioritize regenerative principles, sustainability, and ethical practices.

Regenerative Economy: Advocate for workplace practices that eliminate waste, optimize resource use, and create regenerative products and services.

Regenerative Leadership: Cultivate leadership that values collaboration, empowerment, and long-term impact over short-term profits.

Promote the Common Good at Work: Foster a work culture that supports employee well-being, diversity, and work-life balance, recognizing that thriving employees contribute to a thriving organization. Extend this beyond the company to the community you work in to advance the Common Good.

4. Nation World: Regenerative Governance and Policy

Regenerative Policies: Advocate for government policies that prioritize the Common Good and long-term environmental, social, and economic sustainability.

Equity in Governance: Support inclusive political processes that ensure all voices—especially marginalized communities—are represented in decision-making.

Green Infrastructure: Invest in bioregional regeneration and sustainable infrastructure projects, such as renewable energy, public transport, and climate-resilient buildings.

Regenerative Agriculture: Promote farming techniques that restore soil health, increase biodiversity, and reduce environmental impact.

5. Planet World: Global Regeneration

Ecological Regeneration: Support or participate in global initiatives focused on reforestation, ocean health, and biodiversity conservation. Just stop fossil fuels!

Climate Action: Actively contribute to reducing carbon footprints by supporting renewable energy, conservation, and sustainable agriculture.

Systemic Change: Advocate for systemic global changes, such as transitioning to a circular economy and reducing consumption patterns that harm the environment.

Global Cooperation: Foster international collaboration to address global challenges, such as climate change, poverty, and inequality, with an emphasis on shared responsibility for advancing the Common Good.

If you want to **dive still deeper** - here are 30 actions you can take for each of the 5 worlds (Individual, Community, Work, Nation, and Planet) to create a regenerative life. Each world has tailored suggestions that can guide both immediate and long-term action:

1. Individual World: Personal Regeneration

- ❑ Practice daily mindfulness or meditation to nurture mental well-being.
- ❑ Adopt a plant-based or reduced-meat diet to lower your environmental impact.
- ❑ Reduce energy consumption by switching to LED lights and unplugging unused electronics.
- ❑ Start a composting routine for food scraps.
- ❑ Eliminate single-use plastics by opting for reusable containers and bags.
- ❑ Exercise regularly to maintain physical health.
- ❑ Commit to a zero-waste lifestyle, starting with small items like toiletries.
- ❑ Learn about regenerative practices like permaculture or holistic health.
- ❑ Invest in your mental health by seeking therapy or counseling if needed.
- ❑ Use public transportation, carpool, or bike to reduce your carbon footprint.

- ❑ Practice gratitude by keeping a daily journal of what you are thankful for.
- ❑ Volunteer for causes that promote sustainability or social justice.
- ❑ Limit screen time to improve focus and social interaction.
- ❑ Read books on regeneration, sustainability, and social equity.
- ❑ Cultivate a green space (indoor plants or a small garden).
- ❑ Opt for natural, eco-friendly products for personal care.
- ❑ Declutter your home and donate unused items to charity.
- ❑ Educate yourself on the impact of your purchasing decisions.
- ❑ Engage in reflective practices, asking yourself how your actions contribute to the Common Good.
- ❑ Buy locally produced food and products to support local economies.
- ❑ Use less water by fixing leaks and taking shorter showers.
- ❑ Reduce your reliance on fast fashion by choosing durable, sustainable clothing.
- ❑ Consciously support businesses that follow ethical and sustainable practices.
- ❑ Travel sustainably—choose eco-friendly accommodations or opt for slow travel.
- ❑ Establish clear, regenerative life goals and revisit them regularly.
- ❑ Share your knowledge about sustainability with family and friends.
- ❑ Reduce food waste by meal planning and storing food properly.
- ❑ Switch to eco-friendly cleaning products.
- ❑ Embrace a minimalist lifestyle, reducing unnecessary consumption.
- ❑ Support or donate to organizations that focus on regeneration, social justice, or environmental conservation.

2. Community World: Regenerating Relationships and Social Fabric

- ❑ Start or join a local community garden.
- ❑ Create or participate in local cooperative economies (e.g., time banks or worker co-ops).
- ❑ Organize a community clean-up event.
- ❑ Establish a neighborhood mutual aid network.
- ❑ Support local businesses and artisans.
- ❑ Host or attend community-building events like potlucks or skill-sharing workshops.

- ❑ Volunteer at local shelters, food banks, or nonprofits.
- ❑ Organize educational workshops on sustainability and social equity.
- ❑ Start a book club focused on topics of regeneration and justice.
- ❑ Advocate for safer, greener public spaces.
- ❑ Set up a local tool library for shared resources.
- ❑ Encourage local sustainable food systems by supporting or creating farmers' markets.
- ❑ Build intergenerational connections by fostering spaces for young and old to interact.
- ❑ Start or join a local climate action group.
- ❑ Offer your skills to help others in the community (e.g., teaching, mentoring, repairing).
- ❑ Participate in or organize community-supported agriculture (CSA).
- ❑ Support initiatives that focus on inclusivity, equity, and access to resources.
- ❑ Educate your community about circular economies and how they can participate.
- ❑ Host a "repair café" to teach people how to fix broken items instead of discarding them.
- ❑ Advocate for local policy changes that benefit environmental sustainability and social justice.
- ❑ Create a local resource-sharing platform (e.g., for tools, equipment, or knowledge).
- ❑ Support mental health and well-being programs in your community.
- ❑ Celebrate cultural diversity through community events or festivals.
- ❑ Organize neighborhood walks or activities that bring people together.
- ❑ Encourage local initiatives for renewable energy or clean transportation.
- ❑ Participate in or start a local clean energy project.
- ❑ Offer or take part in financial literacy workshops focused on sustainability.
- ❑ Collaborate on art projects that highlight environmental or social justice themes.
- ❑ Create a local group to promote gender and racial equality.
- ❑ Mentor youth in your community to prepare them for future regenerative leadership roles.

3. Work World: Regenerative Careers and Organizations

- ❑ Advocate for sustainable workplace practices (e.g., energy efficiency, waste reduction).
- ❑ Encourage or implement remote working policies to reduce commuting.
- ❑ Support businesses that prioritize regenerative, circular, and ethical business models.
- ❑ Create or contribute to a workplace sustainability initiative.
- ❑ Push for diversity, equity, and inclusion policies at work.
- ❑ Adopt regenerative design principles in your product or service offerings.
- ❑ Promote fair wages and ethical labor practices within your workplace.
- ❑ Offer mentorship to colleagues interested in sustainable careers.
- ❑ Champion transparent supply chains that focus on sustainability and ethics.
- ❑ Pursue professional development in regenerative fields (e.g., permaculture, renewable energy).
- ❑ Organize or attend work-related workshops on regenerative practices.
- ❑ Implement eco-friendly office practices like recycling and reducing paper use.
- ❑ Contribute to or initiate corporate regeneration projects.
- ❑ Support the well-being of coworkers through mental health resources and work-life balance initiatives.
- ❑ Advocate for employee ownership models like cooperatives or profit-sharing.
- ❑ Encourage regenerative leadership within your organization.
- ❑ Incorporate sustainable procurement practices in your business or team.
- ❑ Develop partnerships with local or international organizations that focus on regeneration.
- ❑ Create inclusive and supportive workplace cultures that value everyone's contributions.
- ❑ Reduce corporate carbon footprints through energy-efficient solutions.
- ❑ Advocate for green building certifications in company headquarters or facilities.
- ❑ Provide paid time off for employees to volunteer with environmental or social causes.
- ❑ Introduce incentives for employees to adopt sustainable commuting options.
- ❑ Support remote or hybrid work models to reduce workplace resource consumption.
- ❑ Foster collaboration across teams to drive innovative solutions for regeneration.

- ❑ Transition to sustainable packaging and materials in company products.
- ❑ Educate employees on sustainability and offer training on environmental issues.
- ❑ Start or support employee-led environmental or social justice committees.
- ❑ Invest in sustainable tech or green innovations within your industry.
- ❑ Promote regenerative supply chain practices to reduce environmental impact.

4. Nation World: Regenerative Governance and Policy

- ❑ Vote for policies and leaders who prioritize sustainability and equity.
- ❑ Advocate for the implementation of renewable energy programs at the national level.
- ❑ Support policies that promote universal healthcare and social safety nets.
- ❑ Campaign for laws that regulate corporations to ensure they adopt regenerative practices.
- ❑ Encourage government investment in regenerative agriculture and land restoration.
- ❑ Advocate for stronger environmental protections and anti-pollution laws.
- ❑ Push for equitable and inclusive education policies.
- ❑ Engage in civic participation (voting, petitions, local government meetings).
- ❑ Support national policies that ensure fair wages, healthcare, and housing for all.
- ❑ Push for comprehensive climate action plans with measurable goals.
- ❑ Advocate for urban planning policies that promote green spaces, sustainability, and resilience.
- ❑ Support policies that regulate harmful corporate lobbying and promote transparency.
- ❑ Promote democratic engagement through greater participation in decision-making.
- ❑ Join or create campaigns to raise awareness about national sustainability challenges.
- ❑ Push for equitable access to clean water, food, and energy for all citizens.
- ❑ Demand regulations for sustainable infrastructure (e.g., green buildings, public transport).
- ❑ Advocate for national debt relief programs and reparations for marginalized communities.
- ❑ Champion environmental justice movements that fight pollution in marginalized communities.
- ❑ Push for government funding for regenerative businesses and green innovation.

- ❑ Support national policies that encourage biodiversity protection and conservation.
- ❑ Get involved in movements advocating for a Green New Deal or similar initiatives.
- ❑ Promote global cooperation on climate change through international agreements.
- ❑ Advocate for data transparency in environmental and social policies.
- ❑ Promote equal access to the democratic process for all citizens.
- ❑ Encourage sustainable public procurement policies.
- ❑ Support policies that incentivize community-driven initiatives and mutual aid.
- ❑ Push for policies that ensure just transitions for workers in fossil fuel industries.
- ❑ Advocate for human rights protections at the national and global levels.
- ❑ Support initiatives that preserve and restore national parks and natural areas.
- ❑ Foster public-private partnerships that drive sustainable infrastructure projects.

5. Planet World: Global Regeneration

- ❑ Support international environmental agreements like the Paris Climate Accord.
- ❑ Promote and invest in clean energy solutions like solar, wind, and hydroelectric power.
- ❑ Engage in tree planting and reforestation projects.
- ❑ Support global NGOs focused on environmental and social regeneration.
- ❑ Participate in global environmental campaigns (e.g., Earth Day, Global Climate Strikes).
- ❑ Advocate for international policies on carbon reduction and environmental justice.
- ❑ Invest in renewable energy technology and companies.
- ❑ Support efforts to protect endangered species and biodiversity.
- ❑ Promote sustainable water management in regions facing water scarcity.
- ❑ Participate in international efforts to combat ocean pollution.
- ❑ Support carbon offset programs to mitigate your own emissions.
- ❑ Push for international debt forgiveness programs for countries impacted by climate change.
- ❑ Advocate for large-scale conservation projects to restore degraded ecosystems.
- ❑ Support fair trade and ethical global supply chains.
- ❑ Participate in global youth movements advocating for climate justice.

- [ ] Push for the implementation of global circular economies to reduce waste and consumption.
- [ ] Advocate for the preservation of indigenous lands and cultures.
- [ ] Join movements fighting against the exploitation of natural resources in vulnerable regions.
- [ ] Educate others globally about regenerative practices and their importance.
- [ ] Promote global solidarity by supporting international aid efforts.
- [ ] Encourage sustainable fashion by supporting brands that prioritize ethical production.
- [ ] Engage in campaigns for the reduction of plastic pollution.
- [ ] Push for greater global cooperation in disaster relief and preparedness for climate change.
- [ ] Engage with international organizations working to combat climate change.
- [ ] Support global food security initiatives, particularly regenerative agriculture.
- [ ] Advocate for eco-labeling and sustainability certifications for global products.
- [ ] Work toward addressing global inequalities related to climate impacts.
- [ ] Participate in global conservation efforts like biodiversity hotspots protection.
- [ ] Support international wildlife protection programs, including anti-poaching efforts.
- [ ] Encourage global dialogue on creating a more just, sustainable, and regenerative future for all.

Here are a few simple, guiding principles for promoting regeneration across all 5 worlds:

1. **Interconnectedness:** Recognize that actions in one world affect the others—what happens in the individual world influences community, work, national, and planetary systems.
2. **Long-Term Vision:** Prioritize sustainability and long-term thinking over immediate gratification or short-term solutions.
3. **Equity and Justice:** Ensure that regenerative efforts are inclusive, providing benefits to all, especially marginalized groups.
4. **Resilience:** Foster systems that are adaptable and can thrive despite changing conditions—whether economic, social, or environmental.

5. **Collaboration:** Work together at all levels—individual, community, organizational, national, and global—to create transformative and regenerative change.

FUNDING REGENERATION PROJECTS

Financing the actions necessary to create a regenerative life across the 5 worlds requires a multi-faceted approach that combines public, private, and community-based financial models. Below are somc strategies to fund these initiatives:

1. Public Financing (Government & Public Sector)

Governments have significant capacity to finance regenerative initiatives. Here's how:

- ❑ Green Bonds & Climate Bonds: Governments and local authorities can issue green bonds to finance large-scale environmental projects like renewable energy, clean transportation, and ecosystem restoration. Investors purchase these bonds, and the proceeds are used specifically for environmentally friendly initiatives.
- ❑ Tax Incentives & Subsidies: Governments may offer tax credits or subsidies to individuals and businesses that adopt sustainable practices—such as tax breaks for installing solar panels, purchasing electric vehicles, or converting to green buildings.
- ❑ Public-Private Partnerships (PPPs): Governments could partner with private companies to fund large regenerative projects. PPPs are effective in financing infrastructure projects, like public transportation systems, renewable energy grids, and sustainable urban development.
- ❑ Climate Adaptation Funds: Governments can set up or contribute to climate adaptation funds, which provide grants for local governments and organizations to develop resilience strategies in the face of climate change.
- ❑ International Funding & Aid: Governments in developed nations can contribute to international climate financing, such as the Green Climate Fund, which helps developing countries mitigate and adapt to climate change.
- ❑ Regenerative Economic Policies: Governments can implement economic policies that prioritize long-term environmental and social benefits, such as carbon taxes or pollution levies, which can fund sustainability programs.

2. Private Financing (Businesses & Corporations)

The private sector plays a crucial role in financing regenerative initiatives. Here's how businesses and corporations can contribute:

- Corporate Social Responsibility (CSR) Funds: Corporations can direct their CSR budgets toward funding sustainability initiatives, such as environmental conservation, renewable energy projects, and community development programs.
- Impact Investing: Private investors can direct funds into impact investments, which prioritize both financial returns and social/environmental impact. Impact funds focus on sectors like clean energy, sustainable agriculture, and fair trade.
- Venture Capital for Regenerative Startups: Venture capital can be directed toward innovative startups working on regenerative solutions, like companies in sustainable agriculture, eco-friendly construction, or waste-to-resource technologies.
- Corporate Sustainability Reporting & Accountability: Corporations can include regenerative goals within their business models, making financial commitments to sustainability and regeneration through transparent reporting mechanisms. This encourages companies to allocate funds towards regeneration projects.
- Green Bonds Issued by Corporations: Similar to governments, corporations can issue green bonds to raise funds for specific environmentally-focused projects, like reducing emissions or creating sustainable products.

3. Community Financing (Grassroots & Local Initiatives)

Local communities can create their own financing mechanisms to support regenerative projects. Here are a few models:

- Crowdfunding & Donation Campaigns: Online platforms like Kickstarter, GoFundMe, or Patreon can help raise funds for community-based sustainability projects. These funds can support initiatives like local gardens, renewable energy installations, or public space restoration.
- Community Investment Funds (CIFs): Local communities can set up investment funds where individuals contribute and pool resources to fund regenerative projects, such as eco-friendly housing or local business incubators.

- Time Banking & Bartering Systems: Instead of monetary exchange, communities can establish time banks, where people trade hours of work instead of money. This can be used to finance local initiatives by contributing time rather than funds.
- Local Co-ops & Mutual Aid Groups: Establishing co-operatives or mutual aid networks where community members pool resources to fund regenerative projects can be an effective way to finance local sustainability efforts.
- Green Local Taxes or Levies: Local governments can implement specific environmental taxes (e.g., on plastic usage or carbon emissions) and reinvest the proceeds into regeneration initiatives like tree planting, public transport, or local food production.
- Social Impact Bonds: Communities can use social impact bonds to attract private investment for social and environmental outcomes. These bonds pay investors a return based on the success of a specific project, such as reducing homelessness or increasing local food production.

4. Philanthropy (Foundations & Charitable Organizations)

Philanthropy may finance regenerative projects, especially those that require long-term investment or focus on underserved communities. Here's how:

- Philanthropic Grants & Funding: Foundations and nonprofit organizations can allocate grants to fund regenerative projects, particularly in education, community development, or environmental restoration.
- Corporate Foundations: Many large companies have corporate foundations that allocate funding to environmental, social, and sustainability initiatives. These foundations can be an important source of financial support for regenerative actions.
- Donor-Advised Funds (DAFs): Individuals can set up DAFs to donate money to charitable organizations focused on regenerative practices, such as conservation groups or social justice organizations.
- Sponsorships & Partnerships: Nonprofits or community groups can seek sponsorship from large companies for specific regenerative projects or initiatives. In exchange for the sponsorship, businesses get visibility and can align their brands with regenerative values.

5. Innovative Financing Mechanisms

There are newer financial models that can help fund regeneration initiatives:

- Blockchain & Cryptocurrency for Sustainability: Blockchain technology can be used to create transparent, decentralized financing systems for regenerative projects. Cryptocurrencies and tokenization can be used to fund projects with environmental or social impact, such as a carbon offset token system.
- Regenerative Investment Funds: Investment funds focused on regenerative finance specifically target companies and projects that are aligned with sustainability, biodiversity, and social equity. These funds help investors align their portfolios with regenerative values.
- Pay-for-Success Contracts (PFS): Governments, nonprofits, or communities can use PFS contracts to finance initiatives with measurable outcomes. Investors provide upfront funding for a project, and the government or nonprofit repays the investors based on the success of the initiative.
- Sustainable Finance Platforms: New digital platforms focus on sustainable finance, offering tools and resources for both individuals and organizations to invest in projects and companies dedicated to regenerative solutions.

6. Leveraging International Institutions & Global Financing

- UN and Multilateral Financing Programs: The United Nations and organizations like the World Bank provide grants, loans, and investments for projects related to climate change, sustainable development, and regeneration, particularly in developing countries.
- Global Carbon Markets & Offsetting Mechanisms: By investing in global carbon markets, governments and businesses can offset their emissions through funding projects that restore ecosystems or implement renewable energy solutions worldwide.
- Climate Funds and International Cooperation: Governments and businesses can access international climate funds aimed at financing global sustainability projects, such as the Green Climate Fund, which supports projects in vulnerable countries. By combining these approaches, you can create a diverse funding ecosystem that supports regeneration on all levels: from individual actions to global change.

We also recommend our magazine *The Regeneration Journal* (www.regenerationjournal.org)

And the website of the **Regenerative Marketing Institute** (www.regenmarketing.org)

At the **Regenerative Marketing Institute**, we offer several guides[243]:

- Regeneration Exploration Guide for Communities
- Regeneration Exploration Guide for Organizations
- Design for Societal Regeneration: Exploration Guidelines
- Regeneration: Organizational Readiness Survey

See also the following websites:

www.wicked7.org << *the project that started this book!*
www.fixcapitalism.com
www.activistbrands.com

JOIN US.

It's time to put away our differences and work together to save our future – if not for yourself, do it for your children.

[243] https://regenmarketing.org/action/

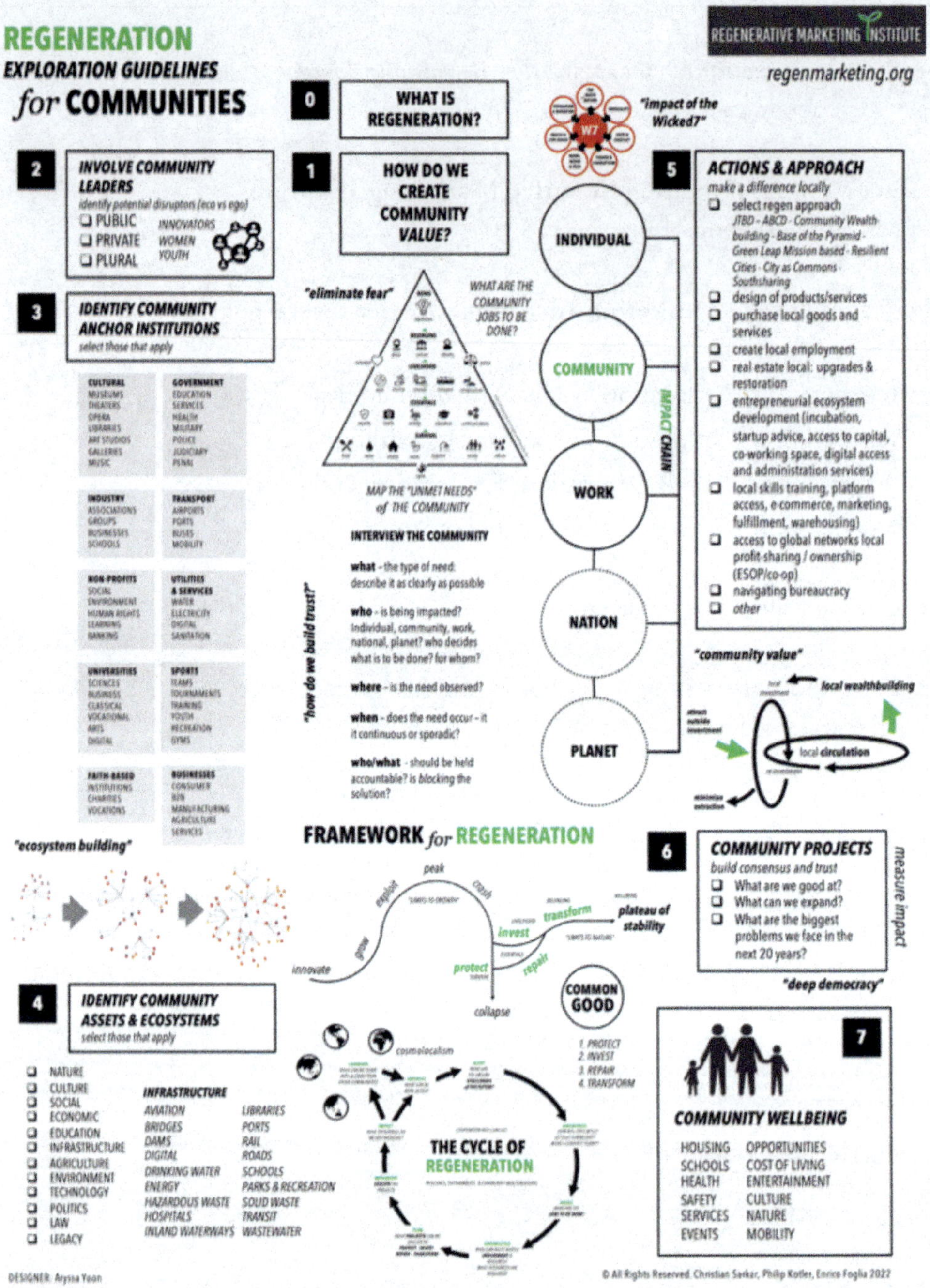

REGENERATION
EXPLORATION GUIDELINES
for COMMUNITIES
REGENERATIVE MARKETING INSTITUTE
regenmarketing.org
0
WHAT IS REGENERATION?
"impact of the Wicked7"
W7
2
INVOLVE COMMUNITY LEADERS
identify potential disruptors (eco vs ego)
❑ PUBLIC
❑ PRIVATE
❑ PLURAL
INNOVATORS
WOMEN
YOUTH
1
HOW DO WE CREATE COMMUNITY VALUE?
5
ACTIONS & APPROACH
make a difference locally
❑ select regen approach
JTBD - ABCD - Community Wealth building - Base of the Pyramid - Green Leap Mission based - Resilient Cities - City as Commons - Southsharing
❑ design of products/services
❑ purchase local goods and services
❑ create local employment
❑ real estate local: upgrades & restoration
❑ entrepreneurial ecosystem development (incubation, startup advice, access to capital, co-working space, digital access and administration services)
❑ local skills training, platform access, e-commerce, marketing, fulfillment, warehousing)
❑ access to global networks local profit-sharing / ownership (ESOP/co-op)
❑ navigating bureaucracy
❑ other
3
IDENTIFY COMMUNITY ANCHOR INSTITUTIONS
select those that apply
"eliminate fear"
WHAT ARE THE COMMUNITY JOBS TO BE DONE?
INDIVIDUAL
COMMUNITY
WORK
NATION
PLANET
IMPACT CHAIN
MAP THE "UNMET NEEDS" of THE COMMUNITY
INTERVIEW THE COMMUNITY
what - the type of need: describe it as clearly as possible
who - is being impacted? Individual, community, work, national, planet? who decides what is to be done? for whom?
where - is the need observed?
when - does the need occur - it it continuous or sporadic?
who/what - should be held accountable? is blocking the solution?
"how do we build trust?"
"community value"
local wealthbuilding
local circulation
"ecosystem building"
FRAMEWORK for REGENERATION
peak
exploit
crash
grow
innovate
invest
transform
plateau of stability
protect
repair
collapse
COMMON GOOD
1. PROTECT
2. INVEST
3. REPAIR
4. TRANSFORM
6
COMMUNITY PROJECTS
build consensus and trust
❑ What are we good at?
❑ What can we expand?
❑ What are the biggest problems we face in the next 20 years?
measure impact
"deep democracy"
4
IDENTIFY COMMUNITY ASSETS & ECOSYSTEMS
select those that apply
❑ NATURE
❑ CULTURE
❑ SOCIAL
❑ ECONOMIC
❑ EDUCATION
❑ INFRASTRUCTURE
❑ AGRICULTURE
❑ ENVIRONMENT
❑ TECHNOLOGY
❑ POLITICS
❑ LAW
❑ LEGACY
INFRASTRUCTURE
AVIATION
BRIDGES
DAMS
DIGITAL
DRINKING WATER
ENERGY
HAZARDOUS WASTE
HOSPITALS
INLAND WATERWAYS
LIBRARIES
PORTS
RAIL
ROADS
SCHOOLS
PARKS & RECREATION
SOLID WASTE
TRANSIT
WASTEWATER
cosmolocalism
THE CYCLE OF REGENERATION
7
COMMUNITY WELLBEING
HOUSING
SCHOOLS
HEALTH
SAFETY
SERVICES
EVENTS
OPPORTUNITIES
COST OF LIVING
ENTERTAINMENT
CULTURE
NATURE
MOBILITY
DESIGNER: Aryssa Yoon
© All Rights Reserved. Christian Sarkar, Philip Kotler, Enrico Foglia 2022

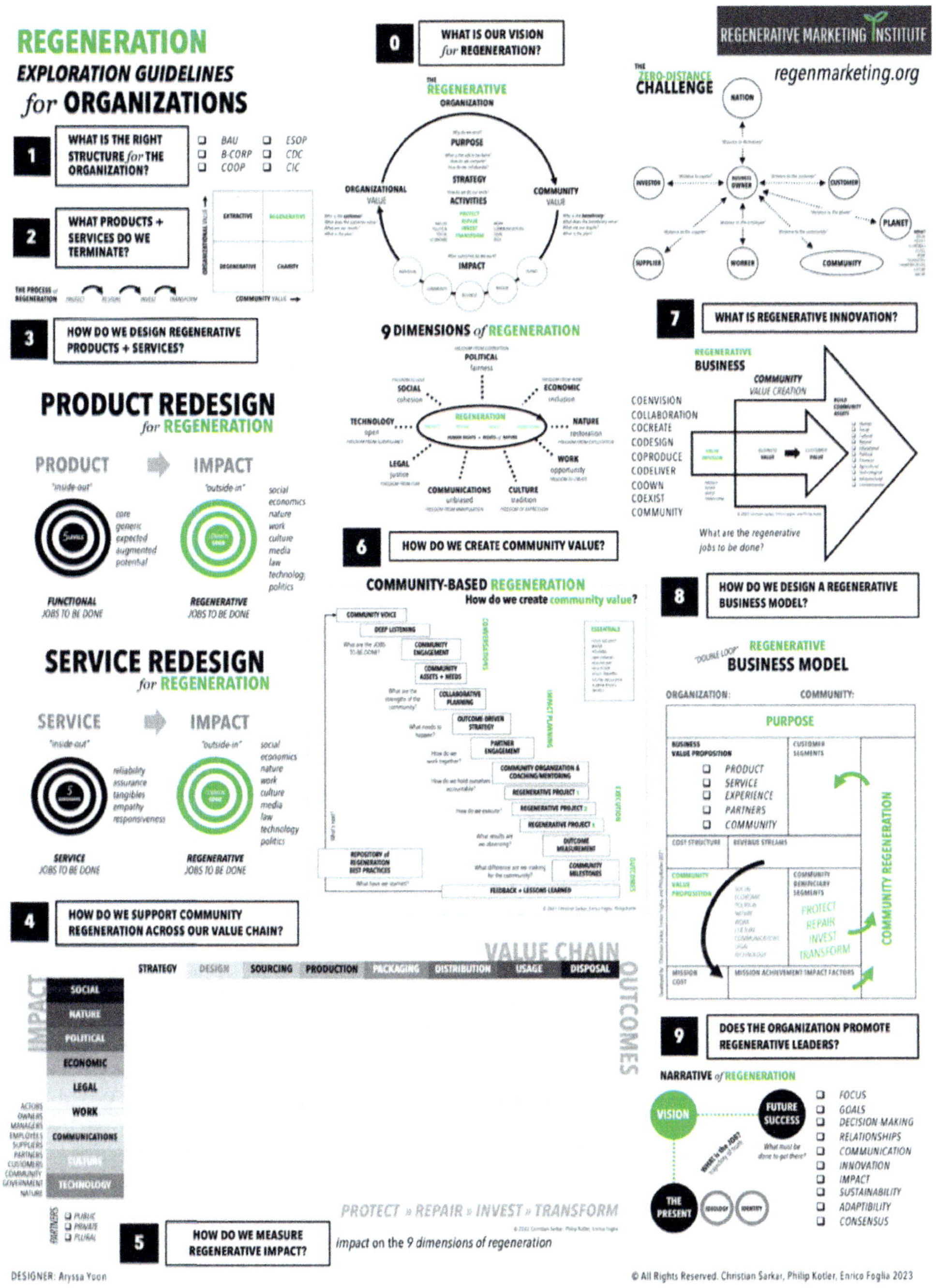

REGENERATION
EXPLORATION GUIDELINES
for ORGANIZATIONS
1 WHAT IS THE RIGHT STRUCTURE for THE ORGANIZATION?
BAU
B-CORP
COOP
ESOP
CDC
CIC
2 WHAT PRODUCTS + SERVICES DO WE TERMINATE?
EXTRACTIVE
REGENERATIVE
DEGENERATIVE
CHARITY
ORGANIZATIONAL VALUE
COMMUNITY VALUE
THE PROCESS of REGENERATION
PROTECT
REPAIR
INVEST
TRANSFORM
3 HOW DO WE DESIGN REGENERATIVE PRODUCTS + SERVICES?
PRODUCT REDESIGN for REGENERATION
PRODUCT
IMPACT
"inside-out"
"outside-in"
core
generic
expected
augmented
potential
social
economics
nature
work
culture
media
law
technology
politics
FUNCTIONAL JOBS TO BE DONE
REGENERATIVE JOBS TO BE DONE
SERVICE REDESIGN for REGENERATION
SERVICE
IMPACT
"inside-out"
"outside-in"
reliability
assurance
tangibles
empathy
responsiveness
social
economics
nature
work
culture
media
law
technology
politics
SERVICE JOBS TO BE DONE
REGENERATIVE JOBS TO BE DONE
4 HOW DO WE SUPPORT COMMUNITY REGENERATION ACROSS OUR VALUE CHAIN?
VALUE CHAIN
STRATEGY
DESIGN
SOURCING
PRODUCTION
PACKAGING
DISTRIBUTION
USAGE
DISPOSAL
IMPACT
SOCIAL
NATURE
POLITICAL
ECONOMIC
LEGAL
WORK
COMMUNICATIONS
CULTURE
TECHNOLOGY
OUTCOMES
ACTORS
OWNERS
MANAGERS
EMPLOYEES
SUPPLIERS
PARTNERS
CUSTOMERS
COMMUNITY
GOVERNMENT
NATURE
PARTNERS
PUBLIC
PRIVATE
PLURAL
PROTECT » REPAIR » INVEST » TRANSFORM
5 HOW DO WE MEASURE REGENERATIVE IMPACT?
impact on the 9 dimensions of regeneration
0 WHAT IS OUR VISION for REGENERATION?
THE REGENERATIVE ORGANIZATION
PURPOSE
STRATEGY
ACTIVITIES
IMPACT
ORGANIZATIONAL VALUE
COMMUNITY VALUE
9 DIMENSIONS of REGENERATION
POLITICAL
fairness
SOCIAL
cohesion
ECONOMIC
inclusion
TECHNOLOGY
open
NATURE
restoration
LEGAL
justice
WORK
opportunity
COMMUNICATIONS
unbiased
CULTURE
tradition
REGENERATION
6 HOW DO WE CREATE COMMUNITY VALUE?
COMMUNITY-BASED REGENERATION
How do we create community value?
COMMUNITY VOICE
DEEP LISTENING
COMMUNITY ENGAGEMENT
COMMUNITY ASSETS + NEEDS
COLLABORATIVE PLANNING
OUTCOME-DRIVEN STRATEGY
PARTNER ENGAGEMENT
COMMUNITY ORGANIZATION & COACHING/MENTORING
REGENERATIVE PROJECT 1
REGENERATIVE PROJECT 2
REGENERATIVE PROJECT 3
OUTCOME MEASUREMENT
COMMUNITY MILESTONES
FEEDBACK + LESSONS LEARNED
REPOSITORY of REGENERATION BEST PRACTICES
CONVERSATIONS
IMPACT PLANNING
EXECUTION
OUTCOMES
ESSENTIALS
REGENERATIVE MARKETING INSTITUTE
regenmarketing.org
THE ZERO-DISTANCE CHALLENGE
NATION
INVESTOR
BUSINESS OWNER
CUSTOMER
PLANET
SUPPLIER
WORKER
COMMUNITY
7 WHAT IS REGENERATIVE INNOVATION?
REGENERATIVE BUSINESS
COMMUNITY VALUE CREATION
COENVISION
COLLABORATION
COCREATE
CODESIGN
COPRODUCE
CODELIVER
COOWN
COEXIST
COMMUNITY
What are the regenerative jobs to be done?
8 HOW DO WE DESIGN A REGENERATIVE BUSINESS MODEL?
"DOUBLE LOOP" REGENERATIVE BUSINESS MODEL
ORGANIZATION:
COMMUNITY:
PURPOSE
BUSINESS VALUE PROPOSITION
PRODUCT
SERVICE
EXPERIENCE
PARTNERS
COMMUNITY
CUSTOMER SEGMENTS
COST STRUCTURE
REVENUE STREAMS
COMMUNITY VALUE PROPOSITION
COMMUNITY BENEFICIARY SEGMENTS
PROTECT
REPAIR
INVEST
TRANSFORM
MISSION COST
MISSION ACHIEVEMENT IMPACT FACTORS
COMMUNITY REGENERATION
9 DOES THE ORGANIZATION PROMOTE REGENERATIVE LEADERS?
NARRATIVE of REGENERATION
VISION
FUTURE SUCCESS
THE PRESENT
WHAT is the JOB?
What must be done to get there?
FOCUS
GOALS
DECISION MAKING
RELATIONSHIPS
COMMUNICATION
INNOVATION
IMPACT
SUSTAINABILITY
ADAPTIBILITY
CONSENSUS
DESIGNER: Aryssa Yoon
© All Rights Reserved. Christian Sarkar, Philip Kotler, Enrico Foglia 2023

DESIGN *for* SOCIETAL REGENERATION

EXPLORATION GUIDELINES

REGENERATIVE MARKETING INSTITUTE

regenmarketing.org

0 WHAT IS THE MISSION *of* REGENERATIVE DESIGN?

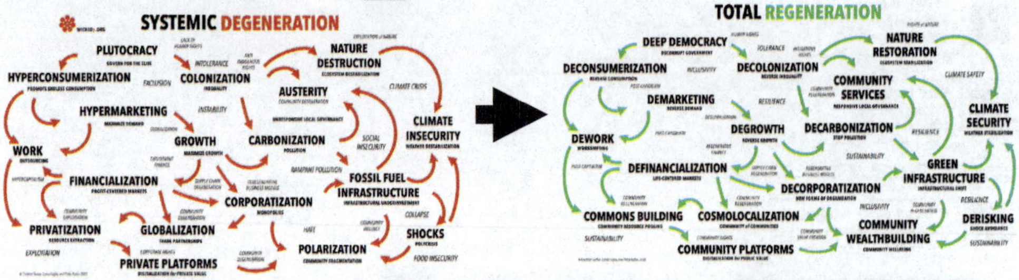

1 WHO IS THE CUSTOMER *for* REGENERATIVE DESIGN?

REGENERATIVE DESIGN is *design for the* **COMMON GOOD**

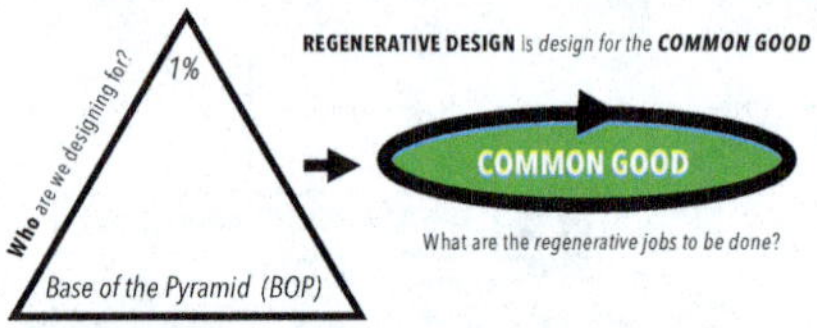

What are the *regenerative jobs to be done?*

2 WHAT IS THE SCOPE *of* REGENERATIVE DESIGN?

THE PROCESS *of* **REGENERATION** — PROTECT → RESTORE → INVEST → TRANSFORM

across **9 DOMAINS** *and* **5 WORLDS** — HUMAN RIGHTS + RIGHTS *of* NATURE

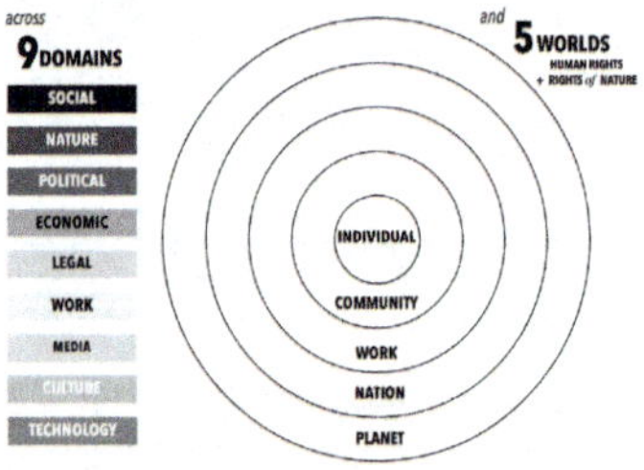

9 DIMENSIONS *of* REGENERATION

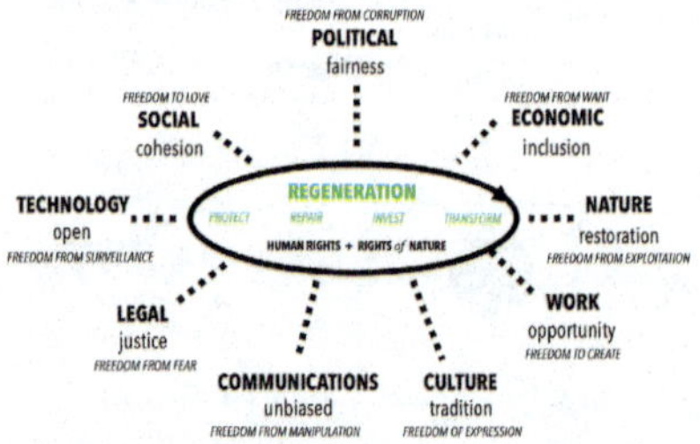

DESIGNER: Aryssa Yoon

3 WHAT ARE OUR GUIDING PRINCIPLES *for* REGENERATIVE DESIGN?

10 PRINCIPLES *of* DESIGN JUSTICE

h/t Design Justice Network

1. We use design to **sustain, heal, and empower** our communities, as well as to seek liberation from exploitative and oppressive systems.
2. We **center the voices of those who are directly impacted** by the outcomes of the design process.
3. We **prioritize design's impact on the community** *(and planet)* over the intentions of the designer.
4. We view **change as emergent from an accountable, accessible, and collaborative process**, rather than as a point at the end of a process.
5. We see the role of the **designer as a facilitator rather than an expert**.
6. We believe that **everyone is an expert based on their own lived experience**, and that we all have unique and brilliant contributions to bring to a design process.
7. We **share design knowledge and tools** with our communities.
8. We work towards **sustainable, community-led and -controlled** outcomes.
9. We work towards **non-exploitative solutions** that reconnect us to the earth and to each other.
10. Before seeking new design solutions, **we look for what is already working** at the community level. We honor and uplift traditional, indigenous, and local knowledge and practices.

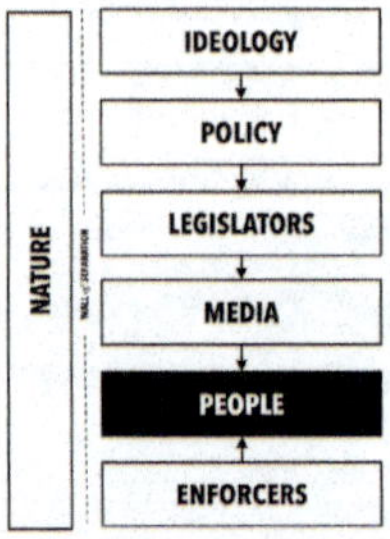

4 HOW DO WE DESIGN A REGENERATIVE ECONOMY?

ECOLOGICAL ECONOMICS	DEGROWTH	DOUGHNUT ECONOMICS	COMMON GOOD ECONOMICS
Steady-state or sustainable economics	System of planned contraction	Regenerative and distributive economics	Community-based regeneration
Shared ownership of resources and production	Shared ownership of resources and production	Shared ownership of resources and production	Community and hybrid ownership
Social equity and ecological sustainability	Social justice and ecological sustainability	Social justice and ecological sustainability	Social justice and ecological sustainability
Emphasis on steady-state	Emphasis on reduction of consumption and production	Emphasis on balance between social and ecological systems	Emphasis on fulfilling social and ecological needs
Sustainable resource use	Reduced resource use	Regenerative resource use	Socially just resource use
Negative externalities are internalized	Externalities are minimized through reduction of consumption and production	Negative externalities are minimized and positive externalities are maximized	Externalities are minimized through socially just economic practices
Government intervention to internalize externalities and ensure sustainable resource use	Government intervention to limit consumption and promote social welfare	Government intervention to ensure regenerative and distributive systems	Community-based regulation with Government incentives
Emphasis on social equity and ecological sustainability	Emphasis on social justice and ecological sustainability	Emphasis on social equity and ecological sustainability	Emphasis on social justice and ecological sustainability

5 HOW DO WE NURTURE THE SHIFT *to* REGENERATION?

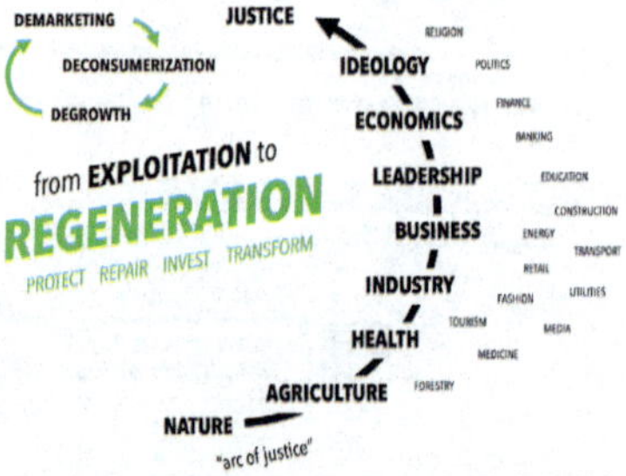

REGENERATION
ORGANIZATIONAL READINESS SURVEY

REGENERATIVE MARKETING INSTITUTE

REGENERATIVE CULTURE: The Mission

What is your company's understanding of the permacrisis? The Existential Threat? Does your organization have a sense of urgency in the face of societal disruption, planetary tipping points, overshoot, i.e., the world's wicked problems?
Does your company understand the linkage between strategy and the Common Good? Do you integrate societal impact, environmental trends, and business strategy with performance?

REGENERATIVE LEADERSHIP: The "Spirit of Performance"

Who in the leadership team is championing the company's shift towards regenerative practices? How do we get leadership buy-in to build organizational capability and commitment in terms of regeneration?
How is the company ensuring that regenerative principles are embedded across all departments, from R&D to operations? How is regeneration being incorporated into all aspects of the business and is cross-departmental collaboration happening?
How does your organization build distributed leadership capabilities? What is the role of ego-centric managers? Can your leaders share power? Are they rewarded for consensus-building and shared decision-making?
How do you engage employees and stakeholders in promoting and adopting regenerative practices? Understanding how you foster internal and external buy-in gives us a sense of the cultural alignment around regeneration.

REGENERATIVE STRATEGY: Intent and Vision

What is your company's long-term vision for becoming a regenerative company? How deeply is regeneration integrated into your corporate strategy and long-term goals? Do you have a regen-strategy map to guide decision-making?
How does you define regeneration in the context of its business and technology offerings? Can you clarify your interpretation of regeneration to ensure alignment between your goals and your approach?
What specific goals or milestones has you set to measure progress in adopting regenerative practices? Do you have concrete, measurable targets? Who sets them and how?

COMMON GOOD

REGENERATIVE INNOVATION: The Role of Technology in Regenerating the Common Good

Do you understand the Jobs-to-Be-Done for community and societal regeneration? How does outcome-driven-innovation apply to your regenerative aspirations?
How do you plan to use existing technological capabilities–AI, IoT, cloud, quantum computing–to drive regeneration? How can technology be leveraged to support regenerative strategy and outcomes? Projects?
What role do you see your company playing in developing technologies for ecosystem restoration or nature-based solutions? Are you investing in tech solutions directly aligned with ecosystem regeneration?
Are there ongoing R&D projects focused on regenerative solutions? What does your innovation pipeline include, and how focused are you on breakthrough solutions for regeneration?

REGENERATIVE BUSINESS MODELS: Investments in Regenerative Impact

How does your organization plan to adapt its business model to support regenerative outcomes? Are your transforming your value proposition to be regenerative? Beyond traditional business operations?
Do you have a "double-loop" business model for community value-creation? Have you mapped out the connections between profits and investments in regeneration?
What percentage of your R&D and investment is allocated toward regenerative technologies or projects? Financial commitment is the key indicator of how central regeneration is to your strategic focus – can you tell us about this?
How do you balance profitability with long-term regenerative outcomes? Have you built consensus on how to manage the tension between short-term financial goals and long-term regenerative benefits?

REGENERATIVE METRICS: Accountability and Reporting

What metrics are you using to measure the success of organizational regenerative initiatives? How do you track progress and ensure accountability for regenerative goals?
How do you plan to report on your regenerative activities, both internally and to external stakeholders? Transparency is key - how committed are you to public accountability?
What frameworks (e.g., ESG, B Corp, SDGs) guide your approach to regeneration? The best organizations build their own effective framework or guidelines as they benchmark and structure their regenerative initiatives.

REGENERATIVE PARTNERSHIPS: Ecosystem Building for Trust and Collaboration

What partnerships has your company formed (or is planning to form) to advance its regenerative goals? Strategic alliances with governments, NGOs, or sustainability organizations indicate the seriousness of your commitment.
How do you collaborate with communities and stakeholders in regions where regenerative projects are being implemented? Do you engage local communities and ensure your approach is inclusive and aligned with the needs of those most affected by environmental degradation?
Are there specific industries or sectors your organization is focusing on to drive regenerative change? Where can your organization have the greatest impact–whether it's urban infrastructure, technology, energy, or agriculture.

SOCIETAL IMPACT

What legacy does your organization want to leave as a regenerative business, and how do you envision your impact on society? What are your aspirations for contributing to regeneration globally?
How do you plan to involve future generations in its regenerative journey? What initiatives do you have for education, talent development, and fostering regenerative leadership for the future?

SCALING REGENERATION

How do you plan to scale your regenerative initiatives across different geographies and industries? Scaling is critical for long-term impact. Do you have a plan for creating regenerative impact across the world?
What role do emerging markets play in your regenerative strategy? What are you learning from the edge? Regenerative projects in developing regions will highlight new reverse-innovation opportunities

OBSTACLES TO REGENERATION: Challenges and Risk Management

What are the main challenges your organization faces in adopting regenerative practices, and how are you addressing them? How do you identify potential hurdles? What are the capabilities you need to make a difference?
How do you managing the risks associated with transitioning to regenerative models, particularly in industries that might resist change? Can you help industries understand the disruptions they face? Can you quantify the impact of regenerative approaches in various sectors (e.g., manufacturing, energy)?

THE FINAL WICKED PROBLEM: HUMAN STUPIDITY

Across the annals of time, an influential factor has impeded the advancement of human well-being and joy. This force wields might surpassing that of the Mafia or the armed forces. Its ramifications resonate on a global scale, spanning from the highest echelons of corporate power to the corners of your neighborhood tavern.

That force is **human stupidity.**

Carlo M. Cipolla, noted professor of economic history at the U.C. Berkeley, wrote an important book – ***THE BASIC LAWS OF HUMAN STUPIDITY***[244] – in order to detect and neutralize its threat.

Stupidity is a complex problem, for many reasons. Here are Cipolla's **five laws of stupidity**:

1. Always and inevitably, **everyone underestimates the number of stupid individuals** in circulation.

2. The probability that a certain person (will) be stupid is **independent** of any other characteristic of that person.

3. A stupid person is a person *who causes losses to another person or to a group of persons while himself deriving no gain and even possibly incurring losses.*

4. **Non-stupid people always underestimate the damaging power of stupid individuals.** In particular, non-stupid people constantly forget that at all times and places, and under any circumstances, to deal and/or associate with stupid people always turns out to be a costly mistake.

---

[244] https://web.archive.org/web/20130216132858/http:/www.cantrip.org/stupidity.html

5. A stupid person is the **most dangerous** type of person.
Here's how Cipolla charted stupidity:

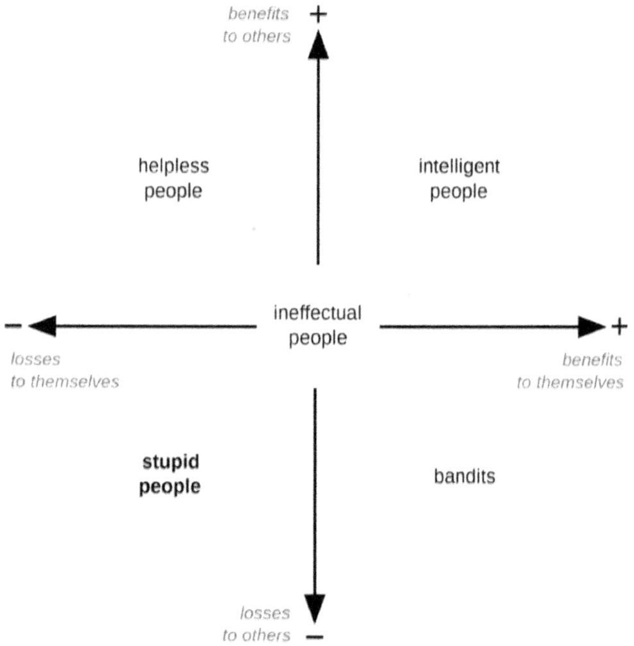

The chart gives us four groups of people:

- *Helpless people* contribute to society but are taken advantage of by it
- *Intelligent people* contribute to society and leverage their contributions into personal benefits
- *Stupid people* are counterproductive to both their and others' interests
- *Bandits* pursue their own self-interest even when this poses a net detriment to societal welfare (most of our billionaires?!)

An additional category of *ineffectual people* exist at the center of the graph!

What's really interesting is that Cipolla applies his **Theory of Stupidity** to the *rise and fall of Nations.*

"Whether one considers classical, or medieval, or modern or contemporary times one is impressed by the fact that any country moving uphill has its unavoidable **σ** fraction of stupid people. However, the country moving uphill also has an **unusually high fraction of intelligent people** who manage to keep the **σ** fraction at bay and at the same time produce enough gains for themselves and the other members of the community to make progress a certainty."

And,

"In a country which is moving downhill, the fraction of stupid people is still equal to **σ**; however in the remaining population one notices among those in power an **alarming proliferation of the bandits** with overtones of stupidity (sub-area B1 of quadrant B in figure 3) and among those not in power an equally **alarming growth in the number of helpless individuals** (area H in basic graph, fig.1). Such change in the composition of the non-stupid population inevitably strengthens the destructive power of the **σ** fraction and makes decline a certainty. And the **country goes to Hell**."

We can also rightly add that the ***stupid Nation*** is one which has *abandoned the Common Good.*

NOTE: Prof. Cipolla retired from UCB in 1991, and died on September 5, 2000, in Pavia, Italy. His heirs have tried to assert control over the text of **THE BASIC LAWS OF HUMAN STUPIDITY**, *but it was released to the public domain, and cannot be retracted.*

Stupidity is worst under authoritarian states. **Dietrich Bonhoeffer** wrote this[245] before he was executed at Flossenbürg concentration camp:

'**Stupidity is a more dangerous enemy of the good than malice.** One may protest against evil; it can be exposed and, if need be, prevented by use of force. Evil always carries within itself the germ of its own subversion in that it leaves behind in human beings at least a sense of unease. *Against stupidity we are defenseless.* Neither

[245] **Dietrich Bonhoeffer**, from 'After Ten Years' in Letters and Papers from Prison (Dietrich Bonhoeffer Works/English, Minneapolis, MN: Fortress Press, 2010.

protests nor the use of force accomplish anything here; reasons fall on deaf ears; facts that contradict one's prejudgment simply need not be believed- in such moments the stupid person even becomes critical – and when facts are irrefutable they are just pushed aside as inconsequential, as incidental. In all this the stupid person, in contrast to the malicious one, is utterly self-satisfied and, being easily irritated, becomes dangerous by going on the attack. For that reason, greater caution is called for than with a malicious one. **Never again will we try to *persuade the stupid person with reasons*, for it is senseless and dangerous.**

'If we want to know how to get the better of stupidity, we must seek to understand its nature. This much is certain, that it is in essence not an intellectual defect but a human one. There are human beings who are of remarkably agile intellect yet stupid, and others who are intellectually quite dull yet anything but stupid. We discover this to our surprise in particular situations. The impression one gains is not so much that stupidity is a congenital defect, but that, under certain circumstances, **people are made stupid or that they allow this to happen to them.** We note further that people who have isolated themselves from others or who live in solitude manifest this defect less frequently than individuals or groups of people inclined or condemned to sociability. And so it would seem that **stupidity is perhaps less a psychological than a sociological problem.** It is a particular form of the impact of historical circumstances on human beings, a psychological concomitant of certain external conditions. Upon closer observation, it becomes apparent that *every strong upsurge of power in the public sphere, be it of a political or of a religious nature, infects a large part of humankind with stupidity.* It would even seem that this is virtually a sociological-psychological law. The power of the one needs the stupidity of the other. The process at work here is not that particular human capacities, for instance, the intellect, suddenly atrophy or fail. Instead, it seems that under the overwhelming impact of rising power, humans are deprived of their inner independence, and, more or less consciously, give up establishing an autonomous position toward the emerging circumstances. The fact that the stupid person is often stubborn must not blind us to the fact that he is not independent. *In conversation with him, one virtually feels that one is dealing not at all with a person, but with slogans, catchwords and the like that have taken possession of him. He is under a spell, blinded, misused, and abused in his very being.* Having thus become a mindless tool, **the stupid person will also be capable of any evil and at the same time incapable of seeing that it is evil.** This is where the danger of diabolical misuse lurks, for it is this that can once and for all destroy human beings.

'Yet at this very point it becomes quite clear that only an act of liberation, not instruction, can overcome stupidity. Here we must come to terms with the fact that in most cases a **genuine internal liberation** becomes possible only when **external liberation** has preceded it. Until then ***we must abandon all attempts to convince the stupid person.*** This state of affairs explains why in such circumstances our attempts to know what 'the people' really think are in vain and why, under these circumstances, this question is so irrelevant for the person who is thinking and acting responsibly. The word of the Bible that the fear of God is the beginning of wisdom declares that the internal liberation of human beings to live the responsible life before God is the only genuine way to overcome stupidity.

'But these thoughts about stupidity also offer consolation in that they utterly forbid us to consider the majority of people to be stupid in every circumstance. It really will depend on whether those in power expect more from people's stupidity than from their inner independence and wisdom.'

"A series of pictures might be painted that should illustrate the History of a natural scene,
as well as be an Epitome of Man–showing the natural changes of Landscape
& those effected by man in his progress from Barbarism to Civilization,
to Luxury, the Vicious state or state of destruction and to the state of Ruin & Desolation.
The philosophy of my subject is drawn from the history of the past, wherein we see
how nations have risen from the Savage state to that of Power & Glory
& then fallen & become extinct..."

Thomas Cole

http://www.explorethomascole.org/tour/items/71/series/

The Course of Empire: The Savage State
Thomas Cole, The Course of Empire, 1833-36. Oil on canvas, The New-York Historical Society.

The Course of Empire: The Arcadian or Pastoral State
Thomas Cole, The Course of Empire, 1833-36. Oil on canvas, The New-York Historical Society.

The Course of Empire: The Consummation of Empire
Thomas Cole, The Course of Empire, 1833-36. Oil on canvas, The New-York Historical Society.

The Course of Empire: Destruction
Thomas Cole, The Course of Empire, 1833-36. Oil on canvas, The New-York Historical Society.

The Course of Empire: Desolation
Thomas Cole, The Course of Empire, 1833-36. Oil on canvas, The New-York Historical Society.

APPENDIX:
ANSWERS from AI (ClimateGPT)

As part of the Wicked7 Project, we were given access to **ClimateGPT**, a planetary-scale AI engine which is trained on the literature of wicked problems [**https://climategpt.ai**]. ClimateGPT is designed to enhance human decision-making by offering robust climate information to researchers, policymakers, and business leaders. It shows how climate change is not just about meteorological events, but how it is impacting people.

We asked it to explain the *root causes* for each of the Wicked7 problems. *We also asked it to explain the plans and track record of the world's largest oil companies and their commitment to meeting their climate goals.*

You can download the 101-page document here >> www.wicked7.org/climategpt.pdf

THE LAST WORD

George Tsakraklides
– one of our favorite commentators on the state of the world –
tsakraklides.com

George Tsakraklides
@99blackbaloons

Our civilisation is no longer run by humans, but by profit. Society has become a money machine with no blood, no pulse, and no other preoccupation than to monetize itself and the original humans who created it. Within this dystopian context, even humans have turned themselves into products: they need to be bought and sold so that they can exist. They need to be used to have a purpose. And they need to lie about themselves in order to be loved.

As witnessed during the industrial revolution, aggressive commoditisation across manufacturing resulted in inferior quality consumer goods, significant loss of human life, as well as loss of human consciousness. Now, thanks to technologies that are already racing past us, this model of commoditisation and value erosion is extending to areas which we thought profit could never touch: social services, mental health, our very attention span and need for human contact, and most importantly, our civil liberties and access to information. Our lives are being held captive online, sold out and replaced by cheap alternatives enabling the economic necrosystem to draw its greatest profits ever. As every aspect of existence becomes a single-use commodity in the global consumaverse, our life is both diminished and shortened: workers are only as good as their last burnout, relationships as good as the last iOS Tinder update, and democracies as strong as the number of Taylor Swift albums they lasted for.

But the biggest damage has been the commoditisation of truth. When news are engineered in AI information nurseries, paid for by the highest bidder and unleashed like forever chemicals into the river of media vomitus, then truth is the little fish in the river that never stood a chance. The media has become nothing but a broadcast channel for global capitalist interests, where zombie journalists and puppet politicians regurgitate the same lies again and again until they become true. As our planet accelerates towards a civilisation-ending climate crisis, reality is being banished from existence. It is labelled as terrorism and put on mute to protect the profits. Climate activists are given jail sentences longer than real terrorists, democracy is reduced to a sugary breakfast cartoon show with plenty of product placements, and Gaza manages to outshine Auschwitz as the first ever concentration death camp with live cameras on set. If you are searching for the truth, then your safest bet is to assume that everything you're being told is probably a lie.

This was all perpetrated by global capital: an entity which operates across borders, time zones and language barriers. Our collective failure to panic, to sound the alarm against the planet's polycrisis is testament to the nerve-paralyzing effects of consumatronic narcissism, meaningless work and entertainment distractions which keep us constantly occupied within this colourful theme park modern business has meticulously curated for us. Our future depends on claiming back our consciousness, and whatever is left of our humanity, from the system which tried to profit from them.
#ClimateCrisis #consumatrons

2:44 PM · Sep 9, 2024 · **20.9K** Views

THE LAST CARTOON

Brenna Quinlan *– one of our favorite cartoonists –* ***www.brennaquinlan.com***

ABOUT THE AUTHORS

PHILIP KOTLER is Professor Emeritus of Marketing at the Kellogg School of Management, where he held the S.C. Johnson & Son Professorship of International Marketing. Kellogg was voted the "Best Business School" for six years in *Business Week's* survey of U.S. business schools. It is also rated as the "Best Business School for the Teaching of Marketing." Professor Kotler has significantly contributed to Kellogg's success through his many years of research and teaching there.

He received his Master's Degree at the University of Chicago and his PhD Degree at MIT, both in economics. He did post-doctoral work in mathematics at Harvard University and in behavioral science at the University of Chicago.

Professor Kotler is the author of over 105 books including: *Marketing Management: Analysis, Planning, Implementation and Control,* the most widely used marketing book in graduate business schools worldwide; *Principles of Marketing; Marketing Models; Strategic Marketing for Nonprofit Organizations; The New Competition; High Visibility; Social Marketing; Marketing Places; Marketing for Congregations; Marketing for Hospitality and Tourism; The Marketing of Nations; Kotler on Marketing, Building Global Biobrands, Attracting Investors, Ten Deadly Marketing Sins, Marketing Moves, Market Your Way to Growth, Winning Global Markets, Confronting Capitalism, Democracy in Decline,* and *Advancing the Common Good.* He has published over one hundred and fifty articles in leading journals, several of which have received best-article awards.

Professor Kotler was the first recipient of the American Marketing Association's (AMA) "Distinguished Marketing Educator Award" (1985). The European Association of Marketing Consultants and Sales Trainers awarded Kotler their prize for "Marketing Excellence". He was chosen as the "Leader in Marketing Thought" by the Academic Members of the AMA in a 1975 survey. He also received the 1978 "Paul Converse Award" of the AMA, honoring his original contribution to marketing. In 1989, he received the Annual Charles Coolidge Parlin Marketing Research Award. In 1995, the Sales and Marketing Executives International (SMEI) named him "Marketer of the Year." In 2011, he was given the title of being a Legend in Marketing; in 2012, he was #1 on the Management A-List of Academics; in 2013 he became the first recipient of the William L. Wilkie American Marketing Association Foundation's "Marketing for a Better World" Award for significant contributions to marketing theory and practice; also in 2013, he was inducted into the Management Hall of Fame; also in 2013, he became the first recipient of the Sheth Foundation Medal for Exceptional Contribution to Marketing Scholarship and Practice.

Professor Kotler has consulted for such companies as IBM, General Electric, AT&T, Honeywell, Bank of America, Merck and others in the areas of marketing strategy and planning, marketing organization and international marketing.

He has been Chairman of the College of Marketing of the Institute of Management Sciences, a Director of the American Marketing Association, a Trustee of the Marketing Science Institute, a Director of the MAC Group, a former member of the Yankelovich Advisory Board, and a member of the Copernicus Advisory Board. He is a Member of the Board of Governors of the School of the Art Institute of Chicago and a Member of the Advisory Board of the Drucker Foundation. He has received honorary doctoral degrees from the Stockholm University, University of Zurich, Athens University of Economics and Business, DePaul University, the Cracow School of Business and Economics, Groupe H.E.C. in Paris, the University of Economics and Business Administration in Vienna, Budapest University of Economic Science and Public Administration, and the Catholic University of Santo Domingo.

CHRISTIAN SARKAR is an author, entrepreneur, artist, and consultant. As the co-founder (with Philip Kotler) and editor of *The Marketing Journal*, he continuously scours the world of marketing for new insights and next practices.

With Enrico Foglia and Philip Kotler, he is a co-founder of the *Regenerative Marketing Institute* – a research and advisory institution dedicated to community development and renewal. He is the co-founder of *The Regeneration Journal* – an online resource for regenerative practices.

He is also the founder of Double Loop Marketing LLC, a marketing consultancy, and Ecosystematic, an ecosystem strategy advisory.

He is involved in numerous non-profit and public-education projects, including The Wicked7 Project, FIXCapitalism.com and the $300 House Project. He is on the advisory board of several startups, non-profits, and universities.

In 2021 Christian was named to the *Thinkers50 Radar* of global management thinkers primarily for his work on brand activism.

Previous books:

- ❑ *Regeneration: The Future of Community in a Permacrisis World*
  with Philip Kotler and Enrico Foglia
- ❑ *Brand Activism: From Purpose to Action*
  with Philip Kotler
- ❑ *Losing our Democracy*
  with Philip Kotler
- ❑ *Inclusivity: Will America Find Its Soul Again?*
  with Michael Gordon

WICKED INDEX

FOR UPDATES VISIT WICKED7.ORG

Printed in Great Britain
by Amazon

59135496R00216